GeekDoctor
Life as a Healthcare CIO

John D. Halamka, MD, MS

HIMSS Mission

To globally lead endeavors optimizing health engagements and care outcomes through information technology.

Printed in the U.S.A. 5 4 3 2 1

Requests for permission to make copies of any part of this work should be sent to:
Permissions Editor
HIMSS
33 W. Monroe St., Suite 1700
Chicago, IL 60603-5616
nancy.vitucci@himssmedia.com

ISBN: 978-1-938904-55-4

The inclusion of an organization name, product, or service in this publication should not be considered as an endorsement of such organization, product, or service, nor is the failure to include an organization name, product, or service to be construed as disapproval.

For more information about HIMSS, please visit www.himss.org.

About the Author

John D. Halamka, MD, MS, is a Professor of Medicine at Harvard Medical School, Chief Information Officer of Beth Israel Deaconess Medical Center, Chairman of the New England Healthcare Exchange Network (NEHEN), co-Chair of the national HIT Standards Committee, a member of the Massachusetts HIT Council, and a practicing emergency physician.

As Chief Information Officer of Beth Israel Deaconess Medical Center, Dr. Halamka is responsible for all clinical, financial, administrative, and academic information technology serving 3,000 doctors, 14,000 employees, and two million patients. As Chairman of NEHEN, he oversees clinical and administrative data exchange in Eastern Massachusetts. As co-Chair of the HIT Standards Committee, he facilitates the process of electronic standards harmonization among stakeholders nationwide. As a member of the Massachusetts HIT Council, Dr. Halamka engages the stakeholders of the Commonwealth to guide the development of a statewide health information exchange.

Contents

Foreword

By Aneesh Chopra

Senior Fellow, Center for American Progress, and
Former US Chief Technology Officer (2009-2012)

There has never been a better time to be an innovator in healthcare than in the post-HITECH and ACA era. And for entrepreneurs and industry veterans alike, there isn't a better go-to advisor than Dr. John Halamka. He is among the few health IT leaders with success in three sectors of our economy—public, private, and academic. No matter the role you find yourself playing in the industry, you will surely find inspiration in John Halamka's words. I certainly have.

I first met John while riding the M2 shuttle bus between Boston and Cambridge. We were both graduate students with a shared passion for the (positive) impact technology and innovation could have on the healthcare delivery system. On one of our trips, he shared the story of Careweb, a web-based application he conceived to simplify access to patient data when a caregiver needed it most. His project couldn't have come at a better time. His employer had recently merged with a neighboring hospital and faced the daunting budgetary challenge of integrating the legacy medical records systems that didn't interoperate. Vendors at the time had pushed for a full-system replacement, at a cost they simply couldn't afford. Rather than give up on their integrated vision, Halamka showed the system leaders that they could achieve a great deal of its functional equivalence simply by using Internet-based technologies to publish each legacy system's data accessible by clinicians at the point of care. His idea worked, and earned him a promotion to serve as health system CIO.

That same creative, yet frugal spirit has defined John over the decades since we first met. As our nation's first Chief Technology Officer, I reunited with

John to help drive a public policy agenda to upgrade the nation's health IT infrastructure—not for the sake of adoption, but rather its use as a foundation for achieving health reform, especially the journey towards better population health. No matter the specific topic at hand, Halamka would find a voice for those entrepreneurs seeking a more welcoming path to participate, one with lower barriers that didn't compromise on standards or quality. His leadership to embrace more participatory channels in policy making from blogs to more virtual meetings opened up the Washington, DC-based policy meetings to everyday frontline workers in healthcare, injecting an implementation spirit in policymaking.

In the pages to follow, you will get a better sense of the industry's current and future challenges, but also an appreciation for how we will confront them. Halamka's ideas on leadership and family might be your favorite topics in the book, as innovation is often more than the specific technologies or ideas, but rather the context in which they are generated. Regardless, this is a must-read for anyone wishing to apply his or her talents to address our nation's biggest economic and fiscal challenges. Are we up to the task? If enough of us embrace Halamka's vision, I'm confident we will be.

Introduction

By John D. Halamka, MD, MS

Over six years ago, I began writing a daily blog to share my thoughts, experiences, and concerns about the healthcare IT industry. I soon found that my career as a CIO was hard to separate from my life as a human, so my blog evolved into a mixture of work, family, and personal reflections describing my attempt to navigate a rapidly changing world.

Many have asked me why I blog. Am I an IT exhibitionist? Do I feel my opinions need to be heard? Am I seeking the attention of my colleagues? No. My reasons are more selfless.

Each day I receive more than 1,000 emails including many questions about technology, policy, and government. Although I try to answer each one, it's much more effective to share the answer publicly so that teams of people can read about my failures, successes, and unsolved problems, avoiding the pitfalls I encountered.

CIOs are not the most popular leaders. They are often accused of saying "no" to every new request. The reality is that we're all humans trying to survive in a resource-constrained work environment. I'm hopeful that my blog illustrates the personal crises, tough choices, and constraints that make the job of the modern CIO nearly impossible. It may be that my colleagues and stakeholders do not agree with my decisions, but the blog illustrates the choices I had, the path I chose, and the reasons why.

I've said in several blogs that my goal in life is to make a difference. If I can share experiences of my wife's cancer, my father's death, and my daughter's development into a resilient young woman, I'm hopeful that others facing similar emotional events will feel supported.

Thus, the blogging is all about sharing, communicating, and trying to lessen the burden we all face as healthcare IT professionals. As a CIO, you are not alone and should not suffer in silence.

The themes I cover on the IT side include leadership, change management, interoperability, innovation, and security/privacy.

On the personal side, I share my life details, my family's experience with the healthcare system, the challenge of modern parenting, and the joy of running a small family farm.

I've carefully selected the blog posts that I believe will have the most lasting value for IT professionals, aspiring leaders, and anyone trying to create work/life balance.

I hope my experiences make a difference in your life.

Chapter 1

Leading Healthcare IT Organizations

When I was young, I thought that being a leader meant having power and authority. When I became a leader, I realized that I had accountability but not much else.

I've watched leaders rise and fall. I've experienced autocratic leaders, servant leaders, angry leaders, visionary leaders, and charismatic leaders.

Leadership is not about making decisions and expecting everyone to follow your guidance. Leadership is about convening, facilitating, and communicating. In the posts ahead you'll find that leadership is more about creating a guiding coalition based on informal authority than it is about power and exerting authority over your subordinates. I hope you all evolve into creative leaders and are so respected that people want to listen to your ideas.

In the posts ahead you'll find that leadership is more about creating a guiding coalition based on informal authority than it is about power and exerting authority over your subordinates.

What Is Leadership?

Thousands of books have been written about leadership. I've posted many blogs about my leadership lessons learned as a chief information officer (CIO). As I

1

mature, my view of leadership has become increasingly clear. Here's what I look for in a leader (and what I aspire to do myself):

1. Guidance—A consistent vision that everyone can understand and support.

2. Priority setting—A sense of urgency that sets clear mandates for what to do and, importantly, what not to do.

3. Sponsorship—"Air cover" when a project runs into difficulty. Communication with the board, senior leadership, and the general organization as needed.

4. Resources—A commitment to provide staff, operating budget, and capital to ensure project success.

5. Dispute resolution—Mediation when stakeholders cannot agree how or when to do a project.

6. Decision making—Active listening and participation when tough decisions need to be made.

7. Compassion—Empathy for the people involved in change management challenges.

8. Support—Trust for the managers overseeing work and respect for the plans they produce that balance stress creation and relief.

9. Responsiveness—Availability via email, phone, or in person when issues need to be escalated.

10. Equanimity—Emotional evenness that is highly predictable, no matter what happens day to day.

When my daughter asks me what I do every day, I tell her that I provide guidance and priority setting for my staff, resolve disputes, and continuously communicate. Of the ten items above, Resources is the only item I cannot personally control, since organizational processes beyond my pay grade set budgets (which always seem to mismatch supply with demand—it's a curse of IT).

When I think about the best times in my own career, the real breakthroughs occurred when leaders created a sense of urgency, provided resources, and broadly communicated. These circumstances led to such innovations as the Mycourses educational portal at Harvard Medical School, the widespread adoption of provider order entry in CareGroup hospitals, and implementation of the Beth Israel Deaconess Medical Center (BIDMC) disaster recovery data center.

Maybe we should add "optimism" as the 11th characteristic of leadership. Colin Powell says that optimism is a force multiplier.

Healthcare reform will give us all many opportunities for leadership. We'll have increasing Volatility, Uncertainty, Complexity and Ambiguity ahead, and by embracing the ten characteristics above, I'm confident we will succeed.

Maybe we should add "optimism" as the 11th characteristic of leadership. Colin Powell says that optimism is a force multiplier. When workload seems overwhelming, budgets look bleak, a complex project struggles toward completion, or a key staff member departs, a leader will buoy morale by offering words of encouragement that inspire optimism. When I think of the great leaders in history, optimism in the face of seemingly impossible odds (Winston Churchill at the Battle of Britain, Franklin D. Roosevelt in the Great Depression, John F. Kennedy during the race to the moon) has made it possible for people and nations to accomplish things never believed possible. ■

For Everything There Is a Process

I've written a number of related blog posts on the theme of respecting your colleagues, neighbors, and family: "The Greatest Good for the Greatest Number," "Your Karma Balance," and a "Plea for Civility."

A related topic is the way we should react when issues are escalated to us. No matter what the issue, always remember that there is process for every situation, no matter how emotional or urgent. Here's what I do when faced with a challenging issue:

1. Escalated issues are usually complex and difficult to resolve by email. This means that either you pick up the phone or schedule a quick meeting with stakeholders. It's generally best to schedule such meetings rapidly to prevent further misunderstandings and angst. At the meeting, the role of the leader is to listen and accept responsibility, even if the situation is not directly caused by you or your staff. When I've had challenging conversations with vendors, I'm always impressed by chief executive officers (CEOs) who take an active role in problem resolution, even when responsibility for the root cause is not always clear.

2. Build a reasonable path forward. The challenge of being a leader is that demand for resources—staff time and budgets—always exceeds supply. I have to be careful not to over promise and under deliver. Thus, I'll work with the stakeholders to develop reasonable next steps which include short-term wins, governance committee discussions, and phased delivery of solutions in the long term.

3. Instead of saying "no," say "not now." Sometimes it's tempting to just say "no" to a request that sounds unreasonable, untimely, or

nonstrategic. A better approach is to gather the scope of the request, submit it to a governance committee, and then let the prioritization take place by a group representing many institutional interests. The answer back may be a "not now, but in the queue of other institutional priorities," which is more satisfying than "no."

4. You can catch more flies with honey than with vinegar—it is easier to persuade people if you use polite arguments and flattery than if you are confrontational. As a CIO I have complete accountability for all IT-related issues but lack blanket authority. It would be great to be a benign dictator and just say "make it so," but that's not the case. Instead I have to use informal authority, build trust, create consensus and build a guiding coalition. I do that with humor, optimism, and enthusiasm. Doing it by yelling, intimidating, or formal authority may work in the short term, but it destroys trust and loyalty in the long term. I've been a CIO for nearly 15 years using the "honey" rather than "vinegar" approach.

5. Do not throw people under the bus, especially your own staff. I've experienced some leaders who are quick to place the blame on someone else as a way of deflecting responsibility. It's always awkward to be in a meeting when someone, often without warning, is identified as the root cause of a problem. To me, people are rarely the root cause—it's the project management and the governance that were flawed and enabled people to do the wrong thing. Thus, I never shoot the messenger or point fingers at a person. Instead, I ask how we can all do better by changing the way we work.

Everyday I conduct several challenging meetings. I know that there will be confrontations, tough questions, and even misunderstandings based on incomplete information. However, going into every meeting, I know there is a process to resolve every issue without requiring me to counter emotion with more emotion. ∎

> *Going into every meeting, I know there is a process to resolve every issue without requiring me to counter emotion with more emotion.*

Formal Authority

I was recently told by a newly promoted IT leader, "I have a great new job with more responsibility but lacking more authority." I responded that none of us really have authority or, if we do, we seldom use it.

In thinking about my own leadership life recently, I've had to make numerous decisions based on incomplete and contradictory information from stakeholders.

If I said something like, "I'm the CIO and a Senior Vice President. Since I hold the top technology job, I have authority over all technology decisions and by command we will do X," my stakeholders would lose all respect for me.

Every week, I'm handed complex issues with "he said/she said" controversy. It would be easy to resolve the issues with a simple "formal authority" email to remove the issue from my queue. And my decisions would be completely wrong.

Although listening to each side of the story takes time, it's the only way to understand the nuances and technical complexity to make a sound decision. Email is not a good way to resolve controversy.

Email is not a good way to resolve controversy.

First, I identified the stakeholders on each side of each issue and called them. After listening to their input, I outlined a governance process with objective criteria to evaluate the options. The stakeholders agreed to the process, the criteria, and the authority of a governance workgroup to make a decision.

Then, we set up meetings or phone calls during which all the stakeholders could speak with each other, make their points, and come to consensus. If consensus could not be achieved, then a vote would be taken. If the vote was a tie, I would decide based on pros/cons assigned to the objective criteria.

Using this approach, we've brought most of the issues to closure and I've not had to use formal authority.

One consequence of this approach is that it does not create passionate winners and losers. It does not make the CIO the bad guy. When the next issue arises, stakeholders will trust the process and not even remember the controversies of the past.

When I was young, I believed that leaders had it easy—they had such power that they could just exercise their authority to make decisions and get work done.

The reality is that the more responsibility and visibility you have, the less formal authority you can exercise.

So next time you get promoted, accept the mantle of leadership knowing that you're accountable, but your only true power is leveraging the trust of your stakeholders.

And remember, for everything there is a process. ■

An Open Access Scheduling Model for Healthcare Management

Wouldn't it be great if we could solve today's problems today?

Every day I receive over 1,000 emails. A small number of those emails are complex problems that require multi-stakeholder coordination. Although I can try to solve such problems via email, my rule is that if more than three rounds of emails go back and forth about an issue, it's time to pick up the phone or have a meeting.

> My rule is that if more than three rounds of emails go back and forth about an issue, it's time to pick up the phone or have a meeting.

However, scheduling a meeting among senior managers in a large organization can take a month. By that time, the issue has either become a much larger problem, or the opportunity to rapidly move forward has been lost. So much for nimble decision making.

How can we improve this situation?

I suggest we learn from the Open Access Scheduling model used in primary care.

Patients who are sick today do not want an appointment in three weeks: they need to be seen today.

In the past, clinicians noted they were so busy that their calendars were backlogged weeks to months.

But wait—if you see 15 patients per day, a backlogged calendar does not imply you are seeing more patients. Why not work through the backlog and then leave 50% of the calendar open each day for the patients who are sick each day—solve today's problems today.

The same approach can be applied to our administrative lives. Each day there are challenges created by customers, employees, and the external world. If we left 50% of our calendars open each day for solving today's problems today, we would reduce stress, enhance communication, and improve efficiency. We could even develop metrics for senior executives which measure "time to problem resolution" as a means to drive incentive compensation.

Today, we pay doctors for quantity of care delivered instead of quality. Healthcare reform is intended to change that. Administratively, we should be paid for the problems we solve, the chaos we eliminate, and the processes we improve. ■

Volatility, Uncertainty, Complexity, and Ambiguity

In the era of healthcare reform, when accountable care organizations, global payments, and partial capitation are the buzzwords filling board rooms, healthcare executives are wondering what to do next.

The answer came from Dr. Gene Lindsey, President and CEO of Atrius Health, during a retreat.

It's about accepting and managing "VUCA":

V = Volatility. The nature and dynamics of change, and the nature and speed of change forces and change catalysts.

U = Uncertainty. The lack of predictability, the prospects for surprise, and the sense of awareness and understanding of issues and events.

C = Complexity. The multiplex of forces, the confounding of issues, and the chaos and confusion that surround an organization.

A = Ambiguity. The haziness of reality, the potential for misreads, and the mixed meanings of conditions; cause-and-effect confusion.

The common usage of the term VUCA began in the military in the late 1990s, but it's been applied to corporate and non-profit leadership by several authors, especially Bob Johansen, former CEO of the Institute for the Future.

I recommend two books by Johansen: *Get There Early*[1] and *Leaders Make the Future*.[2]

Johansen suggests that strong leaders turn volatility into vision, uncertainty into understanding, complexity into clarity, and ambiguity into agility.

He concludes that:

1. VUCA will get worse in future.

2. VUCA creates both risk and opportunity.

3. Leaders must learn new skills in order to create the future.

Dr. Lindsey and I discussed these ideas and he added two of his own:

1. Leaders need to turn ambiguity into action. How many times have you heard, "I do not have enough data to make a fully informed decision." Not acting makes you a target in a VUCA world.

2. Johansen notes that the most difficult VUCA competency for the future is "commons building." Dr. Lindsey related this to Don Berwick's concept of the medical commons. Berwick, when he was CEO of the

---

1   Johansen B. *Get There Early: Sensing the Future to Compete in the Present.* San Francisco: Berrett-Koehler Publishers; 2007.

2   Johansen B. *Leaders Make the Future: Ten New Leadership Skills for an Uncertain World, Second Edition.* San Francisco: Berret-Koehler Publishers; 2012.

Institute for Healthcare Improvement (IHI), wrote about the need for a medical commons to accelerate the Triple Aim in healthcare. He wrote, "Rational common interests and rational individual interests are in conflict. Our failure as a nation to pursue the Triple Aim meets the criteria for what Garrett Harden called a 'tragedy of the commons.' As in all tragedies of the commons, the great task in policy is not to claim that stakeholders are acting irrationally, but rather to change what is rational for them to do. The stakes are high. Indeed, the Holy Grail of universal coverage in the United States may remain out of reach unless, through rational collective action overriding some individual self-interest, we can reduce per capita costs."

Let's explore the issue of "commons building" with a healthcare IT example. Fifteen percent of the lab and radiology tests done in Eastern Massachusetts are redundant or unnecessary. Ensuring all test results are available electronically among all providers (especially between competing organizations) will cost millions in electronic health records (EHRs), health information exchange (HIE), and interface implementation. Thus, we'll have to spend money to reduce all our incomes. It's the right thing to do, but the medical IT commons will be at odds with individual incentives in a fee-for-service world. The right answer is to change the incentives and pay individuals for care coordination, not for ordering more tests.

I've thought about Dr. Lindsey's comments and realized that I've had my own VUCA challenges in the past, as well as many VUCA challenges in the present.

Let's turn back the clock to 2008. The Obama campaign suggested that EHRs and HIEs were the right thing to do. We had all the signs that ARRA[3] and HITECH[4] would be coming, but large-scale EHR rollouts require significant lead time. We had to act. BIDMC decided that Software as a Service (SaaS) EHRs were the right thing to do and created a "private cloud." The concept of the private cloud really did not exist in 2008 and we did not know enough to predict it. We just did what we thought was right—keep all software and data on the server side rather than in the doctor's office. Today, people look at our Community EHR SaaS model and congratulate us on our foresight to build a cloud. I'll be honest: it was not planned or forecasted. We just had intuition based on the market forces and technology trajectory we saw and we guessed. I would really like to say we built a private cloud on purpose. It was a serendipitous guess. In the future, there may be cloud providers that offer business associate agreements for high-reliability, cost-effective, secure EHR hosting. We should think about migrating our private cloud to such services in the future.

---

3   ARRA = American Recovery and Reinvestment Act of 2009.

4   HITECH = Health Information Technology for Economic and Clinical Health Act.

Several years ago, BIDMC decided to focus our clinical systems efforts on computerized provider order entry (CPOE), medication reconciliation, HIE, quality measurement, and advanced ambulatory function instead of inpatient clinical documentation or nursing workflow. Meaningful Use Stage 1 was a perfect reflection of what we did. I had no influence on the Policy Committee's focus, nor did we have amazing insight. It was a best guess.

ICD-10, new payment models based on quality, and care coordination with incentives to share savings are the new normal, and pressure to reduce cost via guidelines/protocols/care plans will increase. Our governance committees will have to make hard choices about what not to do in the VUCA world of the next few years. Maybe the future is going to include more ambulatory and intensive care unit (ICU) care, with ward care moved to home care. We'll have to guess again where the puck is going to be.

As a leader, my time needs to be divided among federal, state, and local initiatives so that my governance committees, my staff, and I can make the guesses for the future. None of us knows what healthcare reform will bring or what the reimbursement models will really be. However, we need to act now to be ready for the next two years. That's VUCA.

On occasion I tell my wife that someday the VUCA I face every day will get better. She reminds me that it will only get worse. If I'm doing my job properly, I will accept and manage the VUCA, so that my staff can focus on the work we need to do to stay on the cutting edge. ∎

Dispute Resolution in Healthcare

At a recent conference, I was asked an interesting question. If there is a dispute about any data in healthcare—EHR, PHR (personal health record), or HIE—how is it resolved?

eBay does millions of transactions via the Internet and it has automated, web-based dispute resolution workflows. Can healthcare learn something from eBay?

I attended a workshop in Washington, DC, called "Online Dispute Resolution in a Technology-Oriented Healthcare World."

The attendees were evenly split between representatives of the healthcare, dispute resolution, and computer science communities.

The goals of the meeting were to:

- Identify the key risks of disputes in the networked health information technology environment

- Identify the best practices in avoiding and resolving such disputes and the need for new dispute prevention/resolution approaches in problem areas

- Identify the computing and other research challenges inherent in supporting these practices

As the work I've done with e-Patient Dave[5] illustrates, personal health records should have a process for resolving data issues.

Here are a few lessons learned from that conference:

1. There's a need to web-enable dispute workflow in healthcare. As e-Patient Dave pointed out, I did not hear about any data concerns regarding personal health records, likely because there was no easy way to raise the issue. Hospitals have policies regarding medical record disputes. Generally the workflow involves writing letters, making phone calls, and resolving disputes via committee. As the country implements more electronic records and shares more data (with patient consent) among more stakeholders, we need to embrace automated dispute resolution workflows such as those used by eBay. In healthcare, the issues are complex because the medical record is a legal record and there are many compliance issues involved in annotating it. However, I can imagine adding a comment field to the problem list which could be electronically annotated by the patient, so a clinician examining the record could understand the patient's point of view if data is disputed. In our medication reconciliation application, we give clinicians the ability to make notations about patient compliance with medications (e.g., discontinued, taken infrequently, changed to a different medication). I can imagine gathering this input directly from patients.

   Thus, the work of the dispute resolution community working with the healthcare data community will be to think through the workflow that can be supported via web-based dispute resolution tools, while still ensuring the non-repudiability of the medical record and complying with federal, state, and local medical record policies.

2. For issues that cannot be resolved via automated tools, an electronic escalation to an ombudsman is a reasonable workflow. Complex issues are generally more easily resolved when two people speak directly rather than virtually. However, a web application could be used to identify the issues, exchange background information, and schedule the discussion.

3. If there is assertion of malpractice or harm caused to the patient, then workflows involving risk management and insurance organizations are appropriate.

---

5 e-Patient Dave, or Dave deBronkart, is a former cancer patient and blogger who, in 2009, became a noted activist for healthcare transformation through participatory medicine and personal health data rights.

As a result of this conference, I will be more sensitive to the need to consider the modes of failure in electronic health records, especially those which are shared with patients, and the desirability of automated dispute resolution workflow. ■

The Work of Worry

As I've taken on more responsibility for more organizations, I've discovered that more authority does not lead to more power. It leads to more responsibility. Translated into a simple statement: when everything goes right, many people get the credit. When anything goes wrong, the leader is responsible.

> *When everything goes right, many people get the credit. When anything goes wrong, the leader is responsible.*

This creates what I call the "Work of Worry."

The burden of ensuring that every aspect of your job—human resources, budgets, customer service, reliability, security, and strategy—is optimized requires constant vigilance and daily management attention.

For example, each night before I go to sleep, I mentally run through every one of my direct reports and ask myself what issues are unresolved, what projects are going off track, what budgets are at risk, and what strategies need adjusting. I make a list and then sleep on it. In the morning, when I'm refreshed, I send out email and schedule meetings to address everything on the list.

This means that no issue remains unaddressed for more than a day. There may be a multi-week process needed to resolve some issues, but at least that process is initiated in a timely way.

When leadership is not a job, but a lifestyle and every aspect of the organization's performance becomes the responsibility of the leader, the work of worry can be intense. It can become challenging to balance responsibility/anxiety with family life, free time, and maintaining a positive mood.

So if you are thinking that your leader's work is not always visible, consider the time that is spent on the "Work of Worry" and ensuring that the organization does the right thing, all the time. ■

Conservation of Aggravation

The first law of thermodynamics tells us that energy is neither created nor destroyed; it is simply converted from one form to another.

For IT professionals, I believe in the first law of project dynamics: aggravation is neither created nor destroyed; it is simply converted from one project to another.

As a CIO, I oversee 200 projects a year. Following are a few examples of "Conservation of Aggravation."

In 2003, we had a growing problem with spam and I received many requests each day to implement a centralized spam filter. We initially tried Spam Assassin, but found that it could not distinguish between advertisements to enlarge body parts and physician referrals to clinics for diseases affecting body parts. In a medical environment we wanted very few false positives (real mail marked as spam), so we implemented Brightmail. Now I receive many requests a day to loosen the spam filters, which are blocking important business email such as eBay receipts, newsletters from professional sports organizations, and casual email conversations (Subject: Hi!) from friends and relatives. Aggravation has been conserved.

In 2002, Beth Israel Deaconess experienced a 1.5-day network outage when a misperforming application flooded the network and overwhelmed the spanning tree algorithm in our older network gear. In 2003, SQL Slammer and other Microsoft-related security issues caused server downtime. I spent a year creating highly redundant state-of-the-art networks, server clusters, and virtualized central storage. Uptime 2004–2008 has exceeded 99.9% for all applications and services. On rare occasions, I need to take down a segment of the network to upgrade hardware or firmware. Trying to find an acceptable 15-minute window to take down IT services is nearly impossible. Sunday at 4 am? We could have trauma patients arriving in the ER then. By creating complete reliability, we have made downtime unacceptable. Aggravation has been conserved.

In 2006, we implemented electronic prescribing for our clinicians. We replaced unreadable handwritten paper and free-text typing (take some Tylenol) with structured, standards-based, secure electronic messaging from doctor to pharmacy. Clinicians welcomed the idea of more accurate, safer medication practices, requiring fewer callbacks from pharmacists with questions about handwritten scripts. However, clinicians rapidly discovered that older prescriptions, written before the new system required structured prescribing, had to be retyped because the computer could not automatically convert "take some Tylenol" to "take Tylenol 1-2 tabs every 4-6 hours as needed for pain." They wanted accuracy and ambiguity to be acceptable simultaneously. Aggravation has been conserved.

In writing this, I feel so much better that I've shared the challenges of being an IT professional. Will this catharsis lead to less aggravation? Nope. Within 48 hours of this blog being published, 25 salespeople will call and email me about spam solutions that block all bad emails but allow eBay/sports/casual email, about highly reliable infrastructure components that require no maintenance, and about e-prescribing systems that do everything for everyone. Some of these sales offers will make it through the spam filter. (Do these folks believe that CIOs have the time to read unsolicited sales emails?) Some salespeople will pester my assistant to the point that she whimpers in frustration. I have no doubt that aggravation will be conserved! ∎

How to Be a Great Boss

In my career, I've reported to CEOs, professors, doctors, and deans. I've had good bosses and bad bosses. I've had bosses who have leveraged me as a strategic asset (my current bosses do) and others who have not.

In my opinion, there are ten characteristics that make a great boss. These are based on my own reporting experiences and are the behaviors I try to use with staff I supervise.

> *There are ten characteristics that make a great boss.*

1. Responds rapidly—In general, employees escalate issues when they feel anxious, conflicted, or powerless. When an employee asks for clarification of a strategy, help with a political conflict, or a decision about resource allocation, bosses should respond rapidly with a decision, so that the boss is not the rate-limiting step to progress. A boss does not need to carry a Blackberry, but should acknowledge every email the same day it was sent, even if the resolution will take a little longer. My personal goal is to clear my inbox completely before bed each day, ensuring every issue is responded to and resolved if possible.

2. Embraces process—Every problem, even a crisis, can be resolved by initiating the right processes. Each organization should have budget processes, position control (new hire) processes, governance processes, communication processes, conflict resolution processes, and human resource processes that can address every issue. If a boss cannot respond immediately with the resolution of an issue, he/she should identify the processes needed to bring it to closure. Giving employees definitive directions about which processes to pursue and guidance about how to pursue them is a great way to resolve complex issues.

3. Micromanages and macromanages—Some projects are so complex and require such alignment of stakeholders that the boss needs to get involved with the details of the people, budgets, and project plan. Most projects require just general oversight of progress. A boss

should get involved in the details when asked to help, but otherwise should follow project progress at a high level, leaving the details to those experts who are immersed in the project specifics.

4. Empowers—A boss should use his/her authority to support direct reports, giving them the freedom to execute their projects per their best judgment while giving them the political support they need to be effective. As a project sponsor, the boss can help with stakeholder alignment, project vision, and building a guiding coalition in support of the project.

5. Provides resources—Staff counts and operational budgets should be increased yearly based on workload, strategic plans, infrastructure demands, and compliance requirements. Of course, most organizations are resource constrained, so it may not be possible to fund all new staff needed. But since each project is a function of scope, time, and resources, the boss needs to pay attention to resources to avoid turning a "lean and mean" organization into a "bony and angry" one.

6. Stands by you in good times and bad—One of the great joys of IT is that the organization rarely gets credit for the thousands of things it does right, but is often criticized for the few things that go wrong. A boss needs to acknowledge employees with personal thanks and praise when things go right and support them when things go wrong. The organization should not punish the individual but should ask how processes can be improved to avoid bad outcomes. Whenever we have downtime, project delays, or budget overruns, we improve our processes to reduce the likelihood of future problems, supporting our employees completely along the way.

7. Communicates consistently—I would much rather hear often from a boss about strategy, priorities, politics, and rumors than be surprised with sudden changes in direction or given emergent deadlines. Everyone in the organization is happy to work hard, but they need the flexibility to plan their own schedules and control their own destinies. I try very hard to communicate to all my staff via blogs, email, town meetings, and very predictable priority setting. With consistent communication, I will never be accused of "priority deficit disorder," a corollary of attention deficit disorder which occurs when executives and organizations forget the priorities for year-long projects half way through them.

8. Delegates and trusts—A boss must build a trustworthy team of people and delegate the details to them. I try to master the technical and process details of all our major projects but as my authority becomes

broader, my depth of understanding of the details shrinks. My teams support each other and I watch their progress. Unless I see someone on the team impeding the work of others, I leave the team alone to execute the projects using the standardized processes we have established together.

9. Has boundless energy and enthusiasm— Bosses should be your greatest fan and marketeer. They should show real passion for your work and tell the world about it. An optimistic, highly visible, and energetic boss keeps the employees optimistic, visible, and enthusiastic. Of course, the boss should also respect the need for downtime and temper that boundless energy during employee vacations, family time, and weekends.

> *Bosses should be your greatest fan and marketeer.*

10. Focuses on the trajectory and not the position—Every day the organization will have some new need for an IT project that is deemed critical for quality, safety, compliance, profitability, or customer satisfaction. Governance committees need to triage these using objective criteria. More often than not, new projects will be placed in a queue behind existing priority projects. The boss must realize that on any given day, 10% of the organization will feel that their needs are not being addressed, but that over time, all projects get done based on the prioritization of governance committees. If the track record of the organization is that projects get done consistently and needs of stakeholders are addressed year to year in a way that keeps most people happy, the trajectory is good. I especially apply this concept to audits. Every kind of audit—security, governance, strategy review, or specific technology—will identify dozens of opportunities for improvement. Every year gets better and better, but the position is never perfect. That's a great trajectory.

Let's hope you have a great boss. If not, keep the faith. The one constant in this world is change and over time you'll have one. In the meantime, be the best you can be by using the ten behaviors described above with your staff and you'll succeed. ∎

Running an Effective Meeting

My daughter and I once talked about my jobs. I gave her the long explanation about what I do: strategy, structure, staffing, and process optimization. She asked for the elevator speech version and I said, "Basically, I run a lot of meetings."

Running an effective meeting takes a lot of energy. The meeting organizer is responsible for the logistics, bringing together the right people, ensuring all stakeholders are heard, managing the interactions, and documenting the results. Many meetings are not a good use of time. Here's columnist Dave Barry's analysis:

"Compare the modern corporate meeting to a funeral, in the sense that you have a gathering of people who are wearing uncomfortable clothing and would rather be somewhere else. The major differences are: (1) usually only one or two people get to talk at a funeral; (2) most funerals have a definite purpose (to say nice things about a dead person) and reach a definite conclusion (this person is put in the ground); whereas meetings generally drone on until the legs of the highest ranking person fall asleep."

Here's my guidance for running an effective meeting:

1. Organize the meeting in the most painless way possible. Outlook invitations work well for folks who have a lot of flexibility in their calendars or who are always working in a single location. For executives who attend meetings 12 hours a day and who travel between several corporate locations, automated invitations just do not work. I cannot be in Los Angeles for breakfast and Boston for lunch. Outlook invitations do not take into account travel time, location, and the general pace of the day. In my view, there are three effective ways to organize a meeting:

    a. Propose four or five possible dates/times and circulate them via email among the attendees/administrative assistants. Determine the "must have" attendees at the meeting. Based on the best fit of the "must haves," select a date/time. Just about all meetings can be organized this way.

    b. If urgency is required, get all the admins on a conference call and do a real-time reconciliation of calendars for the best fit. A use case for this is a meeting to discuss a strategic opportunity with time sensitivity.

    c. If real urgency is required, just set a date and time and ask everyone to cancel their other commitments. A use case for this is a Joint Commission visit. Just drop everything you're doing.

    Using endless "reply to all" emails among a large group of attendees to schedule a meeting generally does not work. For a senior leader, trying to organize a meeting yourself, without administrative coordination, is very problematic, since there is a lot of communication required to find the best fit among many schedules.

2. Food and drink are real motivators to attend a very early, lunch time or very late meeting. Be kind to your attendees. They are giving their time to you and have very busy schedules. We are all under such time pressure that the only near-term free times in our calendars are breakfast, lunch, and dinner. If you use those times, bring refreshments.

3. Arrive early and begin the meeting promptly. Meetings take a lot of energy to organize. Time is the one commodity that people cannot make more of. If the meeting organizer arrives late, it's a sign of disrespect. Begin and end the meeting on time. The attendees will appreciate it.

4. Circulate meeting materials, including a formal agenda, ahead of time. I've attended several meetings without a clear understanding of who is attending, the purpose of the meeting, the desired outcome, and any preparation I should do ahead of time. Circulate an agenda a few days before the meeting containing:

   a. The attendees, location, and call-in number (for remote attendees)

   b. The overall purpose of the meeting

   c. The items to be discussed, identifying the main presenters

   d. The background briefing materials to help with decision making

   The meeting is likely to be much more productive.

5. Ensure everyone has a chance to speak and interact professionally. As the master of ceremonies of the meeting, the convener must prevent hegemony of any one speaker and should rapidly quash any emotional outbursts. It's fine to criticize ideas in a meeting but not to criticize or attack a person. I often use humor, real-time compromise, and personal stories of similar past controversies to bring out the best behavior in everyone. If I know that a meeting has potential landmines, I'll openly state them at the beginning of the meeting and give permission to everyone to openly discuss them in a non-judgmental forum.

6. Put your mobile devices away. During long meetings that I run, I will very occasionally (once an hour) scan the inbox on my Blackberry for downtime messages, urgent notices, email from the CEO, etc., but I will never use the Blackberry to respond to an issue while I am running a meeting.

7. Adhere to the agenda. Running a meeting requires focus. If there are tangential discussions, bring the focus back to the agenda. If there are

private sidebar conversations, bring them into the whole meeting. The only way for the meeting to move forward is with everyone listening and progressing through the agenda.

8. Do a mid-meeting summary. Halfway through the meeting, I take a checkpoint. Are we on track; what have we decided thus far? I summarize the main points of agreement and the remaining items on the agenda, so we can bring closure to the work we've done thus far and move forward.

9. Own the last two minutes. The last two minutes of the meeting are the most important. The convener should review all the decisions made, the next steps decided upon, the resources committed, the timelines, the deliverables, and most critically, the paths not chosen (e.g., we will not do this project, spend this money, pursue that opportunity). By ending the meeting with an overall summary, all will leave the meeting with a common understanding of the consensus, even if some do not agree with it. The last two minutes can make or break the meeting by ensuring there is no ambiguity about the meeting's results. With a clear summary, all participants will understand the value of the meeting and their role in the meeting events.

> *By ending the meeting with an overall summary, all will leave the meeting with a common understanding of the consensus, even if some do not agree with it.*

10. Send a follow-up email summary with minutes. Even with a great last two-minute summary, some stakeholders will have selective memory. It's best to memorialize the last two minutes of the meeting in meeting minutes, and circulate to all meeting attendees and stakeholders. Also, take the time to thank those who attended the meeting and praise them for their work.

By following these steps, you maximize your meeting time, optimize communication, and maybe even reduce the number of meetings needed because of your remarkable efficiency running the process! ∎

Resolving Conflict

I've written about leading change and managing personnel transitions, and the next in this series is resolving conflict. Most people do not enjoy conflict and want highly contentious situations to resolve themselves. Sometimes this works and sometimes it ends in chaos. I am convinced that to be a successful CIO, you must embrace conflict.

Here's the approach I use to resolve conflict:

1. Listen before talking. I find that many conflicts are the result of poor communication. Just understanding the issue deeply can resolve many conflicts. Being proactive by learning more about controversial situations early in the conflict is much easier than getting involved after the situation escalates.

2. Never use email to resolve complex issues. Anytime I receive long email threads about an issue, I call a "time out" and schedule a meeting or conference call.

    > *Never use email to resolve complex issues.*

3. Pick up the phone to diffuse emotion. Anytime I receive an emotional email, I do not respond via email. I pick up the phone, even if I know the conversation will be painful. Most people react differently in a person-to-person conversation than in email.

4. Never send an emotional email or make an emotional statement. If I ever feel a negative emotion while writing an email, I save as draft. Although an emotional email may feel like an effective weapon, it wins only the battle, not the war. Emails last forever, can be circulated widely, and make conflict resolution much harder in the long run. My experience with emotion, written or spoken, is that no one who responds to any issue with anger looks good while doing it. Those with polished executive presence are always emotionally neutral when dealing with conflict.

5. Take a walk in the woods, a technique named after a famous story in which international negotiators at loggerheads over a nuclear arms treaty went for a walk in the woods near Geneva and discovered common interests that led to new solutions. The four negotiation steps developed by the Harvard Program for Health Care Negotiation and Conflict Resolution are the following:

Step one: Self-interests. Each participant articulates his or her view of key problems, issues, and options. Stakeholders are encouraged to actively listen, question, and interact with one another.

Step two: Enlarged interests. The participants reframe their understanding of current problems and possible options with a wider perspective, based on the integrative listening and confidence-building that occurred in step one.

Step three: Enlightened interests. The group is ready to engage in innovative thinking and problem-solving, generating ideas and perspectives that had not previously been considered.

Step four: Aligned interests. Participants build common ground perspectives, priorities, action items, agreement, or plans for moving forward. Depending on the scope of the intended objectives, at this point they recognize the tangible contributions and opportunities accomplished through the meeting.

My "walks in the woods" usually take place at the Elephant Walk Restaurant on Beacon Street in Boston, so if you ever see someone dressed in all black eating a vegan meal at the Elephant Walk, it's a good guess that I'm resolving conflict! ∎

An About Face on Flexible Work Arrangements

In my years as a CIO, I've strongly believed that productivity is best when everyone works in close physical proximity, so that you get the benefit of the "over the cubicle" effect of being able to brainstorm with colleagues ad hoc, respond to urgent issues as a group, and build trust among team members.

But the world has changed, and new factors need to be considered. First, the commuting needed to bring everyone together has become burdensome and expensive. Commutes can now take two hours or more, and gas prices are causing hardship. At the same time, environmental consciousness about the carbon impact of those long commutes is on the rise. Second, Internet connections are becoming faster, more reliable, and cheaper. I have a high bandwidth fiber connection in my basement for $40 a month.

We also have many more means of communication: e-mail, instant messaging, blogs, wikis, WebEx, and videoconferencing. Face-to-face meetings that take weeks to schedule are no longer sufficient for the pace of IT change and the level-of-service demands.

How should a CIO react to this changing landscape? I believe we have to explore the entire spectrum of flexible work arrangements.

Are in-person meetings really necessary? I find that a kick-off meeting to initiate a project works best if the team assembles in person. Collaborators can introduce themselves and build a common framework for working together. Thereafter, conference calls, online collaboration tools, and email are sufficient.

Is 8 am to 5 pm the best way to staff an office? Not if it implies hours on the road each way. If working from 10 am to 7 pm reduces the commute by an hour each way, it's likely that productivity and staff satisfaction will rise.

Is being in the office even necessary? For some jobs, the interruptions of the office may actually reduce productivity. Some structured time in a home office may be preferable.

Of course, there are issues.

A home office needs infrastructure support: networks, desktops, and connections to the corporate phone system. Figuring out the best way to service hundreds of remote locations will require planning and pilots. The technology may not need to be complicated, though. Videoconferencing isn't always necessary, for example, since phone calls and Web-based remote presentation tools are very efficient.

Accountability for employees with flexible work arrangements is key, so you may need management tools to monitor specific project milestones and productivity goals. But you may be pleasantly surprised. In a recent pilot in Massachusetts, a major health insurer found that productivity for 200 staffers working from home rose 20%; only two participants had performance issues.

Equity is another problem. Some staffers, such as those doing direct desktop service or training, need to be on-site. But you can still offer some flexibility, letting them put in four ten-hour days, say, or giving them every other Friday off.

Security and privacy are other concerns, and they loom especially large for me, since my IT organization is part of a large healthcare provider. If protected health data is to be accessible in employees' homes, we will need to investigate biometric devices, re-examine application time-outs, strengthen surveillance of audit logs, and ensure end-to-end security from data center to the home.

We will continue to enhance the technologies, policies, and business processes needed to manage technology professionals in flexible work arrangements. I expect that retention, productivity, and employee satisfaction will rise as time spent commuting falls. I'll write about the progress—from my home office. ■

Removing Complexity

"Fools ignore complexity. Pragmatists suffer it. Geniuses remove it."[6]

Whenever I purchase something for myself or my home, I always think about the complexity that the purchase will add to my life. Adding more stuff to my life can lead to short-term gratification, but it also can lead to long-term maintenance headaches.

The same can be said of information technology. Here are a few examples:

---

6   Quote by Alan Perlis, creator of ALGOL, one of the first programming languages.

1. A few years ago, I had dinner with Steve Ballmer[7] and explained that Microsoft should produce secure, reliable products with fewer features and lower cost. Who really wants their outline reformatted by the Outline Wizard in Word? Who really wants to apply the latest emergency patch that's required because of too much code supporting too many seldom-used features? He explained that I was mistaken since most people use 95% of the features in Office and the average user prioritizes new features over everything else. We agreed to disagree and he returned to Redmond to manage the creation of Vista.

2. At BIDMC, we buy and build software. Every time we buy a commercial product, we need to think about interfaces from our existing systems to the new product and from the new product to our existing systems. All those interfaces add significant complexity, make recovery from downtime more difficult, and increase the cost of support. Recently, a clinician commented that one of our new software purchases really surprised her, since it added complexity, fractured workflow, and inconvenienced many users for the benefit of a few.

3. When we build software, we are often tempted to add all the bells and whistles requested by the user. For each new custom feature, there is a cost of maintenance, additional training, and potential bugs that could compromise stability/reliability. I've been involved in many development projects that eventually became so complex that the software had to be rewritten to ensure usability, security, and maintainability.

4. Customizing commercial packages seems like a good idea to get the buy-in of stakeholders. Over my past decade as a CIO, I've found that stakeholders come and go, and when they leave, all the esoteric customizations they designed are often retired. In fact, many upgrade projects include the retirement of all the previous customizations that became an impediment to life-cycle management of software, added complexity, and over the long term were more hassle than benefit.

5. Best of breed seems like a good idea when you're comparing products based on narrowly focused requirements. We did that with our email system (i.e., Exchange for general email functions, Brightmail for spam protection, McAfee for virus protection, Tumbleweed for secure email transmission, SendMail for SMTP gateways). The end result was a feature-rich system that has been too challenging to maintain and

---

7   Steve Ballmer has served as CEO of Microsoft since January, 2000.

debug. Our next purchase will be an appliance from a single vendor which consolidates spam filtering and security into a single product.

In short, complexity is generally not a good thing. What am I doing to battle complexity?

I try to use the fewest number of vendors possible—one (or at most two) storage vendors, one desktop vendor, one network vendor, and very few application vendors. The more vendors, the greater the integration effort, the increased support and maintenance burden, and the higher the cost.

I aim to avoid customizing commercial software whenever possible. My experience is that customizations are rarely worth the investment. Once customizations are in place and the users really understand the implications to workflow, cost, and impediments to future upgrades, they are no longer so enthusiastic about them.

I use enterprise-wide generalizable tools whenever possible (e.g., one content management system for the web, one means of authentication/single sign-on, one ERP system for all fiscal/administrative functions).

How are we seeing this "removing complexity" idea play out in the industry?

People have adopted Gmail, Google Apps, and Facebook as "good enough" productivity tools.

People are adopting commodity hardware, clustered together using basic Linux operating systems, instead of proprietary niche solutions.

People are using SaaS offerings with thin-client computers running nothing more than a browser. Even Microsoft has embraced the new reality of cloud computing, demonstrating a willingness to eliminate the complexity of its current operating system and application environment.

In the world of IT, simplicity is often more reliable, more secure, and more usable. Whenever I'm tempted to add complexity to address the needs of a few customers, I remind myself that Less is More. Per the Alan Perlis quote above, we should all strive to be geniuses! ∎

An Epidemic of Overtreatment

Healthcare costs in the US are approaching 17% of the gross domestic product (GDP) and may be as high as 20% in the next few years. What is causing the US to have the highest cost and lowest value for the healthcare dollar? Simple—it's overtreatment.

Overtreatment takes many forms—from over-ordering expensive diagnostic tests to the

What is causing the US to have the highest cost and lowest value for the healthcare dollar? Simple— it's overtreatment.

prescribing of expensive and sometimes unneeded therapeutics.

There are many reasons for this. Here are just a few:

1. Incentives are misaligned. Healthcare reimbursement in the US pays for quantity, not quality. This means that clinicians benefit from performing more procedures, hospitals benefit from more diagnostic testing, and the pharmaceutical industry benefits from adoption of new brand name drugs. If you do not believe this to be the case, spend a day in an ambulatory care clinic or a hospital and see what goes on. Ask any resident, fellow, or attending how many tests and treatments are unneeded. We believe that paying for wellness or paying for outcomes will solve this piece of the overtreatment puzzle. If doctors and hospitals had to live within a budget, diagnostic and treatment strategies would change quickly and become less expensive for all of us, with equally good clinical outcomes.

2. We've attended many gatherings at which parents discuss brand name powerful antibiotics and recommend that they become the first-line drug for treatment of anything their children complain about. "Don't accept amoxicillin, go for the Augmentin or Cipro." My daughter has never taken an antibiotic in her life. She's had a few viruses, but no virus is cured by antibiotics. Overtreatment of the pediatric population with powerful antibiotics creates resistant organisms that make children sicker and create a dependency on ever-more powerful antibiotics. The problem with adults is equally severe. Watch the evening news and within an hour you'll hear about a dozen brand name pharmaceuticals treating diseases you've never heard of, but may now suspect you have. The US is the only country in the world that allows "direct to consumer" advertising. We believe this advertising should be regulated to solve this piece of the overtreatment puzzle. Those advertising dollars end up coming out of your pocket too!

3. Some patients are not willing to accept risk or shared decision making with their doctors. They want to begin the evaluation of back pain with an MRI instead of trying a course of gentle exercise and pain meds. Many issues do not have a clean or simple diagnosis. Eat right, exercise, avoid caffeine/nicotine, and let the body heal itself. For many conditions, rest and time cure the problem. Although the healthcare systems of Canada and the UK have their problems, the fact that access to expensive diagnostics is limited enables patients and their doctors to work together on simpler evaluations and therapies as a first step. We need to change the cultural expectation that expensive tests are "first line."

4. As a country the US eats poorly, avoids exercise, drinks an infusion of lattes, and then wants to take a pill to make all the lifestyle diseases go away. Lifestyle issues should be treated with lifestyle changes, not pharmaceuticals or nutraceuticals. Our own experience convinced us of this. I gave up the lattes, the super-sized meals, and began daily exercise 15 years ago. Since that time, my lifestyle diseases have disappeared.

5. Overtreatment begets overtreatment. If a lifestyle disease is treated with pharmaceuticals, it's likely that those medications will cause side effects. The symptoms of side effects lead to further diagnostic testing and more pharmaceuticals are often the result. We know several patients who are on medications for hypertension due to overeating, H2 blockers due to excess caffeine/nicotine consumption, and several medications to treat the side effects of their initial medications. Two or three medications can fast become ten. We've suggested taking a medication holiday with appropriate clinical supervision, redesigning their diets, and beginning daily exercise. The answer we often hear is that taking all those pills, having all those tests, and visiting their clinician often are easier than changing their lifestyle.

6. In a radio interview a few years ago, an attorney asked the question, "Have you ever had a bad outcome or misdiagnosis? I've been holding doctors accountable for 30 years. Call me and we'll get you the cash settlement you deserve." There are bad doctors. There are doctors who are unskilled at surgery or provide very non-standard care. However, most clinicians are trying to do the right thing. Medicine is not an exact science. It's based on experience and probabilities. This means that even the best clinician will miss a rare disease or an atypical presentation of a common disease. As a country, we need to realize that delayed or misdiagnosis will occur despite best efforts and accept a low level of imperfect outcomes instead of forcing every doctor to over treat every patient in the pursuit of 100% certainty. Both patients and doctors together must accept some degree of uncertainty or we will continue to bankrupt our system.

Our economy has lost its competitive edge because our healthcare costs have ballooned to extreme levels due to misaligned incentives, overzealous pharmaceutical marketing, expectations of high-cost testing/therapeutics, excessive administrative costs, and complications due to overprescribing and fear of litigation.

The diagnosis of overtreatment is simple. The therapies are complex. I've proposed a few fixes above and will continue to write about this topic. ■

Lessons Learned from Being a Public Figure

Although I'm not really a public figure, I do enough presentations in my local, state, and federal roles to appreciate the challenges of highly visible corporate and government public figures. Here are my top ten observations:

1. There is no downtime. While on a plane, train, or in any public space, you cannot be freewheeling with your opinions. Your communications must be thoughtful regardless of venue. Emails must be written with the assumption they will appear in *The New York Times*. While going about the activities of day-to-day living, you must always be "on." I've had deep conversations about IT strategy and government policy at the dump.

> *Emails must be written with the assumption they will appear in The New York Times.*

2. You must be a good listener. Public figures are assumed to have power and there will be many opinions about how to best use that power. Employees, colleagues, and the blogosphere will offer continuous advice as to the best path forward. All of this input should be gathered and acknowledged. Since every action you take will be documented and scrutinized, it's important to incorporate multi-stakeholder input into your decision making.

3. You must hold yourself to high standards. Watching the confirmation activities as candidates have been vetted in the new administration, we know that you must be a tax expert, avoid hiring domestic help, and shun association with lobbyists. The good news for me is that my tax returns are simple, I've never had domestic help, and I rarely get out much, so I have few opportunities for any conflicts of interest with lobbyists or other nefarious characters. I married the first woman I dated in college and we're still together. There are no experiences in my life thus far that Dr. Phil or Jerry Springer would find interesting.

4. You cannot be too extreme in your views. Public figures listen to all sides of an issue, then select a path forward that works for most people. In a recent keynote I did with Senator Sheldon Whitehouse (D-RI), he noted that politics are like topography—there are peaks and valleys of political issues. Some mountains, like single-payer healthcare, cannot be climbed in the short term.

5. You rarely use formal authority. In many societies, policy can be made by benign dictators at an accelerated pace without debate. That's not the way policy is made in the US. Whether in institutions like Harvard University or in government, there is a process for everything. A leader

can communicate a vision or assemble a guiding coalition, but rarely can a public figure just declare an action to be done by fiat.

6. It's more about responsibility than power. Public figures take responsibility for all the actions and events that take place in their sphere of influence. My experience has been that lofty positions come with huge responsibility but little power. Many public figures are like the General Secretary of the UN—charged with communicating a vision, organizing people, and moving issues forward, but without significant power to orchestrate rapid change.

7. Your communications will be interpreted in ways you never intended. In my own small world of healthcare IT, I find it interesting to read blogs, articles, and news stories which interpret my actions and comments. People will find support for their own views, will extend my opinions to meet their needs, or will create controversy where none exists. I'm always amused when I read headlines such as, "Was HITSP[8] work shift a political maneuver?" since politics never crossed my mind when I thought about transport standards and simple EHR data content exchange.

8. There will be good days and bad days. As I begin each day, I never know what press, email, and unexpected events will occur. Some days have a relaxed schedule but turn into a firestorm of communication about controversies I did not anticipate. There is no potential for completing a day without some measure of angry emails, hostile phone calls, and unresolved issues. Each day, I look at the trajectory and the issues that were moved more forward than backward. On balance, if I feel that I've done everything possible to bring closure to my open issues, it's a good day.

9. You'll receive credit for things you did not do and blame for things you cannot control. Whenever I'm introduced at keynote addresses, my life summary sounds like I'm super human. The reality of being a public figure is that you'll get credit for many things done by people working for you or done by colleagues working with you. I constantly credit the team and institution with the accomplishments, not myself. Spreading the credit for success is easy since "Success has 1,000 fathers." However, when bad things happen, it's expected that the public figure will accept responsibility, even if the events were not directly controllable. Apologizing with candor and grace is an important skill to have.

---

8   HITSP = Healthcare Information Technology Standards Panel.

10. You cannot make everyone happy. There are so many special interests in the world today that there is no such thing as a policy or idea that everyone will accept. A solution based on 90% consensus means that 10% will feel wronged and will oppose the path forward. The best a public figure can do is listen, facilitate, communicate, and then move forward with the optimal thinking at the time. Even while executing a well-orchestrated plan, there will be naysayers, continued debate, and controversy. The public figure should continue to listen, provide mid-course correction as needed, and support forward progress.

> *The best a public figure can do is listen, facilitate, communicate, and then move forward with the optimal thinking at the time.*

I've known many public figures in my career: Milton Friedman, Edward Teller, Condoleezza Rice. I have some sense of the energy they required just to be themselves. Next time you're feeling angst for a public figure, take a moment to empathize with their challenges. ∎

A Visicalc Moment

If you were an early Apple II or IBM PC user, you may remember the first time you saw Visicalc (1979), SuperCalc (1980), MultiPlan (1982), or Lotus 1-2-3 (1983).

The spreadsheet solves a real problem—it saves time, it empowers its users, and people are more productive using it. No more paper, pencil, and calculators. No more days wasted manually computing "what if" scenarios.

I call this joy from the early days of personal computing a "Visicalc moment."

One challenge we face as we roll out electronic health records to every clinician is that the first time they see an EHR (of any type, from any vendor), they rarely have a "Visicalc moment."

Because we have not marketed the benefits of EHRs to clinicians, they are not sure an EHR saves time, streamlines their workflow, or brings them a better quality of worklife.

There are three ways to motivate most clinicians:

1. Pay them more.

2. Offer them more free time.

3. Apply peer pressure.

How can we leverage these principles so clinicians will have Visicalc moments?

A few thoughts:

1. Electronic medication workflow in an EHR saves time, reduces the number of calls/pages due to unreadable prescriptions, and streamlines the refile process.

2. Templates, macros and voice recognition can speed up clinical documentation. Of course, they must be used wisely to avoid creating inaccuracies that are persisted forever in the record. Electronic clinical documentation can be electronically exchanged between referring clinicians and specialists, leading to a peer preference for those who document electronically.

3. Patient education can be automated by linking problem lists and prescriptions to resources such as UptoDate and Healthwise.

4. Decision support such as automated ordering ensures the safest, most effective therapies are given based on evidence and patient-specific data. It can also be used to generate alerts and reminders in support of pay-for-performance programs.

5. Administrative simplification streamlines the revenue cycle, reducing denials and accounts receivable (AR) days.

Thus, EHRs, especially those offered via the web via SaaS models, can generate income, save time, and keep peers happy.

Let's hope that the future of healthcare IT includes many "Visicalc moments." ∎

The Role of a Leader

I've written many blog posts about leadership and the challenges of running large, complex organizations. Recently, I've thought about how I have personally changed during my 15 years in healthcare leadership positions.

In my early years, the initial challenges were to break through technical barriers by creating prototype applications and demonstrating the possibilities of the emerging web in the mid-1990s.

I then progressed to organization building, devising the strategy, structure, and staffing of a growing IT organization.

From there I evolved to thinking about processes—how to ensure reliability, security, and performance of complex infrastructure and applications.

I then moved on to education—writing and speaking about our efforts inside and outside my organizations.

Where am I today as a leader? I believe I'm a convener.

Whether it's my federal, state, or local roles, my most important leadership task is assembling people with various opinions, some of them very vocal, and achieving a set of priorities, next steps, and policies.

In some ways, I'm becoming less technology focused and more business focused. Many of the technologies that were risky/bleeding edge a few years ago—the web, clouds, clusters, enterprise storage, and thin clients—are now mainstream. My day is less about getting the technology working right and more about ensuring we're using the right technology to meet the needs of business owners. Unfortunately, many business owners do not know what they need, although they have high expectations.

The theme of my next leadership year will be governance.

Of course, there is Meaningful Use, EHR implementation, and privacy policy change—but convening stakeholders via a recognized governance model is a prerequisite to getting those done.

> My day is less about getting the technology working right and more about ensuring we're using the right technology to meet the needs of business owners.

It's painful at times to gather everyone together and hear a multitude of diverse opinions, some of which may be factually incorrect and many of which can be critical. All of us are tempted to 'wait to speak' instead of listen. However, the best way I can serve my staff and ultimately all my stakeholders is to condense the messiness of contentious viewpoints and competition for resources into a well-communicated list of priorities.

The measure of my success should be the projects we decide NOT to do, since great governance will set priorities, and align them with limited budgets and fixed timeframes. A sign of failed governance is saying "yes" to everything, flogging staff until they resign in fatigue, and creating general dissatisfaction throughout the organization because scope is too large and resources are too small.

Convening and governance will be my role as a leader over the next year. Only when I can master that can I progress to my next leadership stage. ∎

Assessing My Own Risk

Leaders often think about succession plans for their direct reports, but what about themselves?

What if I had a serious health problem or accident that impaired my ability to lead my IT organizations? Here's my brief analysis.

Beth Israel Deaconess Medical Center

My role at BIDMC is to document the strategies prioritized by our governance groups, ensure our organizational chart structure is optimized for executing the strategies, and find/retain the best people. I also work on the processes that support our strategy including governance, budgeting, and communication.

In the 1990s, I wrote the code that powered our clinical web-based applications and intranet. At this point, we've retired all the code I've written or transitioned its development/support to full-time programmers. I am no longer a single point of failure for any application or infrastructure. At BIDMC, about 30% of applications are built and 70% are purchased. Occasionally some stakeholders wonder if building a few applications is a risk. It's actually a risk mitigator. We create the "glue" that links together vendor applications via portals and web-based service-oriented architecture approaches. Since we control the front end that clinicians see for EHRs and provider order entry, we can rapidly add features needed for Meaningful Use, healthcare reform, and Joint Commission requirements. We've implemented novel solutions for medication reconciliation, decision support, and health information exchange. Building what is not available in the marketplace and buying products that are mature are the best ways to reduce risk.

Some projects depend upon my strength of will—implementing EHRs for the community, embracing interoperability/standards, and keeping us focused on the large projects that move us forward. If I were to disappear, it is true that efforts to achieve Meaningful Use would slow significantly. As I've discussed in my blog several times, it takes all the energy and reputation I have to ensure all our clinicians—those in academic health centers and those in small community practices—have all the tools they need and training/education they require to achieve Meaningful Use.

In any large, complex organization, satisfaction with IT goes up and down. As resources are pulled into large projects, smaller projects suffer and stakeholders may feel underserved. As compliance requirements, new regulations, Joint Commission mandates, and senior management signature initiatives appear, existing initiatives may be slowed or cancelled. My role is to foster communication, ensure that governance includes all stakeholders, and provide a buffer for my staff from the ups and downs of opinion and changing priorities. If I disappeared, the "tyranny of the urgent" may triumph, preventing IT from staying focused on the functionality needed to achieve Meaningful Use.

Harvard Medical School

At HMS, my role in governance, strategy, structure, staffing, and process was similar to BIDMC. I worked with research, education, and administrative stakeholders to define their priorities and allocate resources. My major projects included building one of the top 100 supercomputers in the world, providing a petabyte of storage to support translational research, and supporting all the interactive media for over 1,000 courses. My role was to balance managing day-to-day issues while also engaging all stakeholders in long-term planning activities. When I left my HMS role, the communication/education of stakeholders and the delicate balance of services among the research/education/administrative communities were the key focus for my replacement.

Overall in my role as CIO, my greatest utility is to provide a common link between the academic/education/research activities of the medical school and the clinical/financial/research activities of the hospital, while also leveraging my state and federal activities to ensure my organizations are early adopters of federal requirements and participants in pilots. My multi-organizational role provides economies of scale, knowledge sharing, and community-wide visibility for IT activities. My absence would diminish these cross-organizational collaborations, slowing down our work.

My role has evolved substantially over the past decade and I've moved from programmer to convener, from a focus on operations to a focus on innovation, and from technologist to policymaker. Senior leaders owe it to their organizations to periodically reflect on their role and how their organization would carry on without them.

> *Senior leaders owe it to their organizations to periodically reflect on their role and how their organization would carry on without them.*

The Year of Governance

If my epitaph had to be written tomorrow, what pithy quote would I select from my blog?

Possibilities include:

"For everything there is a process."

"The happiest stage of life is wherever I am today."

"The nice guy can finish first."

However, if I died today I'd recommend, "Governance is the solution to all your problems." What have I done to improve IT governance?

At Harvard Medical School, we expanded our governance committees to ensure administration, education, and research stakeholders have governance committees which roll up to an executive governance committee of the individual committee chairs. Together, these committees set the departmental and overall IT priorities for the school.

At BIDMC, we created a new overall IT Governance Committee, in addition to the existing subcommittees that prioritize departmentally focused efforts:

- Laboratory Information Systems chaired by the senior vice president/vice president (SVP/VP) overseeing the lab

- Radiology Information Systems chaired by the SVP/VP overseeing radiology

- Enterprise Image Management chaired by the CIO

- Emergency Department Information Systems chaired by the SVP overseeing Ambulatory and Emergency Services

- Critical Care Information Systems chaired by the Director of Trauma, Anesthesia, and Critical Care

- Peri-operative Information Systems chaired by the Director of Perioperative Service

- Inpatient Clinical Applications (includes Provider Order Entry) co-chaired by the Chief Nursing Officer and VP for Clinical Systems

- Ambulatory (WebOM) users group chaired by the SVP overseeing Ambulatory and Emergency Services

- Health Information Management Information Systems chaired by the Director of the Hospital Medicine Program

- Community Information Systems chaired by the Executive Director of the Physician's Organization

- Decision Support Steering Committee chaired by the Director of Business Planning and Decision Support and the Vice Chair of General Medicine

- Enterprise Resource Planning (ERP) Information Systems chaired by the Director of Business Services and the Controller

- Human Resources Information Systems chaired by the SVP of Human Resources

The role of the overall IT Governance Committee includes:
- Communication about prioritization and resource decisions

- Articulating, prioritizing, and monitoring the overall vision for IT at BIDMC

- Achieving the right balance between built and bought systems including adequate staffing for maintenance to ensure high customer satisfaction

Why is governance so important?
- This is the most stressful time in the entire history of healthcare IT in the US. Meaniningful Use requires significant application, infrastructure, and change management efforts.

- This is the time to begin planning for healthcare reform and the new world of accountable care organizations and the electronic systems we'll need for the future.

- This is a time of many new regulatory/compliance mandates including planning for ICD-10, new data protection regulations, and increasing oversight from the Joint Commission/CMS[9]/FDA,[10] etc.

---

9 CMS = Centers for Medicare & Medicaid Services.

10 FDA = US Food and Drug Administration.

Every hour you spend on governance will save you ten hours of future conflict and misunderstanding. ■

Good Consultants, Bad Consultants

In 1998, when I became CIO of CareGroup, there were numerous consultants serving in operational roles at BIDMC and CareGroup. My first task as CIO was to build a strong internal management team, eliminate our dependency on consultants, and balance our use of built and bought applications. Twelve years later, I have gained significant perspective on consulting organizations—large and small, strategic and tactical, mainstream and niche.

There are many good reasons to hire consultants. One of my favorite industry commentators, Robert X. Cringley,[11] wrote an excellent column about hiring consultants. A gold star idea from his analysis is that most IT projects fail at the requirements stage. If business owners cannot define their future state workflows, hiring consultants to implement automation will fail.

I've been a consultant to some organizations, so I've felt the awkwardness of parachuting into an organization, making recommendations, then leaving before those recommendations have an operational impact. Many of my friends and colleagues work for consulting companies. Some consultants are so good that I think of them as partners and value-added extensions of the organization instead of as vendors. From my experience, both hiring and being a consultant, here's an analysis of what makes a consultant good or a consultant bad.

1. Project Scope
Good—They provide work products that are actionable without creating dependency on the consultant for follow-on work. There are no change orders to the original consulting assignment.

Bad—Consultants become self-replicating. Deliverables are missing the backup data needed to justify their recommendations. Consultants build relationships throughout the organization outside their constrained scope of work, identifying potential weaknesses and convincing senior management that more consultants are needed to mitigate risk. Two consultants become four, then more. They create overhead that requires more support staff from the consulting company.

2. Knowledge Transfer
Good—They train the organization to thrive once the consultants leave. They empower the client with specialized knowledge of technology or techniques that will benefit the client in operational or strategic activities.

---

11 Robert X. Cringley is the pen name of technology journalist Mark Stephens.

Bad—Their deliverable is a PowerPoint of existing organizational knowledge without insight or unique synthesis. This is sometimes referred to as "borrowing your watch to tell you the time."

3. Organizational Dynamics

Good—They build bridges among internal teams, enhancing communication through formal techniques that add processes to complement existing organizational project management approaches. Adding modest amounts of work to the organization is expected because extra project management rigor can enhance communication and eliminate tensions or misunderstandings among stakeholders.

Bad—They identify organizational schisms they can exploit, become responsible for discord, and cause teams to work against each other as a way to foster organizational dependency on the consultants.

4. Practical Recommendations

Good—Recommendations are data-backed, prioritized by relative value (cost multiplied by benefit), reflect current community standards, and take into account competing uses of the organization's resources and time.

Bad—Recommendations lack depth. They are products of uncorroborated interviews. They lack factual details and are a scattershot intended to create fear, uncertainty, and doubt. They focus on parts rather than systems. Implementing these recommendations causes energy to be drained away from more strategic and beneficial initiatives.

5. Fees

Good—Consultants use markup factors (amount they charge verses the amount they pay their staff) such as the following: staff augmentation / placement only, with no management oversight = 1.5; commodity consultants, largely staff augmentation, but with "account management" = 1.5-2; consulting / systems integration, project-based = 2-3.5; management consulting / very senior and high-demand specialists = 3.5-4.

Bad—The engagement partner becomes more concerned about billing you than serving you. Meetings appear on your calendar weeks before the end of a consulting engagement to discuss your statement of work renewal. You begin to spend more time managing the consultants than managing the project. Consultants justify a markup factor of 5 or 6 by saying "We're so good that we have high overhead."

6. Balancing Priorities

Good—Complex organizations execute numerous projects every year in the context of their annual operating plans. Although consultants are hired to complete very specific tasks, good consultants take into account the environment in which they are working and balance their project against the other organizational priorities. In this way, the organization can adapt to the changes caused by the presence of the consultant while not significantly disrupting their other work.

Bad—Meetings are consistently scheduled with little advance notice that conflict with other organizational imperatives. Any attention paid to organizational demands outside the consulting engagement are escalated to senior management as being "uncooperative."

7. Quality of Deliverables

Good—The deliverables are innovative, customized to the organization, and represent original work based on significant effort, due diligence, and expertise.

Bad—Material is reused from other organizations. The volume of deliverables is increased with boilerplate. The content seems unhelpful, general, or unrelated to the details of your organization.

8. Managing Project Risk

Good—Risk is defined as the likelihood of bad things happening multiplied by the impact on the organization. Real risks to the project are identified and solutions are recommended/developed collaboratively with project sponsors.

Bad—There is greater concern about risk to the reputation of the consultants than the risks to project success.

9. Respect for the Org Chart

Good—Work is done at the request of the project sponsors. The chain of command and the hierarchy of the organization are respected, so that consultants do not interact directly with the board or senior management unless directed to do so by the project sponsors.

Bad—Governance processes are disrupted and consultants seek to establish the trust of the organizational tier above the project sponsors. Sometimes they will even work against the project sponsors to ensure organizational dependency on the consultants.

10. Consistency

Good—Transparency, openness, and honesty characterize all communications from the consultants to all stakeholders in the organization.

Bad—Every person is told a different story in the interest of creating the appearance of being supportive and helpful. This appearance of trustworthiness is exploited to identify weaknesses and increase dependency on consultants.

I'm the greatest ally of good consultants. Per Robert Cringely's article, we'll bring in a few "Consulting Type A" experts each year for specific well-defined tactical projects requiring deep expertise.

If survival of the fittest applies to consultants, then the good ones should thrive and the bad ones should see fewer engagements over time. However, I'm not sure Darwinian selection pressures apply to consultants, since organizations may have short institutional memories about consulting experiences due to their own staff turnover.

The best you can do for your organization is think about the good and bad comparisons above, then use them to evaluate your own consulting experiences, rewarding those who bring value-added expertise and penalizing those who bring only "PowerPoint and suits." ∎

Regression to the Mean

You may have heard about the *Sports Illustrated* effect, the notion that people who appear on the cover of the magazine are likely to experience bad luck, failure, or a career spiral.

Over the 30 years of my own professional life, I've watched many colleagues become famous, receive significant publicity, then fail to live up to the impossible expectations implied by their fame. They regress to the mean. Nature seems to favor symmetry. Things that rise slowly tend to decline slowly. Things that rise rapidly tend to drop rapidly.

Fame is usually a consequence (good or bad) of invention, innovation, and accomplishment. Fame itself is generally not what motivates a person to accomplish his or her feats. An Olympic athlete is usually inspired because of a highly competitive spirit. An inventor is usually inspired because he/she believes there is a better way. Fame that is the consequence of a feat can affect future behavior. It can become an intoxicant and motivate someone to strive for accomplishments that keep the fame coming.

I've thought about my own brushes with fame.

When I was 18 and started at Stanford, I realized that my scholarships would cover only the first year of tuition. I visited the Stanford Law library, read the US tax code, and wrote software for the Kaypro, Osborne 1, and CP/M computers that calculated taxes. The software shipping from my dorm room generated enough income to start a small company. When the PC was introduced, we were the first to provide such software to small businesses seeking to compute their tax obligations. By the time I was 19, I moved into the home of Frederick Terman, former Provost of Stanford, and the professor who first encouraged William Hewlett and David Packard to build audio oscillators and form a new company called HP. The story of a 19-year-old running a software company and living in the basement of the founder of HP was newsworthy at the time. I did interviews with Dan Rather, Larry King, and NHK TV Japan.

The company grew during my medical and graduate school years, but as technology evolved it did not innovate to take advantage of new platforms, graphical user interfaces, or emerging networks. I sold the company when I began my residency. It eventually closed.

By the time it closed, I was learning to build clinical systems and worked during residency to develop a hospital-wide knowledge base for policies/procedures/protocols, an online medical record, a quality control system, and several systems for medical education. I achieved local fame when the County of Los Angeles voted me the County Employee of the Month, the first time it was given to a physician.

I left residency and began practice at Beth Israel Hospital while doing post-doctoral work at MIT, writing a thesis about using the web to securely exchange medical records. In 1997, using the web was considered risky, unreliable, and insecure, but the recent merger of Beth Israel and Deaconess needed a quick win, so "CareWeb" was born. I became CIO.

In 1999, Dr. Tom Delbanco and others had the idea that patients should be able to access their own records electronically. My team created Patientsite. We were credited with inventing one of the first personal health records.

And the list goes on: the 2002 network outage, early regional healthcare information exchange, harmonizing standards, creating a private cloud for healthcare records, and achieving hospital certification in the Meaningful Use process.

The interesting conclusion of all of this is that in every case, the fame was temporary, and very soon followed by regression to the mean—a stellar performance or innovation became typical/average/mundane.

It's nearly impossible to remain at the front of the race forever—eventually someone stronger, faster, or more nimble will displace you.

In my case, I stopped thinking about my own reputation and fame about 1998, recognizing that every episode of fame is followed by a decline into anonymity—the *Sports Illustrated* effect. What are lasting are great organizations and teams that are constantly reinventing themselves—changing the race they are running.

Steve Jobs[12] said, "We're as good as our last product," and he's right.

If you focus on creating great organizations, which consistently achieve discrete episodes of fame but continuously innovate so that those episodes of

---

12 Steve Jobs was the co-founder, chairman, and CEO of Apple, Inc. until his death in 2011.

rising and falling actually look like a continuous series of peaks, then you can beat regression to the mean.

The organizations in which I work will last for generations. Their reputations transcend anything I will ever do personally. My role is to champion, support, and publicize a few key innovations every year that will keep the organizations highly visible. That visibility will attract smart people and retain the best employees who want to work for a place on a rising trajectory. If I can transform the rise of fame and regression to the mean into a trend that feels like one organizational strength after another, I'll declare victory. ■

Working with the Media

Throughout my adult life, I've had many opportunities to speak with television, radio, and print journalists. I may not always receive good press, but I almost always receive balanced press.

I've learned several lessons along the way:

- It's important not to endorse any product or service. I'm always careful to present my experience in the context of a case study or objective observation. I avoid conflicts of interest by never accepting gifts, travel, or meals from vendors.

- It's important to speak as an individual and not as an organizational representative. I remove my badges and eliminate any organizational logos from the visual field. I emphasize that my comments are personal opinions and do not necessarily reflect the views of any corporation I work for.

- It's important to speak clearly and succinctly, and deliver an unambiguous message. Everyone should be able to understand a 30-second elevator speech about the technology I'm discussing.

- It's important to use personal stories, analogies, and lay language. I often describe my own experience with healthcare and the ways technology would improve my wellness or my family's care coordination.

- It's important to give honest answers. Occasionally, reporters have an agenda and try to put words in your mouth. State your beliefs without being led to a conclusion by redirecting a bad question into a relevant, thoughtful answer.

In the iPad2 release (I'm at 11 minutes 44 seconds into the presentation), here are the points I conveyed:

I have watched clinicians (including myself) using tablet-style devices. They enhance clinician productivity because of their portability (they fit in a white coat pocket), long battery life, and ease of disinfection (alcohol wipes on the screen do not damage the display). They untether clinicians from laptops and carts, are easy to read, and provide the high-definition graphics needed for clinical imaging interpretation.

The nature of the form factor makes it easier than laptops for clinicians to share medical information with patients (such as explaining conditions by retrieving images), improving communications.

My quotes were as follows:

"Sometimes doctors are overwhelmed with data. What we've tried to do on the iPad is to give doctors at the point of care the tools they need at the exact moment the doctor can make the difference."

"We're finding with the iPad that doctors are spending more time with patients. In fact, doctors are engaging patients by showing them images, showing them data on the screen. So it's empowered doctors to be more productive, and it's also brought doctors and patients together."

Some have called this an endorsement. I've followed my own guidelines and described my experience using the device and the behavior of other clinicians I've observed. I did not describe any plan to purchase the devices, nor have I ever received any free iPad products or services.

In a world of YouTube, social media, and blogging, everything I do and say should be considered public. Hopefully, by following my own moral compass and my guidelines for working with the media, I can share my experiences for the benefit of all without compromising my own objectivity. ∎

A Recipe for Success

When I reflect on the times in my career that perfect alignment of environmental factors resulted in high productivity and innovation, the following themes come to mind:

1. A sense of urgency to change—John Kotter's[13] change model starts with creating urgency. A perfect example of this is Meaningful Use. All stakeholders recognize that MU is a high priority requiring complete organizational focus with a well understood timeframe and clear outcomes.

---

13 Dr. John P. Kotter, head of research at Kotter International, developed the "8-Step Process for Leading Change." An authority on leadership and change, Kotter is a frequent contributor to ·The Harvard Business Review, a New York Times best-selling author, a Harvard professor, an ⁻award-winning business and management thought leader, and a business entrepreneur.

2. A clearly defined scope—Often, business owners choose software solutions before they analyze their workflows and define requirements. Automating a broken process does not make it better. The rational way to approach projects is to define an ideal workflow, develop requirements, create specifications for automation, and build/buy products. BIDMC recently designed the medication workflow of the future. Our first step was to assemble all the stakeholders for a three-day retreat to define the ideal functional characteristics without being biased by existing technology or practices. In the next few years, you can expect us to create an automated medication workflow that looks more like a Toyota production system and less like a traditional hospital ward.

3. A guiding coalition of leaders serving as champions for the project and providing ideal leadership characteristics—Leaders need to be positive, visionary, and supportive—not angry, autocratic, and arbitrary.

4. A dedicated implementation team and appropriate funding—How many times have you been asked to do more with less? Eventually you'll do everything with nothing. Your lean and mean teams will become bony and angry. If an urgent project with a tightly defined scope and unified leadership is resourced with dedicated staff, you'll be unstoppable.

5. A timeframe that makes it possible to do the project with enough attention to detail that the result is high quality, well communicated, and innovative—Every project needs to link time, scope, and resources. Nine women cannot have a baby in one month. A fixed scope and fixed resources implies a fixed time. Attempts to artificially shorten the time will compromise scope or quality. A project that goes live at the right time, even if the timeframe seems long, will never be remembered. A project that goes live too early will never be forgotten.

May you all have the time, resources, scope, noble leaders, and urgency you need to succeed. May you be driven by innovation and the desire to make a difference instead of a pugilistic project manager creating fear of failure. May you all have your Man on the Moon moment.

These are the successes we'll tell our grandchildren about. ∎

Characteristics of High-Performing Teams

I've written previously about those times in my career when alignment of leadership and resources led to major achievements. High-performing teams are a prerequisite to such achievement and here are a few characteristics of high-performing teams with which I have worked:

Competence

Domain expertise and an ability to execute assigned tasks are key to ensuring vision is turned into successful implementation. My experience is that "A" players hire "A" players and "B" players hire "C" players. This means that highly competent people surround themselves with skilled people because they do not feel intimidated by having subordinates or colleagues who are smarter, more talented, or more successful. No member of a team can do everything, so having a group of smart people working together creates a sum greater than the parts. On the other hand, incompetent people tend to hire even less competent people to shore up their own egos and self-image. Leaders need to be very careful when retaining marginally performing teams, because incompetent people hiring less competent people can get the organization in trouble very quickly.

> *Highly competent people surround themselves with skilled people because they do not feel intimidated by having subordinates or colleagues who are smarter, more talented, or more successful.*

Trust

As a rock climber, I know that my life depends upon the skill and decision making of my climbing partner. No matter how good I am, a mistake by my partner could kill both of us. Every day I think about my teams and ask if I would trust them to hold my rope. A high-performing team requires a level of trust and confidence that fosters a joy of collective achievement rather than fear of individual failure. Creating an environment of trust has worked for me as a parent and is an essential part of an optimized team.

> *A high-performing team requires a level of trust and confidence that fosters a joy of collective achievement rather than fear of individual failure.*

Communication

I realize that carrying mobile devices creates the burden of being connected 24 hours a day. I do not inflict my own work schedule on any of my teams (my last true day off was in the summer of 1984). However, creating a level of communication among team members that enables rapid escalation and resolution of issues is essential to high performance. Teams should respect the need for time away but arrange coverage such that email, instant messaging, paging, phone calls, and web-based collaboration can be initiated at a moment's notice for resolution of complex issues that are often precipitated by circumstances beyond the control of the team. Teams should create a level of transparency that keeps all members informed of current priorities, strategies, and challenges using blogs, wikis, and meetings (to the extent necessary). Great communication reduces friction, enhances decision making, and reduces unnecessary work.

Loyalty

Highly functional team members are always there for each other. No matter what happens, they do not throw their colleagues under the bus. They give an early heads up when projects or staff members are in trouble. They accelerate decision making by contributing positively to consensus building. They respect hierarchical boundaries, escalating problems by collaborating with team leaders and managers. The result is a team that is deeply loyal to its members rather than focused on highlighting the success of any one individual.

The Greater Good

In my trip to Japan, I discussed priority setting in the Japanese bureaucracy. At times it appears that ministries set priorities based on sustaining their own power and authority. Bureaus within ministries can set priorities in silos. Rarely is the greater good for the country the driving force that unifies budgeting at every level. Highly functional teams think about the overall goals of the organization and craft their plans around those activities which will create the greatest good for the greatest number. There is not siloed thinking about resources, budgets, or achieving individual goals at the expense of the team's goals.

> *Highly functional teams think about the overall goals of the organization and craft their plans around those activities which will create the greatest good for the greatest number.*

High-performing teams are hard to create and sustain, but when they happen, they are to be treasured. There is nothing I will not do for my high-performing teams. ∎

Healthcare Is Different

I'm often asked why healthcare has been slow to automate its processes compared to other industries such as the airlines, shipping/logistics, or the financial services industry.

Many clinicians say that healthcare is different.

I'm going to be a bit controversial here and agree that healthcare has unique challenges that make it more difficult to automate than other industries.

Here's an inventory of the issues:

1. Flow of funds—Hospitals and professionals are seldom paid by their customers. Payment usually comes from an intermediary such as the government or insurance payer. Thus, healthcare IT resources are focused on back-office systems that facilitate communications between providers and payers rather than innovative retail workflows such as those found at the Apple Store.

2. Hiring and training the workforce—Important members of the workforce, the physicians delivering care, are seldom employed by the hospital. This is rare if not non-existent in any other industry. It's as if Toyota built a factory that anyone can use but does not hire or train the workers who build cars. If someone wanted to create a Toyota with wings and an outboard motor, they would have the freedom to do it.

3. Negotiating price—Reimbursement no longer is based on a price schedule hospitals and professionals can control. It is based on a prospective payment model such as diagnostic related groups (DRGs) that someone else designs and dictates. Where else in the US do prices get dictated to a firm?

4. Establishing referral relationships—We cannot market services to those who control our patient flow due to Stark anti-kickback regulations. In other industries, you can build relationships, offer special incentives, and arrange mutually beneficial deals to develop your referral business. In healthcare, it's illegal even when unilaterally funding an action would make things easier for both parties and the patient.

5. Standardizing the product—In most industries, the product or service can be standardized to improve efficiency and quality. In healthcare, every person is chemically, structurally, and emotionally unique. What works for one person may or may not work for another. In this environment, it is difficult to standardize and personalize care in parallel.

6. Choosing the customer—In most other industries, you can choose with whom you do business. Not so in healthcare. If you have an emergency department, you must provide treatment even if the customer has no means to pay.

7. Compliance—Data flows in healthcare are increasingly regulated. What other business, including the IRS, is required to produce, on-

demand, a three-year look back of everyone who accessed your information within their firm.

As I noted in my post about the Burden of Compliance, "The more complex a health system becomes, the more difficult it becomes to find any system design that has a higher fitness."

We are successfully automating healthcare workflows, motivated by HITECH incentives and the requirements of healthcare reform. The seven characteristics above have required vendors to create full-featured software applications and organizations to create complex rollout/funding models that take time. By 2015 we will be there and I will be proud of all we've accomplished, given that the constraints on the healthcare industry are truly different than those on industries which have been earlier adopters of technology. ■

Heathcare Is Different: Part II

After posting "Healthcare Is Different," numerous folks contacted me, agreeing and disagreeing with my points.

Here's a compilation of some additional ways that my readers suggested healthcare is different.

- Domain expertise—The vocabulary, science, and physical skills necessary to practice medicine are very complex compared to most other professions. For example, to become a neurosurgeon requires kindergarten–high school, four years of college, four years of medical school, seven years of residency, and generally a two-year fellowship. That's 30 years of education.

- No second chance—In retail, if a good is defective it can be exchanged. In service businesses, there is the concept of a redo, a repair, or renovation. The concept of "returned goods" does not exist in healthcare.

- Trainees—There's probably no industry that is so inundated with "trainees" as healthcare, especially in an academic medical center. They add a level of inefficiency during the learning process that is required to produce the next generation of healthcare workers. In other industries, trainees come in small streams as you bring in co-ops, interns, etc. They don't come by the hundreds in July of each year.

- Highly regulated and compartmentalized workforce—Healthcare has dozens of professionals whose practice is limited to certain privileges. This inhibits mobility and cross-coverage that could improve the efficiency of the workforce. If demand gets light in cardiology, you can't easily move the clinicians to the gastrointestinal suite.

- Reimbursement and payment process — There is a well-defined commercial code for how payment occurs in most industries. In healthcare, each payer creates its own rules. In aggregate, these rules represent thousands of pages of policies and procedures that a healthcare provider must follow to be paid. For example, Medicare's claims processing manual is over 4,000 pages long and this doesn't include national and local coverage determinations, advisories, and other manuals devoted to specific types of Medicare-sponsored activities. Add to this the claims-processing rules for Medicaid and private health plans and you have an overwhelming regulatory and compliance challenge. A cynical person might suggest that payers and government agencies purposely create rules that no provider can possibly follow, then seek compliance penalties for the arcane rules they created. Providers are in a losing battle to keep up with rules that are in a constant state of flux.

These are all great observations.

My personal goal is to build software and workflow processes that make the complex seem easy, reducing the burden on providers so that they can focus on what's really important — the patient. That's why the work for a healthcare CIO will never be done. ∎

The Importance of Corporate Culture

Can one person make a difference in a large organization? Absolutely.

Although many modern executives operate under such regulatory constraints that they have infinite responsibility but limited authority, a single person can create a corporate culture that impacts everyone's work experience.

What do I mean by creating the corporate culture?

On my flight back from Japan, the in-flight magazine on All Nippon Airlines featured an article about Zappos' corporate culture, noting that the CEO has created an environment which emphasizes fun, creativity, and happiness in the workplace. Happy employees deliver great customer service without needing micromanagement or clandestine monitoring of every conversation.

When evaluating leaders we often think of characteristics such as vision, interpersonal skills, commitment to quality, staff engagement, financial acumen, ability to raise money, and domain expertise.

However, we rarely consider their impact on corporate culture. It can make a huge difference.

In my professional life, I've had two dozen bosses, each with a different style, approach, and culture.

Here are a few questions to ask about your culture:

1. Do you arrive at the office every day thinking about the joy of success or the fear of failure? Are you supported such that a negative outcome is a learning experience that results in policy or process change to improve the organization rather than blaming the person who caused it?

2. Is communication open and transparent, or guarded and reserved?

3. Do managers share accountability and see their role as enabling your success, or are they pugilists who punish unmet goals by screaming louder?

4. Do you have clear expectations for the work you do and clear metrics for success?

5. Is loyalty and trust valued? Is hierarchy respected or is your authority undermined by senior executives who work around you? Would you trust your boss to hold your rope?

6. Do staff feel respect and admiration for their colleagues such that there is a family-like atmosphere in which people will go the extra mile for each other?

7. If someone impedes the work of others through passive-aggressive behavior or scheming for their own self-interest, is it tolerated?

8. Is everyone empowered to make a difference? Are policies and procedures clear so that they know how to make a difference?

9. Are all emails/communications asking for guidance answered promptly?

10. Do you feel positive energy about the possibilities ahead when you wake up each day, or does each day end in a tailspin of emotional exhaustion?

Throughout my career I've worked in positive cultures and negative cultures. I do whatever I can to create a positive culture in the organizations I oversee. It's not always possible to create a positive culture within a larger organization that has a negative culture, but we should all try.

May you always work in a positive culture and if you do not, have the wisdom to seek a better place! ∎

Thoughts on Formal Authority

Here are a few thoughts on the wise use of formal authority (i.e., that job description we were handed when we first became leaders).

In previous posts I've reflected on the fact that none of us really has authority. Instead, we have responsibility and risk.

The work that I do in all my lives—federal, state, local, and my home life as father/husband/son—do not rely on formal authority. They rely on my informal authority to inspire, align, and communicate.

I have never "ordered" a change. The best I can do is to facilitate consensus and follow Harvard Business School Professor John Kotter's principles for change management:

1. Establish urgency.

2. Form a powerful guiding coalition.

3. Create a vision.

4. Communicate the vision.

5. Empower others to act on the vision.

6. Plan for and create short-term wins.

7. Consolidate improvements, creating more change.

8. Institutionalize new approaches.

Relationship building and fostering trust bring me the informal authority I need to lead people through change.

Although the formal authority I have is never used, there are behavioral responsibilities that come with the title of CIO. I have to be careful what I say, whom I speak with, and what I do, because the hierarchy of the organization assigns power relationships to the role I serve. There are five guidelines I've assigned to myself:

1. Respect hierarchical boundaries—If I bypass my direct reports and communicate directly with their direct reports, I always ensure the communication includes everyone in the chain of command. If I did not do this, I would disempower my managers and directors.

2. Communicate consistently with everyone—It's bad behavior to tell different versions of the truth to people based on what you believe various audiences want to hear. By communicating consistently, I create a culture of collaboration. The last thing I want to do is create discord in the organization by encouraging people to work against each other or foster dissension among teams.

3. Work via standard processes—It may seem expedient to invent your own processes, bypass hierarchies, or work around established lines of communication in an effort to accelerate projects. My experience is that such an approach causes confusion, misalignment of priorities, and wasted effort. Just as I respect hierarchical boundaries, I follow standard processes when problems need to be resolved.

4. Communicate broadly and honestly—If there is a problem in the organization, I communicate it to all stakeholders. It is far better to over communicate, even if the news is challenging/difficult, than to work in silos and try to hide failures for fear of embarrassment.

> *It is far better to over communicate, even if the news is challenging/difficult, than to work in silos and try to hide failures for fear of embarrassment.*

5. Work openly and transparently—We've all worked in organizations with office politics that happen behind the scenes. Back channel conversations, blind cc's on email, escalation around hierarchical boundaries, different conversations in the open verses behind closed doors, and undermining the authority of others can occur in any organization. If someone suggests solving a problem by working on it clandestinely, I refuse. Problems should be solved openly and transparently with all the stakeholders in the room.

These are the responsibilities of formal authority. Although you may never use the power you've been given in your job description, your actions every day can impact your peers and your staff in subtle ways. Once you understand that your every word and behavior can inspire, influence, or irritate, you'll have mastered the responsibility of formal authority. ∎

The Healthcare Leader's Dilemma

At a recent IHI conference, I was asked to serve as a panelist for the CEO Summit. We began the day with an inspirational case study from outside the healthcare industry —the transformation of *US News and World Report* from a paper-based subscription model to a diverse web-centric family of products.

In 2007, it was clear that offering a paper-based magazine below cost, subsidized by advertising, was unsustainable. Google's sale of targeted ads at low cost eliminated the business models of many print publications.

US News decided to become a specialized web resource offering news, college ranking, hospital ranking, and car ranking. The advertising on each of these sites is highly targeted and actionable: when a customer clicks on a car, they are redirected to a local car dealer's website. At a time when web-based advertising may be $1.00 per 1,000 clicks, *US News and World Report* can charge $30.00 per 1,000 clicks for qualified car-buying customers.

This transition required layoffs, sale of the paper-based subscription customers to *Time* magazine, and a significant temporary reduction in sales in order to transition to an entirely new business model. The future was unknown and the path to get there was risky. In retrospect, it was exactly the right thing to do.

In healthcare, we are at a similar crossroads.

In an era of healthcare reform, we have three challenging choices:

1. Become a pioneer accountable care organization (ACO) at a time when no one knows exactly what is necessary to succeed, but risks are minimized for early adopters.

2. Wait to become an ACO until the tools and technologies needed to succeed are better known, but risks for failure will be higher.

3. Continue to rely on fee-for-service income and hope healthcare reform is delayed or deferred. If healthcare reform proceeds, fee-for-service income will drop steadily over time, leading to the slow demise of organizations which depend upon it.

Just as it was an educated guess to move *US News and World Report* to the Internet in 2007, moving healthcare organizations to population health/wellness-focused ACOs seems like the right thing to do. Yes, it may result in the downsizing of academic health centers and a reduction of some services like lab and radiology that are more expensive than community-based dedicated labs and imaging centers. However, the future of healthcare looks a lot more promising for community hospitals and outsourced ancillaries than for academic health centers with high overhead costs.

Jim Reinertsen, MD, Senior Fellow of IHI and former CEO of CareGroup, moderated a discussion of these ideas with Derek Feeley, Chief Executive of the National Health Service (NHS) in Scotland, George Kerwin, Chief Executive Officer of President Bellin Health Systems, and me.

We're on a journey from episodic care to coordinated care to patient-directed care. We're moving from fee for service to bundled payments/capitation. Our IT systems are evolving from segmented to integrated to community-based.

Healthcare leaders must make a decision: change now and risk moving too soon, incurring high costs; or wait and risk moving too late, losing your competitive advantage.

In Boston, the healthcare marketplace is evolving so rapidly that our answer is clear—we must move to community-based coordinated care funded through bundled payments/capitation. Implementing this transformation over the next few years will be a challenge for everyone, and along the way we need to ensure that the patient experience is not compromised. We'll need leaders with a vision of the future, a guiding coalition of stakeholder supporters, a sense of urgency from the external environment, and a tolerance for risk. I'm eager to be a part of the next phase in healthcare and look forward to learning from the people who make it happen. ■

Honey or Vinegar?

As a leader, I'm frequently asked to evaluate direct reports, provide guidance to managers, and build consensus among staff with heterogeneous opinions.

There are many ways to approach interactions with superiors, subordinates, and peers.

In my 30 years of working in complex organizations, I've observed different leadership styles with varying degrees of long-term success. I believe it is far better to establish unity, esprit de corps in the foxhole, and boost morale than to create divisiveness, uncertainty, and fear of failure.

> *I believe it is far better to establish unity, esprit de corps in the foxhole, and boost morale than to create divisiveness, uncertainty, and fear of failure.*

My grandmother used to say that, "You can catch more flies with honey than with vinegar," meaning that you can be more persuasive with camaraderie than confrontation.

In the short term, formal authority and fear of job loss can be very persuasive. In the long term, such behavior is likely to result in an "Occupy"-like rally of staff seeking a better organizational culture.

My own experience with "honey" includes five different characteristics:

1. Informal authority—Building trust and exploring possibilities together in a non-judgmental way creates lasting mutual respect and grants a degree of authority that is far more powerful than rule by fiat.

2. Loyalty—I've arranged pay increases and bonuses for staff to recognize special achievements and career growth. The increased payment creates short-term joy but the impact on retention is short lived, since the novelty of the change diminishes over time. Far more important is creating a sense of long-term loyalty that comes with a family-like atmosphere. All for one and one for all.

3. Air cover—In a crisis, you're first on the front line fighting the fight, taking the blows, and protecting those behind you. You're not watching the action from a distant hill or criticizing the troops from an armchair.

4. Good guy can finish first—I'm a strong believer in integrity, honesty, and fair play. I will not hurt my fellow humans to get ahead. My feeling is that those who live by the sword die by the sword.

5. Strong emotion never works—As a parent and as a CIO, I've raised my voice once or twice in 20 years, then felt terrible for doing it. It diminished me.

I'm sure there are those who equate intimidation with leadership, but for me, uniting people in support of a common cause against a common adversary using trust, loyalty, ethics, hard work, and support wins the day. ∎

Servant Leadership

I read every comment posted to my blog and do my best to learn from the wisdom of the community. Two comments made about my "Honey or Vinegar?" post deserve special highlight.

Tony Parham posted a comment comparing management and leadership, quoting the work of John Kotter and Colin Powell:

"MANAGEMENT: Control mechanisms to compare system behavior with the plan and take action when a deviation is detected.

"LEADERSHIP: Achieving grand visions. Motivation and inspiration to energize people, not by pushing them in the right direction as control mechanisms do, but by satisfying basic human needs for achievement, a sense of belonging, recognition, self-esteem, a feeling of control over one's life, and the ability to live up to one's ideals. Such feelings touch us deeply and elicit a powerful response.[14]

"LEADERSHIP is the art of accomplishing more than the science of MANAGEMENT says is possible."[15]

My experience is that as long as a leader unites a team with a clear common goal and enables the team to do their work while supporting their self-esteem and their decisions about scope/time/resources, people thrive. Even recent medical evidence suggests that "honey" and the positive support of a leader yields healthy, productive, and happy staff. Lack of such a leader can lead to negative health and reduced longevity. It seems intuitive that our moods are linked closely to our job satisfaction and that a positive mood improves health, but now we have evidence to prove it.

Katherina Holzhauser, a fellow Stanford graduate from the Czech Republic, wrote to me about servant leadership as part of her philosophy of favoring "honey" over "vinegar."

The important take-home lesson about servant leadership is that the classic organization chart really needs to be rewritten, making staff who interact with customers the most important people in the organization. The role of a leader is to

---

14 John P. Kotter, Professor of organizational behavior at the Harvard Business School.

15 General Colin Powell, former US Secretary of State.

serve and support those staff so that they have the resources and processes they need to optimize customer experiences. I completely agree with the statement that the highest priority of a servant leader is to encourage, support, and enable subordinates to unfold their full potential and abilities. This leads to an obligation to delegate responsibility and engage in participative decision making.

The goals of a servant leader—listening, empathy, healing, awareness, persuasion (which I call informal authority), conceptualization (which I call continuous self-re-examination), foresight, stewardship, commitment to people (which I call loyalty), and building community—are what guide my day-to-day interactions in all aspects of my life.

As we take on more work in less time at faster pace than ever before, let's all strive to be servant leaders for the benefit of those who do the work and serve on the front lines of healthcare and healthcare IT in our quest to alleviate human suffering caused by disease. ■

Leadership Lessons Learned from James T. Kirk

Alex Knapp wrote a brilliant article entitled "Five Leadership Lessons from James T. Kirk" in *Forbes*. For those of us who have watched every episode of Star Trek and can recite every line of dialog from memory, these five lessons are a great distillation of the series.

In a speech about leading innovation, I used the same five points:

1. Never stop learning—Thirty years ago I befriended one of the great thinkers from the vacuum tube era. I showed him the miracle of a modern integrated circuit—one of his most complex tube designs fit into a dime-sized chip. He told me that he was not interested because he could not comprehend the silicon-based technology. As I've told my staff, if I ever become an impediment to innovation because I'm stuck in a technology era of the past, it's time for me to move on.

2. Have advisors with different worldviews—I try very hard not to be dogmatic. I use open source and proprietary software. I use Macs and Windows devices. I run Java and .NET applications. Surrounding yourself with smart people (smarter than yourself), who may have contrary opinions, improves your own decision making. I've always felt that "B" leaders surround themselves with "C" employees who simply reinforce status quo leadership thinking. "A" leaders surround themselves with "A" employees who constantly challenge the status quo.

3. Be part of the away team—It's truly hard for healthcare CIOs to understand the needs of their customers. It helps to be a clinician or partner with a chief medical information officer (CMIO). The best way to truly understand the strengths and weaknesses of your IT organization is to use the applications you purchase or create, "eating your own dog food." This requires leaving the comfort of your office and spending your day in the field. I spend less than an hour a day sitting at my desk—my office is wherever my laptop and iPhone reside.

4. Play poker, not chess—It's important to take educated risks. I bet on the web for healthcare in 1996. Transforming organizations with health information exchange in support of evolving accountable care organizations, patient-centered medical homes, and global payment is the right thing to do.

5. Blow up the Enterprise—Every organization has peaks and valleys. Goliaths fall and Davids rise. In my own career, I've experienced the perfect storm of innovation that results in revolutionary rather than evolutionary change. Sometimes it's clear that an organization should exit certain businesses, downsize and divest to ready itself for the next phase of growth. Being the best "buggy whip" manufacturer is not a sustainable strategy.

Thanks, Alex, for a great article. In the early days of Meaningful Use work, a graphic appeared labeling Dr. David Blumenthal as Kirk, Dr. John Glaser as Spock, and me as Bones (thanks to Brian Ahier for this). It's an honor to be considered part of that crew! ∎

Chapter 2

Implementing Electronic Health Records

Since 2002, my IT teams have provided electronic health records to every owned/closely affiliated clinician of Beth Israel Deaconess, using our home-built webOMR software. We even have a Medical Executive Committee policy mandating the use of EHRs as a condition of practice. 'Use' is carefully defined to adopt Meaningful Use criteria.

Since Stark safe harbor regulations[1] now enable hospitals to fund up to 85% of the non-hardware implementation costs of private practice EHRs, my teams are now expected to provide EHR solutions for all the non-owned, BIDMC-affiliated clinician practices in Eastern Massachusetts. This is a very different project than providing applications and infrastructure to owned clinician practices on a hospital-managed network.

The project planning included the following major issues:

1. Designing governance—My typical steering committees are drawn from hospital senior management, employed clinicians, and hospital staff. The governance of a community-wide EHR system must include members of the physicians' organization, private physicians, community hospital executives, and legal experts.

---

1 The Stark law governs physician self-referral for Medicare and Medicaid patients. The "safe harbor" regulations describe various payment and business practices that, although they potentially implicate the federal anti-kickback statute, are not treated as offenses under the Stark statute.

2. Modeling costs—The 'hydraulics' of the project budget are quite complex. The hospital wants to support implementation for as many physicians as possible but has limited capital. The physicians want as much implementation subsidy as possible since by Stark regulation they have to fund all hardware and ongoing support themselves. The number of doctors implemented, the level of subsidy, and total costs for all stakeholders are interrelated, but each party has different goals.

3. Planning for distributed users—These non-owned clinician practices are widely dispersed throughout Massachusetts and New England in urban and rural settings. Bandwidth varies from 20 Megabit Verizon FiOS connections to 56K dialup. Technology sophistication varies from fully 'wired' clinicians to offices run on 3x5-inch index cards.

4. Managing the project—CIOs traditionally serve hospital-based customers. They may not have the bandwidth or expertise to serve non-owned, geographically dispersed customers.

5. Building a scalable infrastructure—The architecture must be designed to minimize costs, maximize reliability, and support a project scope that is continually evolving.

6. Deploying staff—The existing hospital IT staff is not optimized for supporting networks, telecom, desktop, and application at hundreds of remote locations. The physicians' organization and clinician offices do not have the staff or expertise to execute this project.

7. Creating the model office—A clinically integrated network of providers in a community will want to adopt a standard EHR configuration with common dictionaries to support health information exchange and continuity of care. Standardizing software configuration means standardizing workflow, which requires business process re-engineering. Practice consulting is needed to balance standardization with specialty-specific processes, ensuring that providers buy into the new workflow and staff are appropriately trained.

8. Obtaining all the funding—Once the scope, architecture, staffing, and cost modeling are completed, the funding must be obtained from all of the stakeholders. State and federal governments are not likely to contribute anything. Payers may fund the outcomes of EHR use via pay for performance, but are unlikely to pay for implementation.

9. Specifying the order of implementation—How do we choose the most appropriate offices for pilots and, once those pilots are completed, how do we place hundreds of clinicians in a well-ordered queue for rollout?

10. Supporting the practices—Hospital support models depend upon standardized networks and desktops with end-to-end control over the quality of service. Supporting heterogeneous practices requires on-site, high-touch, higher-cost service.

The posts in this chapter document our experience with implementing EHRs on a large scale in New England. ∎

Governance

The needs of many stakeholders must be balanced to ensure the success of this project. The hospital wants to support as many clinicians as possible using its capital budgets most efficiently. Community clinicians want to minimize the financial and operational impact of the project on their practice. IT staff must manage their hospital-based projects and infrastructure while expanding their scope to new offsite locations.

Governance is critical to establish priorities, align stakeholders, and set expectations. To support this project we created two governance committees: a Steering Committee and an Advisory Committee.

The Steering Committee is comprised of senior executives from the hospital and physicians' organization, since it is truly a joint effort of BIDMC and the Beth Israel Deaconess Physicians' Organization (BIDPO). BIDMC representatives include the CFO, the CIO, the SVP of network development and the IT project manager. Physicians' organization members include the president, the executive director, and the chief medical officer (CMO) of BIDPO. This committee provides oversight of legal agreements, financial expenditures, project scope, timelines, and resources. It is co-chaired by the CIO and executive director of BIDPO, who jointly sign off on all expenditures. The BIDMC and BIDPO boards provide additional oversight of the committee chairs.

The Advisory Committee is comprised of prospective community physician users of the EHR system. Since our community network is comprised of 300 non-owned Boston-based clinician practices in the western suburbs, and clinician practices in the southern part of the state, we have representatives of each group sitting on the committee. The committee focuses on making the project really work for the practices, but also to meet the needs of the physician organization's clinically integrated network model. The role of the committee is to review our "model" office templates, help us prioritize the implementation order of practices, and make recommendations on policies. As with every project, we use our standard project management tools including a charter for each committee.

Since this project is so challenging and requires a precise blend of economics, information technology, and politics, the governance committees are the place to ask permission, beg forgiveness, and communicate progress on every milestone. This is especially true to the complex cost model which shares expenditures equally between the hospital and physicians' organization for implementation, subsidizing private clinician costs to the extent we are able based on Stark safe harbors. As you'll see, the costs are diverse and deciding who pays and how much they pay cannot be done alone by IT, the hospital, or the physicians. It's truly a role for transparent, multi-disciplinary governance committees. ∎

Cost Modeling

Based on the informatics literature, the initial implementation cost of an EHR for private practices averages between $40,000–$60,000 per provider and the cost of maintenance averages $5,000–$10,000 per provider per year. Using these numbers, the total EHR implementation costs for our 300 non-owned clinician practices could be $12–$18 million and $1.5–$3 million per year. Of course, this includes total costs paid by the hospital and by the practices. To understand the economics of the project, we need to inventory all the costs included and who pays those costs. Stark safe harbors provide some guidance here, since Stark separates costs into those which can be shared with hospitals and those which must be paid by the providers themselves. Up to 85% of implementation costs excluding office hardware can be funded by the hospital. Hardware and most ongoing costs must be paid by the providers. We must also consider what costs the hospital should absorb for planning, legal, and infrastructure to offer EHR services to non-owned clinician practices. These startup costs are nearly the same for 30 or 300 doctors, so they are not easily computed on a per-provider basis.

Initial Costs

1. Startup costs to be funded by the hospital:
    - Planning
    - Legal costs
    - Hosting site hardware and operating system software
2. Practice implementation costs to be shared between the hospital and practices:
    - Software licensing fees
    - Technical deployment services and workflow design services
    - Project management costs

- Training costs
- Interface costs
- Data conversion costs

3. Practice implementation costs to be funded entirely by the practice:

- Hardware local to the practice

Ongoing Costs

1. Maintenance costs to be funded by the hospital

- Hosting site staffing and hardware lifecycle maintenance

2. Support costs to be shared per Stark

- Help desk
- Practice consulting support

3. Support costs to be funded entirely by the practice

- Hardware service and support
- Network connectivity

Of course, each of these categories and subcategories has its own detailed analysis. The "hydraulics" of our model must take into account the goals of the stakeholders—the hospital has a fixed capital budget and wants to connect as many doctors as possible. Doctors want as much subsidy as possible. Given the hospital contribution of 'x' million, and a doctor's ability to pay 'y' thousand, we need to compute the subsidy level and number of doctors included in the rollout. To help with this decision, we're dividing our budgets for all the categories above into fixed startup costs and marginal costs to add 100 doctors. We're also categorizing all costs as 'subsidizable' or 'non-subsidizable.'

We'll do our best to achieve economies of scale, negotiate appropriate vendor pricing, and document acceptable service levels. Our governance committees will review the final pricing to ensure we've achieved a balance of hospital costs, practice costs, and service. We'll also refine our cost models by documenting all the costs we experience in our pilots this spring.

Our internal staff and external collaborators are doing a remarkable job documenting the costs. We'll know soon if it is possible to use the capital budgets that the hospital has available to create an EHR product at a price at which clinicians are willing to pay. ∎

Planning for Distributed Users

CIOs of academic healthcare facilities are used to highly controlled and predictable environments. We oversee the quality of service from end to end. Desktops have a managed image with updated anti-virus software. The network is physically secured in closets we control, using fiber and cables we install. Our teams and our management are optimized to deliver services that are consistent and standardized.

The EHR project for non-owned clinician practices requires a different approach. The initial 300 doctors in 173 physical locations spread over 450 square miles have diverse needs and heterogenous access to infrastructure. Some already have computers, and wired and wireless networks. Most do not. Those in rural areas may have limited access to bandwidth, making business digital subscriber lines (DSL) their only choice for connectivity.

The alternatives we considered for serving these geographically distributed users were the following:

- Expand our current IS offsite team which currently focuses on BIDMC-owned clinician practices and those occupying BIDMC leased space. This matrix illustrates the different kinds of physicians we support and the services we currently provide.

- Negotiate group purchasing agreements with vendors and make these available to clinicians, reducing heterogeneity but not providing installation and management of the infrastructure. Physicians could hire local consultants, seek help from family members, or do it themselves.

- Outsource the infrastructure of these practices to a firm specializing in managing the IT needs of independent clinicians.

We weighed the benefits and costs of each approach and elected to outsource infrastructure to Concordant.

Here's our thinking:

- Geographically distributed practices needing 24x7 support would require a large internal team to provide a high service level, weekend coverage, and vacation coverage. Although we are currently planning on 300 clinicians, that number might expand to 500 or 1,000, hence scaling up with agility would be challenging, especially in a job market in which many hospitals are competing for skilled IT professionals.

- Our current offsite group is extremely good and focused on providing infrastructure and application services to sites we operate. Expanding this group to support a very different kind of practice with a very different infrastructure would dilute their current focus.

- Enabling these distributed offices to purchase their own equipment and establish their own local infrastructure could be disastrous. Guaranteeing service levels means that we must have an understanding of the network performance, desktop configuration, and local infrastructure (printers, scanners, fax machines) of each office.

Our plan is to operate a highly reliable hosted EHR, house a commercial co-location facility, and make it available to each of these practices via the public Internet without having to create network or telecom connections ourselves. At each office location, however, the desktops and wired and wireless network will be completely homogeneous and managed by Concordant. We'll leverage the scale of the project to obtain the best discounts possible from hardware vendors. We'll even retire existing office hardware to achieve homogeneity. Help desk services will be staffed by Concordant, so that we will not need to train our existing help desk staff to support these distributed non-owned clinician practices.

We elected not to place servers in any clinician offices since physician offices do not have backup power, environmentally controlled server rooms, or appropriate physical security for machines hosting the data. Our plan is to maintain a central hardware depot, assemble all the equipment needed for an office, deliver it, configure it, and test it. Everyone wants to minimize onsite support, but some onsite service will still be needed for hardware failures and very "high-touch" support. Remote support and monitoring techniques can help, though minimally, since we're implementing a centralized architecture.

It is our hope that a dedicated outsourced infrastructure service, optimized for the needs of the geographically distributed small physician office, will work better and cost less than expanding our existing IS teams or enabling physicians to do it themselves. It also enables us to track costs more closely since there is a strict separation between support for owned sites and non-owned sites. ∎

Managing the Project

As I've indicated in my post about managing IT projects and managing consulting engagements, projects do not manage themselves. Although we've put together a remarkable partnership of vendors and service providers for our EHR for non-owned clinician practices project, it's all wrapped in $1 million of project management, coordination, and "air traffic control." The geographically dispersed set of independent physician practices makes the project that much harder to manage. Our partners for this project are the following:

- eClinicalWorks—A leading provider of practice management and CCHIT[2]-certified EHRs, accessible over the Internet using a smart web client, from

---

2 CCHIT = Certification Commission for Health Information Technology.

anywhere in the world. They will provide the software, training, and review of all our infrastructure designs.

- Concordant—A leading provider of desktop, network, and server hosting services for clinician offices throughout our region. They will provide the hosting center for our SaaS EHR applications, operate our help desk, and deploy all our hardware to clinician offices.

- Massachusetts eHealth Collaborative—Our regional implementer of EHRs with expertise in practice transformation. They will provide for the practice consulting expertise to move clinicians from paper-based workflows to electronic systems.

- Third Brigade—A leading provider of security, ethical hacking, and host-based intrusion protection services. They will ensure we protect the privacy of patient records, since confidentiality is foundational to the entire project.

My internal staff, consisting of a project director, project manager, project coordinator, and design engineer will coordinate all the work done by our partners, design the model office/ideal configurations for the entire rollout, and manage the budget. Our first four pilot sites provided enough experience so that our final project plans and management oversight are the equivalent of a "Starbucks franchising model." We expect that this model will enable us to choose a practice and then six weeks later have them fully up and running with hardware, software supplied from our central hosting facility, training, data conversions, and interfaces. Being able to rollout practices in this timeframe, leveraging economies of scale, and using our partners most efficiently will result (we hope) in low cost and high customer satisfaction, since we'll do all the work with a minimum amount of wasted effort.

A few additional months spent planning, project managing, and piloting will improve the quality of the project immensely and ultimately reduce our costs.

My experience with a project of this complexity is that a few additional months spent planning, project managing, and piloting will improve the quality of the project immensely and ultimately reduce our costs. The expense of doing the project twice to get it right far exceeds an investment in project management to get it right the first time. ∎

Scalable Infrastructure

As I've described, the scope of the project is to implement a highly reliable, secure, feature-rich, well-supported, but affordable EHR for private practices.

This post is about building the scalable centralized SaaS-hosting infrastructure to meet these goals.

A key design requirement for the project is scalability. Our projected customer base is 300 clinicians and we have a fixed startup budget. However, we must design the infrastructure in a way that can cost-effectively support the smallest amount of adopters as well as scale to thousands if our project is wildly successful. We debated two possibilities (metaphorically speaking):

a. Build a hotel, not knowing if anyone will ever check-in

b. Build a housing development, where the limits of expansion are defined only by available land

We decided on choice "b," starting with a robust foundation and adding new equipment and storage as we add clinicians. We standardized our central site equipment on products from HP, EMC, and Cisco, with guidance from our infrastructure partner, Concordant, and our equipment supplier CDW, ensuring it was easy to plug in additional hardware on demand. We invested a significant amount of time designing the central hosting facility, doing it right the first time. Over the years, I've seen CIOs rush through the design phase, only having to rebuild the infrastructure later when application performance did not scale. We partnered with our vendors to build something special, that, if successful, could be a model for other medical centers and communities.

Considerations in designing our hosting infrastructure included:

- Supporting a user base that is remote, unmanaged, and diverse; we need to be able to identify any performance issues via end-to-end monitoring of all components

- Meeting important security and privacy restrictions, as well as addressing liability issues (who is responsible for what)

- Understanding infrastructure costs for (a) start-up, (b) additional capacity that occurs in bursts or steps, and (c) variable requirements as practices go live

- Providing connectivity to external parties (labs, claims, etc.) through interfaces which create additional security and performance complexities

- Addressing the limitations and performance of "last mile" connectivity through publicly available Internet access (DSL, cable, etc.)

The infrastructure choices we made are:

- Virtualized servers—VMware was the natural choice because of the scalability design goals. VM and V-Motion technologies also play an important part in redundancy, failure recovery, and disaster recovery.

- Physical services—We debated rack-mounted verses blade servers and elected to use powerful small-footprint HP rack servers connected to fast multi-tiered storage. We computed the economics of blade servers verses rack-mounted servers and the use of VMware made small powerful rack servers the most cost-effective solution.

- Storage—We purchased a Clariion CX3-20 series storage area network (SAN). We will go live with 11.1TB of total storage (2.1TB of fast, Tier 1 storage for database transactions, and 9TB of secondary, Tier 2 storage for files). A single CX3-20 will allow us to expand in a modular fashion to accommodate up to 1,200 practices. We'll also be leveraging a disk-to-disk backup strategy, using tape only for disaster recovery.

- Network infrastructure—We implemented a high-speed network backbone with multiple paths for redundancy using:

  o Cisco integrated services routers (ISR) 2811s for Internet connectivity

  o Adaptive Security Appliances (ASA) 5520 for firewalling, intrusion protection, and IPSec virtual private network (VPN) client termination

  o Catalyst 4948 switches for server connectivity and layer 3 routing

  o MDS 9000 Series multilayer SAN switches for SAN connectivity

- Security—We incorporated physical, technical, and administrative controls to protect confidentiality, integrity, and availability.

- SSL accelerators—We are using Array Networks TMX-2000, the hardware recommended by eClinicalWorks to optimize web server performance.

- Redundancy and disaster recovery—One of the real challenges to this project is the price sensitivity of our private clinicians. We needed to build a world-class system at a price that all clinicians could afford. Redundancy and disaster recovery are like life insurance—it's a great investment only if you need it. We had to balance our infrastructure investment with total cost of ownership, given the fixed hospital contribution and physician frugalness. In the end we used this equation: Risk = likelihood of bad events multiplied by the impact of bad events.

We believe that it is much more likely that a component will fail than an entire data center be destroyed, so we elected to build a highly redundant infrastructure in a single data center for now, expanding to a secondary data center once we have a sufficient number of clinicians signed up to fund the new infrastructure. Networking gear, servers, power, and cabling are duplicated within a commercial co-location facility. Storage is disk-to-disk redundant. Tapes are moved offsite nightly. Once the hardware is up, we'll work with Concordant, Cisco, EMC, HP, Array Networks, and the co-location facility to test physical hardware and operating system/database software redundancy. Then we'll install eClinicalWorks and run the redundancy tests again. We'll also engage Third Brigade at that time for intrusion/security testing.

We've written a comprehensive disaster recovery plan, and if we lost the co-location facility due to disaster, we would recover the tapes from offsite storage and build a replica of the hosting environment (VMware plays a key role here) and restore the data. The recovery point and recovery time objectives for this plan will be clearly communicated to all who sign up for service. The customer base for our SaaS solution is mainly small practices which operate Monday through Friday, 8 am–6 pm. Our disaster recovery plan includes a solid practice/workflow-specific contingency/downtime plan. We will also perform a mock downtime as part of each implementation.

By creating a highly redundant single data center with rack-mounted servers, two-tiered storage, virtualization, and offsite tape backup, we believe we've balanced scalability, affordability, and maintainability. ∎

Staffing the Project

In this post, I'll discuss the complexities of staffing the project, since we've had to weigh insourcing versus outsourcing, costs, and service levels to arrive at a balanced staffing plan. We've divided the staffing into ten categories and below I describe the strategy for each.

In creating this staffing model, we had several considerations:

- The project scope is not fixed. We're starting with 300 clinician practices and may implement over 1,000. Thus, we need a staffing model which is scalable on demand. We may need to flex the size of our teams up or down depending on implementation schedules.

- In Massachusetts, at this time, it is challenging to hire and maintain healthcare informatics staff because of intense competition among hospitals implementing CPOE/EHRs and local software companies expanding their healthcare IT workforce.

- Outsourcing can be a way to rapidly expand capacity but it requires diligent management and tends to be more expensive than hiring internal staff.

Following are the ten staffing categories we created:

1. Project management and financial management—We have a full-time project director and have leveraged our existing IS fiscal staff to manage the budgets. We will partner with the Massachusetts eHealth Collaborative (MAeHC) to operate a project management office under the direction of our project director but jointly and flexibly staffed with BIDMC and MAeHC personnel. This will allow us to:

a. Complement our existing knowledge of hospital and employed-practice deployments with outside expertise regarding non-owned ambulatory practices.

b. Ramp up staff strength quickly as implementation intensity grows.

c. Ramp down smoothly as deployment transitions to long-term support. This model will also allow us to rapidly and seamlessly plug in the temporary project management and staffing gaps that will inevitably arise during the course of the project.

2. Technical design and engineering—We elected to insource design and engineering for our servers, storage, and network design. We collaborated with our vendors, HP, EMC, and Cisco, as well as our infrastructure implementation partner, Concordant, on these designs. We assigned .25 full-time equivalent (FTE) of the manager of our ambulatory applications group to this task.

3. Central site construction—We elected to outsource construction of the central hosting facility to Concordant for a fixed price. They acquired the co-location space, installed all equipment, and took responsibility for establishing power/cooling/network connectivity to the site. They will also manage the central site during the pilot phase. We are paying for a deliverable rather than paying per diem rates for time or hiring FTEs.

4. Office hardware deployment—We elected to outsource office hardware deployment to Concordant by hiring a team of people which scales in direct relation to the number of offices we are implementing. Purchasing a deployment team rather than working on per diem rates means that we pay for FTEs assigned in direct relation to the deliverables.

5. Practice consultation—We elected to insource and outsource practice consultation. An MAeHC senior consultant will directly manage the practice consultant team, which will comprise both BIDMC and MAeHC consultants. These practice consultants will be assigned to individual practices and will provide end-to-end project management of practice-level implementations, to ensure that all activities associated with the implementation are synchronized. They will also work with individual practices on optimizing workflow and translating that optimized workflow into appropriate software configuration, hardware layout, and training approach. As with the project management function, this is a flexible insource/outsource model that allows us to scale up and down rapidly, tap into existing expertise, and apply it to the project

right away, and maintain an adaptive but robust capability to meet program changes as they arise.

6. Training—We elected to insource and outsource training. eClinicalWorks will provide the training for all our initial pilot sites, then train our trainers. Going forward, a combination of eCW and insourced trainers will serve our sites, with supervision/quality control of all training to be provided by eClinicalWorks.

7. Central site operations—We elected to outsource central site operations to Concordant via a "lights out data center" model coupled with systems and application administration. They provide monitoring tools and problem escalation 24x7 rather than hiring a specific number of staff to manage our installation. This enables us to leverage the fact that they are providing support to other customers and projects, keeping our costs low and avoiding the need for us to hire fractional FTEs to provide data center support. The challenge with hiring internal staff to do this is that we expect data center needs to be higher during our initial implementation because of the build/change activities, then markedly reduce during our steady state operations. Outsourcing this function to Concordant, which spreads FTEs over many customers, enables us to flex our needs easily.

8. Help desk, Tier 1, and Tier 2 support—We elected to insource and outsource telephone support. Concordant will be the initial single point of contact for all phone calls, doing Tier 1 support such as password resets and then triaging Tier 2 support. They will handle infrastructure Tier 2 issues and escalate others (such as EHR best practice questions) to our insourced staff. Our staff will escalate eClinicalWorks-specific issues to eCW as needed. By focusing on resolving as many questions as possible remotely and dividing support between Concordant, our staff, and eCW, clearly defining the tasks of each group, we minimize our costs.

9. Field support—We elected to outsource field support to Concordant, using a shared-staff model. This optimizes our costs, coverage, and flexibility since here again Concordant spreads FTEs over multiple customers.

10. Security auditing—Security has been built into our project from the very beginning as part of our infrastructure design, application configuration, and staffing model. We elected to outsource security auditing to an expert ethical hacking and security firm, Third Brigade, for a fixed price. By hiring an expert group to do this, we provide another layer of vigilance and control, ensuring we have an outside

party validating our configurations, providing host-based intrusion protection, and monitoring our systems.

Thus, by dividing the staffing of the project among the members of our "dream team"—BIDPO/BIDMC, Concordant, MAeHC, eClinicalWorks, and Third Brigade—we have achieved an affordable, scalable, balanced insource/outsourcing staffing model. ■

Creating the Model Office

There are many reasons for implementing EHRs: enhancing quality, clinical integration, reducing redundant testing, and building workflow efficiency with technologies such as e-prescribing.

Today, we have 300 closely affiliated physicians in 150 non-owned practices. Although these doctors are not employed by our system, they are part of the Beth Israel Deaconess Physician's Organization (BIDPO), which is a coordinated provider network of nearly 1,500 physicians. Among other quality and safety measures, BIDPO focuses its pay-for-performance efforts on advanced diabetes care, appropriate radiology test ordering, and use of e-prescribing.

Gathering metrics about physician practices requires consistent clinical and process data about the care delivered. This means that all our practices should maintain ICD9-codified problem lists, accurate medication histories, standard-based result reporting, and structured data about lifestyle choices such as smoking behavior. Unless our clinicians have a consistent way to record this data, quality and pay-for-performance reporting will be impossible since clinicians would implement their own unique ways of recording problems, medications, allergies, and notes.

Hence, we're designing the "model office" configuration for eClinicalWorks 8.0, the version of the EHR software we'll be implementing. This means that before our first go live, we're developing data dictionaries that will be used in all practices. We're loading the decision support rules which will provide identical alerts and reminders to every clinician. We're integrating all the lessons learned from the MAeHC rollouts to design the idealized configuration of each EHR screen which will ensure the best quality data capture and enhance the likelihood that we can do performance measurement as a clinically integrated community of clinicians.

Part of our model office also includes idealized workflow made possible by interoperability. Each office will have the following:

1. New England Health EDI Network (NEHEN) which provides electronic links to our regional payers for HIPAA[3] transactions including benefits/eligibility, referral/authorization, claim submission, and claim status.

2. MA-Share RxGateway for e-prescribing features such as formulary enforcement, community drug history, and routing to retail/mail order pharmacies.

3. Results interfaces for labs and radiology from local hospitals.

4. Ordering of BIDMC-based testing including SafeMed radiology decision support.

5. Quality and performance reporting via build in eClinicalWorks 8.0 data query system. Since our model office includes a standard configuration of all data dictionaries and input screens, we'll be able to use a federated approach to performance measurement. Here's how it works:

   a. BIDPO has been given the authority to collect performance data by all BIDPO clinicians using eClinicalWorks.

   b. BIDPO devises a query such as, "How many patients in each practice with diabetes have a hemoglobin a1c greater than 7?"

   c. At night, while the office is closed, the query runs on each clinician's database.

   d. The aggregate counts (not individual patient-identified data) are returned to the medical director for use in pay-for-performance measurement and medical management.

Creating the model office ensures that patients will receive the same quality care wherever they go, that doctors will be empowered with decision support tools, and that we'll be able to measure performance at all our practices as if they were a single integrated entity.

Creating the model office ensures that patients will receive the same quality care wherever they go, that doctors will be empowered with decision support tools, and that we'll be able to measure performance at all our practices as if they were a single integrated entity. We believe the up-front work to design the model office will make our use of eClinicalWorks more effective, make training easier, and serve as a foundation for all our interoperability efforts. ∎

---

3   HIPAA = Health Insurance Portability and Accountability Act of 1996.

Funding

The hardest part of the entire project is, "What's it going to cost and who's going to pay?" Stark safe harbors allow hospitals to support up to 85% of startup and implementation costs, excluding physician office hardware.

I asked the leaders of every major EHR rollout project in Eastern Massachusetts to comment on their funding models. Here's their feedback by institution:

BIDMC

BIDMC and BIDPO have selected eClinicalWorks as the EHR, have outsourced desktop/centralized hosting to Concordant, and have a combination of insourcing/outsourcing to the MAeHC for practice consultation. BIDMC financial modeling of all these costs is consistent with the industry standard experience of $40,000–$60,000 per clinician, including office hardware. Subsidies will come from BIDMC and local hospitals. With maximum Stark allowable subsidies, our computation of the minimum legal cost per clinician is $15,000, so clinicians will be asked to pay at least that much.

Caritas

Caritas has selected eClinicalWorks as the EHR. Caritas would like to subsidize 85% of the allowable costs. However, Caritas leaves the amount of the subsidy up to local hospital CEOs, since they will ultimately pay the bill and decide which community practices are the most strategic for rollout.

Children's Hospital Boston

Children's and Pediatric Physician's Organization at Children's have selected eClinicalWorks as the EHR and the hospital is hosting the application in their data center, maintaining it via existing IT staff. Six new FTEs in the primary care network will provide practice consulting and implementation services. Children's has outsourced desktop support to The Ergonomic Group. Children's experience has paralleled the BIDMC financial model and has roughly the same cost structure, subsidizing costs to the maximum that Stark allows.

Mt. Auburn Hospital/MACIPA

Mt. Auburn and Mt. Auburn Cambridge IPA (MACIPA) have selected eClinicalWorks as the EHR and the physician's organization is hosting the servers in a co-location facility. The hospital has subsidized allowable costs and physicians are paying for all office hardware. The proportion of subsidy for costs of hosting, licenses, training, and implementation is still a work in progress. Mt. Auburn notes that part of the cost equation should be consideration of loss of productivity during initial implementation. This is a good point and no other organization has computed this as part of the cost equation.

New England Baptist Hospital

New England Baptist Hospital and its physicians have selected eClinicalWorks as the EHR and the hospital is hosting the application in a co-location facility. The hospital has hired four FTEs, managed by the hospital CIO, to assess office needs, install hardware, and implement software. A memorandum of understanding (MOU) has been developed detailing the relationships between the parties, services to be provided, and funding allocation to ensure compliance with Stark. The hospital currently subsidizes 80% of the Stark allowable costs. The physicians are funding their portion of the costs via a combination of payer withholds, physician hospital organization (PHO) funding, and direct physician payment.

Partners HealthCare System

Although currently implementing Epic, Partners HealthCare has offered their home-built longitudinal medical record (LMR) or GE Centricity as the EHR. LMR is hosted centrally and GE Centricity is hosted in clinician offices. As a system, Partners withholds in its pay-for-performance contracts to fund EHRs. EHR adoption is a criterion for remaining in the Partners Community HealthCare Inc. (PCHI) network. No subsidy is provided from the central corporation. However, on the local level, PHOs are subsidizing EHRs. Thus, Partners doctors who are in community receive their subsidy and their incentive through pay-for-performance contracts, which could be a Partners PHO like Newton Wellesley or North Shore, or could be a non-Partners PHO like Emerson or Hallmark.

Winchester Hospital

Winchester Hospital has committed to assist its physicians with the EHR implementation process and has budgeted $5 million, including $1.5 million for a four-FTE implementation support team, portal infrastructure development, and associated connectivity. The remainder of the money is available for affiliated physicians to purchase and host the EHR of their choice. Winchester will subsidize up to 85% of the cost of EHR licenses and implementation. The support team primarily offers project management and is staffed out of a joint venture funded by the hospital and the individual practice association (IPA). Winchester hosts the hardware for the 15 practices that are under the corporate umbrella (Winchester Physician Associates). The remainder of the practices are hosting applications in their offices with support from a number of hardware/networking vendors. The IPA has its own incentive program unrelated to the hospital donation.

Thus, the overall consensus in the community is to subsidize the maximum or nearly the maximum of Stark allowable costs and provide centralized project management with either insourced or outsourced implementation/practice consulting services. Most organizations are providing central hosting in a hospital or co-location facility. ∎

Implementation Order

We'll call this post, "triaging the practices." Since we have 300 physicians in non-owned clinician practices who need EHRs, where do we begin? If new clinicians join the BIDPO during our rollout, how do their practices fit into the rollout?

We need specific triage rules to decide on the order of implementation.

In a for-profit business, some metric like referral volume might be used, but in the non-profit healthcare world, such an approach would be a violation of Stark anti-kickback rules.

In our case, we want to ensure the highest quality care, coordinated through the use of interoperable electronic records. We want to ensure decision support is enabled for those who needed it most. We want to invest our effort into those practices which require the most clinical integration with the hospital to ensure high performance medicine. Based on a quality/safety approach, a rational implementation order would be the following:

1. Primary care physicians are the first priority. PCPs see a high volume of patients and are the "air traffic controllers" for care, ensuring coordination among all the clinicians a patient sees. An EHR enables an accurate problem list, an up-to-date medication list, and alerts/reminders for wellness care. We want every patient's PCP to have the benefits of an EHR. Yes, we know that the first few months of using an EHR will impact a PCP's productivity, but our experience with other EHR implementations is that with appropriate training and a "model office" configuration, productivity rapidly returns to baseline.

2. Specialists who serve as a kind of primary care giver, managing diseases such as congestive heart failure (CHF), cancer, and diabetes, are also a priority to be early EHR users. Tracking diabetes care requires data coordination among endocrinologists, ophthalmologists, and vascular surgeons. Obstetricians/gynecologists are primary care givers. Chronic diseases such as chronic obstructive pulmonary disease (COPD) and CHF require coordination among pulmonologists, cardiologists, and PCPs. Specialties that require significant care coordination with primary care givers or deliver primary care themselves include cardiology, ophthalmology, ob/gyn, dermatology, orthopaedics, urology, gastroenterology, surgery, pulmonary, neurology, endocrinology, vascular, and rheumatology.

3. As we are rolling out EHRs to these PCPs and specialists, it's likely that new clinicians will become affiliated with BIDMC. As we plan our rollout calendar, we will need to stay flexible so that new PCPs get priority and the specialists who most benefit from care coordination are placed ahead in the queue.

This approach to triage ensures that patients and providers get the maximal benefit from our efforts as we rollout practices per month. Refinements include:

- PCPs with a closer geographical location to BIDMC/a local hospital go first, since they have the most data interoperability needs.

- Clinicians near retirement may choose not to be early adopters and may want to remain paper-based.

- Some practices may more easily adapt to new technology than others and should go sooner.

The hospital and the physician organization finalized the triage rules based on quality, safety, and data-sharing benefits, so it is very clear that we are Stark compliant and can easily explain to every physician in a non-owned clinician practice when their EHR will be implemented based on objective criteria. So far, so good. ∎

Support

The subject of this post is support after go live and ongoing operational funding. As with my post about implementation funding, I've asked all the implementers of EHR projects in Massachusetts to comment on their plans.

BIDMC

At BIDMC, we'll provide a central help desk (Concordant), outsourced desktop/ network support (Concordant), and ongoing application support (internal staff, MAeHC, and eClinicalWorks). Clinicians will pay a fixed monthly rate for this service. We'll centrally contract for all these services, so the cost will be as low as possible. BIDMC may pay for the ongoing operation of the centrally hosted eClinicalWorks system (e.g., rent in the co-location data center, server support staff); this is still under discussion.

Caritas

Caritas is evaluating their strategy for ongoing support. They are considering the possibility of reassigning members of the implementation team to support as implementation is completed. They have not yet identified a specific funding model for support, but are considering an approach similar to BIDMC.

Children's Hospital Boston

Children's will provide a similar model to BIDMC. The help desk function and first-tier application support will be outsourced to a third-party vendor (The Ergonomic Group). They will escalate to eClinicalWorks as necessary. Ergonomic will also manage and support network operations at each of the practice sites. Children's will support the central hosting site hardware and infrastructure. Children's will also support all network operations inside the core data center. Clinicians will pay a fixed monthly rate for this service.

Mt. Auburn Hospital/MACIPA

Mt. Auburn/MACIPA will provide a central help desk and ongoing hardware/application support. They are currently retraining clinicians to help them increase the utilization of the product, given that during the initial training there is only so much a physician can absorb. They also intend to hold classes at the IPA periodically. Post-live financial support is still being discussed.

New England Baptist Hospital

NEBH will provide an outsourced help desk, ongoing hosting, and application support. Clinicians will pay for non-MEDITECH interfaces, software maintenance, and connectivity/support to billing companies.

Partners HealthCare System

Partners will follow the same model as BIDMC, with clinicians funding ongoing support services.

Winchester Hospital

Community physicians will fund ongoing software and hardware support. The team in Highland Management (joint venture between the hospital and IPA) will provide guidance in the development of templates and the use of the system for reporting to meet pay-for-performance goals and clinical integration. Winchester IT will also be involved in the development of interfaces and the transfer of patient data for care delivery. ■

Roles and Responsibilities

As we "market" to practices the idea of using a hospital-subsidized EHR, we need to have all the details ready: the costs, the service levels, and a crisp definition of the roles and responsibilities of each member of our team. Since the project is comprised of five insourced and outsourced groups working seamlessly together (BIDMC, MAeHC, eClinicalWorks, Concordant, and Third Brigade), we need to have unambiguous agreement among our teams as to who will do what, who will be accountable, and who will communicate the handoffs.

When implementing large, complex projects, adding extra details like a roles and responsibility matrix prevents future problems.

To ensure a perfect understanding among all stakeholders, we created a "Roles and Responsibilities Matrix." There are two aspects of this work that are generally useful to other hospital systems implementing EHRs:

1. We've defined all the component parts of an implementation—from training, to desktop support, to security.

2. We've classified the roles as

    a. Responsible—The person or team that does the work

    b. Accountable—The person or team that reports on the work and is ultimately held responsible for its completion

    c. Consulted—The person or team that provides an opinion when consulted as a stakeholder

    d. Informed—The person or team that is told about the decisions made and progress achieved

Each of the five team members will sign off on the matrix so that there will be no misunderstandings or finger pointing.

When implementing large, complex projects, adding extra details like a roles and responsibility matrix prevents future problems. Assumptions can get teams into trouble. ■

Coming to Terms

Since our community EHR infrastructure is now built, we're in an education and communication phase, explaining to clinicians what it does, what it costs, and what they can expect. All our written and verbal communication must be consistent to ensure we set the right expectations. Part of being accurate is precise definitions of our terms—what is an EMR, EHR, PHR, HIE, RHIO, etc. NextGen markets its product as the NextGen EMR. Does that mean it is inferior to the eClinicalWorks EHR, since an EHR is defined as standards-based and interoperable, while an EMR is defined as a single institution's standalone record? At BIDMC, we're providing a community EHR, we have an institutional EHR called webOMR (Online Medical Record), and a PHR called Patientsite. Patientsite is fully interactive with multiple data sources and Google Health, so we can continue to call it a PHR per the definition below. Here's the summary of the terms we use:

Electronic Medical Record

An electronic record of health-related information on an individual that can be created, gathered, managed, and consulted by authorized clinicians and staff within one healthcare organization.

Electronic Health Record

An electronic record of health-related information on an individual that conforms to nationally recognized interoperability standards and that can be created, managed, and consulted by authorized clinicians and staff, across more than one healthcare organization.

Personal Health Record

An electronic record of health-related information on an individual that conforms to nationally recognized interoperability standards and that can be drawn from multiple sources while being managed, shared, and controlled by the individual.

Health Information Exchange

The electronic movement of health-related information among organizations according to nationally recognized standards. "HIE" is a verb describing a process.

Health Information Organization

An organization that oversees and governs the exchange of health-related information among organizations according to nationally recognized standards. "HIO" is a noun describing an organization.

Regional Health Information Organization

A health information organization that brings together healthcare stakeholders within a defined geographic area and governs health information exchange among them for the purpose of improving health and care in that community. ■

Loss of Productivity

As we implemented EHRs for BIDPO practices, several clinicians expressed concern about the loss of productivity during the first few months post go live.

What's been the experience for private clinicians implementing EHRs in Massachusetts thus far? The Massachusetts eHealth Collaborative implemented practices for 600 clinicians over the past three years and generally found the following:

After three to four months, clinicians started seeing some of the same patients cycle through, and that's when they started to see the productivity benefits of an EHR.

1. There was not a sustained drop in revenue. Indeed, clinicians had the opposite problem with most practices. MAeHC wanted practices to cut back on patient load during training and go live, but most

of them refused because they didn't want a revenue reduction. On eClinicalWorks, most practices that did cut back were back at full-patient load within two to four weeks of go live. MAeHC did have a few (literally 3 or 4 out of 150) practices that experienced a cash flow reduction because their clearinghouse transition went awry (generally due to the clearinghouse vendor). This usually took a short time to resolve and then they were quickly back to baseline.

2. During the first few months after go live, clinicians worked harder than before because they entered selected historical data into their EHRs for upcoming patients and sometimes stayed later to get the same number of visits in as before. After three to four months, clinicians started seeing some of the same patients cycle through, and that's when they started to see the productivity benefits of an EHR.

3. The industry averages on productivity loss are for practices that did not have the type of preparation and end-to-end practice consulting that MAeHC and BIDMC invested in. For the BIDPO rollout, we are leveraging the practice transformation lessons learned from MAeHC. Based on MAeHC's experience and the fact that we've assembled an implementation dream team of the same folks who implemented practices for the 600 docs of MAeHC, we do not believe we will have a significant reduction in billing or productivity. ■

Sharing Data Among Providers

At times, the business case for interoperability is not entirely clear. If data sharing reduces the volume of redundant lab tests, then the healthcare system as a whole wins, but someone loses revenue.

Over the past few years, I've seen a remarkable change in attitude among clinicians in Massachusetts communities. They are demanding data sharing. Here's the history, the specifics of the clinician requests, and the plan for making it happen.

Over the past few years, I've seen a remarkable change in attitude among clinicians in Massachusetts communities. They are demanding data sharing.

When we first conceived our hosted software as a service model to provide EHRs for non-owned clinician practices, we designed one-way interoperability. BIDMC has an ambulatory record called webOMR which contains the problem lists, medication lists, allergy lists, notes/reports, labs, and imaging studies for three million patients. We worked with our community EHR vendor, eClinicalWorks, to create a seamless web service that links eClinicalWorks to webOMR, such that community physicians can securely view BIDMC data from inside eClinicalWorks without having to login again or use a separate application. However, we did not design a link between eClinicalWorks and webOMR to enable a BIDMC hospitalist or emergency department (ED) physician to view individual patient-identified private practice data.

We did design aggregate data sharing such that the medical director of the physician's organization could query private practices to retrieve performance, quality, and outcomes data in support of pay-for-performance contracts.

As we began to communicate the vision of a community EHR, our private practice clinicians started asking three questions:

1. How does a primary care provider send a clinical summary to a specialist?

2. How does the specialist close the loop with the primary care provider by sending an electronic consult note?

3. How does a hospital-based physician such as an ED clinician, hospitalist, or anesthesiologist retrieve patient summary records from private practices?

My initial response was that private practice data sharing is such a novel idea, that it would have to wait until after our EHR rollout was complete to formulate a strategy.

Clinicians were not satisfied with that approach. Thus, we've decided to accelerate our work on private practice data sharing by creating a clinical summary repository.

Here's how it will work.

1. Whenever a patient visits one of our BIDPO community clinicians, the documentation of their visit will be done in our hosted SaaS eClinicalWorks application.

2. Patients will be asked for their consent by the clinician for community data sharing via opt-in consent at the practice level. Consenting at one practice implies that data from that practice can be shared with other practices, but not visa versa.

3. When the encounter is complete, a summary record including problems, medications, allergies, notes, and labs will be forwarded to the eClinicalWorks EHX repository using the Continuity of Care Document (CCD) format.

4. Other clinicians, who are credentialed members of BIDPO, will be able to view summary records from this repository, assuming the patient has consented to sharing that data.

5. An audit trail of all such lookups will be available to enforce security.

Such an approach solves the PCP-to-specialist clinical summary issue, the specialist-to-PCP communication issue, and the hospital-based viewing of private practice records issue. From a technology perspective, it's an elegant solution that reduces the number of interfaces. All practices send their summaries to a repository in a standard format, then all exchange is done from that repository.

A similar approach has been used in the MAeHC pilots in North Adams, Newburyport, and Brockton to enable secure, patient-consented data sharing in those communities.

I'm hopeful that our BIDPO clinicians will be satisfied by our strategy to embrace bidirectional data sharing in this incremental way—sharing data from BIDMC, sharing aggregate private practice data, sharing data among private practices using eClinicalWorks, then sharing data among communities and hospitals. ∎

The Perfect EHR

I support over 3,000 clinicians in heterogeneous sites of care—solo practitioners, small offices, multi-specialty facilities, community hospitals, academic medical centers, and large group practices.

In every location there is some level of dissatisfaction with their EHR. Complaints about usability, speed of documentation, training, performance, and personalization limitations are typical. Most interesting is that users believe the grass will be greener by selecting another EHR.

The bottom line from every product I've used and everyone I've spoken with is that there is no current "perfect" EHR. We're still very early in the EHR maturity lifecycle.

I've heard from GE users who want Allscripts, eClinicalWorks users who want Epic, Allscripts users who want AthenaHealth, and NextGen users who want eClinicalWorks.

The bottom line from every product I've used and everyone I've spoken with is that there is no current "perfect" EHR. We're still very early in the EHR maturity lifecycle.

What is the perfect EHR? I've written about my best thinking, which has been incorporated into the BIDMC home-built record, webOMR (which has dissatisfied users too).

However, after listening to many "grass is greener" stories, I believe that what a provider perceives as a better EHR often represents tradeoffs in functionality. One EHR may have better prescribing functionality while another has better letters, another is more integrated, and another has better support. The "best"

EHRs, according to providers, vary by what is most important to that individual provider/practice, which may not be consistent with enterprise goals or the needs of an accountable care organization.

My experience is that organizations which have given clinicians complete freedom of EHR choice now have an unintegrated melange of different products that make care standardization impossible.

My advice: pick an EHR for your enterprise that meets your strategic goals, providing the greatest good for the greatest number. Apply a maximum effort to training, education, sharing of lessons learned, user engagement, and health information exchange.

There will always be dissatisfaction and a claim that something is better. However, I've never seen a change in product fix workflow and process issues. BIDMC's strategy is to do our best to ensure providers are educated and use their EHR optimally. I do not believe that there is a better choice than our current mix of built and bought products that makes sense for our pioneer ACO and individual providers within the organization. ∎

The Post EHR Era

Over the next few years, the majority of my time will be spent discussing topics such as care coordination, health information exchange, care management, real-time analytics, and population health. At BIDMC, we've already achieved 100% EHR adoption and 90% Meaningful Use attestation among our clinician community. Now that the foundation is laid, I believe our next body of work is to craft the technology and workflow solutions which will be hallmarks of the "post EHR" era.

What does this mean?

I've written previously about BIDMC's accountable care organization strategy, which can be summed up as ACO = HIE + analytics.

> *Over the next few years, the majority of my time will be spent discussing topics such as care coordination, health information exchange, care management, real-time analytics, and population health.*

In a "post EHR" era we need to go beyond simple data capture and reporting — we need care management that ensures patients with specific diseases follow standardized guidelines and protocols, escalating deviations to the care team. That team will include PCPs, specialists, home care, long term care, and family members. The goal of a care management medical record (CMMR) will be to provide a dashboard that overlays hospital and professional data with a higher level of management.

How could this work?

Imagine that we define each patient's healthcare status in terms of "properties." Data elements might include activities of daily living, functional status, current care plans, care preferences, diagnostic test results, and therapies, populated from many sources of data including every EHR containing patient data, hospital discharge data, and consumer-generated data from PHRs/home health devices.

That data will be used in conjunction with rules that generate alerts and reminders to care managers and other members of the care team (plus the patient). The result is a CMMR system based on a foundation of EHRs that provides much more than any one EHR.

My challenge will be to build and buy components that turn multiple EHRs into a CMMR at the community level.

This will require philanthropic funding, in-kind contributions from selected vendor partners, and a willingness to take a risk on creating something that has never been operated at scale in the past.

I wrote previously about the reluctance of healthcare to change and adopt new delivery models.

BIDMC is a unique learning laboratory because 65% of its patients are already in global captivated risk arrangements.

If the CMMR can be created anywhere, it's at BIDMC, which strives to be agile and transparently share all its early experiences with the world. And now to define the requirements! ∎

Chapter 3

On Being a Modern CIO

A few times a year, I'm asked to visit organizations and perform an IT assessment. I know how uncomfortable such activities are when auditors visit me, so I try to be very supportive and transparent with the local CIO. Inevitably, stakeholders will accuse the CIO of being a naysayer, of not meeting their needs, and of spending too much operating/capital to deliver limited functionality. Since not every CIO in the country can be delivering below the median for CIO performance (by definition), it must be that local stakeholders do not understand the constraints facing modern CIOs. In this chapter, I review the techniques and processes that help CIOs get through their day and keep their jobs. Remember, CIO does not stand for "Career Is Over" or "Cost Is Outrageous."

Service Level Agreements

I was recently asked about our approach to service level agreements (SLAs) at BIDMC.

We develop customer-facing SLAs for every new infrastructure and application as part of our standard project management methodology. We work collaboratively with the application owner and subject matter experts to develop a mutually acceptable process for support escalation, with defined availability and response times.

The end result is a series of documents which outline customer and IS responsibilities, as well as provide enough detail about the application to understand its scope and uses.

The following documents can be found at www.himss.org/geekdoctor.

Customer-Facing Documents:

1. Customer Project and Post Project Responsibilities—This document serves as a foundation for each project and sets customer expectations for support roles and responsibilities.

2. Service Level Agreement—This SLA for a live application illustrates the types of service level documentation we provide.

Internal IT Documents:

1. Business Impact Analysis—A worksheet used by our managers to facilitate discussions with application owners and document service level of objectives based on business requirements.

2. Service Level Objectives—Availability and disaster recovery service levels by class of application.

A few general observations about our SLAs:

1. Much of our planned downtime is now done as a background task thanks to improvements in our configurations. For example, we have clustered servers, redundant network components, and Internet connections, mirrored storage devices, shadowed or mirrored databases, and other improvements that have remarkably decreased the need for disruptive, planned outages.

2. Escalation processes differ slightly for our mission-critical clinical applications, such that downtime over two hours triggers implementation of paper-based downtime procedures.

3. In addition to our own hosted applications, we have a few SaaS applications. Our SLAs with hosting vendors include:

   a. Expected uptime—In some cases this is backed by a well-defined formula that states the goal (e.g., 99.9%), and any other qualifiers such as excluding planned downtime that is done at mutually agreed-upon times. Whatever is set as an uptime goal usually drives the high availability and disaster recovery configurations.

   b. Transaction performance—This traditionally has not been a problem for us, but for applications that may have not been engineered well, it's an important component of an SLA.

c. Escalation—Defining the event levels (priority one, priority two, etc.), contacts, and what response time (phone versus on-site) and repair time can be expected are a key component. Time to repair is usually a tough negotiation in hosted application SLAs.

d. Remedies—This is not usually defined in internal agreements, but is for vendor agreements. The typical remedy is a credit on future maintenance payments, which is not always satisfying if you lose an application for a prolonged period. ∎

Maintaining an Agile IT Organization

I tell my managers that their professional lives will be like a rotating lighthouse. The beam will pass each part of the landscape and sometimes you'll find yourself and your group in the beam.

As strategic plans change, compliance demands arise, and board level priorities create highly visible projects, each team will feel the spotlight and may struggle with timelines and resources. The beam may focus for days or even months on a particular group.

Since all IT projects are a function of time, scope, and resources, when the lighthouse focuses on a group, I'm often asked about increasing FTEs. Getting new positions approved, especially in this economy, is very challenging. I go through an internal due diligence process following the strategy, structure, staffing, and processes approach I use for all IT management.

Here's what I do:

1. **Strategy**—When IT groups are created and position descriptions written, it's generally in response to a strategic need of the organization or mission-critical projects. Strategies change and projects end, so it is important to revisit each part of the organization episodically to ensure it is still aligned with the strategic needs of the organization. Imagine an application group created at the peak of client/server technology. When the spotlight shines on such a group to deliver web-based applications, it may be that the group was never designed to be an agile web delivery department. Thus, I

> *Strategies change and projects end, so it is important to revisit each part of the organization episodically to ensure it is still aligned with the strategic needs of the organization.*

look at the strategy of the organization, the current state of technology in the marketplace/in the community, and the level of customer demand. We can then re-examine the assumptions that were used to charter the group and its positions. For example, two years ago, the PeopleSoft team faced growing demands for application functionality and high levels of customer service. As chartered, our PeopleSoft team was a technology group without staff devoted to workflow analysis, subject matter expertise, and proactive alignment of new PeopleSoft functionality with customer needs. We rechartered the group as a customer-facing, business-analyst driven, service organization backed by a world-class technology team. Given the visibility of our financial projects at that time, the organization was willing to fund expansion of the team.

2. **Structure**—It may be that the team is not structured properly to deliver the level of service needed by the customers. Recently, I worked with my Harvard Media Services team to align job descriptions and hours worked with customer demand. This restructuring was entirely data driven and demonstrated that in order to meet evolving customer expectations, we needed one person to work four ten-hour days, four people to work five eight-hour days, and one person to serve as a line supervisor, scheduling everyone and communicating to customers. The end result was a minimal increase in expense but a complete realignment of our organizational structure with the current needs of the enterprise.

3. **Staffing**—It may be that staff skill sets are perfect for their job descriptions as originally written, but they are no longer appropriate for the current state of technology. Training is critically important to maintain an agile IT organization so that staff can grow as technology grows. Based on expertise, levels of training, and capacity to evolve, staff in a group may be promoted or reassigned to best align them with the current strategy and structure.

4. **Processes**—It may be that customer service issues are related to less than optimal communication or lack of a consistent service process. When the spotlight focuses on a group, I make sure we have optimized and documented our processes to serve the needs of customers.

CIOs should not assume their organization will be static. Technology changes rapidly and customer demands continue to grow. A healthy re-examination of each part of the organization to ensure strategy, structure, staffing, and process are optimized will ensure an agile IT organization that grows and thrives over time.

When the lighthouse beam shines on your group, welcome it as an opportunity to renew! ∎

The Impact of Lean Times on IT Organizations

Times are tough in the US. It's not clear that recent college graduates will find jobs, wages are stagnant, and costs are rising.

What about the impact on IT organizations?

To me, lean times require every company to re-examine itself and validate its priorities. Capital and operating budget processes separate the 'nice to have' from the 'must have.' Discretionary projects are deferred.

Since I have strong belief in IT governance, which suggests that IT strategy should be perfectly aligned with the overall strategy of the company, I welcome this kind of corporate introspection, which results in a very specific list of high-priority projects.

I would much rather have a short list of high-priority, high-business value projects that focus on the basics than a list of ambiguous, speculative projects driven by politics.

Lean times enable the IT organization to catch up, ensure its own processes are optimized, and realign its work with business owners.

There is the risk that resource constraints will tip the IT organization from 'lean and mean' to 'bony and angry,' but ideally, appropriate governance process will align expectations and resource availability so that lean budgets yield realistic expectations of what can be done with existing resources.

Despite the doom and gloom reported on CNN, I would offer the optimistic suggestion that lean times are a positive experience for IT organizations, creating accountability for doing a few new projects really well.

Given the economies of scale that often happen with centralized IT infrastructure and well-coordinated enterprise application projects, lean times can also reduce the number of competitive departmental/local efforts. As I've said previously, there will always be a balance between central and local IT, which is good, but taking the time to carefully plan enterprise resource allocation instead of simply reacting to evolving local efforts is optimal.

Yes, people are hurt by any economic downturn and I will not minimize the negative aspects of recessions. However, it is possible for IT organizations to thrive by focusing on the specific projects needed to ensure the stability of the business in lean times. ∎

Implementing New Applications

I've previously written about selecting new applications and the infrastructure reviews we do whenever new applications are added to BIDMC.

Once an application is selected, my role as a CIO is to set expectations about what happens between product selection and go live. On occasion, some stakeholders think of applications like installing a spreadsheet on their home computer—you just buy the application, type "setup," and then begin using it.

I've even heard of examples in which a CIO tried this. At one institution I visited, they purchased PeopleSoft, copied it to a server, and then "turned it on." To their surprise, it was not used.

We try to standardize the steps between product selection and go live, ensuring that IS manages that process with strong governance oversight by the stakeholders. Here's our framework:

- Hold kick off meeting for all stakeholders

- Identify the business process owner and the individual who makes decisions for the users

- Identify the project manager in IS (note that every project needs a named project manager in IS)

- Obtain agreement on scope (may include phased implementation such as pilots)

- Obtain agreement on timing

- Obtain agreement on staffing and budgets

- Schedule steering and working group meetings

- Identify needed Infrastructure: network impact, servers, storage/archiving

- Acquire the application including negotiation and legal approval of terms/ conditions

- Configure the application and establish any needed interfaces

- Perform integrated testing of the application

- Train support staff and stakeholders on the use of the application

- Go live

- Support and life-cycle manage the application

This framework ensures a successful go live, provides 24x7 support, and ensures the application is maintained over time. Although the process typically takes 6–12 months from start to finish (except for the simplest SaaS applications hosted externally), it's a worthwhile investment if you plan to use the application for decade.

I hope this is helpful to you. ∎

Aligning Clinicians and IT

Each year when I publish the IT operating plan summary, I'm careful to relate the projects to their strategic importance, impact on patients, improvements in quality/safety, and return on investment.

This was nicely stated by Ian Furst who commented on my blog about marketing IT. He noted that a statement such as, "Our goal is to be 100% computerized" sounds like an IT goal. Ideally, goals should start with, "We will improve the patient care/experience/life expectancy with..."

To align clinicians and IT, I have a Clinical Information Systems Steering Committee which includes membership from 11 subcommittees:

- Chair of the Laboratory Information Systems Committee

- Chair of Radiology Information Systems Committee

- Chair of Critical Care Information Systems Committee

- Chair of Inpatient Information Systems Committee

- Chair of Ambulatory Information Systems Committee

- Chair of Health Information Management Committee

- Chair of Community Information Systems Committee

- Chair of Decision Support Information Systems Committee

- Chair of Revenue Cycle Information Systems Committee

- Medical Executive Committee Representative

- Operating Room Executive Committee Representative

I recently presented the work of all these committees to the Clinical Operations Coordinating Committee, the joint administrative/clinician governance of BIDMC. The presentation I used illustrates the major clinical accomplishments for last year, the goals for next year, and plan for future years. Each slide describes the clinical benefit of the projects.

When I execute complex clinical projects each year, I'm typically asked three questions about my approach to aligning clinicians and IT:

Every project must start with a charter that identifies the stakeholders, roles/ responsibilities, purpose of the project, milestones, and metrics for success.

1. What are our biggest challenges running large clinical information systems projects?

Every project must start with a charter that identifies the stakeholders, roles/ responsibilities, purpose of the project, milestones, and metrics for success. The only way to balance scope, timing, and resources is to have an unambiguous definition of who cares about the project, who does the work, why the project will be done, when the project will be done, and how project success is defined. As the project proceeds there will be many requests to expand its scope, add more features, increase the number interfaces, and expand the stakeholder population being served. The committee providing governance to the project, guided by the charter, must resist the change in scope. If change in scope is deemed critical to the project's success, then the charter should be changed to reflect the impact on project timing and resources, ensuring that change is broadly communicated.

2. What are the biggest mistakes?

Projects must ultimately be driven by their business owners, such as the doctors, nurses, and staff who will be using the finished system, not by IT. Having clinician-driven projects ensures the application becomes "the clinician's system" and not the "IT system which administration forced on us." Also, software should not be used to change workflow. Before implementation of the software, business processes should be optimized and workflow documented. Then, software can automate that workflow. If software is used to force behavioral change, clinicians will blame the software for any frustrations they have about the process change.

3. What are the top three best practices to ensure success?

Big bang IT never works. Pilots and phased implementation of applications reduce the risk of failure and ensure the resources are available to respond to any infrastructure or application issues which occur during roll out.

Broadly communicating the benefits of the project and the urgency to implement it really helps with clinician acceptance/adoption.

Project management is key. Ensuring the scope is constrained, milestones achieved, and participants coordinated are prerequisites to a successful project.

As a clinician myself, I use the systems we create. Being a physician CIO/CMIO helps me understand the clinical impact of every project, engage the clinicians in every project, and establish trust with all the doctors and nurses in the hospital. ∎

Marketing IT

The role of the CIO is very operational—keeping the trains running on time, ensuring budgets are sufficient, and aligning IT resources with the needs of stakeholders. One other important task of the CIO is to market the work of the IT department to internal and external audiences. Although IT staff and those involved in IT governance committees are interested in the granular details of projects and their timelines, many audiences want the vision—the big, audacious goals that are really transformational.

To ensure I target the right message to the right audience, I create two documents each year: an operating plan and an "elevator speech." Here's a typical elevator speech to use with senior management and board members:

1. We will lead the country in interoperable electronic health records.

    a. Every doctor in New England affiliated with BIDMC or its associated organizations will have a hospital-provided or hospital-subsidized electronic health record with e-prescribing and connections to our community data-sharing systems by the end of the year.

    b. Every patient will be given the opportunity to have a personal health record by the end of the year.

    c. All inpatient documentation will be electronic and multidisciplinary by the end of the year.

2. We will lead the country in 'social networking tools' for healthcare.

    a. We will launch a new intranet which includes instant messaging (IM), blogging, wikis, and forums by the end of the year, ensuring every doctor and staff member can be an author and publisher.

    b. We will pioneer the concept of the "patient-specific healthcare wiki" for team management of patient medications, documentation of problem lists, and creation of clinical documentation by the end of the year. The idea behind this concept is that an entire community of caregivers should work together to create and maintain the lifetime medical record of each patient. This means that any caregiver should be able to add/amend/correct the patient's lifetime record, with a complete audit trail to identify every source of data and edits.

    c. We will use a combination of personal health records, electronic health records, and social networking tools to ensure continuity of care among all stakeholders in our community.

3. We will lead the country in 'event-driven' medicine.

    a. We will adopt electronic clinician notification systems for our hospital applications based on physician communication preferences (EHR, email, fax, page, cell phone) by the end of the year. These systems will close the loop for laboratory, radiology, discharge, referral, and other important communications needed to ensure safety.

    b. We will deploy business intelligence tools connected to our clinical data marts by the end of the year.

    c. We will embrace next-generation decision support tools from Safe-Med and others by the end of the year, which will provide the business rules to trigger notification of clinicians. This will ensure that clinicians receive just-in-time information to deliver the best possible care. ■

New and Improved

CIOs rarely receive credit for keeping the trains running on time. Instead, they receive credit for implementing new applications and cool infrastructure features. The challenge is that 80% of IT resources are needed to maintain existing applications and infrastructure, leaving 20% of the total IT budget to be spent on new work. When you consider the multi-year larger projects, the "must do" compliance issues, and the tyranny of the urgent, there is very little left over to focus on discretionary innovation.

A cutting edge application can rapidly become a legacy system if the stakeholders feel that IT has lost the ability to respond to the needs of the users. What is the best strategy to keep the users happy and make the organization feel that IT is constantly innovating? Here's my approach:

Establish Strong Governance

Governance committees have three major purposes. They provide a process for prioritizing new requests, establish a team of champions for the application, and provide a forum for education about an application's features and benefits. Whenever I hear that an application is non-intuitive, has ceased to be innovative, or lacks critical features, most of the time it's a governance problem. Do not replace the application; establish a multi-stakeholder governance committee as your first step.

Implement small continuous improvements instead of big bang new applications.

A few times in the history of my organizations, stakeholders outside of IT have decided that wholesale replacement of applications or massive new implementations will solve workflow issues. In each case, the issues turned out to be non-IT process problems or weak governance caused by internal politics. The problem with big bang new applications is that they consume all available IT resources and often require existing applications to be frozen for months (if not years), while the new implementation progresses. Lack of progress in existing applications causes even more frustration and by the time the new application is ready, it's common that needs have changed and the new application is no longer the nirvana it was once thought to be. Making constant small changes in response to constantly evolving customer needs is the best way to achieve satisfaction.

> The problem with big bang new applications is that they consume all available IT resources and often require existing applications to be frozen for months (if not years), while the new implementation progresses.

Communicate Broadly

For the past decade, I've written an email to everyone in the organization at least once a month describing the latest in IT innovations. With the increase in sensitivity to spam and broadcast email, I've replaced that communication with blogging. My posts about "Integrating the Medical Record," "Providing Decision Support," and "Clinical Documentation" were all in response to internal customer questions about strategy, new features, and priorities. I use blogs, emails, and in-person presentations to celebrate IT successes and to educate naysayers.

Enhance the User Interface

Just as many people are attracted to new car models because of changes in style or color, users find a new user interface to be a sign of innovation. Especially with the web, it's important to evolve user interfaces to embrace a modern look and feel. The late 1990s were about lists of links. The early 2000s were about graphical elements and color. The mid 2000s were about clean interfaces with blues and whites. The 2010s are about pastels, brushed steel, and effective use of screen real estate, especially on mobile devices.

Run Focus Groups and Do Surveys

As a corollary to governance, it's important to get feedback from the trenches. Doing usability testing with focus groups and getting candid feedback from a large number of stakeholders via surveys is an effective way to measure the pulse of the organization. When I get detailed feedback, I often find that the issues which are most bothersome to users are the easiest to fix, such as relabeling a button, changing a screen layout, or improving workflow through refinement of a minor feature.

> When I get detailed feedback, I often find that the issues which are most bothersome to users are the easiest to fix, such as relabeling a button, changing a screen layout, or improving workflow through refinement of a minor feature.

Thus, continuous incremental improvement driven by strong governance is the path to success. My governance groups are stronger than ever and the buzz is that "new and improved" applications are rolling out faster than ever. ∎

How to Be a Bad CIO

In my decade as a CIO, I've seen a lot of turnover in the IT industry. Each time a CIO is fired, I've asked around to learn about the root cause. Here's my list of the top ten ways to be a bad CIO:

1. Start each meeting with a chip on your shoulder—Human nature is such that every organization has politics and conflicts. Sometimes these differences of opinion lead to emotional emails or confrontational meetings. If the CIO develops an attitude that presupposes every request will be unreasonable and every interaction unpleasant, then every meeting will become unproductive. I find that listening to naysayers, understanding common ground, and developing a path forward works with even the most difficult customers. Instead of believing that meetings with challenging customers will be negative, I think of them as opportunities for a "walk in the woods."

2. Bypass governance processes and set priorities yourself—Although it's true that some budget decisions must be made by the CIO, such as maintaining infrastructure, the priorities for application development should be based on customer-driven governance committees. Even the best of intentions can lead to a mismatch between customer expectations and IT resource allocation. I recently participated in a meeting to discuss technology problems, when in fact the problem was governance—a lack of communication among the stakeholders, resulting in unclear priorities and unmet expectations. Once the governance is clarified and communication channels established, IT can deliver on customer priorities and meet expectations.

3. Protect your staff at the expense of customer and institutional needs— As a CIO, I work hard to prevent my staff from becoming over stressed. However, I also work with the customers to balance resources, scope, and timing, rather than just saying 'no.' Sometimes organizational priorities will be overwhelming due to sudden compliance issues or "must do" strategic opportunities. I do my best to redirect resources to these new priorities, explaining that existing projects will slow down. My attitude is that I do not know the end of play in the middle of act 1, so I cannot really understand the impact of new priority initiatives until I accept their positive possibilities and start working on the details. Tolerate some ambiguity, accept change, support the institution, and, if a resource problem evolves, then ask for help.

   Tolerate some ambiguity, accept change, support the institution, and, if a resource problem evolves, then ask for help.

4. Put yourself first. I've written that life as a CIO is a lifestyle, not a job— Weekends and nights are filled with system upgrades. Pagers and cell phones go off at inopportune moments. Vacations and downtime are

a balance with operational responsibilities. When I go on vacation, I get up an hour before my family, catch up on email, then spend the day with my family. At night, I go to bed an hour after they do, catching up on the day's events. It's far worse to ignore email and phone calls for a week, then come back to a desk filled with loose ends. Being a CIO requires a constant balance of personal and professional time.

5. Use mutually assured destruction negotiating tactics—Walking into the CEO's office and saying that you will quit unless your budget is increased does not win the war. It may result in temporary victory but it demeans the CIO. Similarly, telling customers that the CEO, chief operating officer (COO), and chief financial officer (CFO) are to be blamed for lack of resources does not make the organization look good. The CIO should be a member of senior management and all resource decisions should be made together by consensus, even if the outcome is not always positive for IT.

6. Hide your mistakes/undercommunicate—My network outage in 2002 resulted in what was called "the worst IT disaster in healthcare history." By sharing all my lessons learned with the press and internal customers, everyone understood the combination of issues and events that caused the problem. I received email from CIOs all over the world explaining their similar problems that had been hidden due to public relations concerns. I have found that transparency and over-communication may be challenging in the short term, but they always improve the situation in the long term.

7. Burn bridges—It's a small world and the best policy is to be as cordial and professional as possible with every stakeholder, even your worst naysayers. A dozen years ago, before I was CIO, I presented to the IT steering committee about the need to embrace the web. I was told by a senior IT leader that they did not care what I had to say since I was not an important stakeholder. A year later, I became CIO and that IT senior leader left the organization within a week.

8. Don't give your stakeholders a voice—Sitting in your office and not meeting with customers is doom for the CIO. Every day, I fill my schedule with meetings in the trenches with all the stakeholders to understand what is working and what is not. I never shoot the messenger when I'm told that our products or services need improvement. A CIO can earn a lot of respect just by listening to the honest feedback from every part of the organization.

9. Embrace obsolete technologies—The CIO should never be the rate-limiting step for adoption of new technologies and ideas. If open

source, Apple products, and Web 2.0 are the way the world is going, the CIO should be the first in line to test them.

10. Think inside the box—Facebook as a rapid application development platform? Empowering users to do self-service data mining? Piloting thin-client devices and flexible work arrangements? Although exploring new ideas will not always result in a breakthrough, it's much more likely to create innovation than maintain the status quo.

Each time you approach a senior manager, a customer, or an employee, remind yourself of the top ten ways to be a bad CIO. By avoiding these behaviors, you may find yourself embraced by the organization for many years to come. ∎

Always Look on the Bright Side

Every day as a CIO, I inevitably receive unpleasant emails. I truly wish I could receive emails like: "The network and the servers have been running flawlessly for the past year. Congratulations on zero downtime."

But alas, no one is likely to send such an email.

The CIO has the challenge of delivering flawless operational performance, while also managing constant change. It's a bit like changing the wings on a 747 aircraft while in flight.

I have an appropriate budget which is prioritized by excellent governance committees, and a yearly operating plan that is only occasionally interrupted by the "tyranny of the urgent" due to compliance, quality, or strategic opportunity mandates, but I still receive daily complaints such as the following:

- "The Spam filters are too lax since I still receive some junk mail, but by the way, you need to let my eBay transactions through."

- "My brother-in-law will offer me a WugaWuga 3000 desktop computer at a cheaper price; why are you using Dell and Lenovo hardware?"

- "I need to surf pornography sites as part of an NIH-funded research study and you should not restrict my academic freedom."

- "My application, although not funded and not reviewed by any governance process, is your highest priority."

- "I did not tell you that we needed network, telephones, desktops, and new applications by next week but now it's your emergency. I'm headed out to my vacation; let me know how it goes."

To all such complaints, a kneejerk response might be:
"Your bad planning does not constitute an emergency on my part."
or

"Every project is a function of funding, scope, and time. You've provided no funding, so your project will either have zero scope or take infinite time."

But the CIO needs to respond:

"Thanks so much for your thoughtful email. There is a process to evaluate your request and I will personally supervise your request during that process. Your peers and the clinical leadership of the entire organization will evaluate your request based on the following:

- Return on investment

- Quality/compliance

- Staff/patient/clinician impact

- Strategic importance"

Every time I have responded to angry email with emotion I have regretted it. Although it may feel good to respond to a negative email with a venomous answer, emotion is never appropriate. I tell my staff that if they ever feel emotion while writing an email, "save as draft." Get someone else to review the response first. Send it after a day of rest.

Rather than judge the quality of every day based on the negative email I receive, I ask about our trajectory. Have we moved forward on our yearly and five-year plan? Has today had ten good things and only five bad things? Do I have my health, my family, and my reputation?

No matter how bad the week, the answer to all of these questions is always yes. Our trajectory is always positive.

With a positive trajectory in mind, a non-emotional response to every issue is easier. If a CIO ever uses profanity, a raised voice, or escalation to the CEO, the CIO diminishes himself/herself.

You can always recover from a bad day, but you cannot always recover from a bad email.

Thus, keep a stiff upper lip, have a thick skin, and run each day based on your trajectory, not the position of your ego. And remember, "save as draft." ∎

Managing Consulting Engagements

In previous blogs, I've mentioned the importance of project management. Every IT project, no matter how large or small, needs an assigned single point of contact for the IT department who can resolve day-to-day project issues and orchestrate communication. As I've said previously, not every project needs a Gantt chart and I'm dubious about the value of centralized project management offices for IT departments, but assigning an IT project manager and using a set of standardized project management tools are very important prerequisites for successful projects.

Consulting engagements need to be managed using the very same approach. All consulting projects need an IT project manager, a steering committee, and a project charter which documents the reason the consultants have been hired. For very politically challenging consulting engagements, the CIO can serve as the catalyst to start the project, but I do not recommend that the CIO serve as the IT project manager. The level of detail required to manage consultants requires more dedicated time than most CIOs have each day.

Here's the structured approach I recommend to manage consultants:

1. Scope—All the stakeholders involved in the consulting engagement must agree on an unambiguous scope for the project. The steering committee for the engagement should meet and agree on this scope before the consultants are engaged. This scope should be described in the project charter along with the governance that will be used to escalate questions about scope. Only by actively managing scope can consulting costs be controlled.

2. Deliverables—The result of a consulting engagement should be clearly described deliverables such as a finalized software product selection, a thoroughly researched whitepaper, or a comprehensive policy. The entire consulting engagement should be managed toward the production of these deliverables, including interim review of drafts as often as possible. Mid-course corrections of interim deliverables are always easier than a wholesale revision at the end of the process.

3. Interview plan—Consultants, no matter how well intentioned, are disruptive to the day-to-day work of an organization since they need to meet with many stakeholders on an aggressive schedule to gather the information they need for their deliverables. The project manager overseeing the consulting engagement should work closely with the consultants to create a draft interview plan. This interview plan should specify the person, his/her role, and the questions to be answered.

4. Inform superiors—The steering committee of the consulting engagement needs to review the draft interview plan, concur with the interview choices, and ensure the managers of the interviewees are informed that the interviews will be scheduled. Typically, the project manager can send an email on behalf of the steering committee to the managers of the interviewees, so that all concerned realize the importance of the engagement.

5. Inform interviewees—The managers of the interviewees should inform them of the purpose of the interviews and the need to schedule meetings with the consultants promptly. Urgent scheduling minimizes the cost of consultant time. The reason I prefer the direct managers to notify the interviewees is that most employees are reluctant to speak

with consultants promptly unless they are told by their managers that they can defer their other work to make time available for the consultants. Circulating a draft list of questions to each interviewee ahead of time is always helpful.

6. Conduct interviews—The interviews should be grouped by physical location to minimize consultant travel time. There are pros and cons to onsite versus phone interviews. Onsite interviews build a sense of team and establish relationships between the consultants and key stakeholders. However, onsite interviews generally require travel and hotel expense. Phone interviews are often easier to schedule and execute. Generally, we schedule the first consultant meetings with key stakeholders onsite and then follow-up meetings by phone.

7. Weekly deliverable check in—Every week, the steering committee (or an executive subset of the steering committee) should meet by phone to discuss the progress of the engagement and the status of deliverables. These weekly meetings are essential to rapidly resolve project roadblocks and clear up any misunderstandings.

8. Daily communication as needed—The IT project manager should be available to all stakeholders by email and phone to respond to daily issues as they arise. Interviews may need to be rescheduled, consultants may step on political landmines requiring escalation, and logistical details may need clarification.

9. Draft deliverable review—The entire steering committee should meet in person at a midpoint in the consulting engagement to review all the draft deliverable work and make recommendations about the final format, content, and timing of the deliverables, ensuring they align with the agreed-upon scope.

> *After each consulting engagement, I summarize the key points from the deliverables so that everyone in the organization learns from the work and understands what we received for our money.*

10. Final communication of the deliverables and next steps—Once the deliverables are completed and reviewed by the committee, they should be broadly communicated to all the stakeholders involved in the engagement. Each interviewee will be more likely to participate in future engagements if they see the results of their input and understand next steps. After each consulting engagement, I summarize the key points from the deliverables so that

everyone in the organization learns from the work and understands what we received for our money.

As a final note, I want to re-emphasize that consultants create a lot of work for internal staff, including those who manage the consultants and those who provide the documents requested during interviews. If anyone believes that consultants can simply parachute into an organization, do their work without disrupting operations, then depart, they have not been on the receiving end of a consulting engagement! ∎

Central and Local Information Technology

A few years ago, I was asked to write an overview about day-to-day IT support, including ideas about expanding services over the next year. One of the most savvy folks in the community responded with a great dialog that illustrates the balance between central and local IT. Although not directly related to healthcare IT implementation, it illustrates the decisions CIOs must make about division of labor between centralized IT organizations and local departmental experts.

1. Networks
Continue to provide high-bandwidth wired and wireless networks to all Harvard Medical School departments. Provide 100-megabit connections to all desktops and 1-gigabit connections as needed, assuming that appropriate Cat 6 wiring is available in the department. In parallel, replace all legacy wiring at HMS over the next five years to ensure all stakeholders have the potential for gigabyte connections.

This level of infrastructure is naturally a central IT (and physical infrastructure) function. However, the requirements are not entirely generic (e.g., different sites have specific network architecture needs). Support for the software side of networking (firewalls) with adequate attention to the particular needs of departments is also essential.

2. Servers
Continue to provide Unix/Linux and Windows server hosting with 24x7 management, operating system patching, and security services for all HMS stakeholders. The offsite data center should be expanded to meet growing demand for server and high-performance computing hosting.

This is one of the areas in which there is the most variation in the benefits of centralization to different research units. Some departments or labs have well-developed IT support staffs and server infrastructure, others have local servers but are poorly staffed, and some have little local support and are reliant on central services. For the first group, having local support staff responsible to a local group and dedicated to the particular needs of the site is a highly effective model. Whether this is consistent with centralized physical location of server hardware remains to be determined. For the other groups, some further investigation is needed to determine whether a centralized or dedicated server model is more appropriate.

3. Storage

Provide 50 gigabytes per user and 500 gigabytes per lab at no charge. Provide storage and archiving services to high-volume users for $1/gigabyte per year. To ensure that storage needs are met for all new faculty, include funding for IT infrastructure such as storage in their recruiting packages. Storage includes 24x7 support for high-speed fiber channel or SATA Network Attached Storage, including appropriate means to attach to this storage for Mac OS X, Linux, Unix, and Windows, as well as web-based online storage. Archiving/backup is also provided as a service.

The proper organization of storage is closely linked to the organization of servers; the physical link between storage and server is still important. Backups might be efficiently provided as a school-level commodity service if competitively priced with an adequate service level for restores, although there are issues of confidentiality and data use agreements affecting some datasets.

4. Desktops

Continue to maintain help desk services, jointly managed with the departments, for support of Windows, Macs, and Linux machines. Provide anti-virus software and operating system updates.

Joint management with departments has been a good model. Some desktop-oriented applications and services are standardized commodities, but assignment of support staff to departments allows them to gain familiarity with the particular needs and configurations of departments and individual users.

5. Applications

Today, the application suite at HMS includes web portals such as Mycourses/eCommons; administrative applications such as FIRST, Room Scheduling, MARS (Medical Area Reporting System), MAES (Medical Area Equipment System), PeopleSoft, GMAS, MADRIS; research applications that run on Orchestra such as Twiki, Matlab, LaserGene, and Endnote; and educational applications such as virtual microscopy, streaming video/podcasting, and simulations.

Email is another crucial service that is best supported at the school level due to the high cost of effectively dealing with spam and malware.

Expand this suite of applications through the enhancement of Mycourses/eCommons to include collaboration services such as instant messaging, WebEx meetings, CONNECTS (a match-making service for equipment, techniques, and scientists), SHRINE (a means of data mining across all Harvard affiliates), and web content management for easy hosting of internal and external websites. Expand this suite of applications to support research administrative and CTSA[1] needs such as IACUC[2] and animal ordering. Expand application support to include informatics services per the BRIC (Basic Research Informatics Core) business plan such as database consulting and web application design.

Some attention should be given to the cost allocation model for these services since some of them are of general use, some are sometimes provided by internally supported staff at departments, and some are of use only to particular groups. However, for the most part the items listed here are of general utility.

6. Disaster Recovery
Currently, HMS maintains two data centers and has significant redundancy in storage, server clusters, and networks. However, it does not have a true disaster recovery center and plan. Hire staff and develop a plan to ensure business continuity in the case of a major data center or natural disaster.

7. Media Services
Provide media services support for the entire school including presentation services, digital photography/videography, and teleconferencing services. The Media Services infrastructure is currently under review and school-wide enhancements will be proposed for next year.

As you can see from this dialog, neither completely central nor completely local is the right model for a research-focused medical school.

At HMS, central organizations provide "heat, power, light, networking, and terabytes"—the utilities needed to empower all the core businesses of HMS: education, research, and administration. Centralizing those utilities which can achieve economies of scale and reliability, while leaving local those areas of science and application expertise unique to each department, has worked well to support all our stakeholders. One of the major central/local collaborations has been the joint hiring of customer service representatives for each department and locating them within the departments they serve. This enables each department to have centrally trained, managed, and budgeted staff but with specific skills to meet each department's academic needs. Similarly, the HMS data center hosts centrally managed servers and storage but also hosts department-specific infrastructure managed by scientists.

This division of labor between the IT department and the scientific community leverages the skills of each, ensuring a positive working relationship, based on a transparent governance model, for all the services we deliver. ∎

---

1   CTSA = Clinical and Translational Science Awards.

2   IACUC = Institutional Animal Care and Use Committee.

Managing IT Projects

I'm often asked how we manage IT projects. Do we have an Enterprise Project Management Office? A tracking Gantt chart for every project?

The answer is that we do not use a one-size-fits-all approach to project management; we use a suite of tools and common principles that we apply as appropriate depending on the scope, risk, and complexity of the project.

Here's my guide to project management:

1. Every project starts with a charter. A project charter clarifies the purpose and urgency of the project which is important for change management. The key leaders, stakeholders, milestones, and risks are clearly stated.

2. Every project gets a single accountable leader. That leader may be the project manager or may have project management staff reporting to him/her. Having a project manager is key to the success of a project. That project manager may use tools such as Gantt charts and workplans, and issue tracking logs. Although some projects are managed through sophisticated Microsoft Project diagrams, most are done on a far less sophisticated basis. Several years ago, we tried to introduce a program management software package and found it to be so burdensome that we dropped it. The main ingredients to our being successful, despite the lack of a PMO, are good managers and good communications.

   Our managers are good at triaging and adapting when unforeseen demands interrupt work plans. They are also good at keeping others informed. There are a few factors that I believe have promoted such good communications:

   a. The tenure of our staff, especially at the managerial layer, has been excellent. They are a well-oiled team and know when the left hand needs to learn what the right hand is doing.

   b. Our office layout promotes communications. We have more conference room space per FTE than any group in the medical center. This has proven not to be a luxury, but a necessity. It makes it easier to hold ad hoc sessions and there are few delays because rooms are available for meetings.

   c. We liberally use conference and bridge calls. Bringing people together periodically to make sure things are moving along is of great value.

   d. We reach out to our vendor partners and other experts when we need assistance. These folks have helped crystallize our plans when complex problems have arisen.

e. We have a very active change management process that also serves to keep the right and left hand communicating. The meetings and email announcements ensure others get the word and are able to weigh in with their advice.

We also tend to select a small number of vendor partners, making technology life cycle planning predictable. We are not constantly shifting vendors, which would drag on our efficiency.

3. Every project has a steering committee with minutes of each committee meeting. Each steering committee is comprised of key decision makers and stakeholders who build a guiding coalition for each project, a key ingredient for change management. We complete each meeting with a summary of who will be accountable for what, and when it will be done. This ensures that the give and take, the digressions, and the range of topics discussed have not confused what has been agreed upon. Every meeting has an element negotiation and we repeat back what was agreed upon to get all parties to acknowledge it.

4. Every project has success metrics which are reviewed frequently. I believe that "The troops do well what their commander reviews." If my top-level IT managers are skilled at asking the right questions about high-visibility projects, but also pay attention to the basics of operations that keep the systems working, it

> *Every project has success metrics which are reviewed frequently. I believe that "The troops do well what their commander reviews."*

carries down to the staff. They know they need to pay attention to the details, keep the project moving, and adhere to agreed-upon deadlines.

Over the past decade we've had a few projects that were over budget or over time. In every case, it was because one of the above steps was not followed. By using these general principles, project risk is minimized and all stakeholders are likely to have a better project experience. ∎

Selecting New Applications

Every week, I'm asked by customers to collaborate with them to choose new applications.

Here's how we do it:

1. First, we take an enterprise view of each application request, since we would much rather consolidate applications and reduce the number of vendors than provide a new niche application for every evolving departmental need. If an existing enterprise application cannot meet the user's requirements, we then survey the marketplace.

2. We do not believe in requests for proposals (RFPs). RFP means "request for prevarication," since most vendors do their best to answer RFPs with as many positive responses as possible. Instead, we review the marketplace, often via the web and by reviewing summary evaluations from KLAS reports. We pick the three or four applications which seem to best meet our stakeholder functionality requirements.

3. Once we have a small number of applications identified, we evaluate them for their suitability in our infrastructure environments using a formal process. In 2003, we created a Change Control Board to orient the infrastructure team to new applications that are being proposed. The forum meets weekly and has broad representation, including help desk, desktop, servers, storage, networking and security staff. Note that this screening sheet evolves as technologies evolve. Two years ago, we would not have asked about compatibility with VMware/ Virtualization technologies. Also, this list is expanded to address those issues arising from bad experiences, so we do not repeat them.

4. Once an application is approved for suitability in our infrastructure environment, application teams then work collaboratively with our customers to do the following:

   a. Manage all vendor relationships including scripted demonstrations, contract negotiation, installation/training, and life-cycle maintenance of the application.

   b. Manage integration with our existing applications. Typically this is done via our eGate messaging engine or via web services, since we have widely deployed a service-oriented architecture.

   c. Define service levels, a disaster recovery strategy, an escalation plan for issues, and division of labor for support of the application. Typically, IS manages the infrastructure and keeps the application running smoothly. Power users in the department document workflow and ensure the application's functionality is optimized to support that workflow.

Over the past ten years, we've found that this collaborative approach with IT, rather than having each department select its own applications, ensures stability, maintainability, and scalability. At this point, most departmental IT systems and staff at BIDMC have been replaced by services from the central IT organization.

It's a win/win for everyone, since costs decrease, quality increases, and the frustration of choosing an application which does not work in our infrastructure has been eliminated. ∎

When to Hire Consultants

I'm sure you've heard the consulting stereotypes.

"For a large sum, they will ask for your watch and tell you what time it is."

"They gather an immense amount of knowledge from the organization, create a splashy presentation summarizing what you already know, then leave the organization taking that knowledge with them to apply to other consulting engagements."

However, there are three specific circumstances in which I hire consultants:

1. As part of change management by having an external group validate the path chosen. Change is hard and sometimes politics in an organization are such that no internal stakeholder can champion the new idea. Bringing in consultants to publicly validate the idea can build transparency and break down barriers. It may sound strange to pay an external party to explain to an organization what it already knows, but sometimes it is necessary. Also, I've seen stakeholders in politically charged situations be more honest and open with external consultants than with their peers. Many staff seem to be happy to tell all to an external party, which can accelerate information gathering.

2. To extend the capacity of the organization for short-term urgent work. I've recently been asked to significantly expand the services offered by IT. All of my existing staff are working at 120% on existing projects. Bringing in consultants for a very focused, short-term engagement will enable my staff to focus on their deadlines while getting extra work done by consultants in parallel. A few caveats about doing this: consultants need to be managed carefully to ensure travel expenses are minimized and the time spent is tightly scoped toward a specific deliverable. This means that consultants will take management time and staff time, so adding one consultant FTE comes at a cost of .5 FTE to manage and provide support for the consultant. Also, the organization must buy into the consulting engagement. I've seen passive/aggressive behavior toward consultants, so stakeholders should ask for the consulting engagement rather than have one forced upon them.

3. As contractors who add new knowledge to the organization. In 2002, I had a serious network outage because there were aspects of network management "that I did not know that I did not know." We brought in experts in network infrastructure and applications (DNS/ DHCP[3]) design. These folks were more educators and contractors than consultants. We now have one of the most resilient networks in healthcare due to their education about best practices.

There are also reasons not to hire consultants:

1. Do not outsource your strategy to consultants. Although many talented consulting firms offer strategic planning, I've not seen business-changing strategic plans come out of outsourcing strategy. Consultants can be helpful facilitators of strategic planning, organizing all the ideas of employees, customers, and senior management, but the strategy should belong to the organization, not external consultants.

2. Do not hire consultants as operational line managers. Sometimes positions are hard to fill and consultants are brought in as temporary staff. This can work. However, hiring a consultant to manage permanent employees does not work. It generates a great deal of resentment from the existing employees and it's hard to sustain because everyone knows their manager is temporary. It's a bit like having a substitute teacher in school.

3. Do not allow consultants to hire consultants. Sometimes consultants are self-propagating. A tightly scoped engagement grows as consultants discover new work for other consultants to do. Keep the consulting engagement focused and move the work to the permanently employed staff in the organization as soon as possible.

On rare occasions, I make myself available for one-day consulting engagements doing comprehensive IT audits of healthcare organizations. When I do this, I donate all fees to BIDMC or Harvard, not accepting any payment for my time. I create an overview analysis of the strategy, structure, and staffing of the IT organization as a guide for the existing management and staff. I hope these efforts follow my guidelines above—bringing external validation, extending capacity, and offering new perspective. ■

---

3   DNS/DHCP = Domain name server/dynamic host configuration protocol.

IT Governance

One of the most important steps a CIO can take to ensure alignment of IT with the business strategy of the organization is to create robust governance committees. It's also the best way for a CIO to satisfy customers, respond to the tyranny of the urgent, and keep the CIO employed!

In the interest of transparency, I'd like to describe my governance successes and failures, plus my plans for IT governance.

At Beth Israel Deaconess, I have committees for each of my major groups of IT customers:

- Laboratory Information Systems co-chaired by the SVP for Operations and the Chief of Pathology (an MD)

- Radiology Information Systems co-chaired by the SVP for Operations and the Chief of Radiology (an MD)

- Critical Care Information Systems chaired by the Director of Trauma, Anesthesia and Critical Care (an MD)

- Inpatient Information Systems (includes provider order entry) chaired by the Senior Director of Clinical Resource Management (an MD)

- Ambulatory Information Systems chaired by the SVP of Ambulatory & Emergency Services (an RN)

- Health Information Management Information Systems chaired by the Director of the Hospital Medicine Program (an MD)

- Community Information Systems chaired by the Executive Director of the Physicians' Organization and the SVP for Network Development (an MD)

- Decision Support Steering Committee chaired by the Director of Business Planning & Decision Support and the SVP for Healthcare Quality (an MD)

- Enterprise Resource Planning (ERP) Information Systems chaired by the Director of Business Services and the Controller

- Revenue Cycle Information Systems chaired by the CFO

This structure worked very well for ten years, ensuring that each application had a lifecycle prioritized by the clinicians and not the IT department. However, a few years ago we needed to make a change. As BIDMC grew into a $1.2 billion organization, an emphasis was placed on achieving an operating margin which would yield the capital budgets needed for expansion. This meant that IT budgets did not grow at the same pace as the clinical budgets and led to competition for IT resources among my governance committees. Existing governance committees set the right priorities within each business area, but we did not have a governance construct to set priorities among all the business areas. Thus, we created an overall IT Steering Committee comprised of the chairs of each of the existing governance committees.

At HMS, I also have committees for each of my major groups of IT customers:

- Administrative Information Technology chaired by the Executive Dean for Administration

- Educational Applications Committee chaired by the Executive Director of Curriculum Programs

- Research Information Technology chaired by the Director of the Research Information Technology Group

Like BIDMC, these three committees functioned very well for five years to ensure priorities were set within the domains of the three core businesses of HMS: research, teaching, and administration. When a new dean of HMS took office and launched a strategic planning process, governance models needed to evolve. Harvard University performed a governance audit of IT departments and the following are the unedited conclusions about Harvard Medical School:

"A school-wide committee overseeing coordination of IT resources among HMS' three primary business groups does not exist. HMS has functioned as three core businesses: research, education and administration. HMS IT has established governance processes for each of these three businesses which have led to a high degree of customer satisfaction.

"As the new HMS strategic planning process creates new projects and stakeholders, the individual governance committees will evolve to align with the new strategic needs, including the creation of a school-wide IT Steering Committee if appropriate. There is a risk that IT resources could be allocated inequitably among the three core businesses and decisions made without the involvement of key business stakeholders.

"The HMS CIO will participate in HMS strategic planning, identifying and documenting governance requirements and school-wide committee needs to ensure appropriate allocation and prioritization of IT resources."

Thus, we established an overall IT Steering Committee at HMS. Bigger committees are not always better committees and creating a committee to objectively balance the heterogeneous needs of research, education, and administration will be challenging. However, I'm very willing to do it if the demand for resources by any one group of customers significantly conflicts with the requirements of other customers.

A few lessons learned from the governance experience above:

In a hospital, it is key that clinicians (MDs and RNs) run the IT governance committees. You'll note that I do not chair any committee other than serving as co-chair of the overall steering committee. My role in that committee is as facilitator only and I do not vote on priority setting.

It's very important to have governance committees that are focused enough to really grasp the details of stakeholders' needs. It may appear that I have too many governance committees, but this is the parsimonious number required to ensure that priorities are set at the application level.

Governance must evolve with the needs of the business. I am a servant of the organizations which employ me and I do not have an agenda of my own. Hence, I will gladly change governance as needed to be maximally responsive to changes in the business environment around me. ∎

It's All About the Workflow

On occasion, the business owners I serve suggest that new software will solve all their workflow problems. Time and time again, we learn that it's not the software that really matters, but good processes. Automating a broken workflow does not achieve a positive result. Re-engineering workflow, then automating it, results in a successful project for everyone.

> *Re-engineering workflow, then automating it, results in a successful project for everyone.*

Here's a tale of my holiday season experience with workflow from an IT perspective.

My wife asked me to return a few holiday items to Target. They had an efficient queuing system set up to enable four clerks to serve a well-ordered line. The process is simple: hand the receipt to the clerk, then hand the items to the clerk. Each receipt is archived for 90 days and has a unique bar code at the top. The clerks do not need to read the receipt; they simply scan the bar code and all the items are retrieved into a local cache. The clerk then scans each returned item and it is checked against the local cache for price, verification of purchase, and the fact that it has not been returned previously. This prevents fraudulent return of items not purchased from Target. Most importantly, Target has decided that this verification workflow is all that is needed to return an item. No manager/supervisor approval is needed, no key is used to open a register, and no credit card is needed. All returns are automatically credited against whatever method of payment was used for the original purchase. By empowering the clerks to process returns this way, the customers are very satisfied, no manual keying of data is needed so accuracy is high, and I'm motivated to buy again from Target, knowing that I can easily return anything I purchase.

My wife also asked me to return ten extra towels/linens to Bed Bath & Beyond. As I entered the store it was clear that the workflow was broken. I found no orderly queue and unclear responsibilities as to who provides specific customer services. I found a very helpful, enthusiastic employee who began to manually match the 16 digit bar codes on my receipt with the bar codes on each towel to verify that I had the correct receipt. Once she manually circled each bar code and initialed them, she then scanned them into the register. She was not empowered to actually process any return transaction, so after 20 minutes of manual paperwork she then paged a manager. The manager was busy so he suggested the supervisor, who was busy ringing up new sales. After trying to interrupt the supervision unsuccessfully, it was clear that another page to the manager was necessary. This time, the manager responded, reviewed the bar codes on each of the towels again, checking the receipt again, then inserting a key in the register to enable a return. I then was asked to produce the original credit card used so that it could be credited. Luckily I had a copy of my wife's Visa card with me. Finally, after 30 minutes, three people and manual paperwork, my ten towels were credited and the $50 dollars was placed back on my credit card. I'm reluctant to purchase from Bed Bath & Beyond again, since I know any return will take more of my time than I have available. Considering the time and gas involved, it would have actually been more cost effective to donate the towels to a worthy cause. The very nice folks at Bed Bath & Beyond said that IT was working on a software solution. Let's hope they re-engineer the workflow first to empower clerks to process returns!

So next time you're told that software will solve the customer's business process problems, be sure to study the workflow first! ■

Leading Change

When I became CIO of CareGroup, I learned an important lesson about leading change.

Just hours after getting the job I decided that we'd embrace a service-oriented architecture (SOA), standardize all desktop/server/storage infrastructure, and implement centrally managed applications. At 8 am the next morning, I was scheduled to meet with my 300 staff members and share with them my vision for the future.

Luckily, experienced leaders counseled me on that first day. I discussed my vision with three board members: Warren McFarlan (Professor at Harvard Business School), John Keane Sr. (CEO of Keane Inc.), and Sam Fleming (CEO of DRI/McGraw Hill). They told me that announcing a strategic plan without engaging all the stakeholders in the process would lead to mixed support and adoption.

Instead of arriving at the 8 am meeting with all the answers, I arrived with questions. I explained to the staff that we wanted to improve customer service, encourage innovation, and ensure our work was aligned with the needs of our stakeholders. I challenged them to tell me what they thought we should do. In the first 30 days of my CIO tenure, I met with every staff member in IS as well as every senior manager in CareGroup to gather their priority lists, synthesize their input, and ensure they had a voice in the future. The result was a new IS operating plan focused on getting the basics done right. We clearly communicated the work to be done, the organizational structure which supported that work, and the right people to staff the structure. The next step was to implement the changes.

I've long been a fan of John Kotter[4] and his work on leading change in organizations. His broad recommendations to effect change include:

    a. Defrost the status quo.

    b. Take actions that bring about change.

    c. Anchor the changes in the corporate culture.

The planning meetings described above defrosted the status quo. The actions I took to bring about change included:

- Create a vision for change—The community came together with a vision of a web-centric organization and I broadly communicated it.

- Establish a sense of urgency—Everyone recognized that IT innovation was essential to coordinate clinical care, improve safety, and enhance our competitiveness, especially after the merger of Beth Israel and Deaconess.

- Elicit executive and peer sponsorship—The CEO declared that medication safety, personal health records, and enhanced communication to all levels of the organization were the strategic goals of the entire organization for that year.

- Communicate vision to implement change—We established steering committees, project charters, project plans, and communication plans.

- Empower employees to implement change—We aligned responsibility, accountability, and authority throughout the IT organization so that managers had the resources and authority they needed to support our improvement efforts. We created a Special Projects team to coordinate the improvement projects without disrupting day-to-day operations.

- Establish short-term goals—We created the first web application in healthcare to share data (with patient consent) among multiple organizations. We created the first web-based provider order entry system, and we created the first personal health record to share all hospital data with patients.

---

4   Dr. John P. Kotter, head of research at Kotter International, developed the "8-Step Process for Leading Change." An authority on leadership and change, Kotter is a frequent contributor to *The Harvard Business Review,* a *New York Times* best-selling author, a Harvard professor, an award-winning business and management thought leader, and a business entrepreneur.

- Encourage additional changes—We created a non-punitive culture in which everyone was encouraged to identify mistakes and opportunities for process improvement.

- Reinforce changes made as permanent—We built standard processes to deliver service, prioritize new projects, and communicate our multi-year plans to the community.

That first year, we implemented strong project management methodologies, eliminated unnecessary work, and focused on getting basic services like email, networks, storage, and electronic result reporting rolled out to everyone in the community. Managing this work required resources, vision, and communication. All the pieces were in place to effect change.

Occasionally, I try to execute a change management project more quickly than usual, bypassing these steps. Whenever I do that I find that adoption of the new technology is delayed, budgets are at risk of overrun, and frustration escalates.

My decade of experience executing change suggests that Kotter was right. Building a guiding coalition, broadly communicating the vision, and celebrating a series of short-term successes really works. I've watched projects without vision, resources, or communication cause pain and anxiety throughout the organization. The good news is that we now know how to execute change and it is the role of senior management to enforce Kotter's principles in every change project. ∎

> *Building a guiding coalition, broadly communicating the vision, and celebrating a series of short-term successes really works.*

Managing Personnel Transitions

As a follow-up to my Leading Change post, one of the most challenging kinds of change to manage is personnel transitions. There are two major kinds of transitions: those which are done to you and those which are done by you.

Regarding changes done to you, the most important role of the CIO is to foster stability while embracing the change that follows a major transition in leadership. Over the course of my tenure as CIO there have been many changes to senior management around me which directly impacted IT. I've experienced the transitions of three COOs, three CFOs, and three CEOs. Each time there is a change in senior leadership, the anxiety in the entire organization is palpable. Everyone wants to know what the change will mean to them. Will their project be canceled or their job eliminated? There is generally a frenzy of activity as many folks in the organization jockey for power or try to resurrect projects that were put on hold by the former administration. The largest transition done to me was ten years ago when I became the new CIO of CareGroup/Beth Israel Deaconess. Although I was an inexperienced leader at that time, I think my basic beliefs about fostering stability were already in place. One of my staff recently sent me a copy of the broadcast email I sent a few hours after taking the job:

From: John D. Halamka MD
12/10/97 01:01 PM
To: IS Employees
Subject: All is well
Folks:

You may have heard that a change is taking place in Information Systems leadership.

I realize that many of you may be feeling anxiety and are wondering what the future holds.

Over the next several weeks, I will get to know each of you, understand your projects and identify your challenges. My role will be to create an environment that empowers each of you. I will begin each conversation with "How can I help you?"

Working together, we can make Information Systems an even better place. We have a great deal of talent in the organization and I look forward to serving, learning and growing with each one of you.

John

Regarding changes done by you, I've personally led several transitions in IT, ensuring that the organization is always optimally structured to support the strategy of the company. Every time I do any reorganization, I've found that communication is key. Communicating often and transparently, engaging all those affected in the reorganization process, really helps. Some organizations do reorganizations behind closed doors and even hire security staff to escort separated employees to their cars. I've never done reorganizations that way. I have treated people with dignity and respect, working hard to ensure their transitions are as painless as possible. There are three ways to transition people:

1. Work together on a separation over several weeks, giving the affected staff the opportunity to move on to a new position outside the organization. This is by far the best approach, since it often leads to new opportunities for the separated employee and can be a win/win for everyone involved.

2. Work with Human Resources (HR) and the affected staff via oral/ written warnings, counseling, and progressive discipline. Whenever I work through a termination via this approach, I follow all HR recommendations to the letter.

3. Termination for cause done precipitously. I am lucky that I have never had to do such a transition. It's very challenging to transition an IT professional abruptly because of the lack of time for knowledge transfer.

Ensuring that no one on the IT team impedes the work of others improves morale, accelerates projects, and minimizes human single points of failure in the organization.

Although managing personnel transitions is not one of the more pleasurable aspects of being a CIO, it is one of the most essential. Ensuring that no one on the IT team impedes the work of others improves morale, accelerates projects, and minimizes human single points of failure in the organization. ■

Time, Scope, and Resources

Over the past few years, the number of new infrastructure project requests has peaked to unprecedented levels. Triage and governance mechanisms work well for applications, but not for infrastructure. Adding a new network port, a new telephone, or a new desktop is viewed as service business that can be ordered on demand, making it very challenging to say "no."

The sudden surge in requests re-emphasized to me the basic law of all IT projects—timeline, scope, and resources are inter-related. If scope increases, timeline or resources must increase. If timeline is shortened, scope must be decreased or resources increased. Increasing scope, shortening timeline while leaving resources constant are not possible.

Of course, we can all work harder. There are 168 hours in a week, vacations can be postponed, and nights/weekends filled. This works in the short term, but is not sustainable.

New FTEs are not typically the short-term answer. Getting new positions raises expectations of delivery capacity but hiring and training new staff take resources from existing capacity, so paradoxically, getting new positions actually reduces capacity for a few months.

This means there is only one short-term answer for unplanned, unbudgeted, unscheduled infrastructure requests—the scope of these requests needs to be reduced/phased, or the time to do them increased.

For my requests this week, I've done the following:

1. Assigned my staff to develop a standard worksheet which outlines the major time-limiting steps (e.g., network connections take 90 days to provision) and thus specifies the minimum lead time for building IS support for a new location.

2. Negotiated a change in scope with phasing—The initial request for a high-bandwidth connection and new telephone system was morphed into a low-bandwidth connection and use of the existing telephone system for now.

3. Reordered priorities—Previous requests were placed on hold in order to service the new 'once in a lifetime' opportunities.

4. Asked for new staff—With the caveat that they will not add to capacity/throughput for six months.

5. Requested governance changes—To ensure a central committee triages and communicates infrastructure requests for new offsite locations.

There is one other strategy that I could employ if this surge in requests becomes chronic. In the past, I've staffed to average workload, not peak workload. This means that staff can put in extra hours for short-term urgent increases in demand. However, I may have to staff to peak so that excess capacity is always available for the continuous infrastructure "tyranny of the urgent." I'm a frugal guy, doing a great deal on a limited budget, so I've never built in excess capacity. ∎

How to Say "No"

I was recently asked to give a lecture about how I say "no" to new project requests. Of course, I have governance committees which help prioritize all IT projects based on:

- Return on investment

- Quality/compliance

- Impact factor—number of doctors, nurses, staff, and patients who will benefit

- Alignment with the strategic needs of the business

Beyond my governance processes, which I will describe further in another post, my top ten list of how to say "no" is more about people than prioritization.

10. Select your change (and what not to change)—I've learned that my hospital organization does not readily accept off-the-shelf enterprise application software. In the past decade, we've stopped a major clinical and a major revenue cycle project because of the limited customization possibilities with vendor-supplied software. To this day, our self-built customized enterprise applications keep customers happy at low cost. Of course, I still buy many departmental systems (lab, critical care, anesthesia, labor and deliver monitoring, PACS,[5] cardiology), but will no longer try to replace our enterprise clinical applications with vendor products. This is an automatic "no" that customers understand.

9. Identify those who will lose and take them to lunch—On a given day, 10% of the organization is not completely satisfied with the triage decisions made by my governance committees. In a world of limited supply and infinite demand, the organization needs to say "no" to many projects. I find that bad news does not travel well via email, hence personal contact is needed to explain many prioritization decisions. I try to make personal contact with those whose projects are not funded/prioritized. Whenever possible, instead of "never," I say "not now" to lower priority projects.

8. Acknowledge the loss—Many people will accept change if the process is transparent, they are involved in the decision, and their losses are acknowledged. Telling folks that you understand the impact of negative decisions and expressing a willingness to work together in the future goes a long way.

7. Over-communicate—Rumors are often worse than the truth. Every Friday I send out a broadcast email to the entire organization explaining issues, good news, bad news, and future plans.

6. Be honest and consistent—I work hard to tell all stakeholders the same message. If everyone hears the good and bad news consistently, the credibility of IT is enhanced.

5. Consensus is not essential—A vote of 500 to 1 is not a tie. If governance works objectively, even politically powerful stakeholders cannot veto prioritization decisions which are in the best interest of the organization.

4. Embrace conflict—Sometimes the right decisions are the hard or politically challenging ones. By expecting conflict every day, the CIO can make decisions more dispassionately. My training as an emergency physician prepared me to approach every situation with balanced emotions. Eliminating caffeine five years ago helped too.

---

5   PACS = Picture archiving and communication systems.

3. Focus on your detractors—Sometimes organizations can be 1,000 points of veto. By focusing on those who oppose projects instead of those who support them, I can use my time most effectively. I'd rather meet with my friends, but my day is optimized when I spend the day with my detractors. Sometimes detractors become friends, but at least all detractors understand the rationale for "no" decisions.

2. The last two minutes of the meeting are the most important—It's very common for politically challenging meetings to end with differing opinions as to what was discussed. Using the last two minutes of the meeting to review all the decisions made and next steps, then memorializing that conversation in written minutes, enhance the communication of "no."

1. You cannot please everyone—I accept that the good of the many outweighs the needs of the few, even if I have to be the "no" guy. ∎

It's Not a Job, It's a Lifestyle

I'm often asked, "What is your job?"

Some may think that being a CIO is all about bits and bytes, buying the latest technology, and keeping up with all the three-letter acronyms of the industry (I use WPA over EAP instead of WEP on my wireless network; what do you use?).

The technology portion of my job is about 15% of my time. The bulk of what I do is organizational, political, and customer relationship management. With hundreds of projects, thousands of customers, and millions of dollars, how do I keep it all straight?

My approach is four-fold:

1. **Strategy**—The information technology department in every organization should not make the business strategy; that is up to the board, CEO, and stakeholders. The IT organization should provide the tactics necessary to execute the organization's strategic plan. For example, if the strategy is to improve quality, the information technology organization can implement e-prescribing, provider order entry, bar-coded wrist bands, and incident-tracking systems. Every year, I approach the strategic planning process by meeting with the CEO, CFO, COO, CMO, Chief Nursing Officer (CNO), and Chief Academic Officer (CAO) to understand their strategic imperatives for the year. The next month, I meet with their direct reports to understand the operational implications and challenges of these strategic imperatives. I then produce an "IS Operating Plan" (note that it is not a strategic plan), which is placed on the web for all stakeholders to

review, and present to my IS steering committees. I have a steering committee for inpatient applications, outpatient applications, critical care applications, operating room/anesthesia, laboratory systems, radiology systems, and health information management (medical records). The chairs of each of these committees plus clinician representatives from the medical executive committee serve on the enterprise-wide information systems steering committee, which ensures coordination of resources among all the projects. Once these committees approve the priorities for the year, we ensure the operating and capital budgets are aligned to do the work.

2. **Structure**—Once the operating plan is in place, I ensure the structure of the organization is arranged to support the projects to be done. Over the past ten years I've done several mini-reorganizations to respond to changing technologies, customer needs, and governance issues. Note that the ideal structure is defined before taking into account the existing staff personalities and skillsets. To build an organization that delivers reliable service over time, I try to avoid single points of human failure, distributing work across many individuals rather than relying on a "lone genius," since reliance on one person is ultimately unsupportable.

    > *To build an organization that delivers reliable service over time, I try to avoid single points of human failure, distributing work across many individuals rather than relying on a "lone genius," since reliance on one person is ultimately unsupportable.*

3. **Staffing**—Once the structure is in place, I ensure we have the best staff possible to populate that structure. I'm a strong believer in training and we try our best, given limited budgets, to hire talented people and continue their education so they remain world-class experts. I'm also a great supporter of co-op programs for college students, bringing in new graduates, training them and hiring them to ensure a constant supply of new talent entering the organization.

4. **Processes**—Finally, once the staffing is in place, I work on the highly repeatable processes that support our workflow. The organization functions most smoothly when policies and procedures are well known by all internal and external to the organization so that I can monitor the performance of known processes, rapidly identifying areas where we can improve service delivery. Metrics I review include infrastructure uptime, electrical consumption, help desk call abandonment rates/

time to problem resolution, budget performance by manager, and performance against project timeline milestones.

At the beginning of each day, I ask myself if the strategy, structure, staffing, and processes are as good as they can be. At the end of each day, I mentally review the issues of the day affecting each of my direct reports and offer mid-course corrections, which are most often organizational and political. I also try to communicate broadly via town meetings, email broadcasts, weekly leadership meetings, and monthly one-on-one meetings with each of my direct reports.

Finally, I try to reserve 50% of my time each day for the important issues of that day. Explaining to a customer or IS employee that I cannot respond to a critical issue for weeks because my calendar is booked far in advance does not work. If I can do today's work today, my calendar has the same number of meetings, but I become a real-time responder to issues before they escalate. Having a Blackberry strapped to my belt 21 hours a day also helps me use my time efficiently and ensures I am not the rate-limiting step in any decision making process.

Of course, I have a family life, personal time, and outside interests, but being a CIO is a lifestyle, not a job. I'm connected to the strategy, structure, staffing, and processes of the organization 24x7x365. ■

The Tyranny of the Urgent

I previously mentioned that I reserve 50% of my schedule for the work of each day and 50% for more longitudinal work. Explaining this balance justifies another post.

Providing cutting edge clinical applications to a hospital is a journey. It requires daily efforts to refine workflow and encourage adoption, but it also requires a multiyear plan to ensure future needs will be met. Three years ago, it was clear that e-prescribing would be very important. However, in 2004, faxing to retail pharmacies was all we had. Today, with the Surescripts connection to retail pharmacies and the RxHub connection to mail order pharmacies, we have fully electronic transmission for 90% of our prescriptions. The only way we were able to support all aspects of e-prescribing including formulary enforcement, eligibility checking, community drug history with drug/drug interactions, and prescription routing was to focus a portion of each day on our long-term goals without being derailed by each day's distractions.

I call the distractions of each day, "the tyranny of the urgent." Everyone believes that long-term goals like medication safety are essential, but each day some stakeholder has a new, mission-critical project that is expected to trump existing priorities. Of course, there are legitimate urgent projects that must be done for quality, safety, compliance, or return on investment, but if we allowed every project proposed each day to defer our multi-year plan, we'd never accomplish our long-term goals.

Thus, I spend 50% of my day on email, phone calls, and the tyranny of the urgent, but reserve 50% of each day for those projects which will create revolutionary change three years from now. To do so requires two kinds of plans.

My operating plan outlines the goals of each year—ensuring that each business owner's strategic priorities are met on a yearly basis. To ensure stakeholders understand the major themes of our yearly operating plan, I produce a thematic summary.

I also have a five-year plan which outlines the "big picture" so that all stakeholders know where we're going year to year. Of course, I watch for major industry trends and refine the five-year plan in response to changes in technology, legislation, and compliance requirements, but in general, the five-year plan is a predictable roadmap of what we'll accomplish over the long term.

Many days, it feels like my job is driven by the contents of my inbox, but in order to create a successful organization, I have to insulate my staff from attempts to change priorities on a daily basis. Instead, my job is to triage the entropy of my inbox into a few short-term urgencies while protecting the operating plan and five-year plan. At times, this triage exercise is challenging and I involve my various governance committees when decisions are politically charged or involve competing stakeholder priorities.

My advice to CIOs is to develop standard escalation processes and use those well-defined processes each day in response to the tyranny of the urgent. Do not let your inbox dictate your strategy or priorities. Keep your eye on the big picture. As Jim Barksdale[6] says, "The main thing is to make the main thing the main thing." ∎

Subject Matter Experts

A challenge in all IT organizations is achieving a balance between central control and local/departmental autonomy. Our approach is to clearly define roles and responsibilities such that IT is responsible for infrastructure, databases, security, interfaces, and data integrity, while partnering with the business owner for subject matter expertise. Here's the detail:

---

6   James L. Barksdale is an American executive who served as president and CEO of Netscape Communications Corporation from January 1995 until the company merged with AOL in March 1999.

There are immediate and long-term elements of an application implementation and the ongoing support of the application that are beyond what the IT department can reasonably be expected to manage, maintain, or support.

These may include, but not necessarily be limited to, customer financial responsibilities associated with managing or maintaining the application; vendor or sales contacts and interactions specific to the product lifecycle, licensing, or application functionality; and user management issues specific to the use, functionality, workflow, or impact of the application.

Some of these responsibilities may be assumed by the customer's or department's management staff ("application owner"), while others may be assumed by a staff member who possesses the depth of knowledge or expertise associated with or required to run the customer's or department's daily operation.

This person is usually referred to as the "subject matter expert" or "SME." The SME is very important to not only assisting in the application's development and implementation, but in also maintaining the long-term use and effectiveness of the application within the department.

The responsibilities outlined below are those that require ownership by the application owner and by the SME. They are specific to financial management, vendor relationship management, or non-technical maintenance and support requirements that can be most effectively handled by the owner or SME. To clarify the use of the term "non-technical": there is no requirement or expectation that the owner or SME will possess either knowledge or understanding about the workstation or server operating system, hardware, or configuration; or the programming, support, or configuration of the software application.

A. Solution/Application Financial Management

- Budget for and procure funds associated with the ongoing management and maintenance of the solution/application throughout its lifecycle, which may include but may not be limited to hardware, software, licensing, maintenance, and support contacts, and other equipment and/or services/agreements that may be required.

- Budget for and procure funds that may be required to secure the services of a third-party vendor(s) for any solution component (hardware or software) that is not supported by the IS department. The sponsor/owner is responsible for all expenses and liability associated with any agreement(s) or service(s) contracted between them and the vendor.

B. Vendor Relationship Management

- Manage vendor relationship and maintain current vendor-related information (i.e., account manager and contact information).

- Maintain product line awareness through routine communications with the vendor or your sales account manager.

- Manage application licensing requirements (identify/forecast needs) and communicate expenses or requirements to your department's financial resource.

C. SME and Use Management

- Possess an understanding of the department's business or clinical workflow requirements.

- Serve as the contact person to whom any HIPAA or compliance issues may be directed, specifically related to the data being entered into the application.

- Serve as the department's liaison to the IS help desk to facilitate IS involvement in basic troubleshooting, problem identification, and escalation paths to technical experts or the vendor.

- Maintain availability as the primary contact to whom the IS department can communicate outages or technology issues that may impact the area's productivity or ability to provide critical services.

- Identify, establish, and maintain downtime procedures to deal with IT outages that may negatively impact the application's availability and potentially the department's productivity or ability to meet its mission or objectives.

- Facilitate departmental user training to ensure efficiency and optimal productivity by providing on-the-job training or working with the vendor to arrange for third-party training.

- Participate with IT staff and vendor representatives in discussions that involve the implementation of application (version) changes that may have an impact on the department's workflow, productivity, or the application's (end-user's) functionality.

- Maintain (working) knowledge of the application user interface (i.e., the ways in which the product is designed to interact with the user in terms of text menus, checkboxes, text or graphical information and keystrokes, and mouse movements required to control the application; as well as report creation/generation and other information about the use of the application that is essential to the day-to-day operation and productivity of the department).

- Perform any routine vendor-recommended or -required user-related performance or integrity checks.

- Create user-specific policies and/or procedures that may be required to address appropriate departmental use and functionality.

- Describe how critical the application is in meeting the mission and objectives of the department in providing services or in maintaining productivity.

- Maintain awareness of vendor-version updates that may impact the department's workflow, productivity, or application's (end-user's) functionality.

- Serve as the primary contact for vendor and the recipient of media related to application upgrades, updates, patches, or other application-related materials or information.

- Work with IS to coordinate/facilitate required software upgrades/updates that may impact departmental/user productivity.

- Provide application-level account management responsibilities that may include defining user access rights or authorizing user accounts.

- Provide on-site first response for end-user issues related to end-user application performance or functionality issues.

The responsibilities listed above are discussed in detail by IT throughout the application's implementation and will be reviewed with the SME when the support level agreement (SLA) is finalized. If, at any time during these discussions, there are items that are unclear, ambiguous, or that cannot be adequately managed or maintained by the SME or a resource within the application owner's department, they should be immediately identified and discussed with the IS manager.

If, during the application implementation or subsequent support discussions, it is determined that the solution/application is identified as being critical to the provision of patient care or to a core or enterprise-wide critical function, the application owner or SME will be asked to identify a backup SME. ∎

The "Cousin Jimmy Syndrome"

I have great respect for my colleagues in the IT industry. It's a challenging profession that requires a mixture of technical knowledge, people skills, and the emotional stability to deal with customer dissatisfaction when technology fails.

However, there's a downside to being an IT professional. No matter how much expertise you have or what your reputation may be, many customers will not be able to distinguish between a polished industry expert and a self-promoting IT groupie.

I call this the "Cousin Jimmy Syndrome."

Here's how it happens. You join a meeting to discuss a major IT project. You talk about issues such as security, disaster recovery, change management, training, and support.

Then someone says, "Oh yeah, we've got 'Cousin Jimmy' doing that." Or Bob who lives in his parents' basement. Or Carol who knows how to use Excel and serves as the "go to" technology guru.

Unfortunately, when Jimmy, Bob, or Carol have an opinion, their colleagues trust them over you, since professional IT organizations may appear less nimble, less focused, and less accommodating than dedicated local experts.

Not to imply that IT professionals in large organizations are perfect—they have their flaws. However, good management and oversight usually creates a culture in which there is division of labor, escalation, and few single points of human failure. Cousin Jimmy does not know what he does not know. His solutions may be fast or cheap but ultimately they are unsustainable, unmaintainable, and unsupportable.

How should the IT professional deal with Cousin Jimmy Syndrome?

1. Let Cousin Jimmy fail—It may take a while, but eventually there will be a major outage, security breach, or data loss. Although this may transiently feel like a win, it's really a loss for the customers. It's a win the battle, lose the war tactic.

2. Make Cousin Jimmy part of your team—This sometimes works and it's worth a try. Success has 1,000 fathers, so if you can create a sense of team in which Jimmy gets all the credit but others do all the work, so be it. The customers win. Of course, it's hard to let Jimmy take the credit for what you've done, but I've learned over the years that anything is possible if you are willing to give others the credit for success.

3. Offer a service so good, so inexpensive, and so reliable that eventually Jimmy moves on—This works much of the time. I believe that hard work, innovation, and honesty eventually pay off and win the game. True, sometimes politics triumph over expertise, but you can outlast the naysayers. By selflessly focusing on the customers, the technology, and your staff, you'll end up with a service that's really hard to beat at any price. Jimmy may be omni-present, but he'll have a difficult time keeping up as technology evolves.

So, when the meetings are awkward, keep your composure, stick to your principles, and put the customers first. Nine times out of ten, you'll eventually beat the Cousin Jimmy Syndrome. ∎

Group IQ

Early in my career, I thought the path to success was making a name for myself—creating software, ideas, and innovation that would be uniquely associated with me. My mentors gave me sage advice to ban the "I" word from my vocabulary and to focus on developing high-functioning organizations. A single individual can come and go, but organizations can scale to enormous size and last beyond the strengths, weaknesses, and longevity of any one person.

Many books have been written about building organizations—*Built to Last, In Search of Excellence,* and *The Innovator's Dilemma,*[7] but the idea I find most compelling was described in a recent *Boston Globe* article about Group IQ:[8]

"Group intelligence, the researchers discovered, is not strongly tied to either the average intelligence of the members or the team's smartest member. And this collective intelligence was more than just an arbitrary score: When the group grappled with a complex task, the researchers found it was an excellent predictor of how well the team performed."

When I was doing graduate work, I thought that a successful leader should be the smartest person in the room. I've learned that the best leaders hire people who are smarter than themselves. Good leaders revel in the capabilities of teams to exceed the leader's own capabilities. Poor leaders surround themselves with underperforming teams which support the leader's need to feel superior. This leads to the notion that "Grade 'A' leaders hire grade 'A' teams and grade 'B' leaders hire grade 'C' teams."

Group IQ is a great concept. I'm very proud of the way IS teams approach tricky problems, resource allocation decisions, and out-of-the-blue compliance requirements that are unstaffed, unbudgeted, and "must do."

The best metric that teams are high functioning is watching their response to a crisis. Is there infighting? Is there jockeying for leadership when responding to the event? Does one person dominate the conversation?

I've watched time after time when teams of IS professionals come together, each assuming a mutually supportive role. Depending on the issue, the person with the most experience on the team runs the activity. Everyone contributes their ideas and is respected for whatever they say—right or wrong. If there are emotions, the team rallies to support the good ones and diffuse the bad ones. No one is blamed for human error—it's used to improve processes in the future.

---

7   Collins J, Porras JI. *Built to Last: Successful Habits of Visionary Companies.* New York: Harper Business, 2004; Peters TI, Waterman RH. *In Search of Excellence: Lessons from America's Best-Run Companies.* New York: Harper Business, 2006; Christensen CM. *The Innovator's Dilemma: The Revolutionary Book That Will Change the Way You Do Business.* New York: Harper Business, 2011.

8   Johnson CY. Group IQ: What makes one team of people smarter than another? A new field of research finds surprising answers. *The Boston Globe.* December 19, 2010.

My experience with highly functional groups is that people have to be hired for their emotional quotient (EQ) as well as their intelligence quotient (IQ). The only thing you can do wrong during a team activity is to impede the work of others. Criticism of ideas is encouraged, criticism of people is not.

> My experience with highly functional groups is that people have to be hired for their emotional quotient (EQ) as well as their intelligence quotient (IQ).

The only way we could survive 2010, which was a year that tested both patience and stamina, was relying on Group IQ to shrug off the naysayers, maintain course and direction, and keep an upbeat attitude through it all. ∎

Defining Business Requirements

In my roles at various institutions, I've had the opportunity to work with thousands of highly diverse stakeholders. Some are IT savvy; some are not. Some are project management savvy; some are not. Some understand leading practices for their particular departmental functions; some do not.

Here's what I've learned:

1. Automating a dysfunctional manual process will not yield a successful performance improvement outcome. Before any technology project is launched, the business owners need to understand their own process flows and goals for improving them.

> Before any technology project is launched, the business owners need to understand their own process flows and goals for improving them.

2. If business owners cannot define their future state workflows, software is not going to do it for them. Sometimes business owners tell me, "I need to buy a wonderful niche software package from XYZ vendor." When I ask how they will use it, they answer that the software will define their workflow for them.

3. The IT department can impose governance and project management processes to ensure that future state workflows and requirements are defined prior to any procurement processes. However, the business owners who are least experienced with project management methodology will accuse the IT department of slowing down the purchase. One way around this is to create an institutional project

management office outside of the IT department which serves as a bridge between the business owners and the IT organization providing the service. Such an approach adds expert resources to the department requesting automation to lead them through a requirements definition process as a first step. Projects without clear requirements and goals can be stopped before they expend time and money on an implementation that is likely to fail.

4. Some departments will try to circumvent governance prioritization and project management processes by contributing departmental funds, obtaining a grant, or getting a donor to fund their software purchases. Such an approach should not be allowed for many reasons. Software licensing is generally about 20% of the total implementation cost which includes hardware, configuration, interfacing, testing, training, and support costs. Every software implementation is a project and needs to be considered a use of scarce IT resources. It is reasonable to initiate an automation request through a project management office to define business requirements and goals, then present it to a governance process for prioritization, then fund the total project costs via departmental/grant/donor dollars if the project is deemed a high priority for implementation.

5. Creating formal documentation of business requirements, goals/ success metrics, and forecasted financial impact is important to establish ownership of the project by the sponsoring department. Although infrastructure projects such as provisioning networks, desktops, storage, and servers can be owned by the IT department, application projects should never be owned or sponsored by the IT department. The business owner, working with the institutional project management office, needs to drive the implementation to achieve the desired process improvement and ensure appropriate change management. If the project is considered an IT effort, then business owners will claim their lack of requirements definition or process redesign is an IT failure based on poorly designed or implemented software.

Thus, however unpopular it makes the CIO, insist on business owner sponsorship with defined requirements, goals, and accountability for process and people change management. Every project I've been involved in that includes this role for the business owner has been successful. With clearly defined responsibilities and accountability, customer satisfaction with these projects has been high, because business owners feel compelled to make the project a success rather than expect IT to deliver a finished project to them. ∎

Frameworks for IT Management

In the next few years, the transition from fee for service to accountable care organizations/global payments is going to require significant IT change at a time when budgets will become increasingly constrained. We'll have the combination of Meaningful Use, ICD-10, and healthcare reform all occurring at the same time.

IT organizations will be required to demonstrate their value, benchmark themselves against best practices, and justify their actions.

There are numerous frameworks that can support a standardized approach to project scope definition, resource allocation, and service provision.

Although you may not use these techniques now, you should be familiar with them as the pressure increases to absorb increasing demand in the face of decreasing supply.

Here's a brief overview of three leading frameworks:

Information Technology Infrastructure Library (ITIL)

ITIL grew out of work done by the UK government's Central Computer and Telecommunications Agency in the 1980s to document best practices. Since then ITIL has had three major revisions and the current version consists of 26 processes and functions documented in five volumes:

1. ITIL Service Strategy

2. ITIL Service Design

3. ITIL Service Transition

4. ITIL Service Operation

5. ITIL Continual Service Improvement

The primary focus of ITIL is to provide best practice definitions and criteria for operations management. As with any framework there is significant debate about the pros and cons of ITIL. As long as you keep in mind that ITIL is a set of best practices, to be adopted and adapted as best fits your local needs, it can be useful. ITIL does not aim to be comprehensive and universal—use it where it helps maintain your ongoing services.

Control Objectives for Information and Related Technology (COBIT)

COBIT was first released in 1996 by the Information Systems Audit and Control Association (ISACA) and IT Governance Institute (ITGI). COBIT has been used to evaluate security and controls during various audits of my IT organizations. The current version of COBIT has 34 high-level processes, covering 318 control objectives, categorized in four domains:

1. Planning and Organization

2. Acquisition and Implementation

3. Delivery and Support

4. Monitoring and Evaluation

COBIT focuses on the definition, implementation, auditing, measurement, and improvement of controls for specific processes that span the entire IT implementation life cycle.

Capability Maturity Model (CMM)

CMM was originally developed by Carnegie Mellon University researchers as a tool for objectively assessing the ability of government contractors to perform a contracted software project. Now it is applied more generally to any organization's software development processes. The predictability, effectiveness, and control of an organization's software development processes evolve over time through five stages:

1. Initial (chaotic, ad hoc, individual heroics)—The starting point for use of a new process

2. Managed—The process is managed in accordance with agreed-upon metrics

3. Defined—The process is defined/confirmed as a standard business process

4. Quantitatively managed

5. Optimizing—Process management includes deliberate process optimization/improvement

CMM provides a framework for measuring and transforming software development.

What's the elevator speech about these various techniques? They are complementary frameworks. COBIT systematically chronicles a checklist of all the things that an IT organization ought to be doing to implement appropriate controls and security. ITIL explains how. CMM measures the sophistication of the processes used along the way.

I'm very interested in hearing from the community. Do your IT organizations use any aspect of these frameworks? Have they been helpful to you to document the resource requirements of the IT organization and give users a transparent look into the work you perform? ∎

Lessons Learned from Steve Jobs

Shortly after Steve Jobs' death, I spoke with several reporters about his impact on healthcare. In preparing for those interviews, I reviewed Steve's career milestones.

In 1997, Apple Computer was in trouble. Its sales had declined from $11 billion in 1995 to $7 billion in 1997. Its energies were focused on battling Microsoft. It had lost its way.

Steve Jobs made these remarks at MacWorld 1997, a few months before becoming Apple's CEO. He outlined a simple go-forward plan:

1. Board of Directors

2. Focus on Relevance

3. Invest in Core Assets

4. Meaningful Partnerships

5. New Product Paradigm

How can we apply these five ideas to the work we're doing in HIT?

It's clear that health information exchanges across the country are in trouble—CareSpark closed its doors, the CEO of Cal eConnect resigned, and Minnesota Health Information Exchange ceased operations.

Let's consider the application of Steve's principles to health information exchange in Massachusetts.

1. Board of Directors—Governance in general is very important to health information exchange. HIEs need a multi-stakeholder governance body to set priorities, monitor progress, and ensure all stakeholders are engaged. State government and the private sector experts worked together to define roles and responsibilities. The state's HIE coordinator, Rick Shoup, and I presented this consensus plan to the state's HIT Council, the decision-making body established by state regulation Chapter 305. Governance will be done by the HIT Council plus an HIT HIE Advisory Group consisting of payers, providers, employers, patients, academics, and government. This "Board of Directors" of the Massachusetts HIE activities is top notch.

2. Focus on Relevance—HIEs can do many things. They can push data among payers, providers, patients, and public health. They can create master patient indexes, record locator services, and registries. However, what will the market pay for today? At the moment, simple secure transport that connects every stakeholder with easy-to-use web applications and native EHR interfaces seems to be the answer. Rather than do everything simultaneously, we need to tightly

At the moment, simple secure transport that connects every stakeholder with easy-to-use web applications and native EHR interfaces seems to be the answer.

focus on just secure routing, making the next few years the era of the state "information highway."

3. Invest in Core Assets—Massachusetts already has production HIEs that serve the business needs of several customers. We have NEHEN, CHAPS, SafeHealth, North Adams HIE, and the MAeHC Quality Data Center. Rather than reinvent these, we need to focus on the gaps, creating a state backbone that will connect every stakeholder, establishing a network of networks that leverages existing investments.

4. Meaningful Partnerships—The State Medicaid Health Plan includes 14 projects that cover over 90% of the providers in Massachusetts. Since Medicaid is eligible for 90/10 matching funds (90% federal/10% state), it makes great sense to do as much as we can via Medicaid. Multiplying our purchasing power by ten is a meaningful partnership!

5. New Products—Once connectivity from every stakeholder to every stakeholder is in place, we can create novel functionality such as clinical registries and the ability to query data to support the "unconscious in the emergency department" use case. ∎

It Takes a Village

In 2008, four people stopped by my BIDMC office to chat about the future. They were Farzad Mostashari, Todd Park, Aneesh Chopra, and Peter Basch. They had a vision to change the world through technology, EHR adoption, and data liquidity.

Little did I know that, at the meeting, I was chatting with the future National Coordinator for HIT, the future CTO of HHS, the future CTO of the US, and an influential policy thinker at the Center for American Progress.

Since that meeting, I've stayed in touch with them to exchange ideas, seek their advice, and share lessons learned.

In 2009, I became co-chair of the HIT Standards Committee. Little did I know that the HIT Standards Committee would become the most functional, most productive, and hardest working federal advisory committee in the Obama administration. Its experts have helped me enhance IT capabilities in all my technology roles.

In 2010, I worked with Brian Biles and Steven Morrison of the Center for Strategic and International Studies on Japanese healthcare IT policy. Little did I know that the work would become a foundation for earthquake/tsunami recovery IT planning. Brian and Steve inspired several trips to Japan and meetings with numerous government, academic, and industry leaders.

In 2011, I began working with Rick Shoup, Manu Tandon, and Micky Tripathi on health information exchange planning for Massachusetts. Little did I know that together they would create a unified health information exchange strategy for the Commonwealth that integrates public sector and private sector priorities with multiple funding streams into a single, extraordinary work plan. It has become one of my favorite projects.

When I was asked to co-lead a design session for public key infrastructure (PKI) in Massachusetts, I called my friend Dixie Baker at SAIC, my friend Arien Malec at RelayHealth, and my colleagues in government to share their experiences, creating a trust fabric for large groups. Massachusetts will succeed by seeking the wisdom of others.

When I was young, I thought I had to be smart enough to solve every problem myself. In today's world, I'm convinced the best way to make a difference is surrounding yourself with people who are smarter than you. The best solutions take a village.

I've said that my tombstone will hopefully read, "He made a difference." After the past few years of working with smart people, I'm convinced it would be better as, "He was part of a village that changed the world." ∎

The New Metrics for CIO Success

When I began my career as a CIO in 1997, success was function of the basics—email delivery, network connectivity, and application functionality. I personally wrote code, experimented with new operating systems, and created analytics using web servers, structured query language (SQL), and active server pages (ASPs).

Now, CIO success is much more complex to measure.

Infrastructure success can be defined as 99.99% uptime of all systems and no loss/corruption/breach of data. The magical belief in the cloud sets expectations that IT infrastructure should be like heat, power, and light—just there as a utility whenever it is needed in whatever amount is needed.

Application success could be defined as on-time, on-budget delivery of go lives according to project plans. Two important forces make this more complex:

- Consumer software stores set expectations that enterprise software should be easy—we need to fix revenue cycle workflow; isn't there an app for that?

- As the economy forces downsizing and efficiency gains, there's an expectation that workflow automation is a prerequisite to organizational change so there is more pressure on the IT department to deliver application solutions quickly.

This all sounds impossible—deliver massive infrastructure with constant change but keep it entirely reliable and secure. Deliver applications that support business processes in increasingly short timeframes with limited IT and business owner resources.

Thus, the modern CIO is no longer a technologist or evangelist for innovation. The modern CIO is a customer relationship manager, a strategic communicator, and a project manager, delicately balancing project portfolios, available resources, and governance.

Modern CIOs have little time to get infrastructure and applications right, so they must "skate where the puck will be," thinking more like CEOs about business needs and future strategies, so that critical information technology is deployed by the time it is needed.

What am I doing to become a more effective modern CIO?

1. I've defined key business customers (BIDMC senior management and chiefs). I'm meeting with each one to ensure their priorities for the next year and beyond are reflected in the IT operating plan and the five-year IT strategic plan. Planning much more than five years in IT is problematic given the pace of technology change. Working with the governance committees, I will trim this list into those projects that have the greatest impact on business strategy, quality/safety, and efficiency.

2. I'm standardizing communication so that key customers receive monthly updates about their priority projects.

3. I'm defining a process for managing IT projects across the enterprise that includes standardizing the IT Project Intake Process, the IT Project Life-cycle, and Project Management tools (project documentation, project plans, and status reports).

It's my hope that by focusing on customer relationship management, communication, and project management that I will create a positive working environment for the IT staff with a more limited set of well-defined projects and more engaged customers. Doing fewer projects with greater speed and depth which meet the most critical needs of the business is much harder than agreeing to do many niche projects and moving forward slowly on all. Given that the supply of IT resources is likely to be fixed since healthcare budgets are under increasing pressure from healthcare reform, the modern CIO should be judged on demand management and achieving reasonable levels of customer satisfaction despite having to focus on a narrower project portfolio delivered at a faster pace. ∎

The Job of a CIO: Content Versus Context

I recently spoke with a former CIO whom I respect a great deal. We talked about the nature of our jobs, the state of the industry, and the change ahead that is needed to support healthcare reform.

She offered a profound observation: the content of our jobs is great; the context is really challenging.

What does that mean?

Who could ask for better content—cool applications that support life-saving medical care and cutting edge research. Innovative health information exchange, patient engagement, and workflow applications. Multi-million dollar infrastructure, great staff, and interesting problems to solve. During my years as an undergraduate, graduate, medical student, and post doc, I dreamt about such content.

However, the context of being a CIO is a struggle. Don't worry, I'm not depressed or pessimistic—just sharing the observations I'm hearing from other healthcare CIOs.

- You'll create miracles every day (99.99% reliability and great security with a low budget), but you'll not receive credit for everything that works. Instead, you'll be held accountable for the .01% that doesn't.

- No matter what your budget, demand will always exceed supply. Success will be finishing half the projects you've been asked to do. You're unlikely to keep a significant percentage of your customers happy.

- You'll be asked to share more data with more trading partners for more purposes, but be held accountable for all privacy breaches, even though you cannot control many of the data flows. Users will demand controls over their devices, bring devices from home, and expect broad freedoms, but you'll be responsible for any security problems they create.

- The pace of consumer IT change—new products and new services arriving every few months—will create expectations for IT service delivery that far exceed the abilities of a thinly staffed IT organization.

- Regulatory burdens will increase exponentially. Compliance is a must do but customers will not appreciate that work. Twenty percent of your budget will be spent on compliance, 20% on security, and 60% on operations. That leaves nothing for innovation (unless its required for compliance or security). Meaningful Use, 5010, ICD-10, new privacy rules, and healthcare reform will occur simultaneously.

- Every year the amount of infrastructure and applications you support will increase dramatically. However, budgets will increase 2%–3% or stay flat. You'll be asked to do more with less. Before long, you'll be asked to do everything for nothing in no time.

- Healthcare organizations in the US are structurally flawed. Hospitals are essentially hotels with operating rooms and patient rooms that are rented by the doctors. Hospitals (other than Kaiser) do not employ the doctors, so it's a bit like Toyota owning the factory but allowing the workers to build whatever they want. How about a car with seven doors and two trunks? No problem—do what you want inside the factory. IT will be caught in the middle because hospitals and doctors will want technology solutions that may not be aligned.

- You'll need to constantly change systems while keeping them stable and secure. It will be like changing the wings on a 747 aircraft while it's flying.

- Many IT services will not be charged back and the demand for a free service will be infinite. Users will consume whatever computing, storage, and network bandwidth they wish, but you'll be held accountable for provisioning enough to support demand you cannot control.

- Unplanned work will consume 20% of your agenda. Compliance/regulatory change, auditors, and reaccreditation will require urgent redeployment of staff, but you will be held accountable for all the projects that were delayed. You should plan for unplanned work.

Demand management, even with good governance, will be an increasing challenge for CIOs in the future. Here's a bold thought: might the context of being a CIO be nearly impossible in the next few years, requiring us to rethink the way that IT services are planned and delivered in the future?

As I hear more from my fellow CIOs about compliance burdens, overwhelming demands, and impossible expectations, I will continue to speculate about IT organizational models for the future that enable CIOs to improve the context of our work. ∎

The Joy of Success

Life is hard for CIOs with accelerating compliance demands, new security threats, rapidly evolving technologies, and unprecedented demand for new projects driven by the consumerization of IT.

At the same time that CIOs and IT professionals are running marathons, they are being held accountable for events that are not directly under their control. They are not being congratulated for the miracles they create every day, but are being criticized for not moving faster.

What do I mean?

One CIO received a negative audit report because new generations of viruses are no longer stopped by state-of-the-art anti-virus software. Interesting. The

CIO cannot control the virus authors, nor the effectiveness of anti-virus software. No one in the industry has solved the problem, but audit firms revel in creating fear, uncertainty, and doubt at the board level as it enhances the reputation of the auditor.

Another CIO was held accountable for infrastructure demands that were not forecasted, planned, or communicated. CIOs do their best to be proactive, but in the world of big data, past trends may not predict future needs.

Another CIO was given ten goals and five unplanned urgent projects. She completed eight of the planned goals and all the urgent projects, yet was told she only met 80% of expectations.

In a world that expects leaders to continuously perform miracles with constrained resources in limited time, we all need to step back and take our own steps to stop the madness.

With your own staff, celebrate the joy of success and focus on what really matters.

Did you achieve Meaningful Use?

Did you support compliance requirements on time to meet regulatory deadlines?

Did you maintain employee satisfaction and minimize turnover?

If so, you're an IT leadership hero.

Did your board or senior management note that a new application or website launched a few weeks late because you wanted additional testing time to minimize risk?

No one will ever remember.

Did you defer a "nice to have" project because an unplanned "must have" occurred mid year?

Good for you.

Did you have a brief infrastructure failure that led to a major improvement in security, reliability, and maintainability because the staff rallied around a tricky problem caused by a combination of rapid technology change and exponential increases in customer demand?

You'll be stronger in the future because of it.

We have to break the cycle of negativity that makes IT leadership so challenging. Create a culture that thrives on the projects you did well and that does not focus on what remains undone because of circumstances beyond anyone's control.

Leaders at all levels—from board members to team leaders—need to realize that shouting louder does not make the rowing staff move the boat faster.

So celebrate the accomplishments achieved by you and your staff. Our trajectory is good at a very challenging time in history. ∎

The Salesman End Run Around IT

In my 15 years as CIO, I've experienced a gamut of sales techniques—the "end of quarter deal never to be repeated," the "we're your partner and you always get our best price," and the selling of products that don't yet exist.

However, today I experienced one of the most reprehensible—"The Salesman End Run Around IT."

Don't like the answer IT is giving you? Go to the CFO and try to convince financial leadership that IT leadership is squandering budgets.

Here's the redacted email that the salesman sent the CFO.

"From: Storage Sales Specialist at a large company
Sent: Wednesday
To: BIDMC Chief Financial Officer
Subject: Lower Storage Costs
I am the Storage Sales rep for the CareGroup hospitals. We have been working with healthcare organizations that are typically XXX shops and saving them $500,000+ in storage cost and associated resources. We will guarantee that we migrate your current environment to 50% or less storage. The industry leading analyst group Gartner has named our storage as the leader.
Why am I reaching out to you? I met with IT a few weeks ago and they told me they didn't have the time or the resources to evaluate new technology and they were happy with XXX. I know healthcare organizations have to think smarter and get more value out of the IT dollar. Our storage is easier to manage (we have customers who reduce admin by 90%+ with our storage), our storage is faster, highly available (ability to have five 9s reliability for critical applications), and has superior service/support.
Can I schedule some time with you next week to go into detail on how our storage can make your IT budget go further and give your stakeholders the best experience they deserve? Please let me know a time that fits your calendar.
Best Regards,
Storage Sales Specialist at a large company"

I completely respect the challenges of commissioned salespeople and the difficulty that large companies face in a lackluster economy. However, there is no better way to sour a long-term relationship than to bypass the usual lines of hierarchy in an organization via an end run.

This salesperson works at a company I respect a great deal, so I believe this is an example of rogue behavior. However, I welcome your comments and feedback: have you experienced the end run and how have you responded to it? ∎

Crafting Quantitative IT Governance

Over the past few years I've been talking to many industry leaders about the challenge of matching IT supply and demand. Governance committees are essential but are not enough when the number of project requests is so large that they become difficult to triage.

Objective, quantitative scoring criteria can help.

Intel has implemented a Business Value Index that is based on numerical scoring of the following:

- Customer need

- Business and technical risks

- Strategic fit

- Revenue potential

- Level of required investment

- Amount of innovation and learning generated

My colleagues at Stanford have developed a quantitative approach based on a weighted scoring of the following:

- Quality and effectiveness

- User productivity and satisfaction (includes providers, patients, referring MDs)

- Compliance (required by law or external regulatory/accreditation body)

- Patient safety

- Financial

- Scope/urgency

Their process is very robust as described by Dr. Pravene Nath:

"We take all inbound requests, whether captured by helpdesk or in meetings. A clinical informaticist reviews the request and presents it at our scoring committee meeting, which lasts for about an hour each week. The informaticist provides a preliminary scoring, and the group either confirms it, adjusts it, or sends it back for more research. Occasionally a request will be outright denied at the meeting if it just doesn't make sense. We have an appeals process for the requestor but it is rarely used. All requests, regardless of age, are kept in a rank ordered list by priority based on score. The application teams work from the top of that list downward, and they don't pick up anything new from the list until something currently underway is completed. Lastly, we reserve some capacity for fast track (easy items) which can be done even if lower on the list."

BIDMC has prioritized capital projects (IT and others) by scoring the following:

- Return on investment

- Strategic alignment

- Impact factor (employees, clinicians, patients)

- Quality/safety

- Compliance/regulatory

We have policies that require CIO sign off of all IT-related projects to ensure grant-funded/departmental-funded IT projects are prioritized along with institutionally-funded capital projects.

This year, we're looking to expand quantitative IT governance to those projects which are not capital funded and simply use existing staff resources.

I welcome your input on approaches you have used to rank project requests in a way that stakeholders feel is objective, transparent, and fair. ∎

Chapter 4

Security and Privacy

I was recently told that JP Morgan had 8,000 employees in its compliance department. Over the past year, it has added 7,000 more. The era in which we live includes an increasingly complex regulatory/compliance environment, more security threats, and a need to share more data with more people for more purposes. At the same time, Meaningful Use requires health information exchange, and the HIPAA Omnibus rule increases breach penalties and extends the reach of business associate agreements. Balancing security with convenience is harder than ever. This chapter focuses on those projects and processes that can help a CIO reduce risks.

The Top Ten Things a CIO Can Do to Enhance Security

Harvard networks are attacked every few seconds 24 hours a day, 7 days a week. These attacks come from such diverse locations as Eastern Europe and Eastern Cambridge (MIT students). In general, protecting the privacy of three million patient records is a Cold War. Hackers innovate, information technology departments protect, hackers innovate, and the process continues. Providing security is a journey and we have been on the path to security best practices for many years. The following are my top ten recommendations to guide this journey:

1. Policies/governance—Without policies and governance, enforcing security best practices is impossible. Do you allow IM or not? Do you

allow modems to be attached to computers without IT approval? Can data be copied onto a thumb drive and transported off site? Such major policy questions must have definitive answers and sanctions for violating these policies must be enforced.

2. Risk assessment and stratification—Do you consider the HIV status of patients to be the same security priority as protecting the data integrity of the library catalog? Probably not. We have established four classifications of risk:

   **** Internet-connected clinical data which are patient identified. Compromise of passwords could lead to access of thousands of patients' records.

   *** Internet-connected clinical data which are patient identified. Compromise of passwords could lead to access to one patient record.

   ** Internet-connected clinical data which are not patient identified. Compromise of passwords could lead to access of aggregate data without patient identifiers.

   * No patient records available.

   Our journey to enhance security focuses on **** and *** data first. By ensuring our latest technologies and techniques protect our most sensitive data, we apply our people and budgets to the areas of greatest risk.

3. Firewalls—Many years ago, we used the "Blanche Dubois" approach to security—a firewall that empowered academic collaboration but relied on the "kindness of strangers." One of our first security enhancements in the 1990s was to replace our permissive firewall (allow anything except where prohibited) with a restrictive firewall (deny everything except were permitted). During this process we eliminated 99% of our publicly available Internet protocol (IP) addresses, eliminated peer-to-peer traffic, and created a demilitarized zone (DMZ) for our web servers.

4. Intrusion detection and prevention/host intrusion protection— Recognizing that operating systems are patched continuously and that applications have vulnerabilities, there are attacks that take advantage of the time between a patch being released and a patch being applied. We've employed software that provides "zero day" protection—eliminating the kinds of traffic between servers that are suggestive of attacks or questionable behavior. We do this network-wide and on individual servers, especially our web servers.

5. Remote access methods—The security of the network is only as good as its weakest point. Remote access technologies such as SSLVPN,[1] MetaFrame, and Remote Desktop via thin client computing devices minimize the threat of viruses from remote access points. Ideally, all computers accessing protected health information should have up-to-date operating system patches, up-to-date antivirus software, and no software which could compromise the security of the device (e.g., peer-to-peer file sharing).

6. Network access controls—In most institutions, hackers wanting to access a hospital network can walk in the front door, unplug an existing computer, and access the network with whatever nefarious devices they choose. Less malevolent is the traveling vendor who plugs a laptop into the network to do a demo, giving viruses and spyware on that laptop full access to the hospital networks. Technologies such as Cisco's Network Admission Control and Microsoft's Network Access Protection restrict network access to known machines containing the right versions of the right software needed to ensure end-to-end security.

7. Vulnerability assessment—Many healthcare applications have vulnerabilities which can lead to inappropriate disclosure of patient data. Typical vulnerabilities include buffer overflows, SQL/JavaScript injection attacks, and cross-server scripting attacks. Hiring "white hat" hackers to perform penetration testing of mission-critical applications, networks, and operating systems helps identify potential problems before security is compromised. Even if vendors do not repair these deficiencies, host intrusion protection software can mitigate risks by surrounding systems with an extra layer of vigilance, stopping attacks before they start.

8. Provisioning/authentication/authorization—Having robust processes to grant passwords only to qualified users, terminate accounts when staff leave the organization, and enable only the "minimum need to know" access to clinical data are foundational to good security. When passwords are issued, they should be strong (non-English words, mixed case, numbers and letters, greater than eight characters long, etc.), expire at a reasonable interval (at least yearly), and be role-based. Registration clerks should not be able to access medication lists or psychiatric notes, only those demographic data elements needed to perform their duties.

---

1   SSLVPN = Secure sockets layer virtual private network.

9. Anti-virus/anti-spyware—The design of Windows operating systems, in which all internal "services" run as the administrator, creates a vulnerable environment that necessitates the need for anti-virus and anti-spyware software.

10. Audit trails—Authorized internal users can be even more of a threat than external hackers. Collecting audit trails and implementing a program to monitor accesses are essential. Has one account accessed more than 20 patients a day? Has one patient been examined by more than 20 accounts? Who is accessing employee healthcare records? Who is accessing the record of a famous athlete or actress? Audit trails and tools to mine audit data help answer these questions.

These ten areas are a starter kit to appropriate security in a healthcare organization. Security cannot be an afterthought—it is a project that must be resourced. A well-trained and staffed security team is essential to success. To keep our organizations secure, I have a full-time security officer and a team of security professionals maintaining our firewall rules, intrusion detection/ prevention software, and our auditing systems. Compliance with HIPAA is a key motivator to implement good security, but most important is retaining the trust of our patients. We are the stewards of their data and our security systems are the last defense against breaches of confidentiality. ∎

Security for Health Information Exchange

In my role as Vice-Chair of the HIT Standards Committee, I join many of the subcommittee calls debating the standards and implementation guidance needed to support Meaningful Use. Over the past few months, I've learned a great deal from the Privacy and Security Workgroup.

Here are my top five lessons about security for health information exchange:

1. Security is not just about using the right standards or purchasing products that implement those standards; it's also about the infrastructure on which those products run and policies that define how they'll be used. A great software system that supports role-based security is not so useful if everyone is given the same role/

Security is not just about using the right standards or purchasing products that implement those standards; it's also about the infrastructure on which those products run and policies that define how they'll be used.

access permissions. Running great software on a completely open wireless network could lead to compromise of privacy.

2. Security is an end-to-end process. The healthcare ecosystem is as vulnerable as its weakest link. Thus, each application, workstation, network, and server within an enterprise must be secured to a reasonable extent. Only by creating a secure enterprise can health information exchange be secured between enterprises.

3. As stated in #1, policies define how security technology is used. However, the US does not have a single, unified healthcare privacy policy—we have 50 of them since state law pre-empts HIPAA. This means that products will need to have the technology capabilities to support heterogeneous policies. For example, a clinician may have simple username/password authentication, while a government agency might require a smart card, biometrics, or hardware token.

4. Security is a process, not a product. Every year hackers will innovate and security practices will need to be enhanced to protect confidentiality. Security is also a balance between ease of use and absolute protection. The most secure library in the world would be one that never checked out books.

5. Security is a function of budgets. I spend over $1 million per year on security work at BIDMC. Knowing that rural hospitals and small practitioners have limited budgets, we need to set security requirements at a pace they can afford. Imposing Department of Defense 'nuclear secrets' security technology on a small doctor's office is not feasible. Thus, the Privacy and Security Workgroup has discussed the need for minimum security standards, realizing that some users will go beyond these minimums.

Privacy and security are foundational to ARRA and Meaningful Use. Since patients will only trust EHRs if they believe their confidentiality is protected via good security, there will be increasing emphasis on better security technology and implementation over the next few years.

Although some may find increased security cumbersome, our goal of care coordination through health information exchange depends on robust security technology, infrastructure, and best practices. ∎

My Privacy and Security Lessons Learned

Here are my top five lessons learned about privacy and security:

1. Security is not just about using the right standards or purchasing products that implement those standards. It's also about the infrastructure on which those products run and the policies that define how they'll be used. A great software system that supports role-based security is not so useful if everyone is assigned the same role and its accompanying access permissions. Similarly, running great software on an open wireless network could compromise privacy.

2. Security is a process, not a product. Hackers are innovative, and security practices need to be constantly enhanced to protect confidentiality. Security is also a balance between ease of use and absolute protection. The most secure library in the world—and the most useless—would be one that never loaned out any books.

3. Security is an end-to-end process. The healthcare ecosystem is as vulnerable as its weakest link. Thus, each application, workstation, network, and server within an enterprise must be secured to a reasonable extent. The exchange of healthcare information between enterprises cannot be secured if the enterprises themselves are not secure.

4. The US does not have a single, unified healthcare privacy policy: it has 50 of them. That means that products need to support multiple policies (for example, those of a clinic that uses simple username/password authentication and those of a government agency that requires smart cards, biometrics, or hardware tokens).

5. Security is a function of budget. Healthcare providers' budgets vary widely. New security requirements must take into account the implementation pace that the various stakeholders can afford. Imposing "nuclear secrets" security technology on a small doctor's office is not feasible. Thus, the Privacy and Security Workgroup has developed a matrix of required minimum security standards to be implemented in 2011, 2013, and 2015, recognizing that some users will go beyond these minimums.

In debating how to enhance security for all stakeholders without creating a heavy implementation burden, the workgroup developed these ideas:

- All data moving between organizations must be encrypted over the wire. Data moving in an organization's data center should be encrypted if open wireless networks could lead to the compromise of data as it is moved inside the organization. There is no need to encrypt the data twice—if an organization implements appropriate secure wireless protocols such as WPA Enterprise, the data can be sent within the organization unencrypted.

- All data at rest on mobile devices must be encrypted. Encrypting all databases and storage systems within an organization's data center would create a burden. But ensuring that devices such as laptops and universal serial bus (USB) drives, which can be stolen, have encrypted patient-identified data makes sense and is part of new regulations such as Massachusetts' data protection law.

Such proposals strike a delicate balance, for while attaining the goal of care coordination through the exchange of health information depends on robust security technology, infrastructures, and best practices, it can't succeed if safeguarding patients' privacy is unduly cumbersome. ■

Strong Identity Management

In addition to audit trails, a key component of enforcing security policy is ensuring the identity of those who use applications. I've been increasingly focused on strong identity management.

Currently, most systems support username/password with various rules such as those we use at BIDMC:

- Passwords must be at least eight (8) characters in length

- Passwords must contain characters from at least three (3) of the following four (4) classes:

    o English upper case letters A,B,C,...Z

    o English lower case letters a,b,c,...z

    o Westernized Arabic numerals 0,1,2,...9

    o Non-alphanumeric ("special characters") such as punctuation symbols: !,@,#...

- New passwords must be different from previously used passwords

- Under no circumstances should the passwords contain your username or any part of your full name or other easily identifiable information

However, it's clear that something stronger than a username/password will be needed for e-prescribing controlled substances. The US Drug Enforcement Administration (DEA) has insisted upon NIST[2] Level 3 authentication. What do levels of authentication mean?

- Level 1 is the lowest assurance and Level 4 is the highest. The levels are based on the degree of confidence needed in the process used to establish identity and in the proper use of the established credentials.

---

2   NIST = National Institute of Standards and Technology.

- Level 1—Little or no confidence in the asserted identity's validity. No identity proofing is required at this level, but the authentication mechanism should provide some assurance that the same claimant is accessing the protected transaction or data.

- Level 2—Some confidence in the asserted identity's validity. Level 2 requires confidence that the asserted identity is accurate. Level 2 provides for single-factor remote network authentication, including identity-proofing requirements for presentation of identifying materials or information.

- Level 3—High confidence in the asserted identity's validity. Level 3 is appropriate for transactions that need high confidence in the accuracy of the asserted identity. Level 3 provides multifactor remote network authentication.

- Level 4—Very high confidence in the asserted identity's validity. Level 4 is for transactions that need very high confidence in the accuracy of the asserted identity. Level 4 provides the highest practical assurance of remote network authentication. Authentication is based on proof of possession of a key through a cryptographic protocol.

If Level 3 authentication is implemented in healthcare for prescribing controlled substances, strong identity management may be expanded to other aspects of healthcare such as signing notes, signing orders, or gaining physical access to restricted areas.

Given the workflow implications of an added authentication burden, it's important to choose the right technology approach.

There are a wide range of two-factor authentication methods, including security tokens, smart cards, biometrics, certificates, soft tokens, and cell phone-based approaches.

I've had experience with each of these. Here's a summary of my findings:

- Tokens—You'd think tokens would be easy to use, but we had a high login failure rate, challenges with tokens getting lost/destroyed (in the laundry), time synchronization issues (as the battery begins to age, the clock inside the token may begin running slowly), and clinician dissatisfaction with having to carry yet another device. A clinician with multiple affiliations has an even worse problem—multiple tokens to carry around. Token and licensing costs were expensive.

- Smart cards—We use smart cards for physical access and they work well. They are foolproof to use, can be laundered without an issue, and are inexpensive. The only problem with using them in software authentication is the expense of adding smart card readers to our 8,000 workstations. Buying and maintaining 8,000 USB devices is costly. However, they are still a serious consideration, since clinicians like the idea of walking up to a device and using something they already have—a badge—to authenticate.

- Biometrics—Biometrics are convenient because you can just swipe a finger, which you always have with you (we hope). Many laptops have built-in fingerprint readers and the BIO-key software easily integrates web applications into Active Directory. As with smart cards, the only challenge is installing and maintaining fingerprint scanners on 8,000 existing desktops. Biometrics have been very popular with our clinicians and we've had a very low false negative rate (and zero false positives).

- Certificates—Managing certificates for 20,000 users is painful. We've done it and although I am a strong believer in organization-level certificates, I remain unconvinced that user-level certificates are a good idea. Maybe new approaches like Microsoft's Infocard, which presents digitally signed XML-based credentials, will make storage and presentation of cryptographic credentials easier.

- Soft tokens—They are just a software version of hardware tokens running on a mobile device or desktop. Since software must be installed and maintained on each device, they can be a challenge to support.

- Cell phone-based approaches—Harvard Medical School recently implemented two-factor authentication with cell phones as a way of securing password reset functions. It's been popular, easy to support, and very low cost. Companies such as Anakam offer tools and technology to implement strong identity management in cell phones via text messaging, voice delivery of a personal identification number (PIN), or voice biometric verification. Per the Anakam website, their products achieve full compliance with NIST Level 3, are scalable to millions of users, cost less than hard tokens or smart codes, are installable in the enterprise without added client hardware/software, and are easy to use (all you have to do is answer a phone call or read a text message).

Thus, my vote for achieving NIST Level 3 is to choose among smart cards, biometrics, or cell phone-based approaches depending on the problem to be solved and the workflow that is being automated. Although we've not yet implemented cell phone approaches for EHR authentication, I can imagine that our 2011 authentication strategy might be the following:

- Physical access (hundreds of existing doors that have smart card readers)—Smart cards

- Fast-trusted login in the Emergency Department (100 devices that are kept in a closed physical space)—Biometrics

- Generalized two-factor authentication for e-prescribing controlled substances (thousands of devices and hundreds of users)—Cell phone approaches

With strong identity management, our audit trails will have greater value. It will be challenging for a user to claim that he or she was not the person performing the transaction. The combination of trusted identity and complete audit trails is key to a multi-layered defense against privacy breaches. ∎

A Privacy Breach

Beth Israel Deaconess and University of California, San Francisco (UCSF) issued press releases about a complex situation.

An employee of BIDMC who had authorized access to data for quality improvement activities placed clinical data (not financial or social security number data) for approximately 2,900 patients on a thumb drive. The employee left BIDMC and went to work in California for UCSF. While at UCSF, the employee copied the thumb drive to a UCSF-owned laptop in order to demonstrate quality improvement reporting. The laptop was stolen, then recovered. There is no evidence that the data on the laptop was accessed.

BIDMC takes this situation very seriously and notified the patients, Health and Human Services (HHS), and the media.

As with other challenging situations I've discussed such as the CareGroup network outage and the limitations of administrative data, it is my intent to openly share lessons learned with my colleagues and the industry. By writing about the process, I hope to encourage policy and technology improvements at healthcare institutions throughout the country to protect privacy.

A few thoughts:

1. Make sure you have a policy requiring that all mobile storage devices be secured. BIDMC has a written policy and is revising it to be even more restrictive.

2. To further mitigate risk, encrypt all laptops. BIDMC has implemented McAfee Safeboot for this purpose. Harvard Medical School has licensed PGP Whole Disk Encryption for this purpose.

3. Educate employees about the policy and technology best practices to protect privacy. A learning management system is great for this.

4. Sanction employees who violate the policies.

5. Implement new technologies that scan/restrict data transfers in the organization (e.g., scan email for medical record numbers or patient identified-information sent non-securely).

The combination of strong policies, state of the art technology, and education is required to protect patient data.

In this case, an authorized employee took data in violation of policies and placed it on technology not controlled by BIDMC. Likely, the laptop data was not accessed, but you can be sure that additional education, broad communication with patients, and close collaboration with government and the media will be our next steps. ■

Protecting Privacy

As we all implement Meaningful Use Stages 1, 2, and 3, we will increasingly share data among payers, providers, and patients. Protecting privacy is foundational and we should exchange data only per patient preference. How will we achieve that in Massachusetts?

Stage 1

In the first stage of Meaningful Use, there are limited data exchanges: e-prescribing, a demonstration of pushing data from provider to provider, and public/population health exchanges for lab, immunizations, and syndromic surveillance.

These can be achieved using the consent mechanisms we have in place today:

- A clinician asks a patient (or the patient signs a paper-based general consent in the office or hospital) if the clinician can retrieve his or her national medication history from Surescripts during the course of e-prescribing.

- A clinician asks a patient if the clinician can push a summary of his or her care to another clinician such as a primary caregiver/specialist or hospital/primary caregiver data exchange.

Aggregating de-identified data for public health purposes is permitted by HIPAA and ARRA without consent. Since no patient identifiers are involved, there is a reduced risk for privacy breaches.

In our community EHR rollout of eClinicalWorks (eCW) via our private cloud (a physically secure, environmentally controlled, generator-supported co-location facility that is professionally operated and provides all the inbound interfaces needed for Meaningful Use), we've designed our infrastructure to support consent for Stage 1 exchanges.

1. Every practice has its own virtual server, separate eCW software, and isolated database instance. The data is owned and controlled by the practice.

2. De-identified data is used for pay-for-performance and quality reporting, but BIDMC/BIDPO has no access to the provider's EHR or billing system.

3. Data can flow from provider to provider with NEHEN or the eCW push product (peer-to-peer, or P2P), but that is at the provider's discretion after consent of the patient is obtained.

Stage 2

A push architecture supports provider-initiated consent—the clinician can ask the patient before pushing data. Pull requires a different approach. The patient's data-sharing preferences must be stored somewhere so that when data is pulled, only those data elements consistent with patient privacy preferences for that type of clinical encounter are shared.

In Stage 2, I expect that such consent will be federated, stored in various EHRs and community exchanges. At the moment there is no plan for a national health identifier or patient-controlled national consent infrastructure.

In Massachusetts, we have legislation (Chapter 305) and a community standard which require an opt-in consent for data sharing between healthcare organizations.

Some EHR vendors have created consent functionality within their products to support the recording of consent for information exchange. Some community HIEs have created city-wide databases to record consent preferences.

In our community EHR rollout of eClinicalWorks, we've designed our infrastructure to support consent for Stage 2 exchanges.

We use the EHX product from eClinicalWorks, which includes an opt-in consent database, a clinical summary data store, and means for clinicians to pull data across practices if a patient opts in to support it.

This works great for the 1,700 clinicians in BIDPO, but does not support pull transactions across competing organizations.

For that, we need to look to Stage 3.

Stage 3

I believe that Stage 3 will include several community, state, and national data exchanges to support care coordination and population health. It will require master patient indices (given that a national identifier is unlikely). It will require a centralized patient-controlled consent framework.

To ensure we are ready for patient-controlled, centrally managed consent, the state of Massachusetts HIE ad hoc workgroup recommended that we begin work building a central consent management framework now using our ONC[3] HIE funds.

Thus, we'll use provider-initiated consent and patient opt in via EHRs and community exchanges for Stages 1 and 2, but we hope to have a patient-controlled statewide consent infrastructure ready for Stage 3.

Opt-in consent that is patient controlled is the right approach and we need to build the infrastructure to support it. In the meantime, we'll protect patient privacy preferences using the best technology available.

Hopefully, our local, state, and federal policy and technology will converge to support the patient-centric consent that ensures we support everyone's preferences for data exchange. ■

> *Opt-in consent that is patient controlled is the right approach and we need to build the infrastructure to support it. In the meantime, we'll protect patient privacy preferences using the best technology available.*

Authority, Responsibility, and Risk

When I became CIO of CareGroup/BIDMC in 1998, I promised to listen to all my staff and collaboratively embrace technologies that would benefit patients while also enabling employee career growth. The IT team worked together to implement new infrastructure and new applications. Success led to an upward spiral of success. Other groups such as Media Services, Knowledge Services, and Health Information Management joined IS. We continued to grow in scope and capability.

My sense at the time was that additional authority, budget, and span of control were great—more was better.

However, in my years as CIO, I've learned that while more authority may bring more opportunities to succeed, it also brings increased responsibility and with it, additional risk.

In a world of increasing regulatory pressures and compliance requirements, the likelihood of something bad happening every day in a large organization is high. The larger your role, the larger your risk.

> *In a world of increasing regulatory pressures and compliance requirements, the likelihood of something bad happening every day in a large organization is high. The larger your role, the larger your risk.*

---

3   ONC = Office of the National Coordinator for Health Information Technology.

Today in my BIDMC role I oversee the following:

- 83 locations

- 18,000 user accounts

- 9,000 desktops/laptops/tablets

- 3,000 printers

- 600 iPads

- 1,600 iPhones

- 450 servers (200 physical, 250 virtual)

- 1.5 petabytes of storage

...Serving over a million patients.

If one employee copies data to a USB drive and loses it, a potential breach needs to be reported. If one workstation is infected with malware that could have transmitted clinical data to a third party, a potential breach needs to be reported. If one business associate loses an unencrypted laptop, a breach needs to be reported. Since HITECH took effect, 30,750 such breaches have been reported. All breaches are the CIO's responsibility.

- If one IT project is over time or over budget, it's the CIO's responsibility.

- If one IT employee goes rogue, it's the CIO's responsibility.

- If one server, network, or storage array fails, it's the CIO's responsibility.

- If one application causes patient harm, it's the CIO's responsibility.

Life as a CIO can have its challenges!

At the same time that responsibilities are expanding, the number of auditors, regulators, lawyers, compliance specialists, and complex regulations is growing at a much faster rate than IT resources.

There are three solutions:

1. Spend increasing amounts of time on risk identification and mitigation.

2. Reduce your responsibility/accountability and thus your risk footprint.

3. Find a nice cabin in the woods and homestead as far away from regulatory burdens as possible.

I'm doing #1—about 20% of my day is spent on matters of risk, compliance, and regulation. I'm doing #2 by transitioning my CIO role at Harvard Medical School to a successor. #3 sounds appealing but I'm not there yet!

As healthcare CIOs face new regulations for e-prescribing of controlled substances, FDA device safety requirements, 5010 implementation, ICD-10, new privacy rules, and Meaningful Use Stages 1, 2, and 3, the magnitude of the challenges ahead may at times seem overwhelming. I sometimes long for the days when all I had to do was write innovative software and create a nurturing environment for my staff!

There are three negative consequences that can result from overzealous regulation:

1. The joy of success can turn into a fear of compliance failure.

2. Compliance can create such overhead that we lose our competitiveness.

3. We'll become less entrepreneurial because the consequences of non-compliance, such as loss of reputation, penalties, and burden of responding to agencies enforcing regulations, become a deterrent to innovation.

For now, I have accepted the risks that come with all my responsibilities, but at some point, the balance may become more challenging to maintain. As we move forward, I hope that policymakers in Washington and at the state level will be mindful of the unintended consequences of regulatory complexity. ■

Meaningful Consent

One major issue facing private and public health information exchanges is how to ensure patients' privacy preferences are respected by obtaining their consent before data is shared.

I met with a multi-disciplinary team of attorneys, vendor experts, and IT leaders to discuss BIDMC's approach to private HIE consent.

After two hours of discussion, here's what we agreed upon:

- Patients and families should be able to control the flow of their data among institutions. The ability for the patient to choose what flows where for what purpose is "meaningful consent."

- To achieve "meaningful consent," we will ask all the patients of our 1,800 BIDMC-associated ambulatory clinicians to opt in for data sharing among the clinicians coordinating their care.

- Patients may revoke this consent at any time.

- Consent for patients under 18 years old and not emancipated will be sought from their parents. Upon turning 18, the patients themselves will select their consent preferences.

- The process for sharing data will function as follows: authorized clinicians with a need to know clinical information for treatment, payment, or operations will electronically request a view of data from a community practice using our "magic button" protocol.

- Only patients shared in common between the two organizations can be queried.

- All requests will be audited.

- Data will be displayed from organizations at which the patient has opted in for disclosure of their information. There will not be a "break the glass" feature to override patient privacy preferences (or lack of preferences).

- We feel that asking for opt-in consent to disclose data is the most patient-centric approach to protecting privacy and we agreed to do it for all our community practices, both private and owned.

This practice mirrors what the Massachusetts public HIE will do as it evolves from a "push" model to a "pull" model over the next few years. Starting this month, we'll record opt-in consents at the BIDMC community level, but by 2014 all consents will be recorded at the state level.

Opt-in consent to disclose with the ease of opting out at any time will work well for private and public HIEs. ∎

The BIDMC Mobile Device Encryption Program

I've written extensively about the Bring Your Own Device (BYOD)/Consumer IT challenge. Here's the message we sent to employees:

"Information Systems will be conducting an aggressive campaign to ensure every mobile device is encrypted. This initiative applies to all staff and students. The program is mandatory and required for any mobile device used to access BIDMC-related systems, programs or documents, including email, clinical applications and administrative documents such as financial spreadsheets, grant information or staff lists.

"Many of you participated in last month's program regarding smartphone devices used to connect to the Exchange email system using ActiveSync. These devices now require password protection. Look for more information soon on new smartphone encryption and 'auto wipe' requirements.

"Securing Laptops and iPads

"The next stage of work is encrypting laptops, iPads and other tablet computers. It will proceed in two phases.

"The first phase, beginning this week, focuses on institutionally owned laptops and iPad-type tablet computers. Other versions of tablet computers will be addressed in a later phase. Service depots will be set up in and around the main campus. The first location will be the Center for Life Sciences (CLS). This building was chosen because it has the largest population of laptops and iPads.

"We appreciate the cooperation of staff of CLS, especially because they are the first to undergo this new process. The CLS experience will guide IS planning for the entire medical center. We will coordinate our encryption program with Research Administration's research equipment inventory project, eliminating redundant phone calls to investigators.

"What You Need to Do

"Prepare Your Device—Prior to dropping off the laptop or iPad at the service depot, delete unneeded applications and data. All valuable data and important files, email, applications and other documents stored on the device should be backed up to your network home directory. Do NOT back up the data to an Internet cloud service such as Apple's iCloud, or DropBox. Storing protected health or personal information on these sites is against corporate security policy.

"Schedule an Appointment—Information Systems will contact staff for which records show you have been issued an institutionally funded laptop or iPad.

"Leave the Device—Encrypting a device may require several hours depending on the method used. For this reason, you will be expected to leave the device at the service depot. Every attempt will be made to complete the work within the same business day.

"Pick Up the Device—Upon returning the device, depot staff will brief you on what work was done and your on-going responsibilities for maintaining the security of the device. You will be asked to start the device from a cold boot and verify it is in working order.

"What IS Will Do

"Intake—To qualify under HIPAA/HITECH 'safe harbor,' full-disk encryption is required. On arrival at the service depot, an initial assessment of the device's configuration will be done to determine the most appropriate encryption method, e.g. software- or hardware-based. Some devices have encryption built in, but it needs to be activated. The method used will depend on the make, model and operating system version of the laptop or tablet computer.

"Inspection—The service depot staff will scan the device for malware and vulnerabilities. They will check configuration settings to ensure they comply with corporate security policy such as power-on password, inactivity timeouts, and, for iPads, auto wipe. If time permits, depot staff will apply operating system and third party software patches necessary to eliminate security vulnerabilities. If malware is detected, the device will be cleaned or re-imaged depending on the nature of the malware. The network address of the device will be recorded so IS knows it has been inspected when it appears on the data network. When practical, management (Microsoft SCCM for Windows or Casper for Macs) and anti-virus agents (McAfee EPO) will be installed to allow Information Systems staff to keep the device in good security hygiene throughout its life while in use at BIDMC.

"Inventory the Device for Research—If your computer is one that still needs to be scanned as part of the bi-annual Research inventory required by federal law, a member of the Research Administration staff will scan the inventory tag while it is at the depot—or apply an inventory tag as needed. We are combining these efforts to make it more convenient for users.

"What Is Next?

"The dates and locations for other service depot sites will be announced later this month as IS continues to secure laptops and iPads throughout the medical center.

"Information Systems will periodically check your mobile device to ensure the safeguards are still in place. Additionally, staff must attest, each time their password is renewed, that all mobile devices they use for hospital-related business, including personal devices, are encrypted.

"From this point forward, newly acquired laptop and tablet computers purchased from institutional funds cannot be used to access the BIDMC data network until their encryption status is verified by Information Systems.

"Information Systems will monitor the network for rogue laptop and tablet devices that have not been screened for compliance. If a device is discovered that has not been screened, Internet access privileges will be blocked."

As I've told the press, it is no longer sufficient to rely on policy alone to secure personal mobile devices. Institutions must educate their staff, assist them with encryption, and in some cases purchase software/hardware for personal users to ensure compliance with federal and state regulations. I will continue to write about our lessons learned supporting personal device security enhancements. ∎

> It is no longer sufficient to rely on policy alone to secure personal mobile devices. Institutions must educate their staff, assist them with encryption, and in some cases purchase software/hardware for personal users to ensure compliance with federal and state regulations.

A Novel Idea for Managing Consent

A few years ago, I wrote about representing privacy preferences in an XML form that I called the Consent Assertion Markup Language (CAML).

At a recent HIT Standards Committee we discussed the draft Meaningful Use Stage 3 Request for Comment (RFC), which includes a measure relating to query for a patient's record. The RFC suggests an exchange of authorization language to be signed by the patient in order to allow retrieval of the requested information. Discussion elicited the suggestion that perhaps patient consent preferences might be included as metadata with the data exchanged so that the patient-approved uses of the data—treatment/payment/operations, clinical trials, transmission to a third party—could be respected.

After the meeting, Dixie Baker proposed a simple, scalable, and powerful approach to avoiding the necessity of either exchanging authorization language for signature, and the complexities involved in exchanging patient preferences as metadata. Her suggested approach draws from both the CAML idea with the metadata idea, but simplifies privacy-management for both consumers and providers, while offering the kind of scalability needed for the dynamic, collaborative healthcare environment we envision.

Imagine that, instead of having to fill out a new privacy-preferences form at each encounter, the consumer could select and manage her preferences with a single entity, and at every other encounter, would need only provide the uniform resource identifier (URI) to where her preferences were held. Then, upon receipt of a request for her health information, an EHR would only need to query the privacy-management service at the URI she provided to determine whether the request could be honored. Her preferences would be captured as structured, coded data to enable query, without having to exchange a complete "form" in order to adjudicate an access request. Per the CAML idea, this XML could include query-able preferences about what data the patient consents to exchange with whom and in what circumstances. This set of privacy preferences could be maintained by the patient and would include such concepts as institution-level permission to share data with partner organizations, permission to send data using a health information exchange organization, and approval to use data for certain types of research.

Instead of sending these preferences with the data itself, the metadata header in the Consolidated CDA summary exchange would include a URI that points to the privacy-management service where the patient's privacy preferences are held.

This simple idea—represent patient's privacy preferences/consents in query-able XML at a specific URI—enables an entirely new approach to health information exchange, while making it easier for consumers to make meaningful choices, and manage them over time.

For example:

> *This simple idea—represent patient's privacy preferences/consents in query-able XML at a specific URI—enables an entirely new approach to health information exchange, while making it easier for consumers to make meaningful choices, and manage them over time.*

1. A hospital is "pushed" a patient record from a primary caregiver. The hospital wants to push that data to a specialist. Before any data transfer is done to an outside organization, the URI is retrieved from the metadata and the patient's current consent preferences are applied to the data exchange.

2. An emergency department wants to pull data from multiple data sources to ensure safe, quality, efficient care of an unconscious patient. The URI of service holding the patient's privacy preferences is available from the state HIE, and the data is retrieved from various sources per the patient's preferences.

3. At discharge, the patient's information is to be pushed to the patient and the primary caregiver/referring clinician per Meaningful Use Stage 2 requirements. Before the push happens, the patient's URI is checked for current data exchange preferences.

As we continue to work on a variety of "meaningful consent" approaches and support complex state privacy policy variants, the notion of recording patient privacy preferences in a place that is under the control of the patient and is query-able via a simple XML makes great sense. ∎

Crafting the Security Roadmap

Per the theme of security assessment I've been posting about, part of crafting a multi-year security roadmap is examining technologies and practices that have limited use in healthcare but are widely deployed in other industries.

*   Application security testing—Vendor applications including those with FDA 510k approval may have security vulnerabilities. Testing third-party products with source code analysis tools can reveal defects that are missed by traditional vulnerability scanning software. Related to application testing is third-party vendor management. Testing and verifying the security of cloud-hosted service providers and business associates are becoming a best practice.

*   Data loss prevention—Although many healthcare organizations have strict policies on the use of email, social networking, cloud storage, remote access, and mobile devices, it's increasingly important to have technology in place that enforces policies, preventing users from violating policy by sending data to non-secured locations (e.g., sending patient information to a referring clinician who uses Gmail). Many vendors offer appliances that quarantine, notify, restrict, and manage the flow of email containing person-identified information/protected healthcare information. Related to

DLP is a strategy to prevent use of unencrypted storage devices—thumb drives, DVDs, CDs, etc.

- Adaptive authentication—Critical applications, including email, enterprise resource planning, and clinical applications deserve increased authentication rigor. For example, if a user is not typically outside the US and suddenly logs in from an unexpected location, then the user should be challenged with an additional factor. Approaches could include a secret question or a one-time PIN code sent to a known cell phone. Such applications can also perform a risk analysis of authentication events to detect anomalies, including authentication events using compromised accounts and suspect IP addresses. ∎

Creating a Mature Security Program

While speaking at the ONC annual meeting, I met Leon Rodriguez, Director of the Office of Civil Rights. I now have a broader understanding of the privacy and security enforcement goals of the Obama administration.

In the past, as an operational CIO, an academic studying approaches to health information exchange, and as co-chair of the HIT Standards Committee, I've focused on security technology (FIPS 140 encryption, ASTM audit trail standards, two-factor authentication, remote access, intrusion detection, zero day defense, etc.) and the enabling policies that support best practices.

While this has been effective, as measured by downtime, breaches of devices under IT control, and a balance between ease of use/access restriction, the entire healthcare industry is still on a journey toward security program maturity.

What do I mean?

A mature program uses a framework such as NIST 800 to serve as rubric for stakeholder analysis of risk. Such a framework ensures that stakeholders consider all the elements of risk and not just the ones that are top of mind for experts in the room. Risks can be physical security, mobile devices, human factors including staffing levels that concentrate expertise in too few people, configuration policies, and timeliness of audit log reviews. In the past, many CIOs in healthcare have been given enough security staff to support operations but not enough staff to create the processes, policies, and documentation that reflect a mature, optimized program.

According to the slides Leon presented, the Office of Civil Rights wants to ensure organizations have done a thorough risk analysis. I would recommend doing this yearly. Once the risk analysis is done, stakeholders including boards and senior management should prioritize risk, develop mitigation action plans, and document their decisions.

Leon and the OCR understand that breaches can occur in effective and mature security programs (i.e., no technology can stop an authorized user from using a digital camera to take a photo of protected health information on a computer screen, then sharing that photo inappropriately).

OCR wants to ensure organizations have created a culture of compliance that goes beyond security technologies. It includes education, incident responses, and documented discussion that demonstrate an organization and its staff consider security and privacy to be part of their duty and daily work lives.

Although the press has called the HHS log of reported privacy breaches the "Wall of Shame," Leon does not use that term. A breach is investigated to ensure that the right processes were in place at the affected organization to mitigate risk. The findings are used to educate the entire industry. Fines are issued when organizations do not follow the compliance requirements of HIPAA and HITECH, not because of the breach itself.

My take away from this is that all IT organizations should spend the next few years adding polish to their policies, procedures, documentation, education, and process efforts. BIDMC has embraced NIST 800 for this effort and thus far it is going well.

A final thought: this work takes resources, both capital and operating. However, boards and senior management are likely to be receptive to security resource requests since the cost of noncompliance can easily exceed the cost of the additional people needed to create a mature security program. ∎

Reflections on the Tragedy in Boston

Here are my lessons learned from the Boston Marathon bombings:

1. Risk planning is forever altered.

To me, risk is the likelihood of an event multiplied by the impact of that event.

Risk management for BIDMC IT now uses the NIST 800 framework, so areas of risk are formally enumerated; however, it still requires judgment about mitigation strategies.

> To me, risk is the likelihood of an event multiplied by the impact of that event.

At 2:50 pm on April 15, 2013, seven BIDMC IT staff were volunteering in the medical tent/working at the Marathon finish line, a few feet from the explosions. They were among the first responders assisting the injured. Their work in a medical community gave them the strength to stay calm but could not have prepared them for the scenes of destruction they witnessed. All my staff were safe and unharmed, but given their proximity to the bombs, the outcome could have been devastating.

As we think about risk planning in the future, we'll need to consider the events of that week when told something as innocent as, "The majority of the database administration team is going to volunteer at the Marathon."

2. Secure remote access to all systems is critical to operations.

As we continue to enhance the security of our applications and networks, we're limiting remote access to those with a true need to use systems from off campus. As the events of that week illustrated, we need to plan for future events which shut down the city for five days and require many people to work from home if travel is restricted or a "shelter in place" order is given.

3. We need to consider restrictions on physical access to the data centers.

The restrictions on travel to and from communities plus restrictions on entering/leaving BIDMC were imposed with an unknown duration. Our disaster recovery planning needs to include scenarios such as no staff able to enter the data center and no staff able to leave the data center.

4. We may need to consider novel audit workflows.

We capture every lookup in real time and perform many analytics to ensure patient privacy preferences are respected.

We placed the following message at the top of our intranet for every staff member to see on every page:

"Urgent Reminder for All BIDMC Staff About Patient Privacy

Staff must completely protect patient privacy according to federal HIPAA regulations and BIDMC's own privacy policies. That means:

No sharing of ANY patient information through email, Twitter, Facebook, Flickr or other photo sites, any other social media, phone calls or conversations—or any other way.

Do not look at, or access by computer, medical records or other protected health information (PHI) or personal information (PI) unless you are authorized to access that information AND you need that information to care for the patient.

Send all media calls to the Communications Department or page the Media Relations staff on call.

Violation of these regulations and policies will lead to disciplinary action up to and including termination of employment.

Most importantly, thank you to the overwhelming majority of BIDMC staff who are doing an excellent job of keeping all patient information secure."

Might there be new workflows required in the future such that appropriate individuals are paged/notified within seconds after a lookup occurs? In an emergency/mass casualty disaster, how can we balance the need for increased security/privacy and appropriate access with real-time auditing alerts?

5. The need for health information exchange in a mass casualty disaster is very clear.

When patients have a choice of caregiver—a patient-centered medical home or accountable care organization—a lifetime medical record is likely to be available, supporting safe, quality, efficient care.

The events of that week required patient routing based on acuity, urgency, and availability of resources. BIDMC, Massachusetts General, Brigham and Women's, and Children's did a remarkable job treating every patient, even with incomplete medical information. The Massachusetts Healthcare Information Exchange ("the MassHIWay") is currently in production for "pushing" summaries from organization to organization. That week's events illustrate the importance of our second phase, now under construction, for secure retrieval of information based on a record locator service and a patient consent registry. By the second quarter of 2014, we should have the infrastructure in place to support the kind of data exchanges that would have been helpful that week—a first in the country kind of capability.

IT in general experiences more demands than supply. We learned firsthand how technology can support a disaster. As we think about all the work on our plates, our plans going forward must incorporate our recent experiences. ∎

Chapter 5

Balancing Job and Home Life

I recently met a fellow clinician in the parking garage at 5 am and explained that traffic is much better when you work 5-9 instead of 9-5. He responded that it's great except for everyone at home. My wife and I have been together since 1980. She has all the talents and skills that I lack. Together, we're a complete person.

In all my careers—as entrepreneur, doctor, mycologist, IT leader, and winemaker—I've depended on those around me—my wife, my daughter, my parents, my friends, and my neighbors—to make it all work. I believe that life as a CIO demands a balanced approach to every day. The difference between our jobs and our lives has become increasingly murky. Here's what I do to keep it all in balance.

A Connectivity Holiday

I took a two-week vacation and a connectivity holiday. What did that mean?

I was on the John Muir trail, 50 miles from the nearest cell tower and had no ability to connect to email, the web, voicemail, etc. I left all my devices in the car.

When I returned to Tuolumne Meadows, I turned on my mobile device, downloaded over 1,000 messages, and triaged the email.

If the email was a CC or FYI, I quickly read it and deleted it without responding.

If the email was about a product or from a vendor, I deleted it without reading it. Post vacation, I'll have plenty of time to review products.

If the email was from my staff asking me to help with a project or budget issue, I responded.

If the email was from a customer containing a question or complaint, I responded.

Each day from August 13-22, I used this same technique. The end result was that I sent about ten emails per day. I made no phone calls.

When I reconnected to a network on August 22, I simply highlighted the thousands of email in my inbox and pressed delete.

It was liberating.

I know that I left hundreds of vendor questions unanswered. I also know that I read all email that contained FYIs and that I responded to every customer/staff need. Over the next few weeks, I'm sure I'll receive many resends from folks who wanted a response while I was on vacation, but it will be much less than the thousands I received during that time.

My ability to send ten emails a day and keep the peace while on vacation raises the issue: have we created an email culture that is so overwhelming that we need to spend hours a day just answering email? Maybe a bulk delete—the equivalent of declaring email bankruptcy—is something I should try episodically as a way of cleaning the slate.

If there are issues that have not been resolved or there are areas where I need to intervene, I'll receive another email asking for help.

My experience over the two weeks of my vacation taught me that we are often too quick to send an email, escalate a problem, or delegate simple issues. In the days before email, we may have been more productive just because instant communication was not available and we just worked out problems on our own.

My connectivity holiday also included complete separation from news, RSS feeds, and my blog.

All that keyboard time was replaced with family time and the joy of not knowing what time or day it was.

When I returned, I asked others for a summary of the news of the past two weeks. Nothing was emergent.

I always learn a great deal from vacations—alpine climbing skills, time with family, and a focus on the basics of eating, sleeping, and avoiding sunburn. This year I learned that an email and connectivity holiday is possible.

If I did not respond to your email, send it again if the issue is still important. Otherwise, relish the digital silence!

I'm rejuvenated and have many new ideas for projects, blog entries, and cool technologies. The aura of my vacation will last for a few more weeks and I look forward to challenges of the fall season ahead. ■

How to Take a Vacation as a CIO

I've written that being a CIO is not a job, it's a lifestyle. Given the CIO's responsibilities, is a vacation possible? Can you really unplug? Here's the way I do it:

1. Pick a second in command to run the operation while you are away— Just as a military operation would appoint a commander or watch officer, assign someone else to run the operations while you are away. Broadly communicate that this delegate is in charge and can make decisions in your absence.

2. Email a bit in the morning and at night—When I go on vacation, I do email early in the morning before my family gets up and I email late in the evening after my family goes to bed. This means that I can resolve all issues and keep my email queue empty. When I return to the office, there is nothing waiting for me. A great vacation is one that is easy to return from. The burden of having 5,000 emails and five crises to resolve is high, so I invest a bit of time each day to ensure my desk is empty when I return, minimizing the emotional cost of a vacation.

3. Set expectations with an "out of office" message and enjoy each vacation day—Since I have a Blackberry strapped to my body 21 hours a day, I generally do not use out of office messages. During August, while I'm climbing in Yosemite, I cannot physically answer email most of the day. My out of office message provides the details of my climbing schedule and sets expectations when I will be reachable.

4. Own the appropriate mobile technologies—Every airport I land at has GSM/GPRS[1] or UMTS,[2] ensuring I can connect as needed. During my two weeks of climbing and hiking in August, I will not bring a laptop and will exclusively rely on my mobile device to keep my email queue empty.

5. Avoid major infrastructure changes during your vacation—Change is the most likely cause of downtime. By minimizing major change during your time away, you can reduce the risk of outages during vacations.

6. Pick the time of year when stakeholders are on vacation—If senior management and other major stakeholders are on vacation, there are fewer urgent requests for new projects or issue resolution.

7. Avoid vacations during a time of organizational instability—I've been in organizations with major leadership changes (e.g., CEO, dean, your boss). I recommend avoiding vacations during times of great

---

1   GSM/GPRS = Global system for mobile communications/general packet radio service.

2   UMTS = Universal mobile telecommunications systems.

transition, since you want to be around to defend your position and your department as needed.

8. Be able to return in case of emergency—Last year, the Joint Commission arrived for a surprise accreditation inspection on the first day of my vacation. It was so important to demonstrate our medication reconciliation system and communicate our plans for quality improvement applications that I agreed to travel back from my vacation for a day to ensure we had the best showing possible.

9. Build a partnership with your family—My wife is very tolerant of my various activities, from working long hours to climbing isolated mountains. My wife, daughter, and I spend time together every day and we support each other's lives, realizing that at times the best support is allowing each other time alone.

10. Tolerate ambiguity—Take each day of your vacation as it comes, and go with the flow. If you need to make a critical call, that's okay; your family will forgive you. If you are late responding to important email, that's okay; your customers will forgive you. Staying loosely connected, not disconnected, and reacting to events without worrying about a precise schedule will make your vacation restorative and your return to the office easy.

Using these approaches, I'm able to balance family time, personal time, and work time on vacation in a way that works for everyone. ∎

My Top Ten Rules for Schedule Triage

Here's my approach to triage of my daily schedule:

My meetings are typically scheduled from 7 am to 6 pm, followed by dinner with my family until 8 pm, followed by email, reading, and writing until 1 am. My assistant and I schedule each day using the following rules:

1. Leave 50% of the schedule available for the events of each day—In a complex organization, many operational issues arise each day that are easier to resolve 'just in time' than via meetings scheduled a week later. I try to reserve 50% of my time for real-time response to strategic issues, ad hoc meetings, phone calls, and opportunities, doing today's work today.

> *I try to reserve 50% of my time for real-time response to strategic issues, ad hoc meetings, phone calls, and opportunities, doing today's work today.*

2. Manage vendor relationships—I receive a hundred requests for vendor meetings each day. My assistant triages these. My approach to vendors is that I select a few close vendor partners through exhaustive research and then really cultivate those relationships. If my selected vendor partners need me to alpha test products, speak to their staff about our needs, or comment on their strategy, I'm available to do so. If new vendors cold call me, I cannot take their calls, although I will review their products if they email me information to read asynchronously. My message to new vendors is that I'll contact them when I'm ready to discuss their products based on my review of electronic briefing materials.

3. Evaluate the impact factor—Every day I receive numerous requests to speak, travel, and write. I evaluate the impact factor of each of these requests. How many people will I reach? Based on the audience, what positive change might result? Will there be an opportunity to discuss issues with detractors? As I've said in previous posts, I embrace debate and controversy, since resolving conflict can have great impact.

4. Serve those who serve you—In the course of my jobs at HMS, CareGroup, NEHEN, MA-Share, and HITSP, I depend upon hundreds of people. These people often work long hours, endure inconvenient travel, and sacrifice their personal time to work on projects I lead. I do whatever I can to support them whenever they ask me to speak, attend specialty society meetings, or write articles.

5. Leverage travel—Travel is miserable today. Each year, I fly 400,000 miles and I leverage every minute of that travel. I try to cluster many meetings, speaking engagements, and events around each trip. If I'm on the West Coast, I group all my San Francisco, Los Angeles, and San Diego meetings together into a two-day cluster.

6. Use the interstitial time—Each day is filled with gaps between meetings, walking from place to place, and driving. I use this time as much as possible by filling it with hallway conversations, wireless email, and calls from the hands-free Bluetooth microphone in my Prius.

7. Keep focused on the important issues—The tyranny of the urgent creates distractions every day, but I stay focused on our yearly operating plan and five-year plan. When I look at each week's schedule on Sunday night, I make sure that all the important issues are prescheduled into my week.

8. Debrief after every day—At the end of every day, I review my important issues list and review the progress and next steps on each issue. By

doing this, I minimize the number of forgotten follow-ups and dropped balls.

9. Respond to each email each day—I do not know the answer to every question that I'm asked via email, but I respond to each one with a description of the process I've initiated to get an accurate answer. This ensures that every person who emails me knows that I've acknowledged their question, even if an answer may take a few days to determine.

10. Never be the rate-limiting step—In my schedule there is always time to resolve open issues, settle a political conflict, or answer an operational question. I close every day with an empty desk, an empty voice mailbox and an empty email queue. This enables all my staff to be as efficient and productive as possible since they are not waiting for me.

These ten triage rules work most of the time to keep my schedule sane and stakeholders happy. Of course, there are times when travel cannot be clustered or there are more meetings and urgent issues than hours in a day, but on average, my day is well balanced. ∎

My Top Ten Rules for Email Triage

I receive over 1,000 email messages each day (with virtually no spam, so they are all legitimate) and respond to most via my mobile device. How do I triage 1,000 messages? I use these ten rules to mentally score each email:

1. E-mail marked with a "high importance" exclamation point must pass the "cry wolf" test. Is the sender a habitual "high importance" e-mailer? Are these e-mails actually important? If not, the sender's emails lose points.

2. I give points to high-priority people: my senior management, my direct reports, my family members, and my key customers.

3. I do the same for high-priority subjects: critical staff issues, health issues, and major financial issues.

4. I rate email based on the contents of the "To," "cc" and "bcc" fields. If I am the only person in the "To" field, the e-mail gets points. If I am in the "To" field with a dozen other people, it's neutral. If I'm only cc'd, it loses points. A bcc loses a lot of points, since I believe email should always be transparent. E-mail should not be used as a weapon.

5. I penalize email with emotional words, capital letters, or anything less than civil language.

6. I downgrade email messages longer than five screens. Issues that complex require a phone call.

> *I downgrade email messages longer than five screens. Issues that complex require a phone call.*

7. Email responses that say only "Thanks," "OK," or "Have a nice day" are social pleasantries that I appreciate, but move to the bottom of my queue.

8. Email with colorful backgrounds, embedded graphics or mixed font sizes lose points.

9. I separate email into three categories: that which is just informational (an FYI); that which requires a short response; and that which requires a lengthy, thoughtful response. I leave the lengthy responses to the end of the day.

10. More than three emails about a topic requires a phone call or meeting. Trying to resolve complex issues via an endless ping pong of emails is inappropriate.

These ten rules really help me navigate my 1,000 emails each day.

If we actually automated the rules above and senders realized that their email had to be truly relevant to get read, folks might think twice before pressing "send." The less important matters can wait until the next staff meeting. With some enforced discipline, we may be able to learn how to better communicate with one another more effectively and get back to our creative work.

One more truly controversial idea: companies that send bulk email should be forced to pay before an email gateway delivers their mail. How many newsletters have you really "opted in" for? A micropayment fee system will keep companies honest about their opt-in and unsubscribe policies by aligning financial incentives. ■

Status Emailicus

My day is spent running meetings—staff meetings, steering committee meetings, and various kinds of national/regional/local governance bodies.

Over the past year I have noticed a trend in all these meetings. The number of emails that people receive each day exceeds their ability to respond to them, so they develop "status emailicus"—a bit like status epilepticus (persistent seizures) but it involves retrieving a Blackberry, iPhone, or other mobile device from its holster every 15 seconds throughout the meeting.

The end result is continuous partial attention. You'd like to believe that everyone is participating in the discussion, especially if complex issues are being debated. Ideally, when consensus is achieved, everyone leaves the meeting marching to the same tune. However, by multi-tasking in meetings, we see every other frame of the movie. We miss the subtleties of conversation and critical details that may later turn into deal breakers.

> *However, by multi-tasking in meetings, we see every other frame of the movie. We miss the subtleties of conversation and critical details that may later turn into deal breakers.*

How do we solve this problem?

We could throw away our mobile devices, but that ignores their positive aspects. My travel to Washington is possible because I can use my mobile device for command and control of all the projects I'm running, even while in planes, trains, and automobiles.

One option is to reset expectations. Email is not the same as instant messaging. A five-minute response time throughout the day works only if there are no meetings to attend.

Another option is to realize that we all work eight hours a day in meetings/calls and eight hours in email. We could limit meetings to 30 minutes in duration—enough time for efficient discussion, but not too long to result in overwhelming email backlog. Following each 30-minute meeting, we could get a 30-minute recess to act on decisions made and catch up on emails.

I'm trying to reserve 50% of my time to address the issues that arise each day. Maybe that will reduce my need to check email during meetings.

The bottom line is that email overload exists and we can

a. Ignore it and hope it goes away.

b. Continue to let email run our lives and distract our every waking moment.

c. Take control and organize our email responses by reserving a part of each day, outside of meetings, for timely email responses.

I already sense that people are beginning to rethink the way they manage connectedness. Twitter's popularity is decreasing, instant messaging is on the wane, and social networks seem less of an obsession.

I welcome your thoughts—just don't email me. :-). ∎

Wag More, Bark Less

I recently saw a profound bumper sticker: "Wag More, Bark Less."

These are words to live by.

Barking may yield short-term gains, but wagging builds lasting relationships. When leaders bark, it diminishes them.

All my lives—as a parent, husband, and CIO—benefit from wagging.

As a father, there is the formal authority of parenthood. However, I rarely use formal authority and instead create a loving environment based on mutual respect and open communication. It worked with lions in *Born Free* and it works well in our household.

In the office, outbursts of emotion may win the battle, but lose the war. Employees, customers, and bosses rapidly tire of emotional liability. A decade ago, a hospital CEO began swearing during a senior management meeting in an effort to demonstrate authority. Within a year he was gone.

In my blogs over the past year, I've suggested that we're the Greatest Health IT generation, that these are the good old days, and that we're all suffering from stress acceleration. Despite the stress, the lack of sleep, the traffic, the cold, and the economy, we all need to keep our composure.

I recently had a storage issue that could have escalated into a yelling match between my staff and the vendor staff. Instead of barking, I used it as a teachable moment to bring the teams closer together, strengthening the relationship, and enhancing the channels of communication. This effort to wag instead of bark laid a foundation for years of collaboration to come.

As a parent, as a CIO, and as a human, I cannot think of any situation that is made better by barking than wagging.

So next time you're given the choice, remember the outcome of the bark versus the wag. A bark may be satisfying for the short term, but a wag is the sign of leadership, stability, and expertise for the long term. ∎

> *A bark may be satisfying for the short term, but a wag is the sign of leadership, stability, and expertise for the long term.*

The Greatest Good for the Greatest Number

In my career I've had many roles. I've been a consensus builder and a disruptive innovator. Sometimes I'm a leader and sometimes I'm a follower.

No matter what I've done in academia, industry, or government, I've been guided by a few basic principles:

- *The Boston Globe* test (customize to the locale of your choice)—If your actions were published as a front page article, would they seem fair and reasonable to the average reader?

- The Sister Mary Noel test (my second grade teacher at St. James Catholic School)—If you had to explain your actions to Sister Noel, would you pass her sense of right and wrong or be rapped on the knuckles with a ruler?

- The Sunday night phone call with parents test—When you describe your week to your mom, will your actions seem noble?

- The Senate testimony test—When describing your actions to a Senate panel, is there any reason to say, "I have no recollection of those events, Senator."

- The Greatest Good for the Greatest Number test—Will your actions have a lasting impact on your organization, your state, or your country without direct personal benefit? Although it's true that actions on behalf of others can indirectly bring notoriety to you, fame is not the primary motivation for what you do.

Unfortunately, in our modern society many people I encounter seem more interested in their fame, their fortune, and their reputation.

It could be the economy. It could be competition for resources. It could be a biased sample selection.

How many people have you encountered today who put their co-workers, neighbors, and society first?

When the topic of healthcare reform is discussed, the first question is, "What will it mean to my benefits, my costs, and my retirement?" rather than, "What will it mean for the 32 million uninsured, future generations, and our nation's competitiveness?"

We're only on this planet for 80 years. We cannot take anything with us. If happiness can be measured by making a difference during our short tenure, I hope that more people will ask big picture questions focused on the world around us rather than the size of their house, the speed of their car, or the stylishness of their bling.

I'm not suggesting that we have blind faith in authority or that we all embrace socialism as the solution to every policy problem.

I am suggesting that we move beyond a narrow self focus in all that we do. We should evaluate policy with the lens of the greatest good for the greatest number in our communities, states, and country. We need to move past special interest thinking, including our own.

Change is hard and fear of the unknown can be unsettling. I strongly believe that the good guy (or gal) can lead a life in which accounts received exceed the balance due (borrowed from a Janis Ian song).

If we guide our behavior each day based on choices that look good to *The Boston Globe*, Sister Noel, our moms, public scrutiny, and our fellow humans, the world will be a better place. ■

Wisdom from Xena: Warrior Princess

My family is a "nerd herd," a "gaggle of geeks," a "den of dorks." We do not watch television, but we do occasionally watch DVDs of cult series such as Babylon 5, The Prisoner, Doctor Who, The Secret Adventures of Jules Verne, and Xena: Warrior Princess.

Last night, we watched an episode in which Xena (Lucy Lawless) described her secret to winning competitions/battles/confrontations: "Act, do not react."

Today, while speaking to my staff about a few challenging projects, I realized the wisdom of this statement.

When I think about challenging projects with difficult-to-please customers, negative emotions may start to flow. You know what I mean—the emails with subject lines or "From" addresses that you dread reading. The meetings you do not want to attend. The politics that are impossible to successfully navigate.

Reacting to any situation when you've already biased yourself with negative emotions leads to less-than-perfect thinking and communication. All that stimulation of the sympathetic nervous system (fight or flight response) leads to a dry mouth, a racing heart, and scattered thoughts.

Instead, if you think about the endpoint you want to reach—a successful project, a better technology, a completed implementation—and take the actions needed to achieve this result, you'll be thoughtful, calm, and reasoned.

Here's an example. Rolling out EHRs to 1,700 clinicians including all the capabilities and workflow redesign to achieve Meaningful Use is a change management challenge. Along the way, there will be naysayers, raised voices, and criticism. There may even be mean-spirited personal verbal jousting.

We know what actions we need to take—implement a practice every week between now and the end of the year. Follow our proven model office configuration. Build the interfaces and interoperability needed for care coordination, patient engagement, and quality measurement. By keeping our focus on the "act" and not the "react" to the few naysayers, we get closer to our goal every day, without emotion or negativity.

So next time you have a difficult project, difficult people, or difficult politics, think about the wisdom of Xena: "Act, do not react."

You'll feel better and achieve your goals. ■

The Stresses of Modern Life

In recent articles, I've reflected on the way humans treat each other in our modern era, competing for resources, attention, and priority.

In my lifetime, I've seen major changes in the nature and quality of life. A few observations:

- When I was in college, faxes, FedEx, and email did not exist. Fast communication meant a land line phone call.

- The pace of each day was limited by the number of in-person encounters you could have.

- Real estate was relatively inexpensive and houses in places like Marin County and Palo Alto could be found for $150,000.

- Debt was something to avoid.

- When I was growing up, a McDonald's meal cost a dollar and consisted of a small hamburger, 4 ounces of fries, and 8 ounces of Coke with sugar, not high fructose corn syrup. It was under 500 calories.

- Doctors were respected members of the community. Lawsuits were rare.

- There was no expectation that you'd have a car, a VCR, a flat screen TV, and an iPod. You spent what you could afford and accepted the fact that you lived within your means.

- No one had peanut allergies.

- People took responsibility and accountability for their actions. If you chose to bathe with a toaster and died, your family would not sue the toaster manufacturer for making an unsafe product.

- Government was a safety net for truly critical emergencies, not day-to-day life.

I realize that the items above are filtered through the haze of imperfect 40-year-old memories.

However, I really do believe that something has happened in modern society that makes each day distinctly different from my childhood experience in the 1960s.

- Instant communication means that anyone can email the CEO and demand immediate action for their personal projects.

- Someone else is always to blame for everything that goes wrong.

- A baseline quality of life includes much more than in the past and if you cannot afford it, credit cards can provide it for you.

- Stress is a badge of courage.

- Information overload is the accepted norm.

When I was an undergraduate at Stanford, Herb Caen[3] wrote many columns about the changes that took place in the 20th century that reduced the quality of life from his perspective—food, culture, and human interaction.

I hope that at some point, modern society stops and reflects about the nature of our day-to-day lives and realizes that we need to rethink our priorities, for example:

- Replace reality TV with a good book.

- Treat your fellow humans with humility and respect.

- Communication can be asynchronous and you do not need to wander through life with a mobile device in your hand.

- Treat meals as an experience, not as refueling.

- Understand that this is the only life we have and we should savor it, not be stressed by it.

After a recent particularly difficult day, I asked my wife if Ted Kaczynski's[4] Montana cabin was still available. Of course, as I age, access to medical care will be important and cabin life would be a bit challenging, but the concept of wilderness life without an Internet connection is intriguing!

No matter how challenging the stresses of modern life, as long as I remember that for everything there is a process, there will always be a path forward. ∎

Simplifying Life

Here's my thinking on simplifying life:

1.1 Starting out

In my 20s I believed success was measured by the amount of stuff you owned, the size of your house, the style of your car, etc. Luckily, by the age of 25 I realized these were all superficial and began a life-long process of living simply—owning the minimum of clothing, electronics, real estate, etc.

My daughter has embraced these values and at 17 she does not own any designer clothing or trendy "must have" consumer goods. By her own design, her bedroom is a minimalist tatami room with a futon, kotatsu (a low wooden table), and clothes storage.

---

3   Herb Caen (pronounced 'Cane') was a San Francisco journalist and columnist who wrote about daily life, politics, gossip, and his beloved San Francisco. He died in 1997 at the age of 80.

4   Theodore John "Ted" Kaczynski, also known as the "Unabomber," is serving life in prison for sending deadly mail bombs. Previously a math professor at UC Berkeley, in 1971, Kaczynski retreated to a remote cabin without electricity and running water in Lincoln, Montana, until his capture and arrest in 1996.

1.2 Home and family life

When I was in my 20s and had a larger home, I spent all weekend maintaining the home and garden. My belongings owned me; I did not own them. Complexity and quantity bring maintenance burdens, so I did not have free time to just enjoy the world around me and live an examined life.

Today, my only maintenance tasks are keeping indoor plants watered, supporting our seasonal traditions of planting fruits and vegetables, and the basics of keeping a house in good condition.

Our family life is simple. I married the first woman I dated. We have one child. We gather for dinner together every night (wife, daughter, father-in-law, me). We visit the Sierra in August. We spend Columbus Day weekend near Mt. Monadnock. On occasion we travel to Japan together. We do not have nor want a vacation home, a boat, an RV, or yearly events that require a significant planning burden.

My business clothing is all black. My outdoor clothing is red and black. Everything I wear is made by just a few manufacturers: Arcteryx, Vegetarian Shoes, and Injinji. On average, my clothes last five years.

Our foods are all simple vegetables: no meat, no eggs, no dairy. We rarely eat out.

1.3 Finances

We live in a small home without a mortgage. We avoid consumer debt. We save as much as we can.

1.4 Work

In each of my jobs, I have strong direct reports with very little turnover. We all work hard to put governance processes in place that minimize conflict and simplify resource allocation.

I try to minimize travel. 2009–2010 required a day or two per month in Washington to support ARRA/HITECH efforts, but in general I try to avoid airports.

My workday routine is a morning walk with my wife, followed by a BIDMC/Harvard time from 8 am–6 pm, followed by a family dinner, followed by writing in the evening—it's generally very predictable.

1.5 Technology and communications

I own a Blackberry Bold 9700 and a MacBook Air—no other technologies or gadgets to maintain and support.

1.6 Personal health and well being

As a vegan for ten years, I've been able to keep my body mass index at 20. My seasonal activities—hiking, biking, kayaking, skiing, and climbing—keep me exercising outdoors. Avoiding caffeine keeps my mood even.

1.7 Time spent with others

Morning walks with my wife, winter hiking with my friends, and multiple visits to my parents in California ensure I'm always sharing my thoughts, feelings, and fears with others.

Having lived many lifestyles as an adult—from Silicon Valley entrepreneur to winemaker to doctor—I can say that the journey is truly more important than the destination. Living simply along the journey enables you to savor the details of existence along the way.

Of course, I would never criticize anyone for wanting to try a complex, high-burn rate lifestyle. However, once you've experienced all the options, I suspect that you too will decide that less is more. ■

The Year of Living Anxiously

I've written many blog posts about the lack of civility in modern society, the uncertainty in the economy, and the mismatch among scope, resources, and time in organizations facing profitability pressures.

The next year will be a year of living anxiously (a reference to a 1982 Peter Weir film[5]).

As I think about the increased conflict, tension, and uncertainty we face every day, what are the causes?

- Increasing competition from a global economy at a time when the US is losing its leadership role in math/science/engineering.

- Increasing mismatch between the cost of living and wages earned.

- Increasing costs of healthcare as a percentage of the gross domestic product.

- Increasing costs of compliance/regulation/legal fees; we are a very legalistic society and we've created substantial increases in overhead over the past few decades to cover lawsuits/risk mitigation/legal consultation.

- Structural issues with our economy. Robert B. Reich, Secretary of Labor in the Clinton administration, wrote a fascinating article in *The New York Times*, in which he notes, "In the late 1970s, the richest 1 percent of American families took in about 9 percent of the nation's total income; by 2007, the top 1 percent took in 23.5 percent of total income."[6]

---

5 "The Year of Living Dangerously," directed by Peter Weir, was set in Indonesia during the overthrow of President Sukarno.

6 Reich R. How to end the great recession (Op-Ed). *The New York Times.* September 2, 2010.

Instead of creating dozens of entry level jobs, we're paying hedge fund traders to put hot tubs in their Lear jets. There is something very wrong about this.

Believe me, I'm not nostalgic for the simpler times of the 1970s—I'm realistic about the challenges and realities of the 21st century. However, there is a point at which we cannot continue the pace of work, the rate of consumption, and the lifestyle we've come to expect.

While the next year is filled with stimulus fund projects causing people to work harder and faster, while the efforts to accelerate HIT in the US create more change management anxiety, and while people feel increasing tension to compete with each other for budgets, I will endeavor to stay true to my own beliefs:

- The nice guy can finish first.

- Treating people fairly is the right thing to do.

- You can lose the battle and still win the war.

- Expressing negative emotion in leadership or business context diminishes you.

- Joy comes from relationships and experiences, not from owning more stuff.

I never know what tomorrow will bring or how my business and personal life will evolve. By staying calm, honest, and altruistic, I'm convinced good things will happen.

In the next year, try to reduce the anxiety level in your workplace. Let's hope it's contagious! ∎

Forming, Storming, Norming, and Performing

In my Palos Verdes High School AP US History class (1979), I studied the writings of Alexis de Tocqueville, the Frenchman who observed American life and then wrote about Democracy in America. Ask anyone what he said, and you'll hear some variation of "America is a nation of joiners."

In my career as an IT leader, I've convened many groups, governance bodies, and new organizations. As new groups gather, everyone wants to participate to avoid being left out of the new, new thing.

The Forming is easy, but soon after, as issues such as governance, strategy, business/operations, and priorities are discussed, there's Storming.

Everyone wants to ensure their point of view, their authority, and their visibility is preserved. In large, multi-stakeholder organizations, this can be challenging.

Eventually, a stable governance group emerges, priorities are developed by consensus, and relationships are fostered, creating a level of stability—the Norming of the greater good.

Once everything is humming, the group begins Performing, embracing change and achieving its goals.

This Forming, Storming, Norming, and Performing pattern is called Tuckman's Stages of Group Development.[7]

Here's my advice on Tuckman's stages:

When you're forming or joining a new group, expect conflict. Don't fear it and don't fight it. Acknowledge it and work with it. Conflict (the "Storming") can create a sense of urgency among participants to solve problems. Conflict can lead to stronger relationships and catalyze change.

> *When you're forming or joining a new group, expect conflict. Don't fear it and don't fight it. Acknowledge it and work with it. Conflict (the "Storming") can create a sense of urgency among participants to solve problems.*

During the Storming phase, the only thing that can hurt your reputation is a public outburst of emotion. As I've said many times before, for everything there is a process that will resolve today's problems. A year from now, no one will even remember today's problems.

Our job as leaders is to navigate the conflict that comes with Storming, listen to the stakeholders, and steer the group toward Norming. It takes time and energy. It takes patience.

I recently talked to a colleague about a particularly emotional public meeting that had dozens of highly charged stakeholders. My colleague did not remember the nature of the conflict, but did remember that I listened, acknowledged the speakers, and suggested a process to move us forward.

As long as you know to expect conflict whenever you form a group, you can remain unaffected by it.

Put another way—your adversaries win only if you let them get to you.

Go forward and Norm! ∎

Losing the Battle But Winning the War

In a typical year, I'm given hundreds of challenging controversies to resolve. I'm not sure if it's the economy, healthcare reform, or the uncertainties of an election

---

7   Bruce Tuckman, an American psychologist who conducted research in group dynamics, developed these stages which he thought were phases necessary and inevitable for teams to grow.

year, but in general, the modern era has had more emotion, discontent, and chaos than most years.

Whenever I'm asked to play Solomon, I always ask myself: do I want to win the battle or win the war?

I could use formal authority to force a short-term outcome.

I could raise my voice, leverage my reputation, or utilize negative commentary (think political advertising) to win the day.

All such victories are temporary and I would never use such tactics.

Imagine that I forced customers to use a technology solution without gaining their buy in. I'd win the battle. Inevitably, the users would try as hard as they could to make the project fail, blaming all negative consequences on the products I mandated. I'd lose the war.

It is far better to take the long view, devising a solution that stakeholders will embrace as their own and feel motivated to make successful.

The day-to-day battles rarely matter. The trajectory over years is the best measure of success.

Similarly, in the world of technology, if you go live a few months late because you focused on user acceptance, no one will ever remember. If you go live too early to meet an arbitrary deadline, no one will ever forget.

Thus, pick your battles. Ignore most of them. Keep your eye on your long-term vision and work toward it incrementally, focusing on change management and stakeholder alignment.

It's the war, not the battle, that people will remember long after you're gone. ∎

A Glass Half Full

My daughter recently wrote an essay that began, "We cannot see our own eyes. The perception of ourselves comes from the reflections of others—how we're perceived and treated by the world around us."

Later in the essay she laments that the modern world seems to embrace bad news, negativity, and criticism rather than joy, optimism, and gratitude.

I agree with her.

This has been a particularly strange year filled with audits, new compliance requirements, and regulatory review. Negative commentators have been granted more airtime than those trying to make the world a better place. We have become a nation that thrives on sensational news, usually to someone's discredit.

There may come a time when we spend more time defending our work to consultants, regulators, and naysayers than doing it.

I wonder if it is possible to reverse this trend.

Imagine the following: instead of a statement with an accusatory overtone such as, "Forty percent of clinicians in Massachusetts do not have an electronic health record. Clearly the state has challenges."

How about: "Sixty percent of clinicians in the state have an electronic health record, making Massachusetts one of the most wired regions in the country. For the remaining 40%, there is a step-by-step plan to achieve 100% adoption by 2015. Massachusetts is the only state to mandate EHR adoption as a condition of licensure by 2015."

Instead of highlighting a small number of flaws in a person, a team, or an organization, I would rather celebrate their strengths. Then in the context of a positive trajectory, discuss the ways they could be even better.

> Instead of highlighting a small number of flaws in a person, a team, or an organization, I would rather celebrate their strengths. Then in the context of a positive trajectory, discuss the ways they could be even better.

I rarely see this approach. Instead, there is a focus on what is not done, not planned, and not budgeted, sometimes declaring risk without providing a benchmark as to the real current state of the industry.

For example, what if an audit or consulting report declared, "IT has not implemented flying cars."

Senior management or board members might think they should worry about IT management, IT planning, or governance processes.

Of course, no one in the country has implemented flying cars and the first production vehicle is not expected for years.

Business owners facing their own operational challenges might say, "We cannot move forward with our workflow redesign because IT has not deployed the flying cars needed to support our automation needs."

Thus, IT becomes the bottleneck, the area of scrutiny, and point of failure.

Consultants might even be hired to analyze why IT has not implemented flying cars and make recommendations for accelerating the flying car program.

Of course, there are numerous other projects that deserve time, attention, and resources before flying cars are even considered.

So what's needed to make this better?

First, we need to eliminate our default tone of negativity. The quality, safety, and efficiency risks we have today were there last year. Somehow we still delivered appropriate care. They are focusing on the trajectory, making each day better than the last.

I've recently rewritten several reports to take this more positive, optimistic approach. Instead of a gap or failure mode analysis, I created a trajectory analysis and mitigation analysis.

If we persist with a negative approach in the way we interact with others and manage our organizations, our work lives will continue to change for the worse. How so?

A recent *New York Times* column relates the modern world to life in a zombie film in which we spend each day shooting zombie after zombie in a war of attrition until the zombies are all gone or we become one of them. Think of your email, your cell phone, and your meeting schedule as a daily battle against zombies and you'll see the author's point.

As my daughter said, we define ourselves based on the reflections we see from others. If others are negative, we become negative. If others highlight the positive, the good, and the trajectory to become even better, we will do the same.

Thus, each one of us can make a difference. Start tomorrow with a glass half full and soon, those around you will see the world for what it can be instead of what it is not. ∎

500 Meetings a Day

In the early 1980s when I was running a small software company while attending Stanford as an undergraduate, my business activities were limited to the number of phone calls I could receive in a day. At most I could have five to ten teleconferences.

Now, with email and social networking, all of the limits on synchronous group interaction have disappeared and I have limitless meetings per day. When you count the emails I send, the blog comments I respond to, and the Twitter/Forums/Texts/Linked In/Plaxo/Facebook interactions, I can have 500 meetings a day.

What does that really mean?

One of my staff summarized it perfectly when I asked him what keeps him up at night:

"The flow of email and expectation upon us all to respond quickly has become more challenging for me than probably most because of the great diversity of areas that I cover. I've been making changes and removing myself from unnecessary support queues (previously used to monitor day-to-day), delegating as much as possible, and making the needed staffing changes."

The demands of 500 virtual meetings a day on top of the in-person meetings result in what I call "Continuous Partial Attention." A one-hour in-person meeting implies that you're 50 virtual meetings behind by the end of the face-to-face time, forcing attention spans to fade about ten minutes into any in-person meeting. The modern electronic world has removed all barriers to escalation and facilitated scheduling. Anyone can interrupt anything 24x7x365. Instantaneous frictionless communication is analogous to the revolution in the publishing industry in which anyone can be an author/publisher/editor without any triage.

What's the best strategy for dealing with this communication overload? Here's a few I've experienced:

a. Declare an end to the madness and stop doing mobile mail and texting. Some senior executives have taken an inspiration from the Corona beer advertisement and thrown their smartphone into the ether.

b. Put up a firewall around your schedule. One of my staff published an "out of office" message this week. When I asked him about it, he said, "I'm just trying to take some time and my outgoing message is helping to filter out the emergencies from the last-minute stragglers who want something that doesn't really need attention until after the break as I'm trying to finish up the necessary end-of-year items."

c. Accept the chaos and schedule around it, creating an open access schedule that reserves half the workday for the asynchronous, unplanned work of each day.

d. Ignore your emails. Some senior executives just never respond and have inboxes with thousands of unanswered emails.

e. Delegate email management. Some executives delegate email to trusted assistants who separate the wheat from the chaff, escalating only a few emails a day to the executive they support.

At the moment, I still do (c), but I must admit it's getting more challenging. I receive over 1,000 emails a day and try to respond to each one, but for the past six months, I've been deleting every unread email that begins:

"Hi, I'm Bob at xyz.com and our products..."

or

"Hi, I'm a venture capitalist and I'd like an hour of your time to..."

Hopefully, I'm answering my critical asynchronous communications in a timely way and only ignoring those communications which are a lower priority. At 500 email and social networking responses per day, I'm approaching the limits of my bandwidth, which I never thought would happen.

I do my best and clear my queues every night before sleep. If I've somehow missed you in my 500 meetings a day, please let me know! ∎

Business Spam

Our spam filters remove the Nigerian businessmen and Viagra ads from my email stack. However, it's really challenging to auto-delete legitimate business email from major companies that I would just rather not read.

Business spam (BS) is what I call the endless stream of chaff filling my inbox with sales and marketing fluff. If a colleague emails me about a cool new emerging technology, I'm happy. If a trusted business partner gives me a preview of a new product and offers me the opportunity to beta test it, I'm thrilled. If Bob at XYZ.com describes their cloud-based, software as service, offshore, outsourced, app store-compliant product line that's presented in PowerPoint (i.e., does not yet exist except in sales and marketing materials), I press delete as fast as I can.

Since there are multiple domains that can be used to reach me: bidmc.harvard.edu, caregroup.harvard.edu, caregroup.org, etc., many email list sellers vend five or six variations of my email address, resulting in five or six copies of each life-changing offer in my inbox.

Now I know why some say email is dead. Email is a completely democratic medium. Anyone can email anyone. There are no ethical or common sense filters. The result is that business spam will soon outnumber my legitimate email.

Social networking architectures offer an alternative. I'm on Facebook, Twitter, LinkedIn, Plaxo, etc. In those applications, individuals request access to me. Based on their relationships to my already trusted colleagues and my assessment of their character, I either allow or deny access. Once I "friend" them, appropriate communications can flow. If the dialog becomes burdensome or inappropriate, I can "block" them.

In order to stay relevant, email needs to incorporate social networking-like features. It should be easy to block individuals, companies, or domains that I do not want to hear from. Today, when a vendor ignores my pleas to remove me from their email list (demonstrating a lack of compliance with anti-spamming policies), I ask our email system administrator to blacklist their entire domain, preventing the flow of their business spam across the enterprise.

My advice: send your customers a newsletter describing your products and services. Ask them to opt in to receive future messages. If they do not respond, stop sending them.

For those of you who use unsolicited business email as a marketing technique, beware. Your message is not only diluted by the sheer volume of companies generating business spam, but it also creates a negative impression among your recipients.

My advice: send your customers a newsletter describing your products and services. Ask them to opt in to receive future messages. If they do not respond, stop sending them.

It's just a like a Facebook request—you pick your friends and your friends pick you.

The alternative is that all your communications will be deemed business spam and blocked at the front door. Do you really want all your customers to say your emails are BS (business spam)? ∎

Can Social Media Be Harmful to Your Career?

Everything I write is personal, unfiltered, and transparent. Readers of my blog know where I am, what I'm doing, and what I'm thinking. They can share my highs and my lows, my triumphs and defeats.

Recently, I had my blog used against me for the first time.

In discussing a critical IT issue, someone questioned my focus and engagement because I had written a post about single malt scotch on June 2 at 3 am, recounting an experience I had Memorial Day weekend in Scotland.

I explained that I write these posts late at night, in a few minutes, while most people are sleeping. They are not a distraction but are a kind of therapy, enabling me to document the highlights of my day.

I realize that it is overly optimistic to believe that everyone I work with will embrace values like civility, equanimity, and a belief that the nice guy can finish first.

If Facebook can be used against college applicants to screen them for bad behavior and if review of web-based scholarly writing can be used by legislators to block executive appointment confirmations, what's the right way to use social media to minimize personal harm?

There are three possibilities:

1. Ignore the naysayers—blog, tweet, chat, IM, and wiki as you wish!

2. Give up—the world is filled with angry people who can stalk you, harass you, and criticize you. Better to keep your thoughts private.

> *Write what you think, back it up with evidence, and temper your emotions—assume the world will read everything you write and have an opinion, but transparency and communication, as long as they are fair, is the best policy.*

3. Write what you think, back it up with evidence, and temper your emotions—assume the world will read everything you write and have an opinion, but transparency and communication, as long as they are fair, is the best policy.

I've chosen #3.

Why did the person criticize me for blogging about single malt?

I have three ideas:

1. Maybe he or she did not understand that I blog only for a few minutes at the end of my 20-hour day, when all work and family responsibilities are done to the extent I can do them. Hence, my blogging does not detract from anything else I do.

2. Maybe he or she cannot accept that I've done everything I can to serve my customers in the 20-hour day before blogging. In that case, it falls under my leadership principle, "You cannot please everyone."

3. Maybe life is not fair and I should be judged by different criteria than other people. When I was 15, I wrote in my journal, "If you are judged using rules that are inherently unfair or unreasonable, then you should realize that the game cannot be won. Stay true to your values, work hard, and all will be well." No matter what people say or how harshly they criticize me, even when their ideas are not factual, I will stay true to my values—not pursuing fame or fortune, but simply trying to make a difference.

So the answer to the question is yes, blogging can hurt your career. However, if you take the high road, you'll always get to where you want to be. ■

Decision Fatigue

We're all suffering from information overload. More projects with fewer staff on shorter timeframes mean more email, texts, blogs, online meetings, and phone calls.

We make more decisions and have more accountability than ever before. Regulatory complexity and the need for risk management have increased. We're pressured to make decisions faster and there is less tolerance for mistakes. Making all those decisions in a high-stakes environment like healthcare leads to decision fatigue, that numbness you feel at the end of an overloaded day when you decided what to spend, whom to hire, and what to do, hundreds of times.

I believe decision fatigue is an escalating threat to our ability to manage the events of each day and keep balance in our lives.

When I think back on my early career as a leader in the 1980s, there was no email, no overnight shipping, and limited numbers of fax machines.

Issues were escalated by writing and mailing a letter. The time it took to compose, type, mail, and deliver a letter meant that many problems solved themselves. Since the effort to escalate was significant, many problems were never escalated.

Today, everyone can escalate everything to anyone. The barrier to communicating is nearly zero and communication is real time. There is no mail room or team of middle management filters between you and the CEO.

This creates an interesting conundrum for leaders. Should everything be answered in a very timely way with Solomon-like decisions about every issue? Should everything be ignored unless truly emergent with the hope that someone else will solve the problem? Should everything be deflected to those in middle management who would have read paper-based mail?

My goal is to never be the rate-limiting step. That means that I make hundreds of decisions every day. Some are right and some are wrong, but they are the best answers given the information that I have. In the IT industry, timely action that is good enough is often more important than a delayed perfect action.

Thus, at the end of every day my brain is whirring with thousands of inputs, and hundreds of decisions made. I'm not physically tired after any workday, but I can feel mentally tired from decision fatigue.

The problem with decision fatigue is that the quality of decisions can diminish as the quantity of issues increases.

There are two ways to address decision fatigue:

1. Reduce the scope of your authority and hence the decisions you need to make and the risks you need to manage.

2. Spread decisions over a wider group of people, reducing the volume of decisions that fall to any one person.

#2 depends upon having a great boss who is supportive, responsive, and willing to share decision-making risk with you. #2 also requires a great staff whom you can empower to make decisions on their own.

Thus, I make the decisions that I am uniquely qualified to make, while pushing others up and down the organizational hierarchy so that risk is mitigated (seeking approval up the org chart) and trusted staff are given the resources and authority to solve problems on their own (delegating down the org chart).

Here's an example of how I managed decision fatigue today. Between 3 pm and 4 pm, I was asked to make several decisions:

1. The regional poison control center sought my input on a mushroom ingestion case. A one-year-old had taken a large bite from a mushroom growing in a backyard. Since I uniquely have mushroom toxicology knowledge, this was my decision. The mushroom was a harmless Lactarius Fragilis and I decided that the child would be fine.

2. A leak in the Longwood Medical Area chilled water supply caused a five-degree rise in our disaster recovery data center. What should we do? I ensured that all appropriate facilities and IT people were organized to address the problem, and asked to be informed if the

temperature exceeded 90°F. The incident management decision making was delegated to others.

3. A researcher in one of the Harvard buildings suspected that the network had been hacked because www.ups.com was unavailable. Should I page security and networking staff to urgently investigate this on a holiday weekend? I used my Blackberry to replicate the problem and escalated it to IT security, who found the problem was unrelated to our network/DNS servers. The incident management decision making was delegated to others.

In the next few months, I'll be finishing the Operating Plan for BIDMC IS, so there will be plenty of decision making to spread among governance committees and executive management.

One other cure for decision fatigue that I recommend is a "time out." On my way home in the evening, I stop at our community garden space to sit on the small bench we've placed there, eat a few cherry tomatoes wrapped in basil, and watch the birds peck at our sunflowers. I leave my Blackberry in the car. By the time I get home, the decision fatigue of the day has passed, so when my wife and I discuss dinner choices, I'm ready to act boldly. ■

My Non-Linear Workstream

In the era before smartphones, texting, social networks, and blogs, I had a predictable day.

I could look at my week and count the meetings, lectures, phone calls, writing, and commuting I had to do.

Although my schedule was busy, I could schedule exercise time, family time, and creative time.

Today, I would not describe my work day as linear or predictable. I do as much as I can, attending to every detail I remember, and hope that by the end of the week the trajectory is positive and the urgent issues are resolved.

Here's what I mean.

Since there are no barriers to communication, everyone can communicate with everyone. Every issue is escalated instantly. Processes for decision making no longer involve thoughtful steps that enabled many problems to resolve themselves. We're working faster, but not necessarily working smarter. We're doing a greater quantity of work but not necessarily a higher quality of work.

Everyone has a mobile device and their thoughts of the moment can be translated into a message or phone call, creating a work stream of what amounts to hundreds of "mini-meetings" every day.

As issues are raised over the wire, the follow on cc's result in a volley of messages, thoughts, and more "mini-meetings."

The linear part of our work streams—face-to-face meetings, presentations, and travel—interrupt the non-linear work streams running through our digital lives. Watch how many people use their mobile devices while in meetings and lectures. Watch how many people need their Blackberry pried from their hands by flight attendants as planes are taking off. Each day has turned into two work days—the linear one which is scheduled and the non-linear 24-hour flow through our devices and social networking applications.

Each day has turned into two work days—the linear one which is scheduled and the non-linear 24-hour flow through our devices and social networking applications.

I do my best to resolve every issue and declare closure on the events of each day. However, I find myself waking up from my few hours of sleep with a full queue of tasks because our non-linear work stream is no longer bounded by a work day.

What are the solutions to the overload we are all currently experiencing?

1. We could eliminate the concept of one-hour meetings, one-hour lectures, and airline travel, realizing that much of what we need to do can be accomplished in tweets, emails, instant messages, and calls. The non-linear work stream becomes our work and we stop trying to schedule a linear workday in the middle of it.

2. Alternatively, we can realize that the non-linear work stream is ultimately unsustainable, tossing our mobile devices as in the Corona beer commercial.

3. We could begin to reduce the non-linear work stream by de-enrolling from Twitter, Facebook, Google+, LinkedIn, Plaxo, and instant messaging. We could maintain just a single email account and triage it well.

I'm not sure which answer is right, but I do believe that the conflict between our linear and non-linear work streams has reached the point at which we all have "continuous partial attention," and are unable to focus more than a few minutes on any one linear task.

I write my blogs in the middle of the night because that is the only moment when the non-linear work stream dips to a point that I can capture my thoughts in a single burst of uninterrupted writing.

It's clear to me that our work lives and styles are evolving. Might there be a day when "work" is plugging into a network and managing the stream of communication, decisions, and ideas for nine hours a day, then unplugging and turning the stream over to the next person on shift? Sounds very Metropolis, but I'm not sure any of us can return to the linear work streams of the past. ∎

Where Have All Our Heroes Gone?

Does it seem to you that we've lost our sense of wonder and our respect for heroes?

The press is filled with stories of flawed or fallen heroes, but little praise for the tireless work done every day to make the world a better place.

In the Northeast, two million people lost power due to an act of God—an early winter storm. One week later, a few thousand were still without power. Local politicians demanded answers from power companies to explain why it took so long and why their planning for the unexpected storm was so poor. As an infrastructure provider myself, I can tell you that utility workers have done a heroic job—deciding what work would restore power most quickly based on a Pareto analysis, doing the main/trunk/substation work rapidly, and leaving the most remote parts of the grid for last. It's been 24x7, cold, wet, and physically demanding work. They've done their best and I respect the people who did the work.

Steve Jobs, a remarkable person, was brilliant and charismatic, but could be overly demanding, emotional, and less than perfect with his family and personal relationships. His death was met with initial shock and an outpouring of respect. After a week, the press turned to the dark side of Steve's personality. The sainthood of Steve Jobs was very short.

I'm an eternal optimist and believe that mankind is basically good. However, I cannot help but believe that society has lost its perspective when we spend time tearing down our heroes, highlighting their mistakes, and reveling in Schadenfreude[8] when someone falls from grace.

Everything regresses to the mean, but wouldn't it be best to capture people at their peak of creativity and remember them for what they did right? Of course, we can learn from their mistakes and failures, but we do not need to perseverate on their nadirs when their zeniths are where they had the most impact.

As someone who lives in operational roles 24x7x365, I can say that it is very hard to achieve and maintain perfection. I've written that I do not have power or authority—what I really have is risk of failure.

I would rather celebrate success, learn from failure, and acknowledge those human beings who have made a difference.

---

8 Schadenfreude is a feeling of enjoyment that comes from seeing or hearing about the troubles of other people.

The héroes in my life are my wife, my daughter, my parents, economist Milton Friedman, Steve Jobs, former HIT National Coordinator David Blumenthal, former Harvard Medical School Dean Joseph Martin, my second in command at BIDMC, John Powers, CEO of the Massachusetts eHealth Collaborative Micky Tripathi, and the current head of CMS, Don Berwick. I'm sure each has had moments of incredible success and events they would rather forget. They have all been inspirational to me.

So for one day, let's celebrate our heroes, flaws and all. Let's ban all news about Lindsey Lohan and Kim Kardashian.

If we try hard enough, maybe our sense of wonder and magic will return. ∎

Work-Induced Attention Deficit Disorder

When you're in meetings or on phone calls, are you focused in the moment or are you distracted by emails, text messages, or social networking traffic?

When you're reading a 20-page whitepaper, RFP, or article, can you finish it?

When you're writing a presentation or article, can you keep your thoughts flowing or are they interrupted by the urge to check your email or mobile device?

Part of the problem is the expectation that we're all connected 24x7 and should respond in near real time.

Part of the problem is an addiction-like behavior caused by a need to feel connected to other people.

Part of the problem is the pace of change that makes us work two days for every workday—one with scheduled meetings and one with unscheduled electronic messaging.

Do you find that your ability to explore issues in depth has diminished over time because of the need to react to the constant flow of input?

When I write, I close my email client and put away my mobile devices. I often do this between 2 am-4 am when the tide of incoming messages is low.

I collect my thoughts and write in a single stream, weaving together ideas from my previous compositions when possible. I have been able to keep my 1,000+ posts integrated in my mind by writing in the early morning darkness.

However, my reading has suffered. When I was younger, I could sit in my old Morris chair underneath a Pendleton blanket and finish a book cover to cover. Today, my reading is more web-like: I cover a topic and then jump to a different topic until I've rapidly covered the important messages from a book instead of reading it at a relaxed pace cover to cover.

The nature of our work has induced a kind of attention deficit disorder.

To explore this idea further, I looked at my calendar for this week. Across my jobs and volunteer efforts, there are a few dozen critical projects with due dates in January. Ideally, my schedule should block out time to focus indepth on each of these major efforts.

Instead, my calendar demonstrates that I've delegated the "depth" to others in order to achieve a "breadth" of oversight which includes only a few minutes per critical project per day. The rest of the time is spent on urgent problem solving, unplanned work, and reducing the tension of change caused by the modern pace of activity, which is challenging for many people to process.

My blog posts taken collectively often paint themes. I'm hoping that I can restore depth, reduce breath, and begin to reform my brain into the linear path of an expert instead of the hyperlinked random walk of a dilettante.

In a world when a five-minute YouTube video is too long for the average audience and a 140-character message has replaced a thoughtful paragraph, we all need to ask if living each day with continuous partial attention is an improvement.

I, for one, am willing to say that our modern work style is an emperor with no clothes, and we need to recapture our focus in order to solve the complex problems ahead. ■

Only Handle It Once

In my previous post on Work-Induced Attention Deficit Disorder, several commenters asked how I stay focused and productive, speculating that I leverage my limited need for sleep.

Although having a 20-hour day helps, the real secret is that I end each day with an empty inbox. I have no paper in my office. I do not keep files other than those that are required for compliance purposes.

The end result is that for every document I'm asked to read, every report I'm ask to write, and every situation I'm asked to manage, I only handle the materials once.

What does this mean?

In a typical week, I'm asked to review four or five articles for journals. Rather than leaving them to be read at some later time or reading them, then deferring the review, I read and review them the day they are assigned. This enables me to read them once and write the review very efficiently, since all the facts are fresh in my mind.

I'm asked to review budgets for various grants, state, and local projects multiple times per week. I read the budget, ask questions while the numbers are at my fingertips, and await responses.

In my 1,000+ emails each day there are 10 to 20 that require detailed responses. I leave these to the end of the day when I know I'll have uninterrupted time. I write the responses and send them while all the details of the issues are clear to me.

Paperwork does occasionally find its way to my desk. Since all payroll and all purchasing functions are electronic at BIDMC, the paperwork I have to do is mostly for external regulatory agencies. I read the paperwork, answer everything, and give it to my assistant to package and mail.

Each day I'm asked to find time for calls, meetings, lectures, travel, and special events. I look at my calendar in real time and respond with availability—making a decision on the spot if I can or cannot participate.

The end result of this approach is that I truly handle each issue, document, or phone call only once. It's processed and it's done without delay or a growing inbox. I work hard not to be the rate-limiting step to any process.

Yes, it can be difficult to juggle the "Only Handle It Once" (OHIO) approach during a day packed with meetings. Given that unplanned work and the management of email has become 50% of our jobs, I try to structure my day with no more than five hours of planned meetings, leaving the rest of the time to bring closure to the issues discussed in the meetings and complete the other work that arrives. It's the administrative equivalent of open access clinical scheduling.

It's tempting, especially after a long and emotionally tiring day, to break the OHIO principle. However, doing so only removes time from the next day and makes it even more challenging to process the incoming flow of events.

One last caveat: OHIO does not mean compromising quality or thoughtfulness. Simply passing along issues to others without careful consideration does not increase efficiency. I focus on doing it once to the best of my ability. For larger projects, I use my "handle it once" approach to set aside a defined time on the weekend when I can do them in one sitting.

OHIO: give it a try and see if the free time it creates enables you to regain depth and counter the evils of work-induced attention deficit disorder. ∎

The Magic of Doing One Thing at a Time

I've previously written about multitasking and work-induced attention deficit disorder.

I've also written about the burden of having two workdays every 24 hours: one for meetings and one for email

Yesterday, I received a post from the *Harvard Business Review*[9] that summarizes these issues very well.

It highlights the problem and a series of solutions.

---

9   Schwartz T. The magic of doing one thing at a time. HBR Blog Network, March 14, 2012.

Nearly half of employees report the overwhelming stress and burden of their current jobs, not based on the hours they work, but the volume of multitasking— too many simultaneous inputs in too little time. They've lost the sense of a beginning, middle, and end to their day, their tasks, and their projects. There is no work/life boundary.

As a case in point, I'm writing now while doing email and listening to a Harvard School of Public Health eHealth symposium. Am I being more productive or just doing a greater quantity of work with less quality?

The author of the post points to evidence that multitasking increases the time to finish a task by 25%. He also notes that our energy reserves are depleted by a constant state of post-traumatic stress induced by our continuous connectivity.

He suggests three strategies:

1. Rather than multitask, reduce meeting times to 45 minutes, leaving 15 minutes for email catchup and transition.

2. Do not expect and do not support the notion that email should be a real-time activity.

3. Take breaks and ensure there are boundaries between work and non-work activities.

He suggests three personal best practices:

1. Do your most important task of the day without interruption first thing in the morning. That's what I've done for years.

2. Create specific dedicated time for long term, creative thinking.

3. Take vacations.

A great HBR post. Unless all of us declare that the multitasking emperor has no clothes, continuous partial attention will only get worse. ∎

The Importance of Giving Your Time

I've written about servant leadership and the special gift of sharing time with others. (It's hard to believe that my father and I enjoyed that day meandering the mountains of Northern California just five years ago).

My wife recently emailed me a *New York Times Magazine* article entitled, "Is Giving the Secret to Getting Ahead?" It really resonated with me.

Every day I receive numerous requests from students, colleagues, and community collaborators for meetings, phone calls, and speaking events.

Just as the *New York Times* article suggests, I do not see these requests for my time as a distraction that gets in the way of my job. I see serving the healthcare IT community and the stakeholders throughout the world as my job.

It can be fatiguing to serve so many people in so many contexts, but time spent sharing a vision or helping break down a barrier makes a great difference to everyone involved. The power of ideas communicated with clarity and enthusiasm may have a disproportionately positive effect when the perfect storm for innovation occurs due to an alignment of people, processes, and possibilities.

I try every day to help and serve those around me, without an expectation that my energy and time will have a specific payback.

However, enough odd coincidences happen to me that I know my time is having an impact. Last week I was having breakfast at the Cambridge Hyatt with a few Canadian healthcare executives and a person I have never met approached our table and said, "Thank you for writing about Unity Farm and my condolences on the death of your father."

When random strangers are affected by the things you do, the thoughts you think, or the words you write, you know that your time is well spent.

My advice: when a young person asks for mentoring, a colleague asks for career advice, or a community contact asks you to speak to a group of concerned stakeholders, say "yes." Giving your time is your best opportunity to make the world a better place. ∎

> *When a young person asks for mentoring, a colleague asks for career advice, or a community contact asks you to speak to a group of concerned stakeholders, say "yes." Giving your time is your best opportunity to make the world a better place.*

What Matters

I've been at Beth Israel Deaconess Medical Center for nearly 20 years. I'm sometimes asked why BIDMC has been and will continue to be my long-term career home.

The answer is simple: it's a foundation for what matters.

1. Colleagues matter—Loyalty to my staff is the number one reason I stay at BIDMC. Together we've shared the network outage of 2002, security challenges, first in the country Meaningful Use attestation, hundreds of innovative application go lives, and the creation of a world-class cloud computing infrastructure. The average tenure of IS people at BIDMC is 17 years. Many have been here over 30 years. Turnover is never more than 10% per year across all IS divisions.

2. Mentoring matters—The real-world experience of operating large-scale applications and infrastructure at BIDMC enables me to share lessons learned with students and professionals all over the world.

Whether I'm doing a Harvard Business School case study, helping a government in Asia, or empowering young investigators by connecting them to collaborators, it is my experience at BIDMC building and buying technology that gives me a broad base of successes and failures to share.

3. Patients and providers matter—Creating technology for technology's sake is not as impactful as using technologies to achieve policy goals. BIDMC is a learning laboratory with 250,000 active patients, 3,000 doctors, and 2 million patient records. Every day we can iteratively improve quality, safety, and efficiency by listening to our stakeholders and testing new technologies in production environments.

4. Innovation matters—BIDMC has a unique blend of built and bought technologies that enable us to control our own destiny. If a new Meaningful Use idea needs to be piloted, a new technology investigated, or a new workflow trialed, we can move with agility, often without dependency on vendors. When a vendor wants to accelerate innovation by testing new technologies, we can be a development partner. Many commercial infrastructure and application products had their start at BIDMC.

5. Culture matters—For 30 years, BIDMC has been impatient with the status quo. The complaints we hear from our stakeholders often relate to problems that other organizations have not yet thought about. There is never time to rest on our laurels. At times it seems that memories of our successes fade fast, but the culture of impatience ensures we get rapid adoption of whatever new features we introduce.

While on the plane returning from Osaka, I spoke with a gentleman who has worked in many companies throughout his career. At this point he's decided that he needs a company of the right size, right leadership, and right structure to empower problem solving—he has no tolerance for people and organizations that impede progress. For me, BIDMC has all the characteristics which are foundational to a satisfying career.

As I reflect on my time in Japan, my most influential moments were those I spent teaching, talking with colleagues, listening to others' experiences, connecting people for collaboration, and sharing meals. BIDMC provides to me a base of operations that enables these international experiences, national committee membership, and regional cross-institutional cooperation.

Life is complex, budgets are limited, and people are diverse. Our careers will have their frustrations when there is competition for resources, ever-increasing regulatory pressure, and accelerating change. However, if you have great colleagues, remarkable students, a learning lab, a capacity to innovate, and a supportive culture, you have all the ingredients you need for a career home where you can make a difference. That's what matters. ∎

Chapter 6

Innovation

Over the weekend, while working in the orchard, I found a small garter snake trying to eat an enormous toad.

Did the toad not realize that by wriggling its feet, it could easily escape? Was the toad unaware of the impending threat? Might the toad have given up and thought that the end was inevitable?

Did the snake not realize that the toad was much larger than it could possibly digest? Garter snakes have special jaw hinges that allow them to swallow things wider than their bodies. Was the snake so optimistic about the benefits of an enormous meal that it was willing to discount the risks it faced in the swallowing process? Might the garter snake have seized the opportunity because the conditions were right for eating the toad slowly over time?

As is often the case, I tried to find deeper meaning in this encounter with survival of the fittest. On a daily basis, I examine my life, asking who I am, where I've been, and where I'm going.

In my early years as CIO, I did not know the risks I faced, what I had to lose, and whom I might upset along the way. I was the garter snake. Out of this period came new advances in interoperability, patient portals, and clinical applications. Everything was developed in a disruptive rapid-cycle improvement fashion.

Today, might I have become the toad?

Have I become too risk adverse in a world of enhanced regulatory enforcement? Have I evolved from the innovative rogue to the keeper of the status quo? Have I become too attached to the customer relationships I've formed, the incumbent vendors I've chosen, and the strategy I have shepherded for 15 years?

In analyzing my behavior, I do not believe I've become the toad quite yet, but I am very sensitive to the warning signs.

In 1996, when I was faced with impossible tasks for which there was no technology, no standards, and no policy, the answer was simple—create them and if they failed, try again.

In 2013, with auditors reviewing my every project, government agencies scrutinizing my process maturity, and boards wanting to minimize risk, how can we reduce the barriers to innovation?

I do not have a complete answer, but I have an idea.

I would like to begin raising funds from inspired philanthropists, grateful BIDMC patients, and partner companies to create what I'll metaphorically call the "New Organization for Transformative Outside-the-Box Application Development" (NO TOAD).

Of course, we'll continue innovating in all my operational BIDMC IT groups, but somehow NO TOAD has to be constructed and chartered to do work unconstrained by convention, risk adversity, or anxiety about the things that create overhead in 2013 and did not exist in 1996 such as the following:

- Project management offices

- Application development methodology

- Communication and milestone reporting

- Operational oversight during workflow design and development

- Business readiness

- Policies, procedures, and guidelines documentation

- Training and education plans

- Cutover planning

- Functional/performance testing approach

- End-to-end and user-acceptance testing

- System support plans

- Infrastructure and controls

- General and organizational controls

- Physical and logical controls

- Program change controls

- Disaster recovery and business continuity plans

Is this possible? I think so.

We'd create a large de-identified data set that could be openly used by developers without fear of violating HIPAA.

We'd isolate devices from the hospital network to enable freedom and experimentation with technology not allowed in a high-security production environment.

Prototyped code would be reimplemented into production software using formal approaches only after it had proven its value.

By design (a separate LLC?), NO TOAD would be considered outside the scope of healthcare audit and regulatory burdens.

Projects would be audacious, aggressive, and agile. Many would be expected to fail. The culture would be high risk, high reward, without concern for the limitations of current healthcare policies or technologies.

Lessons from Bell Labs, Steve Jobs' reality distortion field, and Google's 20% freethinking policy[1] would guide the selection of ideas to pursue.

Over the past few months I've joined a number of BIDMC philanthropy activities, building awareness of the unique culture that is BIDMC and the amazing, talented people who work there.

My challenge is now to incubate a true learning laboratory for BIDMC that can enable garter snakes who are not intimidated by the impossible tasks ahead. Think of it as healthcare IT unchained.

If it works, I'll happily tell people that the entire idea was inspired by a concern that we've become prisoners of risk avoidance and a toad that decided the status quo was unchangeable.

NO TOAD: an idea whose time has come.

The posts in this chapter chronicle all my thoughts about innovation. ∎

The Innovator's Challenge

I've written many blog posts about our efforts along the path to ICD-10 that will enhance our inpatient clinical documentation. We're hard at work planning the improvements we think are foundational to support care coordination, compliance, and quality measurement goals.

It's very challenging to create tools which simultaneously enable rapid, accurate, and complete clinical documentation. We've deferred radical redesign of inpatient documentation for several years awaiting the alignment of technology, policy, and urgency to create the perfect storm for innovation.

BIDMC has had many firsts—early personal health record adoption, first in the country attestation for Meaningful Use, innovation in the use of web-based

---

1 Google allowed its employees to use up to 20% of their work week to pursue special projects. For every work week, employees could take a full day to work on a project unrelated to their normal workload. Google claimed that many of their products in Google Labs started out as pet projects in the 20% program.

provider order entry, rapid adoption of iPads, and one of the first vendor-neutral image archives.

Sometimes we're a leader and sometimes we're a follower. Deciding which to be is the innovator's challenge.

BIDMC decided to ignore the entire client/server era in the mid-1990s. As others were creating Visual Basic, Filemaker Pro, Delphi, and Access front ends to applications, we continued the use of roll-and-scroll terminal emulators. When the web appeared, we jumped in with both feet and moved all our clinician-facing applications to thin-client, cloud-hosted, web-service architectures in 1998. That approach has served us well. It still feels modern.

Recently we completed the implementation of a next-generation electronic medical administration record (EMAR) using iPhones, iPads, and an Amazon-like shopping cart motif for choosing medications. In the past, other organizations were first with EMAR designs, but they had to use computers on wheels and cumbersome user interfaces because the technology was not quite ready for a more streamlined approach.

We feel the same way about clinical documentation. Offering clinicians an enhanced word processor does not result in orderly, complete, and readable documentation. On the other hand, forcing structured input of every clinical observation may yield high-quality data, but usability will be poor. We're working with four different companies to create next-generation documentation tools that we think will benefit inpatient documentation the same way that waiting for the iPhone/iPad benefited EMAR.

Characteristics of this new approach include the following:

- Natural language processing—The ability to prospectively or retrospectively identify key concepts in unstructured text

- Clinical documentation improvement—The ability to pop up templates just in time that offer structured input in the middle of unstructured text (e.g., laterally and specific bone names for fractures)

- Vocabulary crosswalks—Linkage between problem lists, documentation, and billing diagnoses based on mapping SNOMED-CT to ICD-9, ICD-10, and CPT

- Metadata markup—Near real-time SNOMED-CT markup of unstructured data so that structured clinical concepts are embedded within typed or dictated documents

- Computer-assisted coding—Suggesting ICD-10 codes to clinicians or coders based on the markup in current notes combined with structured data extracted from past notes

- Also, we've considered social documentation (group authoring) and patient-generated data.

As with many IT innovations, our stakeholders will feel that we lag existing commercial products while we're in the midst of developing these new ideas. However, once we go live with the finished product, incorporating cutting edge built and bought technologies, no one will remember the days of the hybrid medical record that today includes many electronic features but paper-based progress notes.

Although the paperless hospital is about as realistic as the paperless bathroom, we will substantially reduce paper on our inpatient units in the next 18 months. As a CIO, I look forward to the day when we've closed the last gap in our self-built systems compared to commercial EHRs so that our users can revel in the innovation rather than describing the greener grass available elsewhere. Luckily, we're as good as our latest go live and we're confident now is the time to implement advanced approaches to clinical documentation. Tolerating impatience until technology, policy, and urgency align is what makes an innovator successful. ■

Decision Support Service Providers

I've recently written about decision support and speculated on the ways we can transform data to information to knowledge to wisdom.

Over the past few weeks, I've seen a convergence of emerging ideas that suggests a new path forward for decision support. Application service providers offer remotely-hosted, high-value SaaS applications at low cost. I believe we need decision support service providers (DSSP), offering remotely-hosted, low-cost knowledge services to support the increasing need for evidence-based clinical decision making.

BIDMC has traditionally bought and built its applications. Our decision support strategy will also be a combination of building and buying. However, it's important to note that creating and maintaining your own decision support rules requires significant staff resources, governance, accountability, and consistency. Our Pharmacy and Therapeutics Committee recently examined all the issues involved in maintaining our own decision support rules, and you'll see that it's an extensive amount of work. We use First Data Bank as a foundation for medication safety rules. We use Safe-Med[2] to provide radiology ordering guidelines based on American College of Radiology rules. Our internal committees and pharmacy create and maintain guidelines, protocols, dosing limits, and various alerts/reminders. We have two full-time RNs just to maintain our chemotherapy protocols.

Many hospitals and academic institutions do not have the resources to create and maintain their own best practice protocols, guidelines, and order sets. The

---

2   Safe-Med later changed its name to AnvitaHealth and was acquired by Humana.

amount of new evidence produced every year exceeds the capacity of any single committee or physician to review it. The only way to keep knowledge up to date is to divide the maintenance cost and effort among many institutions.

A number of firms have assembled teams of clinicians and informatics experts to offer these kinds of knowledge resources. UpToDate maintains world-class clinical information with thousands of authors reviewing literature and providing quarterly revisions. Safe-Med has a large team of experts codifying decision support rules and building the vocabulary tools needed to make them work with real-world clinical data. MedVentive provides the business intelligence tools needed to create physician report cards and achieve pay-for-performance incentives.

However, none of these firms can plug directly into an EHR in a way that offers clinicians just-in-time decision support.

Here's a strawman for the way a DSSP should work:

1. A hospital or clinic selects one or many DSSPs based on clinician workflow needs, compliance requirements, and quality goals.

2. EHR software connects to DSSPs via a web services architecture, including appropriate security to protect any patient-specific information transferred to remote decision support engines. For example, an EHR might transfer a clinical summary such as the continuity of care document to a DSSP along with a clinical question to be answered.

3. A clinician begins to order a therapy or diagnostic test. The patient's insurance eligibility and formulary are checked via a web service. The patient's latest problem list, labs, and genetic markers are compared to best practices in the literature for treating his or her specific condition. A web service returns a rank-ordered list of desirable therapies or diagnostics, based on evidence, and provides alerts, reminders, or monographs personalized for the patient.

4. Clinicians complete their orders, complying with clinical guidelines, pay-for-performance incentives and best practices.

5. The decision support feedback is real time and prospective, not retrospective. Physicians get continuing medical education (CME) credit from learning new approaches to diagnosis and treatment.

In order to do this, EHR vendors must work with DSSPs to implement the uniform architecture and interoperability standards needed to integrate decision support into EHR workflow. I would be happy to host a Harvard-sponsored conference with all the stakeholder companies to kick off this work.

Of course, some may worry about the liability issues involved in using a DSSP. What if clinicians comply with flawed guidelines or fail to comply with suggested therapies and bad outcomes occur?

Based on my review of the literature, I believe decision support liability is a new area without significant case law. The good news is that there are no substantive judgments against clinicians for failing to adhere to a clinical decision support alert. As a licensed professional, the treating clinician is ultimately responsible for the final decision, regardless of the recommendations of a textbook, journal, or DSSP. However, as clinical decision support matures and becomes more powerful and relevant, I believe that there could be greater liability for not using such tools to prevent harm.

This blog entry is a call to action for EHR vendors and emerging DSSP firms. It's time to align our efforts and integrate decision support into electronic health records. Working together is the only affordable way for the country to rapidly implement and maintain high-quality decision support. ∎

Designing the Ideal Electronic Record

I recently keynoted a Department of Veterans Affairs (VA) meeting via teleconference (part of my effort to reduce travel, improve my carbon footprint, and be increasingly virtual) on the topic of designing the ideal EHR.

A simple question was posed to me: If I had infinite resources, infinite time, and no legacy compatibility issues, how would I design the EHR of the future?

Here's my answer:

General

The web is the way. Given the 24x7 nature of healthcare, the need for physicians to be in many physical locations, and the multitude of clinician-computing devices, the ideal EHR should be web-based, browser-neutral, and run flawlessly on every operating system. I highly recommend the use of AJAX techniques to give physicians a more real-time interactive experience. Client/server may have some user interface advantages, but it's just too challenging to install thick clients on every clinician-computing device. Citrix is an expensive and sometimes slow remote access solution. Native web works.

Data in medicine is stored hierarchically (i.e., a patient has multiple visits with multiple labs, with multiple results). This is a tree of data with the patient as the root and the lab values as the leaves. Using a hierarchical database such as InterSystems' Cache ensures that data for clinical care is stored in this tree format and thus can be very rapidly retrieved, ensuring fast response times for clinician users. For population health, clinical research, and performance reporting, relational databases work very well. Thus, I recommend a hierarchical database for the clinical care applications and relational data marts for the research applications.

The ideal EHR should incorporate decision support in laboratory, medication, and radiology ordering. EHRs should include "event-driven medicine" alerts about critical clinical issues and patient-specific reminders about preventative/wellness care. Event-driven medicine is the transformation of data into information, knowledge, and wisdom based on decision support, business rules, and timely notification of clinicians.

> *The ideal EHR should incorporate decision support in laboratory, medication, and radiology ordering. EHRs should include "event-driven medicine" alerts about critical clinical issues and patient-specific reminders about preventative/ wellness care.*

The EHR should include an easy-to-read clinical summary of all active patient problems, medications, visits, and labs and should be able to export this summary to personal health records such as Google Health, Microsoft HealthVault, and Dossia.

Problem Lists

Problems should be entered via an electronic pick list of vocabulary-controlled terms using SNOMED CT. The community of caregivers—PCPs, specialists, ED physicians and hospitalists—should be able to maintain this problem list collectively, using social networking type tools. Call this "Wikipedia for the patient." All caregivers should be able to associate notes and medications with entries on the problem list, making it easy to filter notes by problem and discontinue medications that are problem-specific when problems are resolved.

Medications

Medication management features should include e-prescribing for new medications, automatically linked to payer-specific formularies, electronic real-time pre-authorization/eligibility for high-cost therapies, links to lifetime medication history from retail pharmacy and payer databases, and safety checking for drug/drug and drug/allergy interactions. Pharmacy-initiated renewal workflow would reduce calls to the physician's office to refill medications.

Ideally, medication reconciliation features should include prepopulation of the medication list based on the lifetime medication history from retail pharmacy, payer databases, and personal health record applications. Using the same social networking type approach as mentioned with problem lists, all caregivers should be able to update/change/edit/comment on patient medications to keep them current. One click quick picks of commonly used medications should be available to make ordering Tylenol as easy as ordering books on Amazon.

Allergies

Allergies should be recorded by caregivers using vocabulary-controlled entries for therapeutics, foods, and environmental substances. Reaction type and severity should be codified as well as the identity of the allergy observer/documentation source (e.g., did the patient self report that his mom saw a rash to penicillin 30 years ago or did an ICU nurse watch the patient anaphylax to penicillin?).

Visits
Each visit should be documented with a reason for the visit (symptoms or problem), a pre-existing condition flag if the patient has had this before, a diagnosis, a list of therapies given, and the follow-up arranged.

Notes
Notes should be entered via structured and unstructured electronic forms. All text data should be searchable, so that physicians can easily locate old notes. Templates that are disease-specific and macros that are specialty-specific should be available to make documenting easier. Voice recognition for automated entry of free text should be available. Workflow for signing notes and forwarding notes to other providers should be easy to use.

Laboratory Results
Laboratory results should be displayable in several ways: by date, by class of lab, by single result trended over time, and in screening sheet format. Screening sheets are lists of disease-specific lab results combined with decision support. For example, a diabetic screening sheet would include glucose, hemoglobin a1c, lipids, recent eye exam results, podiatry consults, and urinalysis. Alerts and reminders should be generated based on disease state, lab value, and trends.

As results are delivered, especially important results, clinicians should electronically sign an acknowledgment of lab result notification, ensuring that appropriate next steps are taken for patient care.

Radiology Results
As mentioned in a recent blog on image management, all "ologies" should be stored in one place in the EHR and all should be viewable with a single electronic viewer. Radiology, cardiology, GI, pulmonology, echo, vascular, and gynecology images should be easily viewable and these images should be managed according to business rules (e.g., retained as required for medical record compliance, archived when no longer relevant).

Orders
Electronic ordering should include medications, oncology management, laboratories, radiology, and general care (e.g., ordering home care supplies, wheelchairs). Orders should automatically be routed to the department and staff responsible for executing them.

Health Information Exchange
The EHR should be able to retrieve medication lists and clinical summaries from outside institutions as part of local/regional health information exchange. EHRs should be able to send data to personal health records and receive patient-

entered data, especially telemetry data from home devices like glucometers, and from personal health records.

Data Marts

Every night, data from the EHR should be exported to data marts for appropriate use with institutional review board (IRB) approval for clinical trials, clinical research, population health analysis, performance measurement, and quality improvement.

At BIDMC, we're continuously improving our systems and we're well on the road to achieving much of this functionality. Of course, we'll never be done because the goal of the ultimate EHR is a continuously evolving target. ∎

Embracing Innovation

I'm in the prime of my capacity to adapt to mental and physical change. I crave innovation just as I crave my weekend time climbing ice and scaling mountains. However, I know that my mental and physical capacity to embrace change are likely to diminish over time.

My grandmother (who passed away in the 1990s) spent her youth learning the Palmer method of perfect handwriting. When I learned to type in sixth grade and began typing all my correspondence, she could not embrace the notion that cursive handwriting was an anachronism.

As a college student, I had the privilege of living with Dr. Frederick Terman, former Provost of Stanford University and the person who brought Bill Hewlett/ David Packard together in the 1930s. Dr. Terman was known for his foundational work in radio engineering, especially the creation of novel amplifier circuits. One night in the early 1980s, I brought Dr. Terman an integrated circuit that cost under one dollar and did the work of his most complex radio engineering designs in a single device smaller than a dime. I proudly explained that his foundational work made this integrated circuit possible. His response was that he could not understand the technology inside the device and thus he had no interest in it.

Recently, in her Nobel acceptance speech, Doris Lessing[3] explained that the Internet is destroying creativity and intelligence because it enables anyone to be a publisher and it removes rigorous training in the history of literature as a barrier entry to authorship. Although I have the greatest respect for anyone who earns a Nobel prize, these statements reminded me of my conversation with Dr. Terman. Just because the new forms of social networking, blogging, wikis, and instant messaging are different than previous forms of scholarship does not mean they are inherently flawed. In the past, I would not have shared my experiences as

---

3   Doris Lessing was a British novelist, playwright, and poet who won the Nobel Prize for Literature. She died on November 17, 2013 at the age of 94.

CIO with everyone because the barriers to writing a book about it were too great. Now, anyone can benefit from my decade of successes and failures as a CIO for free, anytime, anywhere. In a sense, the Internet has democratized access to knowledge.

My commitment to my staff is that if I ever become the rate-limiting step in adoption of new technologies, then it will be time for me to go. In the meantime, bring on the AJAX, the continuous data replication, host-based intrusion protection, and all the new acronyms that cross my desk every day. I may not immediately understand every new technology, but I look forward to being a student, learning about the latest innovations, for life. ∎

A Chip in My Shoulder

I'm often asked about the radio frequency identification (RFID) chip containing my medical records which is implanted in my right arm.

As a physician and chief information officer, I felt qualified to evaluate the medical, legal, moral, and privacy aspects of the device. After using the device for three years, I am not an evangelist for implanted RFID, but I believe it can be valuable for some patients who understand the risks and benefits. My implantation process in December 2004 was simple—a five-minute office procedure, which included disinfection of the implant site on my upper right arm, a few cubic centimeters of lidocaine, and insertion of the injector into my subcutaneous fascia. I did not experience pain, bleeding, or any post-procedure infection. The implant is not palpable, does not migrate, and has no physical side effects such as itching, irritation, or changes in skin appearance. The RFID device does not impede my activities; even while rock or ice climbing I have hit the implant site many times without any problems. The device is undetectable by airport security metal detectors and hand scanners.

One possible side effect is that my RFID device can be scanned by retail security systems using 134.2 kHz RFID technology, the frequency of my implant. I have had experiences at Home Depot and Best Buy where my device seemed to set off the anti-theft systems. My personal data are not readable by such systems, but they may be able to detect the presence of an implanted RFID tag.

Given my experience, what are the risks and benefits? The medical risks of any implant are infection, pain, keloid formation at the puncture site, and reaction to the local anesthetic. There are quite a range of nonmedical risks. After my implant, I received many emails saying that I had become a "Borg" and had lost some of my humanity because I was now a hybrid human/machine. Some emails even referred to the Book of Revelation, noting that I now carried the number of the Beast. Thus, chip carriers have a risk of being social outcasts.

The chip holds a static and unencrypted 16-digit number, which is used to point to a website containing personal health record data. The web-site requires a username and password, ensuring appropriate security. It is conceivable that a person on a subway could scan a patient's number without their knowledge and steal their medical identity by creating an identical chip and implanting it. This is a very theoretical risk because hospitals are not widely using implanted RFID chips as a means of identification. If the implanted chip were used for security purposes, such as opening a door to a secure area, the person who scanned the patient on the subway could replay the RFID signal and gain access to the secure area. Again, this is purely theoretical since implanted RFID devices are not often used as security authenticators.

If these are the potential risks, what are the benefits? Since we have no universal health identifier in the US, there is no simple way to uniquely identify a patient at all sites of care. The result is a fractured medical record scattered in inpatient, outpatient, laboratory, pharmacy, and emergency department sites. The implanted RFID devices enable patients to establish healthcare identities and become the stewards of their own data. The patient can assemble a reconciled medication list, a complete problem list, and a list of diagnostic study results, and then apply personal privacy preferences—for example, deleting information about mental health, HIV, or substance abuse. This patient-controlled record is available to treating clinicians in the case of emergency via the implanted device.

It is a personal choice whether or not to be fitted with an RFID device, but for some patients such a record has value. For example, such devices may be particularly helpful for a patient with Alzheimer disease who cannot give a history, a patient prone to syncope who may not be initially conscious during an emergency department visit, or a very active person who engages in extreme sports activities and could be noncommunicative due to injury.

I believe that in the near future, patients will own their medical records and be the stewards of their own health data. Implantation of RFID devices is one tool, appropriate for some patients based on their personal analysis of risks and benefits, that can empower patients by serving as a source of identity and a link to a personal health record when the patient cannot otherwise communicate. ∎

Safe-Driver Discounts for Technology

Automobile insurers have long seen the sense of giving drivers an incentive, in the form of safe-driver discounts, to avoid taking risks when they're behind the wheel. In healthcare, more and more payers are rewarding doctors for the quality of care they deliver and not the quantity. Aligning incentives with outcomes makes good sense.

Vendors of technology should follow those examples and revise their pricing models for yearly hardware and software maintenance contracts. If they rewarded customers who adhere to best practices, they would essentially pay customers for their performance.

As a CIO of multiple companies, I have to sign off on a lot of maintenance contracts every year. These contracts have a list price, and there's usually a discount that the manufacturer passes along to the value-added reseller (VAR). The VAR decides how much of the discount to pass along to customers. No extra consideration is given to customers who abide by the vendor's best practices for the implementation and management of its products.

But why not? Why not give technology buyers the equivalent of a safe-driver discount? If customers were given incentives to hire highly competent internal staff, follow all the vendor-recommended configurations, and install all the latest upgrades, life would be better for both the vendor and the customer. The vendor would receive fewer support calls and requests for emergency priority service. The customer would get higher reliability, better performance, and lower maintenance costs.

Why not give technology buyers the equivalent of a safe-driver discount? If customers were given incentives to hire highly competent internal staff, follow all the vendor-recommended configurations, and install all the latest upgrades, life would be better for both the vendor and the customer.

Several years ago, we experienced a devastating network outage that led me to change a lot of our practices. Before the outage, my only incentive to adopt best practices was fear of downtime. The cost of support was certainly not a factor. We could make hundreds of support calls and send out an SOS during numerous high-priority emergencies, and the cost would be the same as it would be with a spotless performance record. The outage led me to replace much of our infrastructure, enhance my support team, and ensure that our engineering practices are world class. We now place an extremely low burden on our vendors, but our maintenance discounts for all the technology we operate today don't reflect that.

Here's my idea. Vendors would give each customer a yearly technology safety rating, starting at, say, 100 points. If you miss an upgrade, 10 points would be deducted. Deviate significantly from a recommended configuration and you would lose another 10 points. Make a support call that's due to your lack of appropriate IT staffing and more points would be taken away.

Discounts would no longer be arbitrary. Instead, they would be a direct function of the yearly safety rating. The harder a customer worked to avoid calls for help, the less the maintenance would cost. The best customer of the year could even be rewarded with completely free maintenance.

Of course, there are potential problems with that approach. Vendors could abuse the system by defining best practices as the elimination of all competing products, or they could take away points if customers didn't buy all the optional add-on software they recommend. But such tactics would defeat the spirit of this proposal. Any vendor that adopted them could expect a good deal of pushback from customers; hopefully, they would see that such transparently cynical ploys have no real value.

So let me publicly ask my good friends at Cisco, EMC, Dell, HP, and IBM, "What do you think?" You'll find that my driving record is exemplary. ■

Data, Information, Knowledge, and Wisdom

One of the challenges of being a doctor in the 21st century is information overload. More medical literature is published every year than a doctor can read in a lifetime. As EHRs become more common, doctors can be overwhelmed with data gathered about each patient. Doctors do not want to review hundreds of normal findings; they want to know what is actionable for each of their patients to keep them healthy.

Healthcare CIOs should implement applications which filter data so that it becomes information, transforms information into knowledge, and ultimately provides clinicians with wisdom based on that knowledge at the exact time they need it.

Here's an example. Suppose a patient's blood pressure is 100/50. That's data. Suppose that patient has a ten-year history of blood pressures of 150/100. That's information. Suppose that the patient has a known history of coronary artery disease and is now experiencing chest pain. The sudden drop in blood pressure could indicate a serious myocardial infarction in progress. That's knowledge. It's time to give the patient an aspirin, oxygen, and nitrates immediately. That's wisdom.

Recently, I asked my primary care physician to export my entire history from his EMR system. Although I'm a completely healthy person, the result was a 77-page PDF. The document contains a mix of administrative and clinical data, numeric observations, and unstructured text. It would take a physician about an hour to navigate all this data.

How can we turn this data into information? Over the past few years, my clinical information systems team, led by Dr. Larry Markson, has built "event-driven medicine" into our applications. Events such as changes in medications, patient visits for diagnostic testing, lab results, or newly discovered allergic reactions generate data which can be transformed into actionable wisdom. Here are three examples:

- When a doctor orders a medication at BIDMC, a query is sent to our regional data exchange determining the patient's insurance coverage for pharmaceuticals. Based on the answer, we access the appropriate payer-specific formulary so that all medications are preferentially chosen to minimize cost and maximize effectiveness for each patient. Every prescribed medication is checked against the entire history of the patient's active medications from pharmacy and payer databases throughout the country. Safety issues, guidelines, and best practices are displayed to the clinician, ensuring quality care. When the correct, safe medication in the right dose is selected, it is instantly routed to the pharmacy of the patient's choice, going from the doctor's brain to the patient's vein without any handwriting or human interpretation. All of this happens in real time based on the data found in EHRs, information about trends in body functions, knowledge from decision support databases, and wisdom from the orchestration of all these moving parts behind the scenes via interoperable web services, ultimately providing the best choice for each medication ordered. This week, we just completed our 100,000th medication processed this way.

- When a doctor orders a radiology test at BIDMC, a query is sent to a decision support engine which we co-developed with Safe-Med. Over 1,000 best practice rules from the American College of Radiology and the world's radiology literature are examined, along with patient medications, laboratories, allergies, and demographics, to select the most appropriate radiology test based on evidence. Radiology exams are scored from five stars to one star, balancing efficacy, risk, and cost. If a clinician orders one of these tests, a pre-authorization is sent to the payer in real time and the test is automatically approved. All of this happens in a few seconds, using patient data plus the knowledge from the literature to yield a wise choice for radiology diagnostic testing. One hundred percent of high-cost radiology tests are processed this way.

- When a doctor identifies a chronic disease condition at BIDMC, a decision support "screening sheet" is created to track all the events in a patient's care. Diabetic tracking includes lipids, glucose, eye exams, foot exams, Hemoglobin A1-C, immunizations, and weight. Whenever an event occurs—such as a lab result or appointment—the screening sheet is updated and decision support rules recommend the best practices for diabetic care, filtering all this data into a concrete set of recommendations such as "patient is past due for an eye exam" or "patient should receive pneumovax this season." Clinicians do not need to focus on the raw data; instead they can review suggestions in real time to optimize the care of the patient. This year we achieved all our pay-for-performance goals using this approach.

Like many other projects, the pursuit of event-driven medicine is a journey. Over the next few years, we'll continue our efforts to ensure that clinicians are given the real-time wisdom they need to deliver safe, cost effective, and appropriate care. ∎

Bar Codes, RFID, and Patient Safety

Like most hospitals, BIDMC is focused on maximizing patient safety, quality, and value. Over the past few years, we've implemented provider order entry, guidelines/care plans, and EHRs. However, a great puzzle remains: how do we positively identify our patients so that we are confident they are receiving the correct medications, have the correct blood samples sent to the lab, and receive the right blood products during a transfusion? For example, with perfect identification, we can create an electronic medication administration record that documents that the right patient received the right medication from the right person at the right time.

To accomplish the goal of positive identification of our patients, our staff, and our medications, we spent the past year investigating two major kinds of technology—bar codes and RFID. In different use cases, each technology has its pros and cons. Based on our early work, we have implemented these technologies in various production settings in the hospital with positive results.

Bar codes have been used successfully in industry for decades. The technology is stable and well standardized. Bar codes come in two basic forms—simple linear bar codes and more complex two-dimensional bar codes. Linear bar codes encode a few characters or numbers, such as the 12-digit UPC symbols found on grocer's shelves. Linear bar codes can be used in a healthcare setting to encode a medical record number placed on a patient wristband. Two-dimensional bar codes can encode more complex information such as patient name, age, and gender that could be used to provide details about the patient without requiring a lookup in a hospital information system, which helps provide redundancy in case of hospital system downtime.

Many vendors offer wrist bands and printers which facilitate easy bar-coded wrist banding of each patient upon admission or registration. Bar codes are inexpensive, highly reliable, and generally already used in hospitals. Hence, existing hospital bar code readers can be used. However, bar codes do have limitations. Reading bar codes requires line of sight scanning which means that patients need to be awakened/repositioned each time the bar code needs to be scanned. Linear bar codes must be relatively flat to be read properly, so a wristband wrapped around a premature baby's wrist is problematic. Bar codes generally do not read well when wrinkled, wet, or torn. One positive aspect of this characteristic is that bar codes rarely yield an inaccurate read, but simply do not read at all when damaged.

In our case, we believe that putting both linear and two-dimensional bar codes on wrist bands enables us to take advantage of linear bar-code readers already in use in the hospital, while also preparing us for purchases of future bar-code reading equipment which will read both two-dimensional and linear bar codes. For employees, our security badging software produces a linear bar code on employee badges. For medications, an informal survey of our supply chain revealed that 70% of all medication containers are already bar coded. Although this may help with drug distribution, it does not help us identify unit doses of medications since pills are not yet bar coded. Repacking pills into bar-coded bags is required for positive identification of unit dose medications.

RFID is an evolving technology that is widely speculated to replace bar codes over the next few years. However, RFID in healthcare requires careful examination, because separating reality from hype can be challenging. RFID comes in two basic forms, active and passive.

Active RFID tags contain a battery and transmitter which can be used as a geo-location, constantly providing information about the physical location of the active tag in the hospital. Current active tags are about the size of the pager, require battery replacement every six months, and cost $50 each. As with many new technologies, the size is decreasing, the battery life is lengthening, and the cost per tag is dropping significantly. Active RFID transmitters generally use one of two frequencies—either 802.11b/WiFi (2.4 Ghz) or a proprietary frequency (488 Mhz). The advantage of using WiFi is that the existing hospital wireless network can be used to read tag location. Our experience is that active RFID over WiFi can be rapidly and cost effectively deployed for use cases which require room-level tag location. Proprietary systems that use an active RFID-specific network, such as 488 Mhz or infrared receivers in each room, can provide location to the level of the square meter, but do require the installation of dedicated wiring to support the RFID system. In our case, we believe that active RFID tags are a robust technology for applications which can utilize a pager-size device, such as tracking equipment, tracking patient beds, and tracking staff who are willing to wear an extra pager-sized device. For tracking staff, we specifically worked with managers to ensure that tags would not be used in a punitive way (e.g., to record minutes in the lunch room, trips outside to smoke). Our application of active RFID is currently used for equipment tracking in the ED and has reduced the time to search for ventilators, IV pumps, and EKG devices to near zero.

Passive RFID tags contain an antenna and a chip, but no battery. They can be as flat as a piece of paper and as small as a grain of rice. When a reader provides RF energy which is absorbed by the antenna, the chip is stimulated to broadcast its data. This data could be simple such as a medical record number or complex such as name/gender/date of birth. Examples of passive RFID tags are the Mobil Speedpass used for gasoline purchases, product identification tags used on retail products such as Gillette razors at Walmart, and tags used in libraries to track books.

RFID tags have several advantages over bar codes. They do not require line of sight reading; hence, an RFID reader can be brought near a sleeping patient or a swaddled neonatal intensive care unit (NICU) baby, and can easily read the patient identifier. RFID tags are resistant to moisture, crushing, and tearing.

However, passive RFID is not a panacea. Tags are more expensive than simple printed bar codes. Standards for passive RFID are still in evolution and many different frequencies are used to read different tags (e.g., 125 Khz, 134.2 Khz, and 13.56 Mhz). RFID tags typically have up to a 20% failure rate in manufacture and thus can result in a non-readable wristband. RFID tags are much harder to read if a metal barrier such as aluminum foil exists between the reader and the tag.

Existing passive RFID products include wristbands and implantable chips such as those used to track pets. Human use has been limited and I am one of the early evaluators of the technology.[4] My body is RFID-enabled and when scanned, I emit my medical record identifiers which can be used by authorized physicians to retrieve my medical records via a secure web application.

In our case, we use passive RFID to track NICU babies via RFID wristbands and to track mother's milk stored in tagged containers. A software application and RFID scanner are used to ensure the right infant receives the right milk and to automatically create an audit trail.

Our early work with positive patient identification can be summarized as the following:

- For identification of most patients, we believe linear and two-dimensional bar codes on wristbands are robust, cost effective, and standardized. For staff badges, linear bar codes work well. For NICU babies, passive RFID enables scanning of swaddled infants without disturbing them.

- For identification of medications, we believe linear bar codes of National Drug Code (NDC) numbers on heat-sealable plastic bags provide a practical means to positively identify medications.

- For identification of equipment, specifically for tracking location in real time, active RFID works well. Because of the size and expense of tags, we do not believe active RFID should be used for patient identification at this time.

Thus, a combination of bar codes, passive RFID, and active RFID is working well in our various pilots. No one technology meets the needs of all use cases.

4 Halamka J. Straight from the shoulder. *New England Journal of Medicine*. 2005; 353:331-333.

Although we favor bar codes over passive RFID in the short term, we do expect to eventually replace bar codes with RFID once the technology is more robust, standardized, and cost effective. ∎

Novel Data Sources for Quality Measurement

My definition of traditional data sources that are currently used to measure quality includes administrative claims data aggregated from hospital-based claims databases (for example, BIDMC has an Oracle repository called Casemix), payer-based databases (all have a claims warehouse to support disease management), physician organizations (Beth Israel Deaconess Physicians Organization has worked with Healthcare Data Services to create all payer business intelligence tools), and health data consortia (such as the Massachusetts Health Data Consortium, which offers de-identified aggregated claims to enable institutional comparisons).

New sources of data for quality analysis go beyond administrative data and include EHR, PHR, and health information exchange resources. Here are a few examples:

- At BIDMC all our laboratory, radiology, pharmacy, and care process data are available in business intelligence data marts. We use these internally for scorecards, benchmarking, and workflow improvement projects.

- Massachusetts has a long history of payer/provider collaboration, such as NEHEN. Recently, the Eastern Massachusetts Healthcare Initiative (EMHI) has developed a new set of clinical data exchange use cases to support regional payer/provider collaboration. One of those use cases is the automated exchange of quality data via a secure publish/subscribe web service that eliminates the need for providers to create bulk data extracts for payer quality measures.

- The Massachusetts eHealth Collaborative has created a quality data warehouse for its 600 participating clinicians. This warehouse is so good that the Beth Israel Deaconess Physicians Organization (BIDPO) has elected to use it for aggregating the quality measure data on its physicians.

Surescripts/Rx Hub provides national medication list data that is helpful for clinical care and quality measurement.

- Commercial labs such as Quest and LabCorp are implementing HITSP[5] standards for lab transactions which include the data elements needed for biosurveillance, public health reporting, and quality analysis.

---

5 HITSP = Healthcare Information Technology Standards Panel.

- The Social Security Administration's Megahit pilot demonstrated automated submission of electronic medical records between hospitals and the SSA with patient consent to improve turnaround time for disability claims adjudication.

- The Centers for Disease Control has implemented BioSense, an automated surveillance system for detecting variations in disease frequency using de-identified emergency department and hospital data.

- The Massachusetts Medical Society is working with the Massachusetts eHealth Collaborative (MAeHC) to pilot quality scorecards for its members using the MAeHC quality warehouse.

- Departments of Public Health in Massachusetts receive automated data feeds from local hospitals to enable early detection of outbreaks.

- The Aegis system developed by Children's Hospital uses automated data feeds from Massachusetts hospitals to create real-time influenza prevalence maps.

- A new generation of consumer healthcare devices from the Continua Health Alliance enables remote monitoring of patients in the home, transmitting data to EHRs and PHRs.

- Personal health records including those tethered to an EHR, those sponsored by employers, those hosted by health plans, and vendor-based systems such as Microsoft HealthVault enable patients to aggregate, enter, and manage their own data. PHRs may be an appropriate way to measure quality by asking patients to subscribe/contribute their data to quality measurement organizations. The trusted third-party model in Google enables patients to share data with their consent. Some patients may feel altruistic enough to contribute their data for quality measurement.

- Google Trends shows search-term trends over time. This can be used to quantify searches on symptoms such as flu-related illnesses, providing early detection of changes in the frequency of users searching for fever/cough/flu, etc. It would be interesting to track the Google trend for searches on "Chest pain/heart attack" before and after the introduction of Vioxx as measure of pharmaco-vigilence.

- As part of the Clinical and Translational Science Awards, all Harvard Medical School affiliates must work together as a single virtual unit, sharing data for clinical research. SHRINE[6] is an innovative, web-services-based federated data mining tool that enables clinical research among all the data at all Harvard hospitals with appropriate privacy protection and IRB oversight.

---

6   SHRINE = Shared Health Research Information Network.

All of these new approaches go behind claims data to provide novel indicators that can be used to measure quality. I predict that all these novel sources of data will become increasingly important as stimulus funds become available and clinicians are incentivized based on quality, not quantity, of care delivered. ∎

It's All About the Kilowatts

Although my demand for servers increases at 25% per year, I've been able to virtualize my entire infrastructure and keep the real estate footprint small.

At the same time, my demand for high-performance computing and storage is increasing at 250% per year. With blade servers and 2-terabyte drives, my rack space is not a rate limiter.

It's all about the kilowatts.

Today, I'm using 220 kilowatts. My two-year forecast is over half a megawatt. What are we doing?

1. Measuring and tracking power consuming and growth—At HMS we have two data centers—a primary and a disaster recovery site. Our primary site is .16 cents per kilowatt hour x 140 kW in use (that's an electrical bill of $16,128 per month). Our backup site is .12 cents per kilowatt hour x 80 kW in use (that's an electrical bill of $6,912.00 per month). Unless you understand your power costs in detail, you'll never be able to control them.

2. Forecasting the future—We use data center modeling software from SAP called Xcelsius that enables us to examine the impact of moving servers, adding capacity, changing square footage, adding power/ cooling, etc.

3. Creating tiers of data center power capabilities—Rather than use a one-size-fits-all strategy, we have begun to rent co-location space that includes specialized rooms for high-power density racks (25kw/rack). We can use liquid-cooled cabinets and other specialized technologies to achieve the right power/cooling support for high-performance computing instead of trying to design one room to serve all purposes.

4. Investigating lower-cost alternatives—Google's strategy has been to locate server farms near hydroelectric plants with lower kilowatt costs. We're considering the options in Western Massachusetts along with other collaborators. One challenge of this approach is backup power. What happens to a high-performance computing facility if the hydroelectric power fails? Creating a megawatt of backup generator power is not easy or cost effective. Instead of protecting all our high-

performance computing assets, one strategy is to protect only storage which is less tolerant of power failures. Since high-performance computing cores are often distributed geographically, failure of any one data center could be invisible to the users.

5. Engineering for efficiency—As we purchase new equipment, we examine power supply designs, cooling profiles, possibilities for shutting down unused equipment until it is needed, etc. I expect some of the greatest software and hardware innovates of the next several years to be power-saving technologies, because real estate is no longer the issue. ∎

Rethinking Clinical Documentation

Over the past five years, I have worked with federal committees to select standards for exchanging clinical summaries. But what exactly is a clinical summary?

There is common agreement about the need to exchange codified, structured data for problem lists, medications, allergies, and labs.

However, what is the role of unstructured clinical documentation text?

Some have suggested that unstructured text is hard to navigate, at times repetitious, and challenging for computers to interpret.

I believe the exchange of free-text notes such as operative reports, histories & physicals, ED charts, consult notes, and discharge summaries is very important.

Consider this example:

A 40-year-old male with no family history of heart disease presents to the ED at 3 am with a chief complaint of chest pain and left arm numbness. The EKG is normal, a stress test is normal, labs are normal, and a cardiology consult is completed. The patient is discharged on H2 blockers with a diagnosis of gastritis.

A summary which includes only a problem list and med list may state a problem list of "Gastritis" and a medication list of "Prilosec OTC."

When the patient next visits an ED, no one will know about the cardiology consult, the differential diagnosis considered, and the thought process that led to the diagnosis of gastritis to explain the chest pain. An entire workup will be started from scratch.

There is a great article in the March 25, 2010 issue of the *New England Journal of Medicine*,[7] "Can Electronic Clinical Documentation Help Prevent Diagnostic Errors?" in which the authors note: "Free-text narrative will often be superior to point-and-click boilerplate in accurately capturing a patient's history

---

7 Schiff GD, Bates DW. Can electronic clinical documentation help prevent diagnostic errors? *New England Journal of Medicine*. 2010; 362:1066-1069.

and making assessments, and notes should be designed to include discussion of uncertainties."

I agree.

Notes should be included as part of clinical summaries.

However, we should do all we can to improve the quality of notes.

Over the next year, we hope to try a radically different approach to clinical documentation at BIDMC which we think will leverage all the strengths of the full-text note as described by Drs. Schiff and Bates, without the repetition and navigation issues.

Today's inpatient charges are a collection of SOAP[8] notes written by the medical student, intern, resident, fellow, attending, and consultants largely for billing and medico-legal purposes.

What if the chart was recast as a communication vehicle for the entire team that summarized the day's events and collective wisdom on next steps?

Our answer: a daily wiki entry for each patient authored by the entire team and signed/locked by the attending at the end of each day.

How will this work?

Think of it as a private Wikipedia built inside our clinical systems and hosted in our data center.

> The idea of a daily wiki entry for each patient creates highly readable, succinct documentation authored by the entire team with a medical-legal record of the process that was used to generate it.

Each member of the care team will use our "Team Census" application to view the list of patients for whom the team is responsible.

Clicking on any patient name will bring up the daily wiki. Each member can add documentation, revise existing text, and leverage the work of others on the team until the attending makes the final edits and signs/locks the day's documentation. Just like a wiki, a complete journal shows all edits/changes/deletes, so no information is lost. Importantly, the day's wiki entry has one physical exam, one assessment, and one plan—not 17 repetitive entries saying the same thing that often appears in today's paper charts.

The idea of a daily wiki entry for each patient creates highly readable, succinct documentation authored by the entire team with a medical-legal record of the process that was used to generate it. It's a perfect single document to share with the referring clinician and the patient/patient's family.

After our initial pilot work, I'm guessing we'll also engage the patient and families to add to the wiki, reflecting the shared decision making between the team, the patient, and the patient's family.

---

8   SOAP = Subjective, objective, assessment, and plan.

A daily patient wiki as unified clinical documentation, exchanged with the team, other providers, and the patient. I bet even the free-text naysayers will agree that this should be part of the clinical summary! ■

The Electronic Medical Home

In previous blog posts, I've mentioned an idea that deserves its own dedicated post.

Recently, I delivered the keynote address at the eClinicalWorks National User's Conference in Florida. One of the attendees emailed the following question to me:

"I have a number of questions regarding certain types of patient-level data that might cause us problems in the future of HIE. No one, to date, has been able to answer these and I thought I might ask you.

"The first, and easiest, is how are we going to handle the following situation?

1. "I am seen in Boston as a child and my mother says that I am allergic to penicillin (or pick your drug of choice). The nurse practitioner asks a few questions of my mother, who isn't terribly forthcoming with information but insists that I am allergic. While he/she has reservations, they record it as an allergy in their eClinicalWorks EMR. It goes to the Massachusetts HIE.

2. "I move to Washington, DC, to go to college and the family practitioner hears my allergy story. He asks more detailed questions and decides that I DON'T have an allergy. He records it in his Epic system and it goes to the Washington, DC, HIE.

3. "I get my first job in Dallas. Unfortunately, I wind up unconscious in the Dallas ED and the doctor queries my records—in our future super-connected world, he/she sees that I am both allergic and not allergic to penicillin.

"How do I, as a patient, protect myself from this happening?"

The best way to accomplish this is for each patient in the country to choose an electronic medical home (EMH) which stores a copy of his or her electronic data as gathered by clinicians, pharmacies, labs, payers, and other data generators.

The concept is simple. An EMH vendor would create a URL or secure email address for each participating patient.

The patient would provide this URL or secure email address to every caregiver.

At the end of each visit, test, or hospitalization, the data would be sent securely to the EMH of the patient's choice.

These EMHs could be offered by primary care givers, EHR vendors (such as eClinicalWorks' 100millionpatients.com), or non-tethered EHR vendors such as Microsoft HealthVault.

Over the next few weeks, I predict that even telecoms like AT&T and Verizon will announce eHealth offerings.

All we need to get started is for one of these groups to create simple software capable of receiving clinical data via a RESTful URL[9] or via SMTP/TLS[10] secure email/XDR[11] as suggested by NHIN Direct.

Electronic medical homes nicely solve the problem of consolidating multiple disparate records in one place. They solve the Meaningful Use requirement to deliver summaries and educational materials to patients. They make the patient the steward of his or her own lifetime records, simplifying consent issues for data sharing.

But what if a patient does not want to be the steward of his or her EMH? That's ok. It will give rise to a new professional service, the healthcare knowledge navigator, an expert who manages your EMH on your behalf. This could be a primary care clinician, a midlevel provider, or a trusted vendor.

Here's my challenge to the industry:

Create an electronic medical home using a RESTful URL or the NHIN Direct specification.

As long as you protect privacy, ensure technical security, and obtain patient consent, I will send data to you on behalf of the patient. ∎

Enterprise Image Management

I've written about our multi-year effort to archive all types of medical images in a single storage platform across the enterprise, making every image viewable everywhere to authorized clinicians. Here's an overview of my lessons learned thus far on the journey.

Image systems have been notorious for being isolated pockets of technology. They are often supported by mini-IS sections at the department level. Vendor support requirements have been significant, often requiring a dedicated onsite engineer at larger institutions. Infrastructure components such as storage, network switches, and workstations have often been available only through the image application vendor. Configurations have often been proprietary and have not lent themselves to substitution by technologies of the customer's choice.

---

9   Representational State Transfer (REST) is an architectural style that uses common HTTP operations: GET, POST, PUT, and DELETE, to link together application components.

10 SMTP/TLS = Simple Mail Transfer Protocol/Transport Layer Security.

11 XDR = External Data Representation Standard.

There has been rapid transition from analog to digital imaging, advancements in imaging (32 and 64 slice), and growth in procedure volumes. The desire to archive digital images for medical, research, and legal reasons has increased. The above has made image storage a costly line item in capital budgets.

Thus, rather than continue managing imaging systems as isolated environments, our goal is to create a common storage archive and I've achieved unified departmental support.

Attributes of the archive include the following:

- Low cost—a total cost of ownership less than $1/raw GB initially and less than $.50/raw GB within four years

- Response times that exceed those of departmental archives in use today

- Support for both DICOM[12] and non-DICOM images

- Support for life-cycle image management (purge, compress, tier migration)

- High availability and disaster recovery protection

- Multi-protocol support (CIFS, NFS, REST)

- Central IT management and budgeting

There are many emerging products from companies such as TeraMedica, Carestream GE, EMC, and Dell. There are cloud services available from Symantec, Life Image, and Accelarad. The past few years have seen a gradual migration of image management back-ends from departments to central IS organizations. In the next few years, I expect departmental experts to focus on imaging modalities and specialized front-end applications, leaving servers and storage systems to be managed by IS. ∎

Freeing the Data

I recently presented the keynote address at InterSystems' Global Conference on the topic of "Freeing the Data" from the transactional systems we use today such as enterprise resource planning (ERP), customer relationship management (CRM), EHRs, etc. As I prepared my speech, I gave a lot of thought to the evolving data needs we have in our enterprises.

In healthcare and in many other industries, it's increasingly common for users to ask IT for tools and resources to look beyond the data we enter during the course of our daily work. For one patient, I know the diagnosis, but what treatments were given to the last 1,000 similar patients. I know the sales today,

---

12 DICOM = Digital Imaging and Communications in Medicine, a standard for handling, storing, printing, and transmitting information in medical imaging.

but how do they vary over the week, the month, and the year? Can I predict future resource needs before they happen?

In the past, such analysis typically relied on structured data, exported from transactional systems into data marts using extract/transform/load (ETL) utilities, followed by analysis with online analytical processing (OLAP), or business intelligence (BI) tools.

In a world filled with highly scalable web search engines, increasingly capable natural language processing technologies, and practical examples of artificial intelligence/pattern recognition (think of IBM's Jeopardy-savvy Watson as a sophisticated data mining tool), there are novel approaches to freeing the data that go beyond a single database with predefined hypercube rollups. Here are my top ten trends to watch as we increasingly free data from transactional systems.

1. Both structured and unstructured data will be important.

In healthcare, the HITECH Act/Meaningful Use requires that clinicians document the smoking status of 50% of their patients. In the past, many EHRs did not have structured data elements to support this activity. Today's certified EHRs provide structured vocabularies and specific pulldowns/checkboxes for data entry, but what do we do about past data? Ideally, we'd use natural language processing, probability, and search to examine unstructured text in the patient record and figure out smoking status including the context of the word "smoking" such as "former," "active," "heavy," "never," etc.

Businesses will always have a combination of structured and unstructured data. Finding ways to leverage unstructured data will empower businesses to make the most of their information assets.

2. Inference is possible by parsing natural language.

Watson on Jeopardy provided an important illustration of how natural language processing can really work. Watson does not understand the language and it is not conscious/sentient. Watson's programming enables it to assign probabilities to expressions. When asked, "Does he drink alcohol frequently?," finding the word "alcohol" associated with the word "excess" is more likely to imply a drinking problem than finding "alcohol" associated with "to clean his skin before injecting his insulin." Next generation natural language processing tools will provide the technology to assign probabilities and infer meaning from context.

3. Data mining needs to go beyond single databases owned by a single organization.

If I want to ask questions about patient treatment and outcomes, I may need to query data from hundreds of hospitals to achieve statistical significance. Each of those hospitals may have different IT systems with different data structures and vocabularies. How can I query a collection of heterogeneous databases? Federation will be a possibility by normalizing the queries through middleware. For example, data might be mapped to a common resource description framework (RDF) exchange language using standardized SPARQL[13] query tools. At Harvard, we've created a common web-based interface called SHRINE that queries all our hospital databases, providing aggregate de-identified answers to questions about diagnosis and treatment of millions of patients.

4. Non-obvious associations will be increasingly important.

Sometimes, it is not enough to query multiple databases. Data needs to be linked to external resources to produce novel information. For example, at Harvard, we've taken the address of each faculty member, examined every publication they have ever written, geo-encoded the location of every co-author, and created visualizations of productivity, impact, and influence based on the proximity of colleagues. We call this "social networking analysis."

> *At Harvard, we've taken the address of each faculty member, examined every publication they have ever written, geo-encoded the location of every co-author, and created visualizations of productivity, impact, and influence based on the proximity of colleagues. We call this "social networking analysis."*

5. The President's Council of Advisors on Science and Technology (PCAST) report on Healthcare IT offers several important directional themes that will accelerate "freeing the data."

The PCAST report suggests that we embrace the idea of universal exchange languages, metadata tagging with controlled vocabularies, privacy flagging, and search engine technology with probabilistic matching to transform transactional data sources into information, knowledge, and wisdom. For example, imagine if all immunization data were normalized as they left transactional systems and were pushed into state registries that were united by a federated search that included privacy protections. Suddenly every doctor could ensure that every person had up-to-date immunizations at every visit.

6. Ontologies and data models will be important to support analytics.

Part of creating middleware solutions that enable federation of data sources requires that we generally know what data is important in healthcare and how data elements relate to each other. For example, it's important to know that an

---

13 SPARQL Protocol and RDF Query Language is a query language for databases, able to retrieve and manipulate data stored in an RDF format.

allergy has a substance, a severity, a reaction, an observer, and onset data. Every EHR may implement allergies differently, but by using a common detailed clinical model for data exchange and querying, we can map heterogeneous data into comparable data.

7. Mapping free text to controlled vocabularies will be possible and should be done as close to the source of data as possible.

Every industry has its jargon. Most clinicians do not wake up every morning thinking about SNOMED-CT concepts of ICD-10 codes. One way to leverage unstructured data is to turn it into structured data as it is entered. If a clinician types "Allergy to Penicillin," it could become SNOMED-CT concept 294513009 for penicillins. As more controlled vocabularies are introduced in medicine and other industries, transforming text into controlled concepts for later searching will be increasingly important. Ideally, this will be done as the data are entered, so they can be checked for accuracy. If not at entry, then transformations should be done as close to the source systems as possible to ensure data integrity. With every transformation and exchange of data from the original source, there is increasing risk of loss of meaning and context.

8. Linking identity among heterogeneous databases will be required for healthcare reform and novel business applications.

If patients are seen in multiple locations, how can we combine their history together so they get the maximum benefit of alerts, reminders, and decision support? Among the hospitals I oversee, we have persistent linkage of all medical record numbers between hospitals—a master patient index. Surescripts/RxHub does a real-time probabilistic match on name/gender/date of birth for over 150 million people. There are other interesting creative techniques such as those pioneered by Jeff Jonas for creating a unique hash of data for every person, then linking data based on that hash. For example, "John," "Jon," "Jonathan," and "Johnny" are reduced to one common root name "John." "John" and the other demographic fields are then hashed using SHA-1. The hashes are compared between records to link similar hashes. In this way, records about a person can be aggregated without ever disclosing who the person really is; it's just hashes that are used to find common records.

9. New tools will empower end users.

All users, not just power users, want web-based or simple-to-use client server

All users, not just power users, want web-based or simple-to-use client server tools that allow data queries and visualizations without requiring a lot of expertise. The next generation of SQL Server and PowerPivot offer this kind of query power from the desktop.

tools that allow data queries and visualizations without requiring a lot of expertise. The next generation of SQL Server and PowerPivot offer this kind of query power from the desktop. At BIDMC, we've created web-based parameterized queries in our Meaningful Use tools, we're implementing PowerPivot, and we're creating a powerful hospital-based visual query tool using I2B2[14] technologies.

10. Novel sources of data will be important.

Today, patients and consumers are generating data from apps on smart phones, from wearable devices, and social networking sites. Novel approaches to creating knowledge and wisdom will source data from consumers as well as traditional corporate transactional systems.

Thus, as we all move toward "freeing the data," it will no longer be sufficient to use just structured transaction data entered by experts in a single organization, then mined by professional report writers. The speed of business and the need for enhanced quality and efficiency are pushing us toward near real-time business intelligence and visualizations for all users. In a sense this mirrors the development of the web itself, evolving from expert HTML coders, to tools for content management for non-technical designated editors, to social networking in which everyone is an author, publisher, and consumer.

"Freeing the data" is going to require new thinking about the way we approach application design and requirements. Just as security needs to be foundational, analytics need to be built in from the beginning. ■

Sending Questions to the Data

As hospitals and practices form accountable care organizations, they will accelerate their efforts to build health information exchanges and novel analytics that support community-wide lifetime care rather than siloed episodic care. This requires "freeing the data" from the EHRs, hospital information systems, and laboratories in which it resides.

There are two basic ways to analyze data for a panel or population:

1. Send the data from multiple sources to a central repository for analysis. BIDMC has partnered with the Massachusetts eHealth Collaborative on such an approach to build a quality data center supporting its ACO strategy.

2. Send the question to the data. The new federal Query Health initiative is a standards-based approach that enables standardized questions to be sent to multiple federated databases without moving the data itself.

---

14 I2B2 = Informatics for Integrating Biology and the Bedside.

In Massachusetts, we've implemented such an architecture in two ways:

- I2B2/SHRINE links together the Harvard hospitals (and many other sites nationwide) with query tools supporting clinical trials and clinical research.

- MDPHnet is an ONC-funded Challenge grant which sends questions to data sources, answering public health questions.

  - MDPHnet is being developed under contract with the Massachusetts eHealth Institute to implement a secure web-based query tool which enables predefined and ad hoc queries to be sent to participating sites, including selected practices within the Massachusetts League of Community Health Centers and potentially, Atrius Health.

  - Queries are executed locally, securely returned after optional review, and then presented to the requester and displayed in a variety of ways—heat map, histogram, table, etc. Results contain no patient-identifiable data. Data holders control authorization of requesters and their specific query capabilities.

  - The current focus for predefined reports is syndromic surveillance (e.g., influenza-like illness) and chronic disease surveillance (e.g., diabetes). It can also support other uses, such as pharmacovigilance and quality measurement.

  - MDPHnet uses PopMedNet open source software developed by the Harvard Medical School Department of Population Medicine at the Harvard Pilgrim Health Care Institute, with support from the Agency for Healthcare Research and Quality (AHRQ) and the FDA. Lincoln Peak is co-developer.

There is great synergy among I2B2, PopMedNet, and MDPHnet, since they use a common architectural approach. Query Health incorporates PopMedNet in its design.

MDPHnet uses the Electronic Health Record Support of Public Health (ESP) common data model. ESP was developed by the HMS/HPHCI Department of Population Medicine with support from a CDC Center for Excellence in Public Health Informatics.

The Massachusetts League of Community Health Centers transforms data from their clinical data warehouse into the ESP format. Commonwealth

Over the next few years I believe that for many use cases we will be sending questions to the data instead of sending the data to centralized registries. I2B2, MDPHnet, and Query Health will show us how.

Informatics supports the process as needed. Additional participants will extract data from their EHR and put it into the same schema (ESP), with help from Commonwealth Informatics.

MDPHnet can be readily expanded to cover other data sources such as the I2B2 nodes, which are hosted at over 60 sites nationwide.

Over the next few years I believe that for many use cases we will be sending questions to the data instead of sending the data to centralized registries. I2B2, MDPHnet, and Query Health will show us how. ∎

Another Shade of Blue Button

The Blue Button idea is simple: a large visible button on payer, provider, lab, or pharmacy websites enables patients to download their records in plain text.

The VA has used it extensively. The Office of Personnel Management (OPM) asked all health insurance carriers in the Federal Employees Health Benefit Program (FEHBP) to add Blue Button functions to personal health record systems. OPM administers health benefit programs for the civilian sector of the federal government, including all executive agencies, Members of Congress and their staffs, and the federal judiciary on their websites.

The Blue Button is one of several models of health information exchange being implemented.

I've summarized HIE models as the following:

- View—A website or web service enables authorized patients, providers, or payers to view data in plain text or HTML. A modest amount of programming is needed, but significant attention to security issues is important to protect the website and data sources.

- Push—An EHR sends data to another EHR via the Direct standard. Since this is secure email, a modest infrastructure investment is needed to create directories, certificate management, and gateways.

- Pull—An EHR queries a master patient index/record locator service to identify a patient and the locations of his or her records. The EHR then queries all the data sources to assemble a comprehensive medical history. NwHIN[15] Exchange is an example of such an approach. Significant infrastructure must be built to support and maintain a pull architecture.

Since push and pull models require HIEs, which are still evolving, some organizations, including BIDMC and its affiliates, have temporarily implemented

---

15 NwHIN = Nationwide Health Information Network.

view approaches inside Epic, MEDITECH, eClinicalWorks, and self-built applications.

Here's how the view approach works:

1. The clinician clicks on a button inside his or her EHR. This click launches a query containing name, gender, date of birth, and zip code to a responding EHR. The physician does not need to respecify the patient or log into a separate portal since the patient identity information and security credentials are sent from the querying EHR automatically.

2. The responding EHR checks the security, looks up the patient, and responds with a medical record number if the patient is found.

3. The querying EHR sends a new query incorporating the returned medical record number.

4. The responding EHR launches a web page which displays clinical data for that medical record number.

5. All transactions are audited in the responding EHRs.

Since this approach works like magic, requires no HIE, and is fast/inexpensive to implement, our clinicians have described it as the "magic button."

In effect, it serves as a web-based single sign-on application that retains patient context and enables clinicians to view data from any EHR that adheres to the magic button implementation guide.

We see it as a temporary solution because it does not result in persistent exchange of semantically interoperable data. It simply enables a clinician to see data such as problem lists, medication lists, allergies, labs, radiology studies, EKGs, reports, and notes in remote systems without requiring a lot of training. It's better than having silos of data and sending faxes.

As HIEs come online, push and pull models will enable the same kind of data exchange but will incorporate data from sending EHRs into receiving EHRs, enhancing workflow and improving the integrity of the record.

One other problem with the magic button is that it does not scale very well— we now have buttons for Atrius, Needham, Milton, and eClinicalWorks practices. Clinicians ask patients where they've received care, get their consent to view the data, and click on the appropriate magic button. As we add more affiliates, the number of magic buttons will be hard to manage.

In future pull models, record locator services will keep an index of all the locations where patients have consented to their data being accessed.

But for now, having a kind of Blue Button that enables clinicians to view each other's records with patient consent is truly magic for those who use it. ∎

The Perfect Storm for Innovation

In my career, there have been a few perfect storms, defined as "a confluence, resulting in an event of unusual magnitude."

When I was an undergraduate at Stanford University in 1980, two geeky guys named Jobs and Wozniak dropped by the Homebrew Computer Club to demonstrate a kit designed in their garage. IBM introduced the personal computer and MSDOS 1.0. I purchased an early copy of Microsoft Basic and began creating software in my dorm room including early versions of tax calculation software, an econometric modeling language, and electronic data interchange tools. Every day brought a new opportunity. The energies of hundreds of entrepreneurs created an industry in a few intensely creative months that laid the foundation for the architecture and tools still in use today. A guy named Gates offered me a job and I decided to stay in school instead.

In 2001, when I was first hired at Harvard, a visionary Dean for Medical Education, a supportive Dean of the Medical School, talented new development staff, and a sleepless MD/PhD student came together to create one of the first learning management systems in the country, myCourses. Robust web technologies, voice recognition, search engines, early mobile devices, and new multimedia streaming standards coincided with resources, strong governance, and a sense of

In a few weeks we became the first hospital in the country to certify our EHR applications—inpatient and ambulatory. We became the first hospital to achieve Meaningful Use.

urgency. Magic happened and in a matter of months, an entire platform was created that is still powering Harvard Medical School today.

At BIDMC in 2010, IS Clinical Systems staff and key operational leaders realized that Meaningful Use Stage 1 was within reach if we temporarily put aside other work and focused our energy, creativity, and enthusiasm on rapid innovation, process change, and education. In a few weeks we became the first hospital in the country to certify our EHR applications—inpatient and ambulatory. We became the first hospital to achieve Meaningful Use. More than 70% of our eligible professionals have surpassed Meaningful Use performance thresholds. We had no budget, no dedicated resources, and nothing but strength of will to make it happen. It was one of our finest hours.

In 2011, the Massachusetts public sector (Secretary of EOHHS,[16] CIO of EOHHS), private sector healthcare leaders, and healthcare IT experts had a bold idea—create a public utility that links together all the existing regional health information exchanges, public health, small clinician offices, payers, and patients using modular components procured and initially operated by state government.

---

16 EOHHS = Executive Office of Health and Human Services, Massachusetts.

We aligned forces and in a few weeks created budgets, project plans, a new State Medicaid Health Plan, and a guiding coalition of stakeholders. Political, organizational, and technical barriers were broken down and unbridled optimism rekindled our health information exchange momentum. 2012 was a transformative year in the Commonwealth—truly a perfect storm.

My advice: look for the perfect storms in your own life. Minimize your distractions, cancel unnecessary meetings, and put aside those tasks that don't add value. Take a risk and dive head first into the possibility of creating greatness. I've seen opportunities come and go in my life. No one remembers the mundane. No one forgets the events of unusual magnitude.

Recently, I updated my BIDMC job description to include fostering health information exchange among affiliates, accountable care organizations, and the community. The Massachusetts Health Information Exchange is the next perfect storm in my career and I will devote all of my energies to the confluence being created by EOHHS CIO Manu Tandon, Massachusetts eHealth Collaborative CEO Micky Tripathi, and the dozens of volunteers lending the wisdom to the process. ■

Electronic Health Record Safety

Although EHRs address a variety of safety concerns such as unreadable orders/prescriptions, drug/drug interaction checking, and fostering care coordination, they can create new problems that did not exist with paper. These problems are rare (less than 1% of quality issues reported), but they are important.

For example, a clinician writing a paper prescription for Atenolol, a beta blocker used for cardiovascular diseases, would be unlikely to accidentally write for Ativan, a benzodiazepine used for anxiety.

However, if an EHR presents medications in a pull-down or an AJAX style lookup list, you can imagine a physician selecting the wrong medication by simple slip of a mouse.

Atelvia

Atenolol

Ativan

Atorvastatin

Atovaquone

...

There have been several articles in the literature suggesting that badly designed software (or any software implemented poorly) can cause harm.

At BIDMC, we've used agile development techniques and rapid-cycle improvement processes to enhance usability of systems, especially in response to sentinel events or clinician concerns. Our systems are developed by clinicians for clinicians.

It is challenging to define usability of applications and software quality, so writing regulation (such as FDA device registration/approval) is hard.

Since it will take time to learn how to monitor the safety of EHRs and write enforceable regulation, what can we do in the short term?

> At BIDMC, we've used agile development techniques and rapid-cycle improvement processes to enhance usability of systems, especially in response to sentinel events or clinician concerns. Our systems are developed by clinicians for clinicians.

The ONC report suggests the following:

- Learn—Make it easier for clinicians to report patient safety events and risks using EHR technology. Engage health IT developers to embrace their shared responsibility for patient safety and promote reporting of patient safety events and risks. Provide support to patient safety organizations (PSOs) to identify, aggregate, and analyze health IT safety event and hazard reports. Incorporate health IT safety in post-market surveillance of certified EHR technology through ONC-Authorized Certification Bodies (ONC-ACBs). Align CMS health and safety standards with the safety of health IT, and train surveyors. Collect data on health IT safety events through the Quality & Safety Review System (QSRS). Monitor health IT adverse event reports to the Manufacturer and User Facility Device Experience (MAUDE) database.

- Improve—Use Meaningful Use of EHR technology to improve patient safety. Incorporate safety into certification criteria for health IT products. Support research and development of testing, user tools, and best practices related to health IT and its safe use. Incorporate health IT safety into medical education and training for all healthcare providers. Investigate and take corrective action, when necessary, to address serious adverse events or unsafe conditions involving EHR technology.

- Lead—Develop health IT safety priority areas, measures, and targets. Publish a report on a strategy and recommendations for an appropriate, risk-based regulatory framework for health IT. Establish an ONC Safety Program to coordinate the implementation of the Health IT Safety Plan. Encourage state governments to incorporate health IT into their patient safety oversight programs. Encourage private sector leadership and shared responsibility for health IT patient safety.

Some have questioned the wisdom of moving forward with EHRs before we are confident that they are 100% safe and secure. I believe we need to continue our current implementation efforts. I realize this is a controversial statement for me to make, but let me use an analogy.

When cars were first invented, seat belts, air bags, and anti-lock brakes did not exist. Manufacturers tried to create very functional cars, learned from experience how to make them better, then innovated to create new safety technologies, many of which are now required by regulation.

Writing regulation to require seat belts depended on experience with early cars.

My grandmother was killed by a medication error caused by lack of an EHR. My mother was incapacitated by medication issues resulting from lack of health information exchange between professionals and hospitals. My wife experienced disconnected cancer care because of the lack of incentives to share information. Meaningful Use Stage 2 requires functionality in EHRs which could have prevented all three events.

I am hopeful that ONC's thoughtful safety plan, which leverages the experience of EHRs in use, will appropriately accelerate the benefits of today's Certified EHR Technology while minimizing risks of future EHR products still in development. ∎

Social Documentation for Healthcare

I define "social documentation" as team-authored care plans, annotated event descriptions (ranging from acknowledging a test result to writing about the patient's treatment progress), and process documentation (orders, alerts/reminders) sufficient to support care coordination, compliance/regulatory requirements, and billing.

Here are a few core principles I'd like to see as the foundation of "social documentation" products:

- Incorporates data input from multiple team members, reducing the documentation burden for each participant

- Eliminates redundant entry of the same information by different caregivers (nurse, PCP, specialist, resident, social worker)

- Supports Wikipedia-like summaries (jointly authored statement of history, plans, and decision making)

- Supports Facebook/Twitter-like updates (e.g., "Patient developed a fever, ordered workup, will start antibiotics")

- Incorporates data already present in the EHR such as orders and results without having to redescribe them in narrative form

Accomplishing this is likely to require a modular architecture with some services offered in the cloud, some on mobile devices, and some via new enterprise software that improves upon insecure consumer offerings (such as institution-hosted, HIPAA-compliant instant messaging).

I recognize that implementing "social documentation" at a time when we're implementing ICD-10, Meaningful Use Stage 2, new security imperatives, accountable care organization tools to support care management, and health information exchange may seem overly burdensome.

However, Yogi Berra said, "If you don't know where you are going, you might wind up someplace else."

I believe that our strategy for ICD-10, Meaningful Use Stage 2, new security imperatives, ACOs, and HIEs can incorporate the modules that will be foundational for "social documentation" in healthcare.

If five years from now, Beth Israel Deaconess is known as the birthplace for the "post EHR" care management medical record and "social documentation," I'll have stories to tell my grandchildren. ∎

Chapter 7

Patient/Family Engagement and National Healthcare IT Priorities

The past several years have been challenging for my family. My mother broke her hip. My father died of chronic illness. My wife had breast cancer. All these events illustrated the need for patient and family engagement enabled by healthcare IT. I've been passionate about personal health records and patient-mediated data exchange in the late 1990s when BIDMC implemented PatientSite. Here are my thoughts about patient/family engagement and other national efforts to enhance data sharing among all stakeholders nationwide.

Personal Health Records

The exact definition of a personal health record (PHR) is still evolving, but personal health records hold the promise to make patients the stewards of their own medical data. PHRs may contain data from payer claims databases, clinician electronic health records, pharmacy dispensing records, commercial laboratory results, and patient self-entered data. They may include decision support features, convenience functions such as appointment making/requesting referrals/medication refill workflow, and bill paying. However, most PHRs are not standards-based and few support an easy way to transport records among different PHR products.

The current landscape of PHRs includes four basic models:

- Provider-hosted patient portal to the clinician's electronic health record— In this model, patients have access to provider record data from hospitals and clinics via a secure web portal connected to existing clinical information systems. Examples of this approach include MyChart at the Palo Alto Medical Clinic, PatientSite at Beth Israel Deaconess Medical Center, and MyChart at the Cleveland Clinic. The funding for provider-based PHRs is generally from the marketing department since PHRs are a powerful way to recruit and retain patients. Also, the healthcare quality department may fund them to enhance patient safety since PHRs can support medication reconciliation workflows.

- Payer-hosted patient portal to the payer claims database—In this model, patients have access to administrative claims data such as discharge diagnoses, reimbursed medications, and lab tests ordered. Few payer-hosted systems contain actual lab data, but many payers are now working with labs to obtain this data. Additionally, American's Health Insurance Plans (AHIP) are working together to enable the transport of electronic claims data between payers when patients move between plans, enhancing continuity of care. The funding for payer-based PHRs is based on reducing total claims to the payer through enrollment of patients in disease management programs and enhancing coordination of care.

- Employer-sponsored—In this model, employees can access their claims data and benefit information via a portal hosted by an independent outsourcing partner. An example of this is the collaborative effort of Pitney Bowes, Walmart, Intel and others to offer Dossia, an open-source application which enables patients to retrieve their own data. The funding for employer-based personal health records is based on reducing total healthcare costs to the employer through wellness and coordination of care. A healthy employee is a more productive employee.

- Vendor-hosted—Several vendors serve as a secure container for patients to retrieve, store, and manipulate their own health records. Microsoft's HealthVault includes uploading and storage of records as well as a health search engine. The business model for these PHRs is generally based on attracting more users to advertising-based websites, although the PHR itself may be ad-free.

All of these models will be empowered by data standards for demographics, problem lists, medications, allergies, family history, the genome, labs, and text narrative.

Another aspect of interoperability is interfacing home monitoring devices such as glucometers, scales, blood pressure cuffs, and spirometers to PHRs. At present, most patients using these devices must manually type results into PHRs or call them into a provider because of the lack of uniform data standards in devices, EHRs, and PHRs. The Continua Health Alliance is building a great foundation for this process by working with IEEE, HL7 and other standards development organizations (SDOs) to identify the most appropriate standards to support device interoperability and identify gaps in current standards.

Privacy and security are critical to health data exchanges between PHRs and EHRs. Privacy is the policy which protects confidentiality. Security is the technical means to ensure patient data is released to the right person, for the right reason, at the right time to protect confidentiality. The US currently lacks a uniform privacy policy for clinical data exchange. Local implementations are highly variable and some organizations use opt-in consent; others use opt-out. The PHR can help address this lack of policy. By placing patients at the center of healthcare data exchange and empowering patients to become stewards of their own data, patient confidentiality becomes the personal responsibility of every participating patient. Patients could retrieve their records, apply privacy controls, and then share their data as needed with just those who need to know. Since policies are local, the security standards built into PHRs need to be flexible enough to support significant heterogeneity.

By placing patients at the center of healthcare data exchange and empowering patients to become stewards of their own data, patient confidentiality becomes the personal responsibility of every participating patient.

The evolution of today's paper-based, non-standardized, unstructured text medical record into a fully electronic, vocabulary controlled, structured interoperable document shared among patients and providers will be a journey. Standards are key and recent work in this area now provides the foundation for PHRs. Security technology exists today that is good enough. Early experiences with PHRs demonstrate high patient satisfaction, reduced phone volume to provider offices, and less litigation by patients sharing medical decision making with their clinicians. The time to implement PHRs is now and the only barriers are organizational and political, not technological. ∎

Delayed and Embargoed Results on PatientSite

Today I was asked about the way we display results in our PHRs and the way we transmit results to PHR services like Microsoft HealthVault.

In general, we share everything with the patient immediately, since it is the patient's data.

However, from our many years of supporting PHRs through PatientSite, we've learned that some news is best communicated in person between doctor and patient (e.g., do you want to find out you have cancer on the web or via a thoughtful discussion with your doctor?).

Here are the reports we delay to enable discussion between doctor and patient to occur first. In the case of HIV testing, since special consents are required, we do not show the results in PatientSite at all.

- CT Scans (used to stage cancer), four days

- PET Scans (used to stage cancer), four days

- Cytology results (used to diagnose cancer), two weeks

- Pathology reports (used to diagnose cancer), two weeks

- HIV Diagnostic Tests: never shown

- Bone Marrow Transplant screen, including:
  o HIV-1, HIV-2, Antibody
  o HTLV-I, HTLV-II Antibody
  o NHIV (Nucleic Acid Amplification to HIV-I)

- HIV-1 DNA PCR, Qualitative

- HIV-2, Western Blot; includes these results:
  o HIV-2 AB, EIA
  o HIV-2, Western Blot

- HIV-1 Antibody Confirmation; includes these results:
  o Western Blot
  o Anti-P24
  o Anti-GP41
  o Anti-GP120/160

I hope these rules help others who are implementing PHRs. We want patients to own and be the stewards of their own data, but we also want to support the patient/doctor relationship and the notion that bad news is best communicated in person. ∎

Lessons Learned from e-Patient Dave

I started the week with a blog about the "Limitations of Administrative Data," so it's fitting to end the week with lessons learned and next steps.

e-Patient Dave,[1] his doctor Danny Sands, and I spent many hours in online and phone conversation about the data elements in healthcare that are of greatest use to e-patients. Since the American Recovery and Reinvestment Act (ARRA) requires patients be given access to their electronic data, I have wanted to share all data with patients, both clinical and administrative. It's clear from our discussions that sharing billing data with patients is unreliable for clinical history, and it was a mistake to do that.

Administrative data is a coded summary of the clinical care that lacks perfect specificity and time references (e.g., just because you had a diagnosis of low potassium five years ago does not imply it is a problem today).

Thus, we must be careful about what data we send to PHRs and how that data is presented to patients. Here's the action plan that Dave, Danny, and I developed to optimize the PHR experience for e-patients[2]:

Problem List

This is useful clinical information as long as clinicians keep it current. Danny has done that with Dave's data, so it's Dave's best current source of relevant diagnoses and ongoing treatment.

Plan

Remove our ICD-9 administrative data feed from Google so that the clinician's problem list is the only data which populates the "Conditions" area.

Continue to improve our problem list functionality in webOMR[3] so that it maps to SNOMED-CT, enabling Google and other PHR vendors to provide medical information and decision support based on a controlled vocabulary instead of just free text.

Change the BIDMC Google Health upload screen from "Diagnoses" to "Problem List."

---

1   e-Patient Dave, or Dave deBronkart, is a former cancer patient and blogger who, in 2009, became a noted activist for healthcare transformation through participatory medicine and personal health data rights.

2   An e-patient is a health consumer who participates fully in his/her medical care. Sometimes referred to as an "Internet patient," e-patients see themselves as equal partners with their doctors in the healthcare process. E-patients gather information about medical conditions that impact them and their families, using electronic communication tools (including Web 2.0 tools) in coping with medical conditions. The term encompasses both those who seek guidance for their own ailments and the friends and family members (e-caregivers) who go online on their behalf. e-Patients report two effects of their health research: "better health information and services, and different (but not always better) relationships with their doctors." (Description from Wikipedia: http://en.wikipedia.org/wiki/E-patient.)

3   webOMR is BIDMC's self-built electronic health record.

Medication List

Name (with NDC coding), Dosage/Frequency, Prescription, and Date provide good "data liquidity" of active medications. We will continue to investigate the utility of sending inactive medications.

Allergy List

Name, reaction, and level of certainty of the reaction has worked well. However, Google Health does not display the detailed reaction information. We will either insert this information into the Google Allergy notes or work with Google to add a new field.

Procedures

We do not currently send procedures to Google Health, nor do they appear in PatientSite. However, Dave feels they may be useful to e-patients. We will add procedure name and date as a pilot.

It was a great week of discussion with many lessons learned. We look forward to our ongoing work with e-patients, doctors, and IT professionals. ∎

Open Notes

An important article was published in the *Annals of Internal Medicine* recently about the OpenNotes study, "Inviting Patients to Read Their Doctors' Notes: A Quasi-experimental Study and a Look Ahead."[4]

There are also two accompanying editorials:

- "A Patient's View of OpenNotes"

- "Pushing the Envelope of Electronic Patient Portals to Engage Patients in Their Care"

We're all enthusiastic about expanding this access to all BIDMC patients. Here's the press release that was issued:[5]

"BOSTON—Patients with access to notes written by their doctors feel more in control of their care and report a better understanding of their medical issues, improved recall of their care plan and being more likely to take their medications as prescribed, a Beth Israel Deaconess Medical Center-led study has found.

"Doctors participating in the OpenNotes trial at BIDMC, Geisinger Health System in Danville, PA and Harborview Medical Center in Seattle reported that most of their fears about an additional time burden and offending or worrying

---

4   Delbanco T, Walker J, Bell SK, et al. Inviting patients to read their doctors' notes: a quasi-experimental study and look ahead. *Annals of Internal Medicine.* 2012; 157(7):461-470.

5   Kowalczyk L. Patients benefit from reading doctors' notes study shows. *OpenNotes.* October 1, 2012.

patients did not materialize, and many reported enhanced trust, transparency, and communication with their patients.

"The findings were published in the *Annals of Internal Medicine.*

"'Patients are enthusiastic about open access to their primary care doctors' notes. More than 85 percent read them, and 99 percent of those completing surveys recommended that this transparency continue,' says Tom Delbanco, MD, co-first author, a primary care doctor at BIDMC and the Koplow-Tullis Professor of General Medicine and Primary Care at Harvard Medical School. 'Open notes may both engage patients far more actively in their care and enhance safety when the patient reviews their records with a second set of eyes.'

"'Perhaps most important clinically, a remarkable number of patients reported becoming more likely to take medications as prescribed,' adds Jan Walker, RN, MBA, co-first author and a Principal Associate in Medicine in the Division of General Medicine and Primary Care at BIDMC and Harvard Medical School. 'And in contrast to the fears of many doctors, few patients reported being confused, worried or offended by what they read.'

"The findings reflect the views of 105 primary care physicians and 13,564 of their patients who had at least one note available during a year-long voluntary program that provided patients at an urban academic medical center, a predominantly rural network of physicians, and an urban safety net hospital with electronic links to their doctors' notes.

"Of 5,391 patients who opened at least one note and returned surveys, between 77 and 87 percent reported open notes made them feel more in control of their care, with 60 to 78 percent reporting increased adherence to medications. Only 1 to 8 percent of patients reported worry, confusion or offense, three out of five felt they should be able to add comments to their doctors' notes, and 86 percent agreed that availability of notes would influence their choice of providers in the future.

"Among doctors, a maximum of 5 percent reported longer visits, and no more than 8 percent said they spent extra time addressing patients' questions outside of visits. A maximum of 21 percent reported taking more time to write notes, while between 3 and 36 percent reported changing documentation content.

"No doctor elected to stop providing access to notes after the experimental period ended.

"'The benefits were achieved with far less impact on the work life of doctors and their staffs than anticipated,' says Delbanco. 'While a sizeable minority reported changing the way their notes addressed substance abuse, mental health issues, malignancies and obesity, a smaller minority spent more time preparing their notes, and some commented that they were improved.'

"As one doctor noted: 'My fears? Longer notes, more questions and messages from patients ...In reality, it was not a big deal.'"

"Walker suggests that so few patients were worried, confused or offended by the note because 'fear or uncertainty of what's in a doctor's 'black box' may engender far more anxiety than what is actually written, and patients who are especially likely to react negatively to notes may self-select to not read them.'

"'We anticipate that some patients may be disturbed in the short term by reading their notes and doctors will need to work with patients to prevent such harms, ideally by talking frankly with them or agreeing proactively that some things are at times best left unread.'

"'When this study began, it was a fascinating idea in theory,' says Risa Lavizzo-Mourey, MD, president and CEO of the Robert Wood Johnson Foundation, the primary funder of the study. 'Now it's tested and proven. The evidence is in: Patients support, use, and benefit from open medical notes. These results are exciting—and hold tremendous promise for transforming patient care.'" ∎

Adoption and Implementation of Standards

In the past several years, many standards have been harmonized, many gaps closed, and many controversies resolved. Stakeholders have come together and the conversations have evolved from emotion to problem solving. Some of these standards are widely adopted and implemented. Others are so new that implementations are limited to prototypes and pilots. To me, the work ahead is continued evolution of the work we've done to ensure adoption of the standards is widespread and implementation is accelerated.

The HIT Standards Committee has focused on adoption and implementation.

The theme of Meaningful Use Stage 1 was getting data into electronic form and beginning data exchange via simple architectures—pushing data from organization to organization. As a country, we've done well with Stage 1 data exchanges—laboratories (HL7 2.x messaging, CDA document summaries, UCUM for units of measure, and LOINC for lab names); medications (NCPDP Script 10.x for messaging, RxNorm for medication names); administrative transactions (X12 for content, CAQH Core for vocabulary); and quality (HL7 2.x messaging, CDA documents).[6] Transmission of all this content will be done using common web standards—TLS to establish a mutually authenticated channel for data exchanges

---

6 HL7 = Health Level 7; CDA = Clinical Document Architecture; UCUM = Unified Code for Units of Measure; LOINC = Local Observation Identifiers Names and Codes; NCPDP = National Council for Prescription Drug Programs; CAQH = Council for Affordable Healthcare; RxNorm = produced by the National Library of Medicine, RxNorm is a normalized naming system for generic and branded drugs, and a tool for supporting semantic interoperation between drug terminologies and pharmacy knowledge base systems.

over the Internet, SHA to protect the integrity of data transmissions, and AES to encrypt data for transmission.[7]

The theme of Meaningful Use Stage 2 is enhanced data exchange among payers, providers, and patients, encouraging more participants to get involved in data exchanges using a variety of architectures—push from point to point, publish/subscribe, secure email, and mobile devices.

The theme of future stages of Meaningful Use will be ubiquitous data sharing with patient consent from all stakeholders to all stakeholders. This level of data exchange requires sophisticated consent management and architectures such as pulling from multiple sources that require a master patient index or voluntary universal healthcare identifier.

What evolution will be required for this evolution?

1. Policies that help streamline security frameworks—Currently, HITSP and the HIT Standards Committee have selected standards and implementation guides that can support the entire range of possible policies. This means that the list of standards for authentication, authorization, access control, secure transmission, document exchange, and auditing looks intimidating. Ideally, the Policy Committee and Standards Committee will work together to develop data exchange policies that will narrow the architecture choices and simplify the list of security standards.

2. Common Data Transport—Currently there is little controversy about the secure transmission standards (TLS plus SHA and AES). However, there is ongoing debate among stakeholders about SOAP verses REST and the use of the various IHE profiles to support document exchange— XDS (document sharing in an organization), XCA (document sharing between organizations), XDR (point-to-point document exchange), and XDM (document exchange on mobile devices). Sometimes this debate is framed as large established companies versus small innovative Health 2.0 companies. Ideally, we'll come to a meeting of the minds in which the right tools are used for the right applications. I can certainly appreciate the pros/cons of the various approaches— SOAP has well-developed security tools but is more challenging to implement than REST. In some ways, SOAP is losing popularity among web application developers. IHE[8] XDS, XCA, XDR, and XDM contain pieces of the somewhat-challenging to implement ebRS standards used in the SOAP headers for metadata and message routing. REST is very easy to implement but lacks generalizable security tools, forcing

---

7   TLS = Transport Layer Security; SHA = Secure Hash Algorithm; AES = Advanced Encryption Standard.

8   IHE = Integrating the Healthcare Enterprise.

each implementer to create their own application specific security controls, such as Microsoft and Google have done with their PHRs. We'll discuss this at the HIT Standards Committee.

3. Vocabulary tools—The vocabularies suggested by HITSP and the HIT Standards Committee, SNOMED-CT for problem lists, LOINC for lab names, RxNorm for medication names, UCUM for units of measure, and UNII[9] (for allergies) will be more easily implementable in health information exchanges if mapping tools are created which enable existing proprietary or older code sets to be mapped to these newer standards. This means that existing legacy systems inside an organization can be left untouched and vocabulary normalization can take place as data leaves applications for data exchange to other organizations or registries. We'll discuss this at the HIT Standards Committee. ■

Standards Lessons from the Web

Why has the web been adopted so rapidly? The web has two basic standards—content (HTML) and transport (HTTP).[10] Of course, there are several other supporting standards such as DNS, TLS/SSL, URL syntax, and CSS, but to get started all you need is basic content and transport.[11] You can learn everything you need to know to create a web page in under an hour.

The content standards we use in healthcare such as NCPDP Script for eRx, HL7 2.x/CDA for clinical transactions, and X12 for administrative transactions are fine. There is some debate about the right level of simplification for a clinical summary standard, but I'm convinced that the SDOs will continue to refine clinical summaries in a way that ensures suitable content packages will be available for simple and complex use cases. There is additional vocabulary work to do, but that is already in progress.

On the transport side, let's explore the options:

1. Do nothing and let the market develop a transport mechanism—after all, that is what happened with HIPAA (it specified the content as X12 4010 and left implementation of transport up to the market).

   I do not favor this option. In Massachusetts, NEHEN implemented secure appliances to solve the problem of data transport. We spent

---

9   UNII = Unique Ingredient Identifier.

10   HTML = Hypertext Markup Language; HTTP = Hypertext Transfer Protocol.

11   DNS = Domain Name System; TLS/SSL = transport layer security/secure sockets layer; URL = Uniform Resource Locator; CSS = cascading style sheets.

millions and took years to do this. HIPAA transactions are not as widely implemented as the industry would like, largely because transport standards were missing and implementation guidance for the content was not detailed enough. Of course, you could force everyone to sign up for the clearinghouse/intermediary of their choice, but this creates heterogeneity, click fees, and unnecessary middlemen.

2. Specify all the standards and policies necessary for end-to-end secure transport.

    Thus far, we've stayed architecturally neutral and provided a suite of standards for transport that ensure authentication, authorization, role-based access control, and auditing to support all policy variations. This approach has been a fine starting point, but it needs to be refined via policy so the number of standards can be constrained. For example, a policy which states that audit trails must be available showing who looked at what and when is probably sufficient instead of requiring every organization to implement a standards-based audit trail. It's unclear what the business case is for a completely standardized, interoperable audit trail. Another example: if policy requires segmentation of the record into standard care, HIV care, mental healthcare, and substance abuse care, as well as requires that the application enables patients to record their preferences for release of these four segments, do we need access control standards, or accept that the application adequately protects privacy?

> *Our experience with NEHEN is that policy, data use, and reciprocal support agreements (DURSA), and simple transport standards can facilitate rapid implementation of healthcare information exchange.*

    If policies and certification ensure appropriate application behavior, then point-to-point transport might be as simple as TLS with bilateral certificate exchange at the infrastructure level, substantially reducing the burden of implementation.

Of course, some may argue that an approach that uses simple web standards for securing transmission and leaves other privacy controls to the application cannot ensure "chain of trust" end-to-end security. It is true that each organization and stakeholder would have to decide if they trust the applications used by their trading partners. Our experience with NEHEN is that policy, data use, and reciprocal support agreements (DURSA[12]), and simple transport standards can facilitate rapid implementation of healthcare information exchange.

---

12 DURSA = Data Use and Reciprocal Support Agreement.

3. Deploy appliances that serve as secure gateways between organizations. With policies and over-the-wire security standards, the market can develop appliances that securely transport packages of content. Some may be SOAP-based using CAQH Core or IHE XDS/XDR, and some may be REST-based. The folks at FHA Connect have done a great job creating an open-source application that can serve as such an appliance.

One thing I've learned from negotiation (my "walks in the woods"), is that being dogmatic about one solution is rarely the right answer. Folks who know me often hear the word "parsimonious"—the smallest number of solutions needed to meet the needs of stakeholders. The answer is not 100 variations, but a small number that provides business value—the right tool for the right job. From the work I've seen thus far, I think the transport solutions that will work for stakeholders include the following:

1. For those who want end-to-end standards-controlled secure transport that guarantees integrity of documents—IHE XDS, XDR, XDM, and XCA fulfill the need. These standards are SOAP-based and enable use of web services (WS) security controls, so they are useful for protecting privacy at the standards level.

2. For those who want standards-based security with simple implementation, an appliance such as FHA Connect, NEHEN, InterSystems' Ensemble, or Orion Health's Rhapsody is a very reasonable approach.

3. For those who want a secure channel for transporting data elements such as a problem lists, medication lists, and labs from EHR to PHR, a simple TLS and REST approach is good enough. Ideally, HITSP and the HIT Standards Committee workgroups will provide an implementation guide with standard URIs/query strings so that we'll not have huge variation in REST APIs.[13] Some have used the term "Healthcare Internet" to describe such an approach.

I look forward to the continued work which aligns healthcare transport with every other industry. At some point in the near future, we'll realize that web-centric standards that are good enough for the financial services industry are good enough for healthcare. ∎

Guiding Principles for National Standards Efforts

The HIT Standards Committee developed guiding principles to steer its work. Here's what we think about when we're selecting standards:

---

13 API = application programming interface.

- Keep it simple; think big, but start small; recommend standards as minimal as possible to support the business goal and then build as you go.

- Don't let "perfect" be the enemy of "good enough"; go for the 80% that everyone can agree on; get everyone to send the basics (medications, problem list, allergies, labs) before focusing on the more obscure.

- Keep the implementation cost as low as possible; eliminate any royalties or other expenses associated with the use of standards.

- Design for the little guy so that all participants can adopt the standard and not just the best resourced.

> *Don't let "perfect" be the enemy of "good enough"; go for the 80% that everyone can agree on; get everyone to send the basics (medications, problem list, allergies, labs) before focusing on the more obscure.*

- Do not try to create a one-size-fits-all standard, it will be too heavy for the simple use cases.

- Separate content standards from transmission standards (e.g., if CCD is the HTML, what is the HTTP?).

- Create publicly available controlled vocabularies and code sets that are easily accessible/downloadable.

- Leverage the web for transport whenever possible to decrease complexity and the implementers' learning curve ("healthcare Internet").

- Position quality measures so that they will encourage adoption of standards.

- Create implementation guides that are human readable, have working examples, and include testing tools. ∎

Marketing Interoperability

In the past, it's been challenging to market interoperability because incentives to share data between organizations are often not aligned.

You can imagine the following conversation:

"Hi. I'm from your local health information exchange. You may know that over 20% of lab and radiology tests ordered in our state are redundant and unnecessary. We're solving that problem through interoperability and we need you to invest $300,000 in capital plus $100,000 per year to connect to our statewide exchange.

When it's all working, we'll eliminate all the redundancy, reducing your lab and radiology income by 20%."

Interoperability is great for patients and a benefit to society, but can create a loss of income for some stakeholders. How do we sell it?

> *Interoperability is great for patients and a benefit to society, but can create a loss of income for some stakeholders. How do we sell it?*

1. Health reform—If healthcare reform aligns incentives for wellness and care coordination, stakeholders will be incentivized to share data. For example, if medical error is no longer reimbursed and hospital readmissions become a cost rather than a profit center, care summaries are likely to be shared among providers and data sharing between patients and providers will be used for home monitoring and keeping patients out of the hospital.

2. Meaningful Use metrics/pay for performance—Meaningful Use requires clinical summary data exchange between organizations, e-prescribing, electronic laboratory workflow, quality measurement, and public health transactions. Thus, for organizations to claim their stimulus funds, they must be interoperable. Exchanging data between facilities within an organization does not count. Many private insurers also offer pay-for-performance incentives for reduced readmission rates, appropriate testing, and medication management. The combination of stimulus funds, Medicare Part D funds, and private insurer pay for performance should provide reasonable incentives.

3. Peer pressure—I've seen several types of interoperability "peer pressure" in our communities. Primary care physicians would rather work with specialists who can exchange clinical data, ensuring a closed-loop referral workflow. Specialists who are not interoperable are likely to experience a decline in business. Among hospitals, our local CEOs have decided that healthcare IT should not be considered a competitive asset for any one organization—it should raise the bar for all organizations to improve the health of the population. Thus, each CEO had decided to eliminate silos and share clinical summaries at transitions of care, even if this means exchanging data between competitive organizations.

4. Cost avoidance—The NEHEN network has eliminated paper for 90% of the administration transactions in Massachusetts, taking the cost of claims submission from $2.50 to .25. We've been able to make the return on investment (ROI)/business case for funding interoperability operations based on cost avoidance. Clinical data exchange also has cost avoidance. E-prescribing eliminates the need for staff to process

refills and reduces calls/pages to clarify prescriptions. Malpractice assertions are less likely when care is coordinated among patients and providers. Disease management programs administered by payers and case management activities are more efficient when data is shared electronically.

5. Increased business—Providing interoperable connections in and out of an organization should make that organization a more attractive business partner for clinical collaboration, clinical research, and diagnostic services. I recently was asked to enable data sharing between BIDMC and a business partner. I was told that interoperability was a significant value add to the relationship.

Thus, although there may be a short-term misalignment of incentives caused by reducing redundancy and waste, there are many reasons to implement interoperability for the long term. With new regulations and healthcare reform on the horizon, I'm hoping it becomes a business imperative! ∎

Advice to Health Information Exchanges

With the HIE grants around the corner, many communities are asking me for advice to prioritize their local/regional infrastructure and applications. Here are my recommendations based on leading an HIE for the past several years:

1. Define your business requirements based on the value proposition for participants. This will maximize the likelihood stakeholders will pay for the services they receive, ideally based on gainsharing a portion of their cost avoidance (e.g., if a lab costs $1.00 to send via email and $.20 to send via the HIE, the hospital can pocket $.80 and everyone wins.

2. Ensure you have a business model. Subscription-based is good, since grants are not a business model. Transaction fees are an impediment to commerce—they are a disincentive to using the HIE. A fixed subscription fee encourages maximal use of the HIE.

3. Ensure you have policies for consent, auditing, and authorization of trading partners. Policies constrain technology choices and ensure the exchange is trusted.

4. Start with push transactions. This is a very important point. I've written several blogs about the importance of using the simplest possible standards to achieve the business goal. A RESTful approach which enables clinical data to be pushed from one clinician to another

is simple to implement since it leverages existing standards and capabilities of web servers without requiring mastery of more complex techniques. In Massachusetts we push admission notification, discharge summaries, ED summaries, and other CDA documents. We're currently implementing push of quality data to registries and public health surveillance to the Boston Public Health Commission. The advantage of push is that it does not require a master patient index, since the messaging is provider to provider or organization to organization. Consent is easy since the patient simply consents for the push. Wes Rishel[14] has written several great blogs about this approach, which are important to read as they reflect some of the discussion in the HIT Policy Committee's NHIN Working Group.

5. Have a vision for pull transactions. At some point, the usual ED use case will be mentioned—how do you pull together the entire history of a patient from all the sites from which he or she has received care in a community? You'll need a master patient index, a record locator service (what institutions have records on the patient) and a means to pull summaries from each site. This pull infrastructure is much more complicated and expensive. Consent is much more complex: who can pull what from where and when? Instead of a provider-to-provider push involving two clinicians, pull could result in hundreds of people viewing a record. Push is great, but it really does not help the ED gather data about a patient for life-saving treatment. Eventually we'll need to implement pull.

The five points above plus the work of the HIT Policy/HIT Standards Community should provide the guidance that HIEs need. ■

A History of Our Healthcare Future

When Stage 3 of Meaningful Use is fully implemented, what will our healthcare system look like? Here's my future forward look at the changes in the provider, patient, payer, and researcher experience five years from now:

- Clinicians will become healthcare coordinators, working in partnership with patients to manage wellness using a shared lifetime electronic health record.

- Clinicians will produce a record that is designed to be shared with the patient, instead of just supporting the billing process.

---

14 Wes Rishel is Vice President and Distinguished Analyst in Gartner's healthcare provider research practice.

- Hospitals will compete based on the results they achieve rather than the grandeur of their buildings. Transparency in the reporting of quality and outcomes will transform the healthcare marketplace. Patients will have a much better understanding of quality, cost, and outcomes.

- Patients will undergo fewer tests and take fewer medications because redundant and inappropriate care will be reduced. Healthcare value will improve—higher quality for less costs, since less care is often the right answer.

- Patients will have much more choice as consumers. Access to the electronic records including their genomes will enable personalized medicine— selecting the treatments that best align with their care preferences, risk- taking thresholds, and physiology.

- Payers will reimburse providers for quality rather than quantity since electronic health records will document the care given and not given.

- Researchers will have access to novel data sources (with patient consent) and be able to discover which treatments are the most effective. This knowledge will be integrated into electronic health records and personal health records so that providers and patients can make the optimal care decisions. Today, there is more literature published every year than a clinician can read in a lifetime, so best current evidence is not rapidly incorporated into practice.

Change is hard; technology is easy. As we navigate the stages of Meaningful Use in the years ahead, be prepared for amazing shifts in workflow, process, and behavior that will accompany them. Let's hope we can tell our children the history of how we did it! ∎

The Characteristics of HIE Governance

Here's what stakeholders in Massachusetts have outlined as ideal characteristics of HIE governance:

Guiding Principle—To provide oversight and governance for an effective rollout of HIE across Massachusetts that accelerates and enables a network-of-network approach by tying existing assets to procured services in a unified, transparent, and standards-driven manner while embracing and enhancing the principle of public private partnership.

Specific Principles for Governance

- Principle #1—Enhance trust and credibility by establishing a multi-stakeholder, open, and transparent body.

○ Note—Need to draw a distinction between this governing body and the existing ones and perhaps consolidate to a fewer number.

• Principle #2—Reflect public/private partnership in a way that balances the priorities of regulation, transparency, and common good with the imperatives of value generation, sustainability, and market economics.

• Principle #3—Enhance credibility and trust by adopting best practices that eliminate any conflicts of interest.

○ Manage procurement by groups not having an interest in bidding for services.

○ Govern operational delivery utilizing groups and individuals separate from the community that provides these services.

• Principle #4—Provide a comprehensive platform that merges the tactical task of oversight of HIE rollout with the strategic need for innovation-driven vision setting. Provide the following functions:

○ Setting priorities for HIE procurement

○ Providing oversight of an HIE project/program management office

○ Holding service providers accountable for meeting goals

○ Providing oversight for resource allocation

○ Providing a forum for fostering innovation

○ Being an enabler and accelerator for the adoption of HIE by anticipating and removing roadblocks

A great discussion and a very sound set of governance characteristics. Our next step is to present these ideas to the Massachusetts HIT Council for their feedback and then think about various structures to operationalize HIE governance (e.g., state department, new 501c(3), private sector). ∎

Unconscious in the Emergency Department

I'm often asked, "But when will health information exchange technology be able to retrieve all my records from everywhere when I'm lying unconscious in the emergency department and cannot give a history?"

Here are my thoughts about the trajectory we're on and how it will lead us to supporting the "Unconscious in the ED" use case.

Meaningful Use Stage 1 is about capturing data electronically in EHRs. Getting healthcare data in electronic form is foundational to any data exchanges. At this point, medication lists, problem lists, allergies, and summaries are available from EHRs.

The data exchanges in Stage 1 are simple pushes of data from point A to point B—from provider to public health, from provider to provider, and from provider to pharmacy. There is no master patient index, no record locator service, and no centralized database containing everyone's lifetime health record.

The Stage 1 data exchanges are the right first step. Serving as chair for a Massachusetts health information exchange for 12 years, I can tell you that pushing data from point A to point B builds trust and breaks down political barriers to data sharing. The policy needed to guide push technology is straightforward, since the parties involved in the exchange are limited—the sender and the receiver. Consent can be simple. For a referral, this might be, "Do you permit me to send your data to a specialist so that your care can be coordinated?"

But how are we going to get to a model that supports the pulling of data by emergency rooms?

There are several engineering approaches.

One is to create a master patient index for a state or region so that the identity of patients seeking care is known. Once we have a master patient index, we can build a record locator service to keep track of every site the patient visits. Then we can build a consent repository so that the patient can control what is shared. During an emergency department encounter, summaries can be pulled from those sites listed in the record locator service which the patient has agreed to share.

I know that this approach works, because it is what I implemented at the hospitals of CareGroup in 1997 as the focus of my MIT thesis.

However, it does have scalability problems. Given that there are 500,000 doctors and 5,000 acute care hospitals, the engineering complexity to pull data from multiple, disparate sites is significant and requires that all sites support real-time queries 24x7x365, maintaining the necessary security and robustness to enable such interchange. That's a tall order.

An alternative that is simpler from an engineering perspective and achievable with the Stage 1 push technologies looks like this:

What if payers, providers, and private vendors offered something called "the electronic medical home"? The patient needs to pick some hosting option they trust. Just as Stage 1 of Meaningful Use supports push transactions from provider to provider, the same transactions could be pushed to the electronic medical home designated by the patient. This has the added advantage of providing a means to support the patient engagement provisions of Stage 1 (deliver summaries of ambulatory encounters within three business days, deliver inpatient summaries upon request, deliver lifetime health summaries upon request). If every producer of data (lab, pharmacy, hospital, eligible professional, etc.) pushed a copy of the data they generated to the electronic medical home chosen by the patient, then the patient could become steward of his or her lifetime medical record hosted by the trusted agent of his or her choice. Medical home data would be complete and constantly updated by data producers.

Patients could store their electronic medical home designation on a card in their wallet or on a medical alert bracelet. If patients visited the emergency room of a hospital they had registered at previously, the hospital would have a record of the patient's electronic medical home selection since the hospital would be one of the medical home data sources.

Ok, but what if the patient arrives in the emergency department, naked and unconscious, so there is no electronic medical home designation on his or her body? I can tell you that in all my years of practicing emergency medicine, I have never treated a naked and unconscious patient, but let's think about the scenario.

There could be a national or federated regional database which keeps a record of the designated electronic medical home—an "electronic medical home locator service" that is easy to implement because it only has to point to one place, not to every location which has records about the patient.

When the patient arrives naked and unconscious in the emergency department, assuming someone knows the name/date of birth of the patient, the electronic medical home locator service is queried and once the selection of medical home is known, that one location could be queried to retrieve all of the records.

Finally, just to play out the complete use case to its most absurd, if no one knows the patient identity, then we could suggest the electronic medical home locator service should contain a hash of a fingerprint, so that a biometric—a scan of the patient's finger—could be used to identify the electronic medical home designation and then retrieve the lifetime record summary.

Summarizing

1. In Meaningful Use Stage 1, we implement push transactions. Microsoft HealthVault, hospitals, and payers should create electronic medical home repositories capable of receiving push transactions so that copies of inpatient, outpatient, and lifetime summaries can be sent there. The transport mechanism used to push data to the medical home could be REST, SOAP, or SMTP, just as the NHIN[15] Direct project has suggested. Ideally, electronic medical home providers will issue to each patient a health URL, making it easy for EHRs and health information exchanges to route data to the correct location.

2. When an electronic medical home designation is elected, a copy of the designation and a hash of the patient's fingerprint is sent to a regional or national electronic medical home locator service.

---

15 NHIN = Nationwide Health Information Network.

3. When the patient arrives unconscious, the name and date of birth of the patient are used to query the electronic medical home locator service, retrieve the electronic medical home designation, and then retrieve the lifetime record summary.

4. If the patient is naked and unconscious, a fingerprint scan could be used to retrieve the electronic medical home designation and the records.

5. All of this is empowered by Stage 1 of Meaningful Use as currently written. All that needs to happen is that providers, payers, and vendors need to offer a place to push transactions on behalf of the patient.

Some have suggested that we should abandon the NHIN Connect, NHIN Direct, and Stage 1 push exchanges in favor of an engineering optimal solution of creating one large database of all electronic health records in the cloud.

Sometimes the engineering optimal solution is not the social/policy optimal solution.

The idea of creating a voluntary, opt-in electronic medical home supported by many hosts—payers, providers, vendors, etc.—is achievable and appealing.

In the US, we are wary of any top-down, government mandate. We are suspicious of centralizing anything. Maintaining patient control of healthcare data and letting the market provide multiple hosting options seems like an achievable architecture that builds upon what we have already implemented and the Meaningful Use regulations already in place. ■

Health Information Exchange Sustainability

As Massachusetts works through health information exchange governance, use cases, and procurement to connect all stakeholders in the Commonwealth, it must ensure sustainability by attracting funding from both the public and private sector. What are possibilities?

- Subscription based on value realized—The New England Healthcare Exchange Network (NEHEN) model over the past 13 years has been based on cost avoidance. It used to cost $5.00 per claim to support phone/fax/email/paper workflow. It now costs $.25. NEHEN was funded in its first decade by gain sharing—payers and providers funded HIE by contributing a small portion of their savings. We found that subscription models encouraged adoption and innovation since increased data flows meant more value for the subscription fee. Novel uses emerged such as scanning all payers simultaneously to identify eligibility for patients with multiple or ambiguous coverage. Subscription fees for e-prescribing and clinical exchange are now justified by Meaningful Use requirements, pay-for-performance programs, and evolving accountable care organization needs.

- Transaction fees—In some states, transaction fees have worked because each transaction creates a cost savings. If it costs you $1.00 to print a lab result and put it in an envelope but only a $.20 transaction fee to send it electronically, you'll be motivated to accept the transaction fee and pocket the $.80 savings.

- Assessment—Some states have assessed a temporary fee, such as $.01per claim, to generate the revenue to build HIE capabilities.

- Public funds—Since states can run their Medicaid operations more efficiently with automated administrative transactions, care coordination, diseases management, all payer databases, etc., they are motivated to invest in HIE construction and operation. Also, given the 90/10 federal match for Medicaid system enhancement, states can realize substantial benefit through strategic HIE investment.

- Bonds—Some states have thought about HIEs like highways. A bond measure funds the construction, then "tolls" are charged to pay back the bond. This is a variation on the transaction fee model.

My goal is to maintain the leadership we've shown in HIE and share our experience with the nation for the benefit of all. ∎

Publicity Is Cheap, Privacy Is Expensive

When I was 18 years old, publicity was hard to come by. Media outlets were limited to newspapers with very high editorial standards, television with few channels and very limited news time, and a few high-profile news magazines.

My first 15 minutes of fame came in 1981 when I was interviewed by Dan Rather for a CBS Evening News spot on entrepreneurialism in the Silicon Valley. In 1982, I appeared in *Newsweek*, as a student correspondent at Stanford, writing about religion, politics, and the culturally important trends of the day. In 1983, I appeared in *US News and World Report* in an article about the emerging importance of software.

Today, blogs, wikis, forums, YouTube, Facebook, Twitter, and Google enable fame and publicity without editorial control. Use your phone to take a video of a squirrel doing something amusing and a few minutes later you've got publicity and thousands of people watching your work.

The democratization of information is a good thing. It enables freedom of expression and instant access to news and information. Of course, it's hard to tell fact from fiction, opinion from news, and accomplishment from self-promotion, but it's left up to the consumer to turn data into information, knowledge, and wisdom.

The downside of a completely connected world is that publicity is cheap, but privacy is expensive.

The downside of a completely connected world is that publicity is cheap, but privacy is expensive.

How much effort does it take to not appear on the Internet, not be tracked by vendors maximizing sales by analyzing your browsing behavior, and not be findable from the innumerable legal/property/licensure records available on the Internet?

In 1981, publicity was expensive, and privacy was cheap.

Thirty years later, publicity is cheap, and privacy is expensive.

In another 30 years, it will be interesting to see how the concept of privacy evolves.

My daughter's generation shares everything about their day on Facebook. Maybe the concept of privacy will disappear for most aspects of life, except for those items, like medical records, which are protected via regulation and policy.

My advice to my daughter about privacy is simple—content on the web lasts forever, on the Internet nobody knows you're a dog, and share what you will such that no one gets hurt, including you.

Thirty years ago I had to wait for a call from Dan Rather. Today, I just press "Post." How we balance the expense of publicity and privacy is a question that society will need to continuously evaluate as we become more and more connected. ∎

The Safety of HIT-Assisted Care

I was recently asked by an Institute of Medicine committee to comment about the impact of healthcare information technologies (HIT) on patient safety and how to maximize the safety of HIT-assisted care.

"HIT-assisted care" means healthcare and services that incorporate and take advantage of healthcare information technologies and health information exchange for the purpose of improving the processes and outcomes of healthcare services. HIT-assisted care includes care supported by and involving EHRs, clinical decision support, computerized provider order entry, health information exchange, patient engagement technologies, and other health information technology used in clinical care.

There are two separate questions:

1. What technologies, properly used, improve safety?

2. Given that automation can introduce new types of errors, what can be done to ensure that HIT itself is safe?

To explore these topics, let's take a look at health information exchange. What HIE technologies improve safety and how can we ensure the technologies are safe to use?

At Beth Israel Deaconess Medical Center we exchange many types of data for care coordination, patient engagement, and population health. Below is a detailed summary of the HIE transactions implemented in our recently certified hospital systems.

1. Patient summary exchange for transitions of care—We produce a Continuity of Care Document for each patient handoff (i.e., from inpatient, ED, and outpatient [coming soon]) to home, skilled nursing facilities, or other hospitals. The CCD includes the following:

    o Problems

    o Procedures

    o Medications

    o Allergies and adverse reactions

    o Results

    o Encounters

Safety is improved by ensuring each provider has a complete problem list, medication list, allergy list, and recent results. Such a document is useful for medication reconciliation, drug/drug and drug/allergy decision support, and managing the entire patient by understanding all active problems.

However, summaries exchanged at a point in time are just that—a summary or abstract of the lifetime record that is accurate at a point in time. They do not provide access to the complete record such as inpatient notes, operative notes, history and physicals, and historical data such as discontinued medications or resolved problems. Many clinicians believe that a patient summary at a point in time is good enough for transitions of care, so the risk introduced by abstracting the record into just the salient handoff details may be minimal. A compromise may be a fresh look at what elements should be required for transitions of care. Recently, Massachusetts was awarded an ONC challenge grant to study this question by piloting innovative additions to the standard CCD using CDA templates.

2. Patient summary exchange from EHRs to PHRs—We produce a CCR when a patient initiates a transfer of his or her records from our EHR to the PHR of his or her choice (Google or HealthVault). The CCR includes the following:

   o Demographics

   o Problems

   o Medications

   o Allergies

   o Additional information about people and organizations

Safety is improved by sharing data between providers and patients, making patients the stewards of their own records. This transparency encourages a dialog about treatment plans, patient care preferences, and the accuracy of data in the medical record.

However, most commercial personal health records do not provide for exchange of clinician office notes such as we've piloted in BIDMC's PatientSite OpenNotes Project, nor do they include a consistent way to map EHR data to PHR displays. For example, BIDMC's EHR considers an allergy list entry to be the substance, the reaction, the observer (doctor, nurses, your mom), and the level of certainty. Google considers an allergy to be the substance and a mild/severe indicator. Thus, a transmission of an allergy, "Penicillin, Hives, Doctor, Very Certain" to Google results in "Penicillin" with no other information. Use of an agreed upon list of data elements (e.g., what constitutes an allergy list) for data exchange would resolve this problem.

3. Patient summary exchange for discharge instructions—We produce a CCD with discharge instructions for patients via a multidisciplinary web application used by doctors, nurses, social workers, and case managers. The CCD includes the following:

   o Discharge medications

   o Discharge instructions

   o Final diagnosis

   o Recommended follow-up

   o Major surgical or invasive procedures

   o Condition at discharge

Safety is improved by ensuring patients understand the next steps after they are discharged from the hospital. Inpatient medications are reconciled with outpatient medications, dietary or activity restrictions are noted, and follow-up appointments are documented.

However, at present, Meaningful Use does not require a specific electronic format for patient discharge communications. Patient discharge instructions are generated by humans and include a distillation of the record, not a complete copy of the record. A printed report, a PDF, or a web page all suffice. Although we have used the CCD format, it is not optimized for structured discharge instructions. Likely CDA templates with specific fields for the data elements most commonly used in discharge communications would be better.

4. Patient summary exchange for quality measurement—We produce a CCD with key process and outcomes measures for transmission to the Massachusetts eHealth Collaborative (MAeHC) Quality Data Warehouse. MAeHC computes all our ambulatory Physician Quality Reporting Initiative (PQRI) measures and all our pay-for-performance metrics. The CCD includes the following:

   o Payers

   o Problems

   o Procedures

   o Results

   o Medications

   o Encounters

Safety is improved by providing our clinicians, administrators, and government agencies with the metrics needed to evaluate our process and outcomes quality.

However, quality measures require precise coding of concepts into SNOMED-CT and other vocabularies. It is up to clinicians to translate their observations into the correct structured data and this is challenging. Better tools to automatically map physician plain language into controlled vocabularies would help.

5. Patient data exchange for public health activities—We produce numerous submissions to government agencies to support population health and public health goals. The messages are sent to public health agencies in batch every day based on results filed into patient records. They are exact duplicates of patient results, diagnoses, and immunization records without any loss of completeness.

Reportable lab results are sent to the Department of Public Health and Boston Public Health Commission. Syndromic Surveillance is sent to the Department of Public Health and Boston Public Health Commission. Immunizations are sent to the Department of Public Health and Boston Public Health Commission. Safety is improved through monitoring of results, symptoms, and immunizations in support of public health.

However, syndromic surveillance is limited by the accuracy of the structured signs and symptoms data captured by EHRs. Ensuring that clinician observations are captured in an accurate, structured, and timely way, then transmitted to public health requires more advanced vocabulary tools than exist in many EHRs.

Summarizing my observations:

1. Summary data is an abstract captured at a moment in time. Data corrections/updates are not sent. Thus, data about the patient becomes incomplete and stale over time. However, for the purpose intended, ensuring a transition of care is safe, a point-in-time summary may be good enough.

2. Enhanced vocabulary tools that translate clinician observations into structured data (such as Kaiser's recent contribution of its intellectual property) are useful to convey the meaning of information exchanged.

3. Implementation guides that specify required data elements are important so that receivers can accurately display the information exchanged.

4. Testing approaches already used as part of the certification process validate that data in the EHR is exported into interoperable formats accurately. National Institute of Standards and Technology (NIST) tools ensure that interoperable formats are compliant with standards. The challenge is getting the data into structured electronic form to begin with and deciding what to exchange for a given purpose.

5. Although not specifically discussed above, patient identification can be a challenge given the lack of a national patient identifier or an agreed-upon way to link the same patient's data among multiple institutions. The combination of labs, medications, and summaries from multiple sources might indicate a safety issue. Having a consistent approach to link these records would be helpful.

A number of these issues are part of the PCAST Workgroup discussion: should data be sent in context-rich documents or separated into individual "atomic" data elements? How granular is an atom—is it a problem list, a single problem, or a single field within a single problem (e.g., problem onset date)? How should patient matching be done? How should searching be done? Should data be structured and vocabulary controlled or unstructured?

The Institutes of Medicine (IOM), ONC, and PCAST efforts are raising all the right issues. I believe the Standards and Certification criteria for Stage 1, exemplified by all the standards samples documented above, is moving the country on the right trajectory to enhance the safety of care while ensuring HIT-assisted care is safe. ∎

Breach Fatigue

You've read about recent high-profile privacy breach settlements.

Every day the headlines are filled with so many such security issues that it almost seems like background noise. Just as too much decision support can result in alert fatigue and too many false alarms can result in alarm fatigue, the barrage of security breach news can lead to breach fatigue, causing you to let down your guard.

Forewarned is forearmed, so push aside your breach fatigue and plan for the day when you will have to run your own breach notification. Here's a task list to guide you:

- Immediate response actions

- Report to police department

- Notify legal counsel

- Notify privacy officer

- Notify CEO

- Notify clinical and IT leadership

- Notify board of directors

- Notify liability insurer

- Develop action plan

- Analysis

- Inventory unsecured data

- Draft risk assessment rules (what data in combination is reportable, e.g., name and social security number)

- Finalize risk assessment rules

- Conduct risk assessment

- Complete risk assessment report

- Complete reporting requirements report
  - Regulatory reporting and notifications
  - Define practice strategy/approach
  - Initial communication with practices
  - Notifications
    - Draft notification to media
    - Oral notification to federal/state authorities including approval of notices

- Office of Civil Rights
- Attorney General
- Office of Consumer Affairs

- o Practice approval of media notification
- o Distribute notification to media
- o Complete practice-specific spreadsheets
- o Choose credit monitoring service
- o Complete credit monitoring service contract
- o Prepare patient notices

- Practice-related activities
  - o Initial call
  - o Follow-up visit scheduled
  - o Practice packages complete
  - o Practice packages delivered to practice
  - o Re-identification visits scheduled (to notify patients, you'll need addresses which may not be included in the actual data breached)
  - o Re-identification complete
  - o Patient notifications complete
  - o Patient notifications sent
  - o Attorney General reports filed
  - o Office of Consumer Affairs reports filed
  - o Office of Civil Rights reports filed

- Communications
  - o Prepare talking points for various channels
  - o Staff a communication office (approximately 10% of notified patients will call)

- Remediation
  - o Cross-organizational review of processes and procedures which led to the breach
  - o Remediation of root causes
  - o Security policy updates as needed
  - o Laptop encryption as needed
  - o Additional training as needed

Follow the advice of your privacy officer and your legal counsel completely. Be transparent. Over communicate. Use the event as a teachable moment for your organization and your community. Be humble and apologize. Protect the patients and the providers.

As we continue the journey toward automation of electronic records to enhance safety and quality, we must retain the trust of our patients. Following the plan above will go far to address those events that occur as we all learn how to be better protectors of the data we host. ∎

> *Follow the advice of your privacy officer and your legal counsel completely. Be transparent. Over communicate.*

The Burden of Compliance

In an email noting the challenges of implementing ICD-10, 5010, eRx, EHR, and HIE simultaneously, my colleagues referenced a paper in the *British Medical Journal* by Enrico Coiera.[16] The authors writes:

"Experimental computer modeling has shown that as the number of dependencies increases in a system, the height of the local optimums [of organizational fitness] in a landscape lowers. In other words, the more dependencies there are in a system, the more likely they will be in conflict (through competing demands), flattening the landscape and diminishing the potential for improving system fitness. Thus the more complex a health system becomes, the more difficult it becomes to find any system design that has a higher fitness."

As we draft new regulations that impact healthcare IT organizations, we need to keep in mind that every regulation has a cost in dollars, time, and complexity.

Many people have spoken to me about the burden created by the Accounting of Disclosures Notice of Proposed Rulemaking (NPRM), highlighting three major challenges it creates: (1) an implementation burden that goes beyond the intent of HITECH; (2) an inadequate impact analysis especially on small entities; and (3) administrative overhead that is incompatible with impending budget cuts from the recent debt ceiling compromise plan.

The wording in the proposed rule which summarizes its intent follows:

"These two rights, to an accounting of disclosures and to an access report, would be distinct but complementary. The right to an access report would provide information on who has accessed electronic protected health information in a designated record set (including access for purposes of treatment, payment, and

---

16 Coiera E. Why system inertia makes health reform so difficult. *British Medical Journal*. 2011; 342:d3693.

health care operations), while the right to an accounting would provide additional information about the disclosure of designated record set information (whether hard-copy or electronic) to persons outside the covered entity and its business associates for certain purposes (e.g., law enforcement, judicial hearings, public health investigations). The intent of the access report is to allow individuals to learn if specific persons have accessed their electronic designated record set information (it will not provide information about the purposes of the person's access). In contrast, the intent of the accounting of disclosures is to provide more detailed information (a 'full accounting') for certain disclosures that are most likely to impact the individual."

Here's a commentary based on the feedback I've received.

Challenge 1—Scope Beyond the Intent of the HITECH Act

Protecting privacy is essential to building patient trust in electronic health records and health information exchanges.

To me, the intent of HITECH is to offer patient access upon request to EHR audit trails and HIE audit trails. However, the proposed rule goes beyond that, creating the concept of a "designated record set" and "disclosure logs" while exempting HIE transactions. It's too much and too little at the same time.

The Designated Record Set (DRS) is a super-set of information that includes the electronic health record as well as data housed in many other systems including billing, quality, research, and operational databases. It includes data shared with business associates such as small entities which provide specialty billing, transcription, and other services. By characterizing the accounting requirements around the more broadly defined DRS, the burden of compliance has been greatly increased, requiring new technologies to aggregate audit logs from a broad array of software applications.

Disclosures are broadly defined as the release of patient information to other entities. This means that every access to the DRS by physicians, nurses, allied health, lab, billing, accountants, auditors, legal staff, and numerous other "business associates" which are involved with a patient episode of care within the covered entity, must be logged, aggregated, and reported to patients on demand.

Business associates are extensions of a healthcare provider, plan, or clearinghouse's workforce. An example is a business hired by a physician practice to bill and collect medical fees. Another example is an independent contractor who provides coding or transcription services. Business associates provide a wide variety of services. Some may access content of the DRS as a direct consequence of their role such as a transcriptionist. Some may access DRS content as an incidental part of their role, such as a software vendor performing troubleshooting on a database. Under the proposed rule, each of these must be logged and included in the disclosure accounting.

By requiring providers to create disclosure logs on designated record sets including business associate access, I believe HHS has gone beyond the intent of HITECH.

Challenge 2 – Inadequate Regulatory Analysis

In describing the regulatory impact, HHS understated the expense burden that the proposed rule will impose.

On page 31442 of the May 31, 2011 Federal Register, the proposed rule notes: "We estimate the effects of the requirement for covered entities (including indirect costs incurred by third party administrators, which frequently send out notices on behalf of health plans) to issue new notices of privacy practices, would result in new total costs of $20.2 million."

The accompanying commentary suggests most of the information needed is already available for disclosure logging. This suggests a lack of knowledge of current state of healthcare information systems.

HHS notes costs will be limited because the number of requests for disclosure accounting will be few. However, it's not the number of requests that will drive the cost, but the preparation needed to meet a request whether there is one or one thousand.

In the Federal Register, HHS suggests there are 673,324 entities that will be impacted by these regulations. This is another understatement as it includes only providers, insurance carriers, and third-party administrators. To this count must be added the hundreds of thousands, perhaps millions of businesses and independent contractors that do commerce with one of the 673,324 and receive protected health information under a business associates agreement.

Without counting business associates, this works out to $30 per entity, an absurdly low figure.

With business associates included, the proposed rule will impact more than a million entities. Every business and independent contractor that provides transcription, billing, computer repair, auditing, or other service to a healthcare provider, plan, or clearinghouse will be affected. A high percentage of these are small businesses.

The cost of modifying or upgrading just one software application and educating a two-person staff would easily exceed $5,000 in first-year implementation cost. Many organizations face modifications to dozens of systems, educating thousands of employees, and modifying hundreds of business associates agreements.

Even if only 500,000 firms are affected, at $5,000 each the total cost to implement the proposed rule would be $2.5 billion. A more realistic estimate is in excess of $10 billion.

Challenge 3 – Incompatibility with the Federal Debt Challenge

The debate on the debt ceiling included a discussion of reductions in payments to providers and hospitals. Yet, as currently proposed, the rule adds billions in additional costs.

A 1999 study comparing Canadian and US healthcare costs showed administrative overhead consumed 31% of the US healthcare dollar. In Canada, administrative overhead accounted for only 16.7% of their healthcare costs, nearly half what we require in the US. We cannot add more administrative overhead and hope to reduce Medicare cost without affecting access or quality of care.

The healthcare industry has often been criticized for inefficiencies. What other industry, including the federal government, is asked to produce an accounting, on demand, of everyone who touches data for any reason? It does not occur in banking, brokerage firms, or credit card processors. It doesn't even occur with the Internal Revenue Service.

> *What other industry, including the federal government, is asked to produce an accounting, on demand, of everyone who touches data for any reason?*

To impose such demanding requirements on the healthcare industry at a time when administrative cost reduction is a top priority seems counter intuitive.

In summary:

The rule should be revised to limit scope to that which is needed to support the spirit of HITECH.

The rule should not be implemented until a realistic regulatory impact analysis can be completed.

The healthcare industry will undergo an upheaval as it contends with healthcare reform and reimbursement decreases. It does not make sense to impose significant regulatory burden while constraining supply (Medicare funding) and maintaining all Medicare benefits such that demand will continue to rise.

I look forward to reading the HHS analysis of comments and hope the final rule supports enough auditing to foster patient trust, while realistically constraining the burden on implementers. ∎

BIDMC's Accountable Care Organization Strategy

No one really knows what an accountable care organization is, but many provider organizations want to be one.

As a CIO, I've been asked to create the financial and clinical analytics needed to support high-value care (low cost, high quality), population health, and care coordination across the community.

I believe that accountable care organizations will be based on health information exchange and analytics. BIDMC's approach is to accelerate our health information exchange work and continue our existing work on financial and clinical data warehouses.

Here's how it will work:

There are over 1,800 clinicians in the Beth Israel Deaconess Physicians Organization (BIDPO). Some are owned, some are private. The BIDPO Board of Directors mandated that a certified EHR be in use at every BIDPO practice as a condition of participation in payer contracting efforts. Those payer contracts require "clinical integration"—all clinicians must be knit together by IT. To accomplish this goal, we implemented a cloud-based EHR which was offered to each practice that did not yet have a certified EHR. We required all clinician practices, owned and private, to send a standardized, structured summary of each visit to a central quality registry.

As each encounter is completed and signed, eClinicalWorks, Altos Solutions, and webOMR send a very specific CDA summary containing all the data necessary to compute quality and performance metrics to a statewide Quality Data Center, hosted at the Massachusetts Medical Society and operated by the Massachusetts eHealth Collaborative.

That warehouse is used to generate PQRI measures, the 44 Meaningful Use measures, and ad hoc reporting via web-based business intelligence tools.

For the financial data warehouse, all private payers claims from BIDPO patients are forwarded to a single financial data warehouse where extract/transform/load (ETL) tools are used to normalize the data into a single schema.

Data mining and reporting is done by Healthcare Data Services.

The interesting recent development is that all the clinical data transfers from heterogeneous EHRs pass through the state HIE, such that the Quality Data Center is just a node on the HIE. Anyone can send any data from any EHR using the standards mandated by Meaningful Use.

The state HIE also transmits summaries to the next provider of care, ensuring clinical integration.

Healthcare reform is causing hospitals, practices, payers, and government to align their healthcare IT efforts in support of the data sharing and analytics needed by new reimbursement models.

It's happening very fast in Boston/Eastern Massachusetts.

I'll continue to share all my lessons learned as BIDMC implements an entire suite of IT solutions on the road to accountable care nirvana. ∎

Radiology Image Exchange

In my recent post about the "Standards Work Ahead," I called DICOM[17] a non-standard standard.

This generated numerous email messages, phone calls, and blog comments. Let me clarify what I meant.

DICOM is a great standard that has unified many processes within organizations, linking radiology modalities and PACS[18] systems.

Why do I believe additional work is needed?

My wife visited a hospital near our home for a diagnostic mammogram. It was clear she needed follow-up care with a cancer care team. We decided that Beth Israel Deaconess would be ideal because of its electronic health records and personal health records that would help Kathy coordinate her care. We asked for the images to be transmitted to BIDMC and we were told that we needed to visit the radiology department Monday–Friday 9 am–5 pm for a CD to be created so that Kathy could drive it 20 miles to BIDMC. The CD contained a proprietary viewer that required Windows and hence was not visible on our home computers (all Mac OSX).

What would have happened in an ideal world?

1. An implementation guide for DICOM would specify required vendor-neutral content—a basic set of metadata (patient identifiers, name of the radiology study, imaging techniques used, etc.) that would work with any viewer such as Siemens, Agfa, Philips, GE, Kodak. Any vendor-specific/proprietary metadata would be stored separately from the required basic content, so that extensions do not impact generic viewers. CDs with proprietary viewers and media formats should become a thing of the past.

2. DICOM combines content and transport in a single standard. Although that is great for communication within an organization, it is not sufficient for a health information exchange world that uses the Direct implementation guide (SMTP/SMIME,[19] XDR) for content exchange among organizations. The fact that vendors such as lifeImage, Accelarad, and Merge Healthcare have created their own image-sharing networks suggests that more standards work is needed to create an open ecosystem of image sharing among organizations.

3. We should not require organizations that want to receive images to have PACS systems. Instead, EHRs with vendor-neutral DICOM

---

17 DICOM = Digital Imaging and Communications in Medicine.

18 PACS = Picture archiving and communications systems.

19 SMTP/SMIME = Simple mail transfer protocol/secure-multipurpose Internet mail extensions.

viewers should be able to incorporate DICOM content sent via Direct into patient records.

Thus, our work on imaging standards should build upon the DICOM foundation we have today, but eliminate optionality for a basic set of metadata, ensure that any proprietary extensions to metadata do not interfere with vendor-neutral viewing, embrace simple transport approaches for cross-organizational exchange, and enable even the simplest of EHRs to be participants in image exchange. ∎

Five IT Tactics of Accountable Care Organizations

I recently presented a webinar outlining the IT work ahead to support accountable care organizations.

I recommended five priorities to create a foundation for care management and population health:

1. Universal adoption of EHRs—Every clinician in an ACO needs to record data electronically, ideally using the same EHR vendor (if not the same EHR, then using common pick lists/vocabularies enables data to be comparable across practices). At BIDMC we created a model office workflow to ensure data is recorded by individuals with the same role at the same time in the same processes using the same value sets.

2. Health information exchange—Data should be shared among caregivers for care coordination and panel management. Approaches can include viewing data in remote locations, pushing summaries between providers, or pulling summaries from multiple sites of care. BIDMC has created novel approaches to secure data sharing, as well as participated in many federal and state HIE pilots.

3. Business intelligence/analytics—Once data is collected and shared, it needs to be analyzed retrospectively to identify gaps in care and prospectively to ensure patients receive the right care at the right time during their encounters with clinicians. BIDMC has worked with the Massachusetts eHealth Collaborative to create a community-wide quality data center as well as pilot popHealth to support our analytic needs.

> *BIDMC has offered comprehensive PHRs to all of its patients since 1999.*

4. Universal availability of PHRs—Engaging patients and families in their care, ensuring communication of care plans, and achieving seamless handoffs are essential to keeping patients well. BIDMC has offered comprehensive PHRs to all of its patients since 1999.

5. Decision support services—Care management requires alerts, reminders, pathways, and guidelines. Ideally, all members of the care team will receive decision support inside their electronic record based on enterprise rule sets. At BIDMC, we've used the concept of Decision Support Service Providers to turn data into knowledge and wisdom inside our EHRs and web applications.

Of these five tactics, the biggest challenge is defining the care management rules—what conditions, wellness measures, home care interventions, best practices, and evidence should be incorporated into the point-of-care and analytic systems? Yesterday, at the BIDMC Clinical IT Governance Committee, we agreed to charter a working group of experts to set these priorities so that our care management strategy is well planned and not a random collection of individual projects, driven by individuals with specific niche requirements (squeaky wheels or siloed departmental requests). It's a good start. ∎

The Golden Spike

In 2012, we made history in the Commonwealth of Massachusetts. Governor Deval Patrick and his physician sent the Governor's healthcare record from Massachusetts General Hospital to Baystate Medical Center. It arrived and was integrated into Baystate's Cerner medical record.

The Massachusetts HIE is now open for business.

Immediately following the Governor's record, institutions throughout the Commonwealth sent their own transactions.

The record I exchanged had special significance to my family.

When my wife Kathy was diagnosed with breast cancer (a highly suspicious mammogram) at Newton Wellesley (a Partners hospital), she was told that Massachusetts had no healthcare information highway and she would have to drive her records and images to Beth Israel Deaconess where she chose to seek the care of oncologists, surgeons, and radiation oncologists.

Two months after she began treatment, her health plan called and told her, "We think you have cancer because you have incurred $25,000 in chemotherapy costs since December."

Her out-of-network caregivers had no visibility into her cancer care.

Her care at multiple institutions was not aggregated for quality measurement.

All of that has ended. In front of the press and leaders of Massachusetts, I accessed her BIDMC records, with her consent, and sent them electronically to Partners HealthCare, a payer (Network Health), a private primary care provider (Dr. Ayobami Ojutalayo, MD, at Ruhke Medical Center), and the Massachusetts eHealth Collaborative (a quality measurement and analytics service provider). Within seconds, we broke down silos, demonstrating that care coordination, population health, and quality analytics based on health information exchange is now possible in Massachusetts. EHRs included Partners' LMR, eClincialWorks, a custom payer system, and self-built analytic applications.

Other transactions followed.

Tufts New England Medical Center sent summaries to and received summaries from Vanguard Health Systems New England, illustrating primary care physician to specialist closed-loop workflow. EHRs included Siemens Soarian and MEDITECH.

Boston Children's sent pediatric patient summaries to Atrius Healthcare, a multi-specialty group, illustrating tertiary hospital to primary care giver coordination.

All were successful and were documented in real time on the Twitter stream.

The Governor distributed golden spikes made from actual railroad spikes salvaged from a rail near Promontory Point.

Just as the original golden spike in 1869 issued in a new era of connectiveness, so does the HIT golden spike change business as usual in Massachusetts. We'll continue to build new "bridges," ensuring that every payer, provider, and patient can join the ecosystem. ■

Our Healthcare IT Progress

In a time of EHR naysayers, mean-spirited election year politics, and press misinterpretation (ONC and CMS do not intend to relax patient engagement provisions), it's important that we all send a unified message about our progress on the national priorities we've developed by consensus.

1. Query-based exchange—Every country in the world that I've advised (Japan, China, New Zealand, Scotland/UK, Norway, Sweden, Canada, and Singapore) has started with push-based exchange, replacing paper and fax machines with standards-based technology and policy. Once "push" is done and builds confidence with stakeholders, "pull" or query-response exchange is the obvious next step. Although there are gaps to be filled, we can and should make progress on this next phase of exchange. The naysayers need to realize that there is a process for advancing interoperability and we're all working as fast as

we can. Query-based exchange will be built on top of the foundation created by Meaningful Use Stages 1 and 2.

2. Billing—Although several reports have linked EHRs to billing fraud/abuse and the recent Office of the Inspector General (OIG) survey seeks to explore the connection between EHR implementation and increased reimbursement, the real issue is that EHRs, when implemented properly, can enhance clinical documentation. The work of the next two years as we prepare for ICD-10 is to embrace emerging natural language processing technologies and structured data entry to create highly reproducible/auditable clinical documentation that supports the billing process. Meaningful Use Stages 1 and 2 have added content and vocabulary standards that will ensure future documentation is much more codified.

3. Safety—Some have argued that EHRs introduce new errors and safety concerns. Although it is true that bad software implemented badly can cause harm, the vast majority of certified EHR technology enhances workflow and reduces error. Meaningful Use Stages 1 and 2 enhance medication accuracy and create a foundation for improved decision support. The Health eDecisions initiative will bring us guidelines/protocols that add substantial safety to today's EHRs.

4. Privacy and security—Some have argued that EHRs reduce security by making records available in electronic form, possibly over Internet connections. Efforts to enhance certification of the security of EHRs, encrypt data at rest, and create guidance for EHR modules that interoperate with built-in security will further protect the data that needs to be shared for care coordination and population health.

5. Innovation—Some have argued that Meaningful Use led to the growth of a small number of vendors and dependency/lock in with those vendors. Meaningful Use Stage 2 requires interoperability between vendors, export of data from EHRs to reduce lock in, and standards that will enable a new generation of modular "plug ins." I'm confident that SHARP[20] grant-funded work, like the SMART[21] initiative, will lead to an ecosystem of applications from small vendors—an app store for health.

> *Our mantra should be that Meaningful Use Stages 1 and 2 have created a foundation for query-based exchange, accurate billing, safety, security, and innovation.*

---

20 SHARP = Strategic Healthcare IT Advanced Research Projects.

21 SMART = Substitutable Medical Apps & Reusable Technology (http://smartplatforms.org).

Thus, our mantra should be that Meaningful Use Stages 1 and 2 have created a foundation for query-based exchange, accurate billing, safety, security, and innovation. ∎

The Patient Experience of EHRs

I'm often asked if the use of EHRs diminishes clinician-patient interactions in the exam room.

At BIDMC, Jan Walker and Tom Delbanco have done focus groups with patients about technology. Generally, they found that patients will embrace technology that gives them access to information about their care. At BIDMC, where we have both a patient portal and Wi-Fi throughout the hospital, doctors often arrive at the bedside to find a patient viewing lab results on an iPad, ready with questions about his or her tests.

The literature studying outpatient offices with computers in the exam room suggest computers do not get in the way as long as clinicians are facile with them and maintain eye contact with patients.

Here are excerpts from three articles on this topic:

> "The examination room computers appeared to have positive effects on physician-patient interactions related to medical communication without significant negative effects on other areas such as time available for patient concerns. Further study is needed to better understand HIT use during outpatient visits."[22]

> "Studies examining physician EHR use have found mostly neutral or positive effects on patient satisfaction, but primary care researchers need to conduct further research for a more definitive answer."[23]

> "With the implementation of the electronic medical record—called HealthConnect—in all exam rooms throughout the Kaiser Permanente health care delivery system, how computers in the exam room affect physician-patient communication is a new concern. Patient satisfaction scores were obtained for all primary and specialty care physicians in a large medical center in Southern California to determine how scores changed as physicians started using HealthConnect in the exam

22 Hsu J, Huang J, Fung V, et al. Health information technology and physician-patient interactions: impact of computers on communication during outpatient primary care visits. *J Amer Med Inform Assoc.* 2005; 12:474-480.

23 Irani JS, Middleton, JL, Marfatia R, et al. The use of electronic health records in the exam room and patient satisfaction: a systematic review. *J Am Board Fam Med.* 2009; 22:553-562.

room. Results show no significant changes in patient satisfaction for these physicians. Although concerns were not realized that patient satisfaction might decrease after HealthConnect was introduced, there was also no evidence that introducing an electronic medical record in outpatient clinics increased patient satisfaction."[24]

Clinicians have different approaches to the use of technology in the exam room—iPads, typing into a laptop, or just taking notes, then entering data outside of the exam room. When clinicians and patients work together to ensure safe, accurate, and timely record keeping, everyone wins. Certainly, there may be awkwardness when clinicians struggle with new technology and patients perceive a change in attentiveness. However, it is highly likely that as clinicians spend their entire practice lives using EHRs and all patient records are recorded in EHRs, this awkwardness will disappear. Just as mobile devices have replaced newspapers and magazines as the favored way for adults to access media, the EHR and PHR, as well as the processes needed to use them, will become a standard part of every clinical encounter, supporting rather than detracting from the patient experience. ∎

Patient and Family Engagement in ICUs

My father died in early 2013, and now, with a bit of distance from that emotional event, it's time to further reflect on technology to support patients and families in ICUs.

BIDMC has been speaking with a major foundation about creating a cross-disciplinary, multi-institutional, open-source application to turn critical care data into wisdom for patients and families.

How might it work? Let me use my father as an example.

My father had multiple sclerosis for 23 years, myelodysplastic syndrome for 2 years, and 3 myocardial infarctions since 2009.

When I arrived at his ICU bedside in early March, I spoke with all his clinicians to create a mental dashboard of his progress. It looked something like this:

- Cardiac—History of two previous myocardial infarctions treated with five stents. New myocardial infarction resulting in apical hypokinesis and an ejection fraction of 25%. No further stent placement possible, maximal medical therapy already given.

---

24 Nagy VT, Kanter MH. Implementing the electronic medical record in the exam room: the effect on physician-patient communication and patient satisfaction. *The Permanente Journal*. Spring 2007; 11(2).

- Pulmonary—New congestive heart failure post recent myocardial infarction treated with diuretics, nitroglycerine drip, afterload reduction, upright position, and maximal oxygenation via bilevel positive airway pressure. O2 saturation in the 90s and falling despite maximal therapy (other than intubation).

- Hematologic—Failing bone marrow resulting in a white count of 1, a platelet count of 30, and a hematocrit of 20.

- Neurologic—Significant increase in muscle spasticity, resulting in constant agitation. Pain medication requirements escalating. Consciousness fading.

- Renal—Creatinine rising.

Although I did not have real-time access to his records, I gathered enough data from my conversations to turn this dashboard into a scorecard with green, yellow, and red indicators.

- Cardiac—Red due to irreversible low ejection fraction.

- Pulmonary—Red due to the combination of falling O2 saturation despite aggressive therapy.

- Hematologic—Red due to lack of treatment options available for myelodysplastic syndrome and an inability to transfuse given the low ejection fraction and congestive heart failure.

- Neurologic—Yellow due to the potential for successful symptom control with pain medications.

- Renal—Yellow due to treatment options available for renal failure.

Our proposed project is an automated ICU dashboard/scorecard for patients and families updated in real time based on data aggregrated from the medical record and patient-connected telemetry.

My father had expressed his wishes in a durable power of attorney for healthcare: do not intubate, do not resuscitate, no pressors, no feeding tubes, and no heroic measures.

From the combination of the dashboard, scorecard, and his end-of-life wishes, it was clear that hospice was the best course of action.

I'm a physician with 20 years of practice experience. I'm a CIO with 30 years of data analysis experience. I'm a decision maker with 35 years leading teams.

Making the hospice decision required all of my skills.

Ideally, patients and families should have the tools needed to make such decisions, regardless of their medical sophistication.

Our proposed project is an automated ICU dashboard/scorecard for patients and families updated in real time based on data aggregated from the medical record and patient-connected telemetry. The architecture will be a decision support web service. Hospitals send data in and the web service returns the wisdom of a graphical display.

The project is ambitious and will bring together patients, providers, and IT experts. We look forward to the challenge of creating a patient- and family-friendly dashboard for ICUs. My healthcare navigator service to my father would have been empowered with such a resource. ∎

Chapter 8

Responding to Adversity—When Bad Stuff Happens

I often tell my wife that I look forward to the day when I'm no longer responsible for the bad things that happen to infrastructure and applications in the ever-expanding Beth Israel Deaconess empire. If a computer does not boot, a printer does not print, a flood impacts phone service, a winter storm removes electrical power, or an application is sluggish, I am responsible. Bad stuff happens. There will be sunny days and plagues of locusts. You never know what tomorrow will bring. However, you can adopt a standardized approach that enables you to survive adversity and keep your job.

This chapter presents my advice.

Responding to an Outage

I recently joined my team while troubleshooting a complex infrastructure problem affecting our community EHR-hosting private cloud.

From years of experience doing this, here are my lessons learned:

1. Once the problem is identified, the first step is to ascertain the scope. Call the users to determine what they are experiencing. Test the

application or infrastructure yourself. Do not trust the monitoring tools if they indicate all is well but the users are complaining.

2. If the scope of the outage is large and the root cause is unknown, raise alarm bells early. It's far better to make an early all-hands intervention with occasional false alarms than to intervene too late and have an extended outage because of a slow response.

3. Bring visibility to the process by having hourly updates, frequent bridge calls, and multiple eyes on the problem. Sometimes technical people become so focused that they do not have a sense of the time passing or insight into what they do not know. A multi-disciplinary approach with predetermined progress reports prevents working in isolation and the pursuit of solutions that are unlikely to succeed.

4. Although frequent progress reports are important, you must allow the technical people to do their work. Senior management feels a great deal of pressure to resolve the situation. However, if 90% of the incident response effort is spent informing senior management and managing hovering stakeholders, then the heads down work to resolve the problem cannot get done.

5. Remember Occam's Razor[1] that the simplest explanation is usually the correct one. In a recent outage at BIDMC, all the evidence pointed to a malfunctioning firewall component. However, all vendor testing and diagnostics indicated the firewall was functioning perfectly. Some hypothesized we had a very specific

It's generally true that complex problems can be explained by a single simple failure.

denial-of-service of attack. Others suggested a failure of windows networking components within the operating systems of the servers. Others thought we had an unusual virus attack. We removed the firewall from the network and everything came back up instantly. It's generally true that complex problems can be explained by a single simple failure.

6. It's very important to set deadlines in the response plan to avoid the "just one more hour and we'll solve it" problem. This is especially true if the outage is the result of a planned infrastructure change. Set a backout deadline and stick to it. Just as when I climb/hike, I set a

---

1 Occam's (or Ockham's) razor is a principle attributed to the 14th century logician and Franciscan friar, William of Ockham: the simplest explanation is usually the right one. It is used in a variety of ways as a means to slice through a problem or situation and eliminate unnecessary elements.

point to turn around. Summiting is optional, but returning to the car is mandatory. Setting milestones for changes in course and sticking to your plan regardless of emotion are key.

7. Over-communicate to the users. Most stakeholders are willing to tolerate downtime if you explain the actions being taken to restore service. Senior management needs to show their commitment, presence, and leadership of the incident.

8. Do not let pride get in the way. It's hard to admit mistakes and challenging to acknowledge what you do not know. There should be no blame or finger pointing during an outage resolution. After action debriefs should include a root cause analysis and identify process changes to prevent outages in the future. Focus on getting the users back up rather than maintaining your ego.

9. Do not declare victory prematurely. It's tempting to assume the problem has been fixed and tell the users all is well. I recommend at least 24 hours of uninterrupted service under full user load before declaring victory.

10. Overall, IT leaders should focus on their trajectory, not their day-to-day position. Outages can bring many emotions—fear for your job, anxiety about your reputation, sadness for the impact on the user community. Realize that time heals all and that individual outage incidents will be forgotten. By taking a long view of continuous quality improvement and evolution of functionality, rather than being paralyzed by short-term outage incidents, you will succeed over time.

Outages are painful, but they can bring people together. They can build trust, foster communication, and improve processes by testing downtime plans in a real-world scenario. The result of our recent incident was a better plan for the future, improved infrastructure, and a universal understanding of the network design among the entire team—an excellent long-term outcome. I apologized to all the users for a very complex firewall failure and we've moved on to the next challenge, regaining the trust of our stakeholders and enhancing clinical care with secure, reliable, and robust infrastructure. ∎

Apologizing with Candor and Grace

As readers of my blog know, I've adopted many aspects of Japanese lifestyle in my household—food, music, and clothing.

Learning to apologize is also something I've learned from the Japanese. You'll find a great description in the *Etiquette Guide to Japan* by Boye De Mente.[2]

A typical corporate apology in Japan is accompanied by a low bow, a sincere apology, and a possible resignation.

Atoning for a mistake in the US does not require the loss of your job (or anything more extreme).

Bad things can happen. You may or may not be able to control them.

When bad things happen, here is the approach I use:

1. Encourage openness and transparency in your staff (e.g., do not shoot the messenger). By empowering every person to communicate the events objectively, you'll get to the root cause more rapidly.

2. Ask what can be done to improve the organization rather than blaming any one individual. If an error occurs in medication administration, ask what systems and processes should be improved rather than fire people.

> *Broadly communicate the issue in terms of the lessons learned and continuous quality improvement.*

3. Broadly communicate the issue in terms of the lessons learned and continuous quality improvement. The Institute for Healthcare Improvement (IHI) espouses the Plan, Do, Study, Act (PDSA) cycle. Many IT projects are cutting edge and require incremental fine tuning. We try, we evaluate, we revise, and we try again. Unintended negative consequences during the learning process require full disclosure and an apology.

4. Do not hide information or sugar coat the events. It is far worse to deny the truth, than have to explain the facts later. In a world of instant communication via email, IM, blogs, and Twitter, assume that everyone knows the facts as soon as they happen.

5. Openly discuss the events, their cause, the immediate corrective action taken, and the long-term changes made to prevent the issue from happening again. Declare that you've made a mistake and that you apologize for it. This may be painful and could result in a great deal of short-term publicity, but it's better than a long-term investigation and future disclosure of management misdeeds. Imagine what would have happened to Bill Clinton if he said, "I did have an affair with that woman and it was wrong. I have taken short-term steps to prevent any such incidents from happening again and I will seek counseling

---

2 De Mente BL. *Etiquette Guide to Japan: Know the Rules That Make the Difference*. North Clarendon, VT: Tuttle Publishing, 2008.

from religious mentors and mental health experts to ensure my future behavior is exemplary." The issue would have disappeared in a few weeks.

In my many years of leading change and making mistakes along the way, I've found that great communication, openness, candor, and admission of mistakes, followed by a sincere apology result in healing the organization and bringing rapid closure to the issue. ∎

Troubleshooting Complex IT Problems

Whenever I'm asked to solve an intermittent IT problem such as occasional slowness, occasional lost data, or intermittently failing hardware, the research is often complex.

Here's a brief example of the efforts we employ to solve IT mysteries.

A few weeks ago we were told that the interpreters at BIDMC often received pages with ambiguous call back numbers. At BIDMC, valid numbers are five-digit extensions, seven-digit local numbers, and ten-digit long distance numbers. Interpreters often received four-digit or six-digit numbers that were impossible to call back.

The most obvious explanation for such an intermittent problem that only seemed to occur in one department was human error. Doctors misdialed numbers, assuming the last four digits would be enough to identify their call back number.

We sent out a broadcast email instructing the clinicians to always dial at least five digits.

That did not cure the problem.

We then began a data analysis. Could we relate the bad pages to a particular individual, department or location? We found no correlation.

We then asked if the problem was truly isolated to interpreters. Our data analysis suggested that it occurred regularly in several departments. No others had mentioned it, but the problem was real.

We then asked if the problem was unique to BIDMC, since we share a paging system with other hospitals. The analysis suggested that it was unique to us, since other hospitals did not have the problem.

It seemed unlikely that just our doctors were using the paging system improperly, so we began analyzing all the hardware involved in paging: phones, interface boards, servers, and software. Since some of these components were redundant, we experimented with taking one member of clustered services offline to see if we could isolate a problem in one switch, one signal processor, or one server. Still no resolution.

We then spoke with the manufacturer of the paging software. They had no reports of similar problems. We then spoke to the engineer who wrote the software. He had an idea.

When you use a paging system, the dialog goes something like this:

"Please dial the person you wish to page"

User enters pager number

"Please enter your call back number"

User enters call back number

"Thank you"

Page is sent

Many interactive telephone systems have a "buffer clearing function" that clears any input before users enter numbers to eliminate digits being carried over between voice prompts and to cancel out any background sounds that might have occurred between prompts. This sounds great, but what happens if an experienced user begins to dial immediately without listening for the prompts (i.e., a person dialing very fast, just immediately enters the pager number, then pauses for one second before the "Please enter your callback number" prompt is completed, and enters the call back number). It's likely call-back number digits would be truncated.

We turned off buffer clearing and here's what happened:

------Percent Bad Call Back Numbers------

Pager pre-change/post-change

Russian interpreter 163/493 = 33% 3/244 = 1%

Spanish interpreter 262/959 = 27% 4/404 = 1%

Chinese interpreter 207/1086 = 19% 8/417 = 2%

Of the 15 pages in the post-change group listed as bad, most, if not all, were likely miss-dialed. For example, a couple were "123." Others were bad, but were immediately followed by what appeared to be a correct return page, suggesting the caller knew he or she had entered bad data.

The troubleshooting process was complicated by the fact that truncation occurred only with pagers signed out to other numbers as is the case with Interpreter Services. The "clear buffer" had no impact on pagers not signed out. We tried many times to "type ahead" call back numbers for these and were unable to mimic the problem. It appears to have been a problem only if someone signed his or her pager out to another. It turns out that the buffer clearing software works differently for pagers with a status of "signed out/covered by."

My advice for diagnosing complex operational IT problems is to work stepwise with every layer of architecture, and isolate the problem.

My advice for diagnosing complex operational IT problems is to work stepwise with every layer of architecture, and isolate the problem. Then, follow the advice of Sherlock Holmes in *The Sign of Four*: "How often have I said to you that when you have eliminated the impossible, whatever remains, however improbable, must be the truth?"

Along the way, you may need tools such as OpNet to help isolate every component of hardware and software and gather data. In this case, our usual network-based software tools did not help because the critical connection we needed to check was the traffic between the phones and the interface boards on the paging server. We needed to analyze if the DTMF[3] input coming from our telephone system was providing the correct digits. If the digits captured before hitting the interface boards were bad, we would know it was how the DTMF signals were handled on our side. If the digits differed from what was being logged in the paging server, we would know the problem was with an inside server.

I wish troubleshooting intermittent IT problems was easier, but alas, many modern technologies have so much complexity that it takes all the skills of forensic pathologists to solve the problem.

The folks at CSI would be proud of my team. ∎

Reducing IT Budgets

I've overseen the budgets of several technology organizations, all of which are under pressure to react to a challenging economy. At BIDMC, capital budgets are constrained, operating budgets are being tightly managed, and no staff reductions are planned. How can IT organizations approach operating budget reductions?

1. Engage all your staff—They can identify operational inefficiencies, redundancy, and savings opportunities. Any budget reduction results in rumors, speculation, and fear of job loss. Engaging your staff in the budget process empowers them, informs them, and reduces their worry.

2. Find the low-hanging fruit—Vacancies, travel/training, consulting fees, food/entertainment, and other "nice to have" expenditures are the first places to start any budget reductions. I passionately support training, but when faced with budget cuts, most staff would elect to support salaries and reduce training.

3. Identify service reductions—All IT projects are a function of scope, resources, and timing. Reducing the scope of service and determining

---

3   DTMF = Dual-tone multi-frequency (signaling).

what projects to cancel are an important part of budget reductions. One challenge is that organizations often have short memories. If you offer a budget reduction linked to a service reduction, you may find that the budget reduction is happily accepted but the service reduction is forgotten in a few weeks. In fact, many departments throughout the organization will suggest that budget reductions are possible if more automation and technology are added to their work processes. Reducing service at a time when customers need more service may not be the optimal approach, which I will discuss further below.

4. Extend timelines—Assuming that resources are diminished and scope is already reduced, the last lever a CIO has is to extend the timelines of new projects. Instead of delivering new software this year, delay it to next year. Existing staff can take on more projects only if they have a longer time to do them.

5. Accept risk—Our job in IT is to ensure stability, reliability, and security. Uptime of 99.99% requires multiple redundant data centers, but there is not a precise cookbook as to how this should be done. I have implemented two data centers a few miles apart and not a grid of worldwide data centers. Why? Because risk = likelihood of a bad outcome multiplied by the impact of that outcome. When creating budgets, I decided that the likelihood of a regional disaster which destroys the IT capability of the entire Boston region is small. The likelihood of a single data center fire, flood, or explosion is measurable, so I chose to mitigate that risk. In times of budget stress, a re-evaluation of risk is appropriate. Can network, server, storage, and desktop components be kept for a year or two beyond their usual lifetimes? Can maintenance contracts be reduced or eliminated and mitigated by having spare components handy? Just as with service reductions, the strategy of increasing risk to reduce costs must be widely communicated, so when a failure occurs, everyone understands it was a risk accepted as a result of budget reductions.

In general, I do not recommend fighting budget reductions with overly dramatic stories of doom and gloom. That is not professional. Instead, CIOs should provide for senior management a list of services and a list of risks, then decide collaboratively what to do. This ensures that the CIO and IT are seen as enablers and team players rather than the cause of the budget problem.

Having been through numerous budget reduction experiences over the past decade, I have witnessed the paradoxical effect that IT budgets are sometimes increased when organizational budgets are decreased. Savvy administrators know that economic downturns provide the urgency to re-engineer processes and accomplish politically difficult strategic changes. A short investment in automation can lead to long-term reductions in operating costs. Thus, this downturn may be the opportunity to eliminate paper, streamline labor-intensive manual methods, and consolidate/centralize for economies of scale. ■

Removing the Emotion from IT

Every day as a CIO, I experience a range of emotions—great joy at watching my staff grow their skills, sadness when politics take time away from the fun work to be done, anxiety when the balance between IT supply and demand requires that I must say "not now" to a stakeholder request, and frustration when an unplanned project becomes a priority.

In my 25 years of leading people, one lesson I learn over and over is never to react with emotion to any of these events. How do I do it?

In my 25 years of leading people, one lesson I learn over and over is never to react with emotion to any of these events. How do I do it?

Although I am not a religious person, I use a variation of the idea from Ecclesiastes 3:1 (also set to music in 1952 by Pete Seeger in his song, "Turn!, Turn!, Turn!"): "To every thing there is a season, and a time to every purpose under the heaven."

The IT version is, "To every thing there is a process which will resolve every problem under the heaven."

- A conflict with a customer—Try a kind email. If that does not work, meet face to face. If that does not work, ask your governance committees to consider the issue and develop a compromise that serves all stakeholders.

- A conflict with an employee—Try a kind email. If that does not work, meet face to face. If that does not work, involve Human Resources (HR).

- A conflict with a colleague—Try a kind email. If that does not work, go to lunch. If that does not work, escalate to senior management.

- A conflict with senior management—Try a kind email. If that does not work, meet face to face. If that does not work, ask the CEO. If that does not work, realize that eventually all senior managers move on and through kindness and the support of your stakeholders, you will outlast your naysayers.

Why is the life of a CIO filled with conflict and emotion? Demand for IT increases exponentially but IT budgets increase linearly (about 3%–4% per year if you're lucky). Competition for resources creates conflict and conflict creates emotion.

Every day I receive hostile email, negative phone calls, and political challenges from various customers, employees, and colleagues. As I've said before, if I ever feel emotion, I "save as draft."

I always respond with a positive email, phone call, or meeting suggesting a path forward.

If I were to ever respond emotionally, I would be burning bridges or giving my naysayers documentation to use against me. Healthcare is a small world. Healthcare IT is an even smaller world. The person whom you alienate today may be your boss tomorrow. The person whom you insult may be the decision maker on your next grant or promotion.

In a world of IM and Blackberry, we're all tempted to resolve complex issues with a few keystrokes. Generally that does not work. A supportive, positive email followed by a face-to-face meeting generally does work. Even if you feel the person emailing you is completely unreasonable, do not EVER react with emotion. It can only hurt you.

In addition to my credo that "to every thing there is a process," I also realize that time heals all conflict.

Can you even remember the problems that made you angry one year ago?

Are the people who caused the issue still around?

Does anyone remember the conflict and frustration?

Probably not. Will history record the masterful way you dealt with the conflict? Nope. If you reacted emotionally, will someone have a copy of that email filled with vitriol that you'd rather not see again? Absolutely.

It may take days or weeks to solve complex problems. An emotional email will only make the problem harder to solve.

Recognizing that solving complex problems will take several iterations, you need to accept the multi-step process needed to ensure you get a good outcome. ∎

Responding to Medical Error

IS and the clinical departments of BIDMC have a very strong collaborative relationship. Working together, we first enhance processes, then automate them, since even the best technology is generally not the solution to workflow and communications problems.

Here's the application enhancement we're making as part of a process change in the operating room (OR) to prevent future patient harm.

Standard operating process in the OR includes a "time out" by all OR personnel in the moments before surgery to double check all aspects of safety—equipment, right surgical site, team readiness, etc. Currently the "time out" is documented on the paper intra-operative record, which means that the scrub nurse needs to look at both the paper record and the electronic peri-operative information system during the "time out." We will add a "Time Out" button to the electronic OR journal screen containing the case times. When this button is clicked, we will pop up a window with the "time out" fields. The nurse will fill in the time out information and enter her/his password. We will not allow the nurse to enter an incision time for the case unless the "time out" has been completed, with one exception: we will provide a check box on the time out screen to indicate the time out could not be completed prior to incision due to a life-threatening situation.

The standard process we've put in place to respond to sentinel events is that the root cause is reviewed with the board (PCAC[4] committee) and the Quality Improvement Directors. IS staff work with Quality Improvement Directors to determine which process improvements need to be made, then what additional automation should be added. Using this approach, we've created a balanced way to add new technology at the appropriate time. ∎

The CareGroup Network Outage

On November 13, 2002, at 1:45 pm, Beth Israel Deaconess Medical Center went from the hospital of 2002 to the hospital of 1972. Network traffic stopped. No clinician could order medications or labs electronically. No decision support was available. Luckily, no patients were harmed. Here's the story of what happened and our lessons learned.

In the years after the 1996 merger of the Beth Israel and Deaconess Hospitals, operating losses caused several years of capital starvation (the network budget in 2002 was $50,000 for the entire $2 billion enterprise). Funds were not available to invest in infrastructure, so our network components were beyond their useful life.

However, it was not this infrastructure underinvestment that was the root cause of the problem; it was my lack of enterprise network infrastructure knowledge. I did not know what I did not know. Here are the details:

1. Our network topology was perfectly architected for 1996. Back in the days when the Internet was a friendly place where all internal and external collaborators could be trusted, a switched core (layer 2) that transmitted all packets from place to place was a reasonable design. After 1996, the likelihood of denial of service attacks, trojans, or other malware meant that networks should be routed and highly segmented, isolating any bad actors to a constrained local area. At the time of

---

4   PCAC = Patient Care Assessment and Quality Committee.

our outage, a data flood in one part of the network propagated to every other part of the network—a bit like living downstream from a dam that collapsed. A well-meaning researcher created a Napster-like application that began exchanging hundreds of gigabytes of data via multicast to multiple collaborators. The entire network was so saturated that we could not diagnose the root cause of the data flood. I did not know that a switched core was a point of failure.

2. Our network team was managed by a very smart engineer who did not share all his knowledge with the network team. Much of our network configuration was poorly documented. With the knowledge of our network isolated to one person, we had a single point of human failure. I did not know that this engineer was unfamiliar with the best practices for routed/redundant network cores, routed distribution layers, and switched access layers isolated into VLANs[5] with quality of service configurations to prevent monopolization of bandwidth by any one user or application. We brought in a Cisco partner, Callisma, to document the network, but the network failure occurred before they were finished.

3. I did not know about spanning tree algorithms, hot standby routing protocols (HSRP), and open shortest path first (OSPF). During the outage, I approved configuration changes that actually made the situation worse by causing spanning tree propagations, flooding the network with even more traffic.

4. I did not establish a relationship with the vendor (Cisco) that enabled them to warn me about our vulnerabilities. A relationship with a vendor can take many forms, ranging from a sales-driven vendor/client adversarial relationship to a collaborative partnership. In 2002, Cisco was just another vendor from which we purchased. Today they are a collaborative partner with a seat at the table when we plan new infrastructure.

5. I did not know that we needed "out of band" tools to gain insight into the problems with the network. In effect, we required the network to be functional to diagnose problems with the network.

6. We did not have a robust, tested downtime plan for a total network collapse. When the outage occurred, we rapidly designed new processes to transport lab results, orders, and other data via runners from place to place.

---

5   VLAN = virtual local area network.

7. We did not have a robust communication plan for responding to a total network collapse. Email, web-based paging, portals, and anything that used the data network for communication was down. Voice mail broadcasts using our private branch exchange (PBX) and regular phones (not IP phones) turned out to save the day.

8. When we diagnosed the problem, we explored many root causes and made many changes in the hope that we'd find the magic bullet to cure the problem. In the end, we ended up fixing many basic structural problems in the network, which took two days and eventually solved the problem. A more expedient solution would have been to reverse all changes we made in our attempts to fix the network once we had stopped the internal attack. When a crisis occurs, making changes on top of changes can make diagnosis and remediation even more difficult.

9. We did not have an enterprise-wide change control process to ensure that every network configuration, server addition, and software enhancement was documented and assessed for impact on security, stability, and performance. Today we have a weekly change control board that includes all IS departments, Cisco engineering services, and IS leadership to assess and communicate all configuration changes.

10. I was risk averse and did not want to replace the leadership of the network team for fear that terminating our single point of human failure would result in an outage. The price of keeping the leadership in place was a worse outage. I should have acted sooner to bolster leadership of the team.

> *Without this incident, the medical center would never have realized the importance of investing in basic IT infrastructure.*

Despite the pain and stress of the outage, there was a "lemons to lemonade" ending. Without this incident, the medical center would never have realized the importance of investing in basic IT infrastructure. If not for the "perfect storm," we may have limped along with a marginal network for years.

Today, we receive annual capital funding to support a regular refresh of our technology base, and we are asked to introduce change at a pace that is manageable. People in the medical center still remember the outage and are more accepting of a tightly managed infrastructure such as locked-down workstations, security precautions, disaster recovery initiatives, and maintenance downtime windows.

During and immediately following the event, I presented this overview of the outage to senior management. Shortly after the outage, I worked with *CIO Magazine* to document the events and lessons learned.

I hope that my experience will help other organizations prevent network and other IT outages in the future. ∎

Reacting to Controversy

I've written several posts about the need for civility, good karma, and a thoughtful process for every issue.

I have to react to negativity several times each day. As I review my email, I read numerous reports of challenges, frustration, and dissatisfaction. It's an expected part of being a senior leader in large, complex organizations and being a CIO.

Some of these emails have a controversial he said/she said character.

Responding to them requires tact and diplomacy. I want to support and protect my staff but also want to ensure we improve our processes in the interest of continuous quality improvement.

Recently, I read an article about the Shirley Sherrod case by Steve Adubato,[6] who speaks and coaches on leadership and communication. His observations mirror many of the lessons I've learned when reacting to controversy:

- Don't be so quick to judge if you haven't heard the entire story.

- Due diligence is critical when it comes to communication.

- Realize how dangerous it is to assume.

- Get the whole message.

As my due diligence progresses, I find that many emails have the quality of Roseanne Roseannadanna (for you 1978–1980 Saturday Night Live fans).

People misrepresent the facts, distort the truth to suit their own ends, and highlight events that are in their self-interest and not the greater good.

It's really important to check out the facts from multiple stakeholders before drawing a conclusion.

> *Understanding the facts, having a dialog, and meeting expectations for follow-up resolve most conflicts.*

---

6 Adubato S. Lessons to be learned from Sherrod video. *Nj.com*. July 25, 2010. (Shirley Sherrod was the Department of Agriculture administrator who was fired after the release of a highly edited two-minute, 45-second video clip of a 45-minute speech she gave before the NAACP in 2010.)

It's really important to pick up the phone and talk through the issues, listening and taking an active interest in all sides of the story.

It's really important to suggest next steps, assign accountability, and deliver on your promises.

Understanding the facts, having a dialog, and meeting expectations for follow-up resolve most conflicts.

As with the Sherrod case, once you know the whole story, most controversies are not what they seem. ■

A Customer Emotion Dashboard

The job of a CIO is filled with challenges. There's a delicate balance in constant flux among:

- Short-term urgencies
- Long-term strategies
- Ever-changing compliance/regulatory requirements
- Day-to-day operations
- Budgets

What's the right objective measure of success?

- Uptime?
- On-time, on-budget project performance?
- Positive feedback from your governance groups?

All of these can look rosy, but customers can still be unhappy. The juggling of IT supply and customer demand means that not all projects can be done. The complexity of IT work means that projects will take longer than customers expect. All communications plans, no matter how comprehensive, will still miss some stakeholders. The end result of all of this is customer dissatisfaction.

> *If only 10% of my customers dislike me on a given day, then I've achieved a stellar approval rating.*

A CIO can never achieve 100% customer satisfaction. In fact, if only 10% of my customers dislike me on a given day, then I've achieved a stellar approval rating.

By human nature, we want to make everyone happy and avoid conflict. Here are my top ten leadership principles for surviving as a CIO:

10. Select what to change and what not to change.

9. Identify those who will lose.

8. Acknowledge their loss.

7. Over communicate.

6. Be honest and consistent.

5. Consensus is not essential.

4. Embrace conflict.

3. Focus on your detractors.

2. The last two minutes of the meeting are the most important.

1. You cannot please everyone.

#1 is that you cannot please everyone. There will never be enough budget, enough staff, or enough governance to ensure everything is perfect.

Normally, the naysaying can be addressed through focused customer service, planning, and conversation.

However, it's getting harder now that the economy is challenging and expectations of technology support are escalating (e.g., "I just bought a new smartphone yesterday. How come you do not provide application support for it?").

The level of tension in every sector is increasing. Civility is diminishing.

This means that I must carefully monitor the pulse of all my customers.

I've emailed my staff that at our next leadership meeting, I'd like to develop a new type of scorecard for each major stakeholder group. I will empower my staff to rate the emotional trajectory of each group as red/yellow/green. With such a scorecard, I'll be able to anticipate growing discontent before it escalates and then focus my time and energy on detractors, embracing conflict to proactively change strategy and tactics before it's too late to change.

A customer dashboard based on the trajectory of stakeholder emotion rather than budgets, projects and timelines—I have a feeling that it will be very effective in directing my management focus, especially in trying times. ∎

Preparing for the Future of IT at HMS

The following is the text I wrote to generally announce that I would be leaving my role as CIO of Harvard Medical School to focus on clinical IT at BIDMC full time:

Every day I examine my life and think about the roles I serve. I consider all the unresolved issues in my professional and personal life, then ponder the processes needed to address them.

I think about the next week, the next month, and the next year. Hopefully, I'll be able to skate where the puck will be.

I've recently become particularly introspective about the challenges in healthcare and medicine that lay ahead.

I believe that accountable care organizations, patient-centered medical homes, and the Partnership for Patients/CMS Center for Innovation will create exponential growth in healthcare IT requirements.

My senior leadership at BIDMC knows that we'll need novel approaches to health information exchange for care coordination and population health management. They know we'll need new analytics which include cost, quality, and outcomes. They want new tools to make these analytics available to every stakeholder, both outside and inside the EHR.

Furthermore, state infrastructure to support "push" and "pull" data exchanges will need to be built. The need for federal standards and policies will accelerate.

At the same time, the science of medicine at HMS is becoming more computationally intensive.

The next generation of whole genome analysis requires tools like BFAST[7] that require new approaches to processing and storage infrastructure.

Image analysis also requires new tools such as OMERO for visualization, management, and analysis of biological microscope images.

These and other research tools need to run on petabytes of data maintained on high-performance storage, backed by thousands of processors, numerous specialized graphics processing units, and high-speed InfiniBand connections.

How does this relate to me?

As the CIO of hospitals, the innovation required to support healthcare reform will require increasing amounts of my time.

As the part-time (50%) CIO of HMS, the tools and technology required to support new scientific approaches will require increasing amounts of my time.

How do I ensure the exponentially increasing needs of the customers I serve are best met?

The answer requires a tough decision.

I believe that HMS requires a full-time dedicated CIO with a skill set in highly scalable infrastructure and the tools needed to support emerging science.

Thus, I think it best that I pass the baton at HMS to a new IT leader. I will continue to serve the Dean of HMS as an advisor on strategic projects, especially those which require cross-affiliate and clinical coordination. In collaboration with the IT stakeholders of HMS, I will work to find my replacement.

Once my successor is found, I will take on additional challenges implementing the next stages of Meaningful Use, healthcare reform, and new health information exchange initiatives at BIDMC, in Massachusetts, and nationwide.

Wish me luck! ∎

---

7   BFAST is a universal DNA sequence aligner tool developed at UCLA.

The Pace of Change

My travels in Japan included lectures in Tokyo and Kyoto, sharing lessons learned from the US health information technology national efforts. I highlighted that the Office of the National Coordinator has to balance the desire for innovation with a pace of change that vendors and clinicians can tolerate.

This led me to think about the pace of change that CIOs are experiencing right now. The IT innovations of the past few years have been dizzying and the cycle between the peak of hype to the trough of obsolescence is now measured in months, not years.

Here are some examples of products that have generated huge visibility, achieved market dominance, then faltered:

1. Blackberry—I was one of the earliest adopters of Blackberry technology, using a small pager-like device for short text messages. As each new model was announced, I welcomed the innovations— the evolution from thumbwheel to joystick to track pad, larger color screens, cameras, video features, and voice memo recording. However, in 2011, my mobile device needs have outpaced Blackberry's engineering. I now need a full-featured web browser, a book reader, the ability to zoom/drag via touch screen, and a robust App Store. Until 2010, Blackberry seemed to be unstoppable in the corporate messaging world. Now they are laying off 2,500 people as the iPhone and Android devices rapidly replace Blackberries in consumer and business settings. They tried very hard to introduce new devices such as the Storm, Playbook, and Torch, but came up short as customer expectations exceeded their pace of innovation.

2. MySpace—Remember when personalized portals were hot? At its height, social networking company MySpace had 1,500 employees. It was purchased in 2005 by Rupert Murdock for $580 million. It was recently sold for $35 million. At this point, MySpace does not appear on lists of popular social networking destinations. Given that the value of most websites is based on usage and thus potential for selling advertising, shifts in the market can occur almost instantly. Who knows: in a year or two surfing to today's popular sites such as twitter.com may yield the error "URL not found."

3. Google Health—Google is a great company and I have no doubt that it will continue to succeed. Google+ is a wonderful social networking site that is likely to steal some of Facebook's market share. However, like most technology companies, Google now has to deal with the mire of maintenance that comes with a mature set of highly used applications. More resources are spent on operations and less are available for pure innovation. Smaller, more nimble companies are

likely to outpace Google and will either be acquired by Google or erode Google's leadership position. Many of my friends and colleagues who joined Google a few years ago (when it was considered unstoppable) have now left Google as the company has matured and its culture has changed. The closing of Google Health is just one symptom of the changes in focus that occur when a company is faced with the maintenance and regulatory burdens of maturing products.

4. Microsoft Windows—In 1995, I remember standing in line at midnight in a Torrance, California electronics store to buy one of the first copies of Windows 95. My early Dell computer (a 386 processor) ran DOS and Windows 3.1, so Windows 95/Office 95 was a remarkable innovation. It was stable and easy to use. Windows 98 Second Edition included built-in Internet features and was remarkably fast and reliable. Thereafter, Microsoft has introduced new features, but has not achieved the same kind of game-changing innovation that occurred 1995–2000. How many people stood in line at midnight to buy Microsoft Vista? How eagerly anticipated was Windows 7? How many people brag about their Windows phone or Windows mobile device? The market share numbers tell the story: as of 2011, the majority of Windows computers in the world still ran XP. Microsoft is a great investment—its stock price is low and its product line is very broad. It's Kinect device was the top-selling consumer electronics product over the past year. However, the burden of maintaining compatibility with an operating system developed for the IBM XT era has led Microsoft to lose its edge in a cloud-based, mobile-centric world.

5. Cisco—The CareGroup network outage of 2002 taught me many lessons about network architecture. In response, we installed an updated end-to-end Cisco infrastructure, embraced Cisco technical services, and worked closely with Cisco salespeople to plan the lifecycle of the network. Since then, the purchase and maintenance costs of end-to-end Cisco networks have outpaced Cisco innovation and other companies such as Juniper and HP offer better value on some components. Cisco is laying off 20,000, closing entire businesses such as the Flip camera (a wonderful technology company that Cisco acquired in 2009 for $500 million, then shut down in 2011), and is rethinking its entire consumer product strategy. By becoming a sprawling company and attempting to maintain very high margins, Cisco lost control of its core business. Its competitors are more agile and cost effective.

The general theme is that it's very hard for CIOs to skate where the puck will be when last year's shrewd investment becomes this year's white elephant. A side effect of this accelerating market change is that customer expectations for constant innovation are higher than ever. The CIO gets credit for change, but does not receive kudos for impeccable stability, reliability, and security of the existing infrastructure and application stack.

While I was in Japan I had lunch with a leading Japanese business thinker, Professor Ikujiro Nonaka. He told me, "If you are doing business as usual, you are falling behind."

> *"If you are doing business as usual, you are falling behind."*

Put another way, no matter how good your daily operations, customers measure your performance based on the pace of change.

Later this month, I'll take a few of my senior staff to dinner so we can reflect on this challenge. How can we deliver infrastructure and applications services at an accelerating pace of change for reasonable cost while maintaining staff morale, quality, and compliance with escalating regulatory complexity? I'll let you know what we decide. ∎

Hospital Disaster Planning

In my role as CIO and a Professor of Medicine, I'm asked many questions about the policies, processes, and procedures of healthcare. Here's one I was recently asked about hospital disaster planning. Meg Femino, BIDMC Director of Emergency Management, prepared the answer.

The question:

Your hospital has been placed on alert for receiving patients from a local explosion at a large factory. Reports from the scene are spotty in terms of numbers killed or injured, and you do not know how many patients you may be getting. News reports are calling for casualties in the 100s, but local fire responders are sending in conflicting reports. You need to know what your ED will be receiving, so you can determine whether to close surgery to elective cases and go on ED bypass for regular patients. Rumors are swirling inside the hospital and the chain of command about how severe the incident is and what it will do to your ability to function. What thoughts do you have about how to learn what you need to know in order to structure the hospital's preparations and continue regular functioning at the same time? What resources can you tap in order to learn more accurately about the situation at the scene and what you can expect to come to your ED? How would you manage this situation to cause the minimum disruption to regular hospital functioning?

When faced initially with a disaster situation in a healthcare setting, what do you think your first five steps need to be? Why?

Meg's answer:

This can be a common scenario: early information is always scant, unconfirmed, and conflicting. Due to the mechanism of injury (explosion), chances are traumatic injuries will be present. That is what we would base our initial response on until credible information came in. We would immediately implement the following strategies:

- Activate the Emergency Operations Plan and the Incident Command System.

- Report to Emergency Management Systems (EMS) via our disaster radio how many red (emergent), yellow (urgent) and green (non-urgent) patients we can take. This is only a guide for EMS to distribute patients equally if they can; in a large mass casualty, you get what you get.

- Clear as many patients out of the Emergency Department as we can; admit patients upstairs immediately, discharge others, and make decisions on the rest.

- Alert the trauma teams with numbers expected, injuries, time to ED, and any other pertinent information available.

- Alert the ORs to hold any currently open rooms; do not start any other cases until we have more information and begin to assemble trauma teams. We know from previous drills we can open 17 OR rooms with staffed teams in 2 hours if we have to. This would involve canceling all non-emergent surgeries.

- We would see how many staffed in-patient beds are available in house and prepare for early discharges if we needed to. I call this the "purge to surge."

- Alert the blood bank of potential incoming trauma to prepare for high volume of blood use.

- Open the command center and assemble the incident command team and begin gleaning information.

How we get information and share information during a citywide event:

- The Boston hospitals have an emergency manager on call 24/7 for events like this. We would immediately be in touch with him; he liaisons with other citywide agencies and shares this information with hospitals.

- The TV provides information and usually pictures of the scene so we can get a better idea of the scope.

- The city utilizes WebEOC, which is a software system all hospitals, public safety, public health, EMS, and others are linked into. This system would be active within 15 minutes. Information is shared here across disciplines and is great for situational awareness. We can also share our situation with others, make resource requests, and monitor others.

- Boston also has a medical intelligence center housed at Boston EMS; they would be pushing out information as it becomes available. They would be asking our needs and monitoring the situation.

- We (hospital emergency managers) receive information messages from state agencies via the HHAN (Health and Homeland Alert Network), if they activate the state Emergency Operations Center (EOC), etc.

- We also monitor the disaster radio in the ED; they will update us on how many more patients on scene, where they are going, etc.

We flex our incident command team up or down as needed for response and tailor our response strategies to the needs of the event. As far as the five first steps, I would say the following:

1. Activate the Emergency Operations Plan and notify Incident Command; this brings the team approach to the response.

2. Prepare the hospital for patient surge.

3. Glean information and share information to establish accurate situational awareness.

4. Monitor resources—Find the balance with staffing and burn rates of supply. This allows us to continue treating and know when to call for more.

5. Stabilize the event—Treat those from the event to return the hospital to normal operations. ■

Downtime in 2013 versus 2002

On November 13, 2002, the network core at Beth Israel Deaconess failed due to a complex series of events and the hospital lost access to all applications. Clinicians had no email, no lab results, no PACS images, and no order entry. All centrally stored files were unavailable. The revenue cycle could not flow. For two days, the hospital of 2002 became the hospital of 1972. Much has been written about this incident including a *CIO Magazine* article and a Harvard Business School case.

On July 25, 2013, a storage virtualization appliance at BIDMC failed in a manner which gave us Hobson's choice: do nothing and risk potential data loss;

or intervene and create slowness/downtime. Since data loss was not an option, we chose slowness. Here's the email I sent to all staff on the morning of July 25.

"Last evening, the vendor of the storage components that support Home directories (H:) and Shared drives (S:) recommended that we run a re-indexing maintenance task in order to avoid potential data corruption. They anticipated this task could be run in the middle of the night and would not impact our users. They were mistaken.

"The indexing continues to run and must run to completion to protect H: and S: drive data. While it is running, access to H: and S: will be slow, but also selected clinical web applications such as Provider Order Entry, webOMR, Peri-operative Information System, and the ED Dashboard will be slow. Our engineers are monitoring the clinical web applications minute to minute and making adjustments to ensure they are as functional as possible. We are also investigating options to separate clinical web applications from the storage systems which are causing the slowness.

"All available IS resources are focused on resolving this as soon as possible. We ask that all staff and clinical services affected by the interruption utilize downtime procedures until the issue is resolved. We apologize for the disruption this issue has caused to patients, providers, and staff."

The experiences in 2002 and 2013 were very different. Here's a brief analysis:

1. Although 2002 was an enterprise downtime of all applications, there was an expectation and understanding that failure happens. The early 2000s were still early in the history of the web. There was no cloud, no app-enabled smartphones, and no universal adoption of social networking. Technology was not massively redundant. Planned downtime still occurred on nights and weekends.

In 2013, there is a sense that IT is like heat, power, and light—always there and assumed to be high performing. Any downtime is unacceptable as emphasized by the typical emails I received from clinicians:

"My patients are still coming on time and expect the high quality care they normally receive. They also want it in a timely manner. Telling them the computer system is down is not an acceptable answer to them. Having an electronic health care record is vital but when we as physicians rely on it and when it is not available, it leads to gaps in care."

"Any idea how long we will be down? I am at the point where I may cancel my office for the rest of the day as I cannot provide adequate care without access to electronic records."

In 2013, we've become dependent on technology and any downtime procedures seem insufficient.

2. The burden of regulation is much different in 2013. Meaningful Use, the Affordable Care Act, ICD-10, the HIPAA Omnibus rule, and the Physician's Quality Reporting System did not exist in 2002. There is a sense now that clinicians

cannot get through each day unless every tool and process, especially IT related, is working perfectly.

Add downtime/slowness and the camel's back is broken.

3. Society, in general, has more anxiety and less optimism. Competition for scarce resources translates into less flexibility, impatience, and lack of a long-term perspective.

4. The failure modes of technology in 2013 are more subtle and are harder to anticipate.

In 2002, networking was simple. Servers were physical. Storage was physical. Today, networks are multi-layered. Servers are virtual. Storage is virtual. More moving parts and more complexity lead to more capabilities, but when failure occurs, it takes a multi-disciplinary team to diagnose and treat it.

5. Users are more savvy. Here's another email:

"Although I was profoundly impacted by today's events as a PCP trying to see 21 patients, I understand how difficult it is to balance all that goes into making a decision with a vendor on hardware/software maintenance. However, I was responsible for this for a large private group on very sophisticated IT, and I would urge you to consider doing future maintenance and upgrade projects starting on Friday nights, so as to have as little impact as possible on ambulatory patient care."

My experience with last week's event will shape the way I think about future communications for any IT-related issues. Expectations are higher, tolerance is lower, and clinician stress is overwhelming. No data was lost, no patient harm occurred, and the entire event lasted a few hours, not a few days. However, it will take months of perfection to regain the trust of my stakeholders.

It's been ten years since we had to use downtime procedures. We'll continue to reduce single points of failure and remove complexity, reducing the potential for downtime. As a clinician I know that reliability, security, and usability are critical. As a CIO I know how hard this is to deliver every day. ∎

Chapter 9

On Being a Parent, a Son, and a Husband

Every Thursday I write about personal issues—my family, my farm, my travels, my emotions, and my lessons learned. When my wife was diagnosed with breast cancer, she agreed to share every aspect of the journey publicly with the hope it would inform other families with cancer. When my father became gravely ill, the entire family agreed to share the details with the hope it would inspire others to think about care preferences and planning for end of life. In the posts below I share my highest highs and lowest lows. I have accepted that life is balance, bad things happen for a reason, and there are some things we cannot change. I hope my experiences ease your burden.

We Have Cancer

Cancer. It's a word that creates fear and uncertainty. Many of the doctors I know use the word "hate" whenever they discuss their feelings about cancer.

My wife Kathy was diagnosed with poorly differentiated breast cancer. She is not facing this alone. We're approaching this as a team, as if together we have cancer. She has been my best friend for 30 years. I will do whatever it takes to ensure we have another 30 years together.

She has agreed that I can chronicle the process, the diagnostic tests, the therapeutic decisions, the life events, and the emotions we experience with the hope it will help other patients and families on their cancer treatment journey.

Here's how it all started.

On Monday, December 5, she felt a small lump under her left breast. She has no family history, no risk factors, and no warning. We scheduled a mammogram for December 12 and she brought me a DVD with the DICOM images a few minutes after the study. On comparison with her previous mammograms, it was clear she had two lesions, one anterior and one posterior in a dumbbell shape. I hand carried the DICOM images to the Breast Center team at BIDMC.

On December 13 she had an ultrasound-guided biopsy which yielded the diagnosis—invasive ductal carcinoma, grade 3.

We assembled an extraordinary team of Harvard faculty—a primary care provider (Dr. Li Zhou), a surgeon (Dr. Mary Jane Houlihan), a medical oncologist (Dr. Steve Come), a radiation oncologist (Dr. Abram Recht), a pathologist (Dr. James Connolly), and a skilled breast imaging team. I also contacted my associates from the genomics research community.

On December 16, after my daughter's last final exam at Tufts, Kathy told Lara about the diagnosis. Lara immediately offered her love and support. We also told the grandparents.

Today, Kathy completed a bone scan and chest/abdominal CT. Both are negative for metastases.

We also received the receptor studies from the tumor tissue.

HER-2/neu gene amplification - Not Amplified

Estrogen Receptor - Strong

Progesterone Receptor - Strong

Our next step is to complete the staging via an ambulatory surgical procedure – a sentinel node biopsy to determine if the lymph nodes closet to the tumor have evidence of malignant cells.

Summarizing what we know thus far: the tumor is less than 5 cm, poorly differentiated/fast growing, not yet spread to bones or organs, HER-2 negative and Estrogen/Progesterone Receptor positive. Once the staging is completed, we'll be able to finalize a treatment plan and determine an estimated five-year survival rate.

Likely, she'll begin with chemotherapy to be followed by a left mastectomy.

We'll also explore her genome to understand the risk factors and determine if a bilateral mastectomy reduces future risk.

We'll face many decisions ahead and many emotions. We've already assembled a community of supporters.

One in eight women will develop breast cancer in their lifetime. We never thought we'd be the one.

One in eight women will develop breast cancer in their lifetime. We never thought we'd be the one.

My Thursday blogs for the next six months will document our progress on the healing journey.

Thank you for your prayers and support. ∎

Our Cancer Journey Week 31

Today marks the end of our cancer journey for now, although the follow-up will be life long. In 2012:

Kathy completed chemotherapy with Adriamycin/Cytoxan and Taxol.

- Kathy underwent a lumpectomy of her left breast where the tumor was growing.

- Kathy received 33 doses of radiation therapy over 42 days.

- We sold our home in Wellesley (it closes today), purchased a farm in Sherborn, and moved all our belongings, the contents of Kathy's studio, and her father's belongings to a single location.

- We acquired 8 alpaca, 2 llama (if you count our pregnant guard llama), 12 hens, 1 rooster, and 22 guinea fowl.

So now, it's time for a breather. The month of August has no travel, no visiting family/friends, and a little less chaos in our lives.

We will use our August 8 anniversary (32 years together, married 28) to reflect on where we've been and where we're going. We'll celebrate the trajectory of the past year. There was good and bad, but we're on a very positive path.

Although Kathy still has numbness in her feet and hands, the rest of her body and her mind is in good shape. She's designing our blueberry patch and apple orchard. She's putting the finishing touches on our barn, paddocks, and fences. Her new beginning as a cancer survivor is mirrored by a new lifestyle for our entire family.

I'm a strong believer in the karmic notion that everything happens for a reason. Life is anything but a linear path and you never know what you'll find around the next turn or how one turn will affect another.

To me, success is not measured in fame or fortune, but in relationships you nurture and the difference you make. Our cancer journey has been all about relationships—spouses supporting each other, family supporting family, clinicians supporting patients, my employer supporting its employee, and the broad community (Massachusetts colleagues, acquaintances, and fellow cancer patients) offering unconditional optimism.

So thank you to everyone who has supported Kathy and me since our diagnosis. By all measures, you've made a difference and strengthened every relationship while opening new doors for the future. We are truly blessed to have you around us. We look forward to the day we can invite all of you to our farm for blueberry picking, apple picking, and alpaca watching in celebration of surviving cancer. ■

Going Home Again

Recently, my wife and I flew to Northern California with my daughter to connect her with a group of students traveling to Japan for intensive language study this summer. After dropping my daughter off for her flight to Tokyo, my wife and I drove to every site that played a role in our 30-year relationship.

We met in 1980 at Stanford in the dorm complex next to Lake Lagunita. I was in Granada; she was in Eucalypto. We visited our old dorms and found the forests we walked in replaced with construction over the past 30 years.

In 1982, we served as live-in companions to Dr. Fred Terman, the former provost and Dean of Engineering. We visited his former home, in an enclave of faculty housing, on El Escarpado. It was getting a new driveway, but otherwise had not changed.

In 1983, after Dr. Terman died, we moved to a cabin in La Honda, California, on Shelden Road. Fritz Maytag, the founder of Anchor Steam Brewery, had lived there before us. La Honda had not changed much, and the biker bar called Applejacks was still a popular town gathering spot.

Each night in 1983–1984, we would drive from La Honda to the San Gregorio Stage stop, then to Pompano Beach and onward to Pescadero, a small farming town. We'd talk about the future and speculate where our Stanford education would take us. We did that drive again and stopped at Pompano to walk through the waves around the sandstone cliffs.

We drove north to San Francisco. Even in the late 1980s and early 1990s, we had an affinity for Japan and frequented Japantown in San Francisco. We strolled the shops, restaurants, and markets, nostalgic for the easy access to all things Japanese that is missing from Boston.

In 1984, we moved to Marin County and bought a small home on Rose Avenue, near Panoramic Highway in Mill Valley. That isolated neighborhood of older homes is now filled with expensive new construction. Our starter home is now ten times the price we paid for it. We were both amazed that we commuted through the narrow, steep, potholed roads of upper Mill Valley from 1984–1986. We had a great time back then with hot tubs, star gazing, and weekend sushi dinners, but we would not want to drive the cliffs of Rose Avenue today.

In 1986, we built a home on Mt. San Pedro in San Rafael overlooking China Camp State Park. It was the go-go 1980s, when owning a large home was a sign of success. Our home, Woodcliff, had five pods—a living area, an underground winery, an artist studio, a library/office wing, and a lab space for wine chemistry. We sold the home to Dr. Dean Edell in 1993. We learned many lessons about living large during that era and that led to the simpler existence we have embraced today. The house is still there, although the grape vines have been replaced with fields of lavender and the mountainside is now a destination for mountain bikers who seem at battle with private property owners.

During our Marin County years, I ran a software company called Colossus at 100 Smith Ranch Road while going to medical school at UCSF and graduate school at UC Berkeley. The office space is still there, occupied by another software company.

During weekends, we hiked West Marin locations: Pt. Reyes, Tomales Bay, and Bolinas. We did an eight-mile hike down the Bear Valley trail to Arch Rocks and visited the Tule Elk at Pierce Point. We stopped for dinner in Bolinas, a hidden town without any road signs to identify it. As we drove toward the Palomarin headlands, a rainbow appeared without any clouds or rain.

Would we go back? Would we want to relive the Palo Alto, Mill Valley, or San Francisco of our 20s? The great wines, the energy, and the outdoors of our youth?

Nope.

Northern California is a great place, but today we have different needs.

We're approaching 50 and our focus is on a great education for our daughter, time with family, career, and community service—locally and in Washington, DC.

Just as Northern California was a perfect fit for our 20s, New England is a perfect fit for our 40s and 50s. We have easy access to great educational institutions, healthcare, museums, New York, Washington, and colleagues across the Eastern Seaboard. The outdoors still beckons and we have easy access to hiking, biking, and kayaking. We have local farms and look forward to the variation of four seasons.

Our 60s may bring another set of needs. My daughter will be starting her own family, my parents may need more frequent visits, and our work activities may evolve. It's hard to know what tomorrow will bring, so we're leaving our options open. Maybe a small farm in Vermont? Maybe an ecofriendly cabin with a Japanese lifestyle? If my daughter lives and works in Japan after college, her current dream, then we might create a new life in Kyoto.

> *I would rather move forward guided by the past than try to relive it in the future.*

You can go home again and for me it was a great opportunity to refresh the memories that made me who I am today.

I look forward to each day and the potential it brings. The past is filled with great experiences, joys, and struggles. I would rather move forward guided by the past than try to relive it in the future. ∎

Your Karma Account Balance

It's a tough time for everyone right now.

The economy is troubled, there's an H1N1 flu outbreak, and there's increased competition for scarce resources.

This causes people to be edgy, angry, and impatient.

I encounter a sense of frenzy when I board airplanes, when I search for parking, and when I commute on busy highways.

It's time to dust ourselves off, make the most of each day, and strive for more good karma.

What do I mean?

Conflict happens every day. I have always believed that the nice guy can finish first in any conflict by doing the right thing.

1. By trying to win every competition, you may win the battle of office politics, but lose the karma war. I've found that those who are Machiavellian live by the sword and eventually die by the sword. Thus, do not grandstand, take credit inappropriately, or demean others to enhance your own stature.

    Rather than worrying about fame, fortune, or glory, just try to make a difference.

2. Rather than worrying about fame, fortune, or glory, just try to make a difference. Treat everyone with respect, listen to their concerns, and make decisions based on the greatest good for the greatest number.

3. Use email as a communication tool, not a weapon. If you feel emotion, save as draft and send it later. Never use blind cc's or use email to make others look bad to their superiors.

4. At the end of every day, look back on each open issue and ask if you've moved the issue forward. Many conflicts are not easily resolvable, but can be moved forward over time via gradual change and aligning the interests of stakeholders.

5. Stick to your principles. Integrity, honesty, and consistency should guide your actions.

If everyone looked at the balance in their karma account at the end of every week, the world would be a much more positive place.

Yesterday in a meeting, someone asked how I was doing. My answer was that my 401k may be bad, but my karma account is looking good. I have my health, a happy marriage, a loving daughter, and a set of really interesting challenges that enable me to make a difference.

I do not know where the future will lead, but when I look back in 30 years, I'll feel good about the journey. Along the way I'll be optimistic, kind, and fair. ∎

The Hive Mind

Over the past few years, I've radically redesigned my approach to learning. In the past, I memorized information. Now, I need to be a knowledge navigator, not a repository of facts. I've delegated the management of facts to the "Hive Mind" of the Internet. With Web 2.0, we're all publishers and authors. Every one of us can be instantly connected to the best experts, the most up-to-date news, and an exobyte multimedia repository. However, much of the Internet has no editor, so the Hive Mind information is probably only 80% factual—the challenge is that you do not know which 80%.

Here are few examples of my recent use of the Hive Mind as my auxiliary brain.

I was listening to a 1970s oldies station and heard a few bars of a song. I did not remember the song name, album, or artist. I did remember the words "Logical," "Cynical," "Magical." Entering these into a search engine, I immediately retrieved Supertramp's Logical Song lyrics. With the Hive Mind, I can now flush all the fragments of song lyrics from my brain without fear.

My daughter asked me a question from her chemistry homework about calculating the mass of nitrogen gas gathered over water. I did remember the ideal gas law ($PV=nRT$), but I did not recall how to correct for the partial pressure of water using Dalton's Law. One quick search for "nitrogen collected over water" yielded sample problem sets from colleges that refreshed my memory with all I needed to know.

While writing, I'm constantly looking up words, concepts, maps, and dates. I know how to look for them and where to find them.

There are a few times when the Hive Mind yields surprising results. I wanted to learn more about the stimulus bill's "Healthcare IT Standards Committee." I wanted to check out the "ARRA privacy timeline." Finally, I was looking for information about the "healthcare CIO." All three of these searches returned my own writing as the first hit. The blessing and the curse of Web 2.0 is that blogs are the news and personal opinions can become facts.

At the moment I have a balanced separation between my own mind and the Hive Mind. However, as we use Twitter, Facebook, and LinkedIn, I wonder if the separation between our human mind and our network mind will blur.

I remember an Outer Limits TV episode entitled "Stream of Consciousness" (actually, I found it in Wikipedia by searching Google for "outer limits episode stream") in which everyone in society is connected to the "Stream" and shares a network-connected existence based on information, not knowledge. In the end, the Stream is destroyed and mankind has to re-learn how to think for themselves.

As the closing dialog of that episode notes:

"We make tools to extend our abilities, to further our reach, and fulfill our aspirations. But we must never let them define us. For if there is no difference between tool and maker, then who will be left to build the world?"

Words to live by as we use the Hive Mind of the Internet. ∎

Do Your Best Today

I've written several blogs about being a parent, a husband, and a son.

Today's blog is about a simple statement my daughter made that applies to every one of my roles.

She said, "Do your best today."

These words are important to me.

Life as a CIO is really not a job, it's a lifestyle. I really do not know what each day will bring. There could be great joys of lives saved through the innovative use of IT. There could be budget stresses, conflict, or politics. There could be unexpected new project priorities or a particularly satisfying consensus about a strategic path forward.

As I wrote in my "Setting Expectations" blog entry, it is very challenging to judge the success of each day, each week, or each year because there are few specific objective criteria that meet the definition of success for all stakeholders.

The simple objective way I can judge my progress is by knowing I did my best today.

The simple objective way I can judge my progress is by knowing I did my best today.

- I treated my customers with respect and listened to their needs, even if I could not implement every one of their requests.

- I navigated the politics of every situation without criticizing others or inflating my own self-importance.

- I left the stress at the office behind and brought laughter to our family dinner.

- I put aside my email and helped work through a complex question on my daughter's chemistry homework (why is the surface tension of acetone higher than ethanol despite the hydrogen bonding in ethanol that should create higher inter-molecular forces).

- I supported my employees through challenging decision-making processes.

- I moved forward every project as much as it could be moved, including a new breakthrough in community clinical data exchange.

- I helped my parents choose a new digital television for their kitchen.

- I spoke with the press to speculate on the next steps needed to enhance rollout of electronic health records nationwide.

- I taught a course to MBA students at Boston University who are eager to find opportunities in stimulus-related work.

- I fixed a clogged bathtub drain.

As a parent, I want my daughter to be successful, but my definition of success is mine, not hers. I could tell her, "Get straight As in your honors classes today," or "Do amazing extracurricular activities that appeal to Ivy League Universities." Instead, "Do your best today" empowers her to set priorities—personal, educational, and family. She'll learn to triage the most important tasks and over time she'll learn the joy of success instead of the fear of failure.

We'll all have good days and bad days, high highs and low lows.

Do your best today. You'll be okay. ∎

Measuring Success

Over the past few weeks, I've reconnected with several folks from my past on Facebook and Twitter. It's an interesting end to the story to see what my high school friends have experienced over the past 30 years. There's good news and bad news, happiness and sadness, and occasionally a sense of missed expectations (e.g., "My life did not turn out as planned").

What should we expect from life, especially when we're 16 years old?

Some want fame.

Some want fortune.

Some want power.

Since high school I've discovered that life is much more subtle than that. Life is about finding your passion and committing every day to it.

In my case, I wake up every day and ask:

"How can I make my wife and my daughter happy today?"

"How can I ensure patients will receive the best possible care through the use of the IT systems I oversee?"

"How can I experience some wonder of the natural world—something as simple as watching a plump squirrel meander through my back yard or feeling the wind on my face as I run through a local forest?"

If you're doing what you love to do, have the basics of food/clothing/shelter/health, and have people you care for/care about you, then you're successful.

My daughter will apply to college next year.

Will I measure her success based on an application to Harvard, Stanford, or MIT? Will I feel satisfied only if she becomes a doctor, lawyer, or public figure? Will I demand that she marry into a family with wealth, power, or fame?

The answer is simple: I've told her to find her passion and pursue it with gusto, becoming the best she can be at whatever brings her joy. That could mean Middlebury or Mass Bay (a local community college). It could mean pharmacology or farming. It could mean marrying a member of the Forbes 400 or a forest ranger with a great sense of humor.

We set expectations based on what we believe society defines as success. The problem with this is that society continuously changes the definition. When I was an Emergency Medicine resident, ER was the most popular new series on television and society defined my intended career as glamorous. Then again, society also defined Wall Street as a highly desirable career. Society's expectations are ephemeral.

In my youth, I thought society defined success as the car you drive, the house you own, and the clothes you wear.

Today, I know that none of these things really matter.

Define your expectations as pursuing your passion and you'll not be writing, "My life did not turn out as planned" 30 years from now. For me, life is filled with daily adventures and no particular expectation where I will end up, but the journey will be quite a ride. ∎

Engage with Grace

Recently, you'll find that many healthcare bloggers have devoted their blog to the post below. My wife and I have completed the exercise. In my case, I do not want end-of-life care in a hospital. When I cease to be me through brain injury or diminished mental capacity, I do not want to be supported. I want my ashes scattered from the top of Mt. Scowden on the Tioga Crest.

This guest post was written by Alexandra Drane and the Engage With Grace[1] team.

"We make choices throughout our lives—where we want to live, what types of activities will fill our days, with whom we spend our time. These choices are often a balance between our desires and our means, but at the end of the day, they are decisions made with intent. But when it comes to how we want to be treated at the end of our lives, often we don't express our intent or tell our loved ones about it. This has real consequences. 73% of Americans would prefer to die at home, but up to 50% die in a hospital. More than 80% of Californians say their loved ones know exactly or have a good idea of what their wishes would be if they were in a persistent coma, but only 50% say they've talked to them about their preferences. But our end of life experiences are about a lot more than statistics. They're about all of us.

"So the first thing we need to do is start talking. Engage With Grace: The One Slide Project was designed with one simple goal: to help get the conversation about end of life experience started. The idea is simple: Create a tool to help get people talking. Five questions designed to help get us talking with each other, with our loved ones, about our preferences. And we're asking people to share this wherever and whenever they can ... at a presentation, at dinner, at their book club, just five questions.

"Let's start a global discussion that, until now, most of us haven't had.

Here is what we are asking you: share the five questions at any opportunity with colleagues, family, friends. Think of the slide as currency and donate just two minutes whenever you can. Commit to being able to answer these five questions about end of life experience for yourself, and for your loved ones. Then commit to helping others do the same. Get this conversation started.

"Let's start a viral movement driven by the change we as individuals can effect...and the incredibly positive impact we could have collectively. Help ensure that all of us—and the people we care for—can end our lives in the same purposeful way we live them. Just goal. Think of the enormous difference we can make together."

To learn more please go to http://www.engagewithgrace.org. ∎

The Gift of Time

Time is the one commodity you cannot buy and you cannot make more of. To me, this means that time is our most valuable resource.

---

1 Engage With Grace is a viral movement to help individuals understand, communicate, and have honored their end-of-life wishes.

The role of the CIO is to allocate their time to those people and projects most needing of attention.

Every day, I would really enjoy meeting with friendly, aligned, and supportive stakeholders. I would really enjoy focusing on those projects that are proceeding flawlessly. However, my most limited commodity, time, is best allocated toward those stakeholders who are not satisfied and those projects which are troubled by politics, scope, or technical challenges.

Every day, my staff ask for help with budget issues, strategy clarification, and political questions. The CIO should never be the rate-limiting step. I answer these questions within an hour of their being asked with either an answer or a definite set of next steps. This is a great use of my time.

Every day, my customers ask for new projects, new priorities, or new features. I answer with either a blog entry so that I widely communicate the answer, a personal email, or a set of next steps involving our governance committees to consider the request. This is a great use of my time.

Every day, I receive numerous requests to travel to give presentations to organizations both large and small. I'm always happy to educate, communicate, and collaborate. The challenge is the time involved in travel. Doing a conference call, WebEx, or video teleconference is a great use of time. Sitting in an airport for half a day because of a canceled flight is not a great use of time. I'm hoping our culture changes to the point that everyone thinks about the value of time and does more virtual collaboration.

Every day, I receive 100 requests from salespeople for my time. Money is one thing you can always make more of. Time is limited. As I've said before on my blog, I will not grant my time to cold-calling salespeople who email me about the wonders of their product. Stop trying. As needs arise I'll search the web for technologies and user experiences with them. I'll then contact you.

Money is one thing you can always make more of. Time is limited.

The reason that I mention this entire subject is that recently I reflected on the best gift for Father's Day. Anyone can buy a tie, a CD on Amazon, or the latest gadget. However, the gift of time is more valuable. Here's what I did.

I had a Google Advisory Council meeting in Mountain View from 8 am to 1 pm. My parents live in Southern California. I asked my father to meet me at the San Jose Airport at 2 pm and I picked him up in my rental car. We drove together through the most beautiful places in the Santa Cruz mountains—Crystal Springs Reservoir/Filoli/Alpine Road, Highway 84 to Skyline Boulevard in the Santa Cruz Mountains, La Honda, San Gregorio, Highway 1 to Pigeon Point Lighthouse, and Pescadero. We had dinner at Duarte's, a 19th century restaurant which serves fresh artichoke dishes and homemade pie. We talked about life, goals, the future, family, and challenges. For six hours, we drove, talked, and turned off the cell phones. At sunset we returned to Skyline Boulevard and played flutes together— my Shakuhachi and his Native American flute. I then dropped him off at the airport for his return flight and I spent the night in San Francisco to attend an early morning board meeting.

My daughter and I recently began playing the Native American flute, so that we can have a family gift of time. My parents will join us on a family vacation to Yosemite in August and we'll play music together across three generations.

To me, there is no more profound gift than time. If future Father's Days include the gift of time from my daughter such as a walk in the woods, kayaking on a river, or playing a flute, I'll be completely happy.

Next time you ask how to organize your day, think about the value of your time. Think about the needs of your customers, staff, and family. If you think about your time as a gift and your most valuable commodity, I suspect your schedule may change. I know mine has. ■

Management Lessons Learned as a Parent

Being a parent has taught me more about leadership and management than any of the Spencer Johnson or Peter Drucker books. I've learned patience, communication, and the ability to trust.

Here are my top ten management lessons learned from being a parent:

1. Yelling never has a positive outcome—In my life as a parent, I've raised my voice twice over the past decade and a half. My daughter can remember both times, even though they occurred in the distant past. My outbursts diminished me and had no positive impact on her behavior. In business, if I ever feel that raising my voice would win the battle, I reflect on my life as a parent and hold back, since I know that confrontation ultimately makes the situation worse. As I've said before, "save as draft."

2. Formal authority rarely works—As a CIO, I would never stand in front of a group of stakeholders and say, "You must do this, because I'm the CIO." Standing in front of a teenager and saying, "You must do this, because I'm your father," is just as problematic. Leadership comes from thoughtful discussion, weighing pros and cons, then ultimately arriving at a consensus. Shared decision making between parents and children based on a fair, consistent, and predictable process preserves domestic tranquility. IT governance preserves organizational tranquility in the same way.

3. Give permission to make mistakes—Wellesley and the surrounding western suburbs of Boston have had a number of teen suicides over the past few years. Parents apply such pressure to perform that many teens have irrational expectations of perfection for themselves (e.g., "You can be valedictorian, captain of the squash team, and a Pulitzer Prize winner by the time you're 18"). Making mistakes and learning along the way are the way we learn as children and the way we learn as leaders. In management, I find that setting limits, then offering staff the flexibility to excel on their own, are far more effective than micro-management and a constant threat of management retribution.

4. Communication is key—During a teenager's development, mom and dad may not be perceived as cool, smart, or fun to be with, but this can change by the day. Keeping the channels of communication open as moods change is key. There will be disagreements, but it's less important to win the argument than to ensure you're still speaking when the discussion is over. The same thing is true with customers and employees—I'd rather hear from them about bad news and fix the problem than not hear anything at all.

5. Get the basics right—Why was religion invented? There are encyclopedias written about that topic, but in my opinion, religion was invented to provide a moral/behavioral framework that puts boundaries on human instincts to compete, reproduce, and survive. We do not have a religious household, but we have a moral household. As a parent, I've tried to be a living example that the nice guy can finish first, that theft and aggressive behavior are wrong, and that kindness and consensus win the day. If my examples lead my daughter to make the right choices when faced with tough decisions, then the basic moral framework we've built will be a foundation for her success. In business, setting a tone of expected behavior by being a living example of ethical, fair, and collaborative behavior spreads to staff and customers.

6. You can criticize ideas but do not criticize people—As the brain matures, sensory input is integrated with experience to produce more robust decision making. During that process there will be many experiments, trial/error, and fine tuning. If my daughter makes a decision that I do not agree with, we can debate her ideas but not her abilities. The same is true with employees and customers. I treat everyone with respect, even if I do not agree with their ideas.

7. Build a joy of success rather than fear of failure—When I was a teen and took the SATs, I had no real knowledge of their importance. I arrived a bit late, and did not stress over the outcome. The result

was a scholarship, not because I was smarter than my peers, but because I did not have a fear of failure during the exam. I watch many parents link performance on every test to an admission or rejection from Harvard. Admission to an Ivy League school is equated to happiness. With Lara, we've tried to celebrate success and build a joy of achievement rather than a fear of failure. Thus far, the motivation from within to do well seems much more sustainable than fear of failure imposed by authority figures. Emphasizing growth and achievement among employees creates a higher performance organization than management by intimidation.

8. Delegate responsibility but emphasize accountability—My daughter tends to have the same sleep cycle that I do, often sleeping 4 or 5 hours a night. Her schedule is left up to her to decide, but when the 6:30 am alarm sounds, she is accountable for her decision to go to bed late. Rather than enforce a bedtime and wake time, delegating her sleeping hours to her, but holding her accountable for getting to school on time, awake and alert, has enhanced her decision making. Leadership is the work of worry and it's important to learn accountability early. The more responsibility I'm given, the greater the accountability.

9. Respect innovation—As vegans, my wife, daughter, and I grow beets, carrots, and turnips each year. Last year, when we picked a bucket of carrots, I recommended to my daughter that we use a sieve to wash off the dirt. She had a different idea of laying them out in the driveway and washing them off with a sprayer. I suggested that sieves have always been used and it's the "right way." Her method, although non-standard, was fast, effective, and efficient. Just because business as usual has always worked, there may be better ways. As I tell my staff: If I become the obstacle to innovation, it's time for me to move on.

10. Accept that the best lessons learned come from independence—For my daughter to develop self-esteem, assertiveness, and a willingness to take acceptable risks, she needs to make decisions on her own, even if they are imperfect. If I make decisions for her, she'll be less prepared for life in college and beyond when I may not be present. I give her the best guidance that I can, hope that she develops a strong internal compass, and then let her change from within as she experiences the world. Developing

I give her the best guidance that I can, hope that she develops a strong internal compass, and then let her change from within as she experiences the world.

the next generation of leaders in an organization requires the same approach.

I highly recommend parenting over an MBA. Parenthood teaches humility, selflessness, and self-control. No matter what I do in IT, my daughter will be my greatest legacy. ∎

Outliers

It's too cold for rock climbing and kayaking but not yet cold enough for ice climbing or skiing, so I'm using the time to read through the books on my nightstand and on my Kindle.

I just finished *Outliers* by Malcolm Gladwell[2] (author of *The Tipping Point*), a well written thought piece on what really produces the movers and shakers in each generation.

Darwin would have loved the heady questions raised by this book. Is success more about nature or nurture? What's more important: the Intelligence quotient or Emotional quotient? Is the Stanford-Binet test a useful measure of your likelihood to succeed? Can Harvard really tell the differences among 3,000 valedictorians with perfect SATs applying to college?

Here's my own story put in the context of the book.

When I was 12 years old (1974), my parents went to law school and I spent my free time after school scouring surplus stores in Southern California. Sunny Trading Company on Torrance Boulevard was my treasure trove. For 10 cents I could buy NAND gates, Shift Registers, and LM555 digital timing chips. Reading through National Semiconductor product catalogs and the entire contents of our local library's Dewey Decimal 620-622, I learned digital logic, analog-to-digital conversion, and the basics of microprocessor design.

Then, in 1975, a major breakthrough: the *Popular Electronics* January issue announced the Altair 8800, which made home computing possible and I devoted myself to learning about "personal computers."

I spent my high school years programming in numerous languages from Assembler to Fortran to Cobol to BASIC. I used minicomputers, microcomputers, and mainframe computers. In 1978, I designed the software and hardware for my first experimental medical device—a computer capable of gathering visual and audio evoked potentials, then performing signal averaging and fast fourier transforms in real time.

All of this was possible because I lived in Southern California in the mid-1970s, when surplus stores had cheap integrated circuits and because my local

---

2   Gladwell, M. *Outliers: The Story of Success*. Back Bay Books; 2011.

library gave me access to great books about emerging technology. I truly believe that this foundational portion of my career was more about time and place than me.

From high school I went to Stanford, started a software firm, and began the parallel life of medicine and technology that leads to the present.

> *I truly believe that this foundational portion of my career was more about time and place than me.*

In *Outliers*, Gladwell points out that Bill Gates, Steve Jobs, Larry Ellison, Scott McNealy and Bill Joy—the leaders behind our largest technology companies—were all born in 1955. They were 20 when the *Popular Electronics* issue was published, just completing college (or dropping out of it). They were at the beginning of their careers but without families, a mortgage, or an established job in a traditional technology firm. They were at the right place at the right time to ride the wave of emerging technologies.

Of course, they were smart, but numerous people are smarter. Gladwell concludes that once you are "smart enough," then culture, circumstance, timing, and luck are key differentiators for success.

Our lives are complex paths with daily choices that lead to success or failure. I know that I could have ended up in a dozen different careers, lifestyles, and economic strata. However, as *Outliers* suggests, the world around me shaped my outcome and I can really link my Harvard faculty position to my parents' choice of living near an electronics surplus store in the 1970s.

Outliers is worth reading to understand the external context which shaped some of the most successful people of our generation. ∎

Plea for Civility

It's Thanksgiving Day and we should all take time for our families, our mental health, and a pause from the pressures of the modern world. As I've told my staff, it's been a typical fall—we go from the doldrums of summer to a sprint post-Labor Day with numerous urgent (and sometimes unplanned) projects.

This takes a personal toll. Tempers can flare, and patience can run thin. Civility disappears.

What do I mean by civility?

Webster's calls it "civilized conduct; especially courtesy, politeness."

How was your drive to work yesterday? Put another way—what is the shortest unit of measurable time? Answer: the time between the light turning green in front of you and the person honking behind you.

Did people stop for pedestrians in crosswalks? Did they let you into merging traffic? Did they stop at yellow lights to keep intersections clear and prevent gridlock?

If you boarded a flight yesterday, did passengers wait until their seats or zones were called before standing in line? Did they check their steamer trunk-sized bags so that there was plenty of room in the overhead bins for others with smaller carry-ons? Did the person in front of you avoid reclining their seat so that you could have a more enjoyable flight?

I realize that more people are competing for fewer resources and the economy is less than robust. That does not mean we have to turn each day into our own personal *Lord of the Flies*.

It is my hope that as we enter the holiday season, the pace will slow and we'll be able to do our work in a predictable way, with the scope, resources, and timelines we need to get them done.

Today, raise a toast to the good things we have in life—family, wellness, and the boundless opportunity to make the world a better place. Let's use the Thanksgiving weekend to renew our spirits, prepare for the challenges ahead, and regain our civility.

I'm off to roast the squash and carve the tofu. ∎

Measuring Happiness

It's Christmas Eve and I've put the smartphone to bed, stopped the strategic planning, and set aside the work of worry.

My daughter does not want to discuss upcoming college tours or the cube root of 127. Instead, we're discussing our personal definitions of happiness.

For my daughter, it's the little things that make her happy. The smiles from her friends, the smell of soy hot chocolate, and the idea of sleeping for 12 hours without homework to do.

For me, I measure happiness by looking at my reflection in the people around me. Have my parents had a good year because of something I've done? Has my wife been empowered to pursue her dreams? Has my daughter gained more self-confidence? Do my staff feel good about our trajectory and the stability of their work environment? Do my colleagues feel that I'm a convener who can be trusted to bring people together seeking the greatest good for the greatest number?

Measuring happiness through the eyes of others is imperfect—you cannot make everyone happy. However, you can treat them fairly, positively, and with respect, even if they are naysayers. My metric is to simply ask if I've done my best.

As I sit with my family, a snow-covered wreath hanging on my front door, the smell of chestnuts drafting through the house, sipping a cup of Graham's 1985 Port, and watching *The Polar Express*, I have a sense that my wife, daughter, parents, friends, staff, and colleagues are achieving their own happiness. I'm at peace with the world and thankful for the year that's passed, happy by all measures.

Happiness to you and to all a good night. ∎

Stress Acceleration

When I think back on my high school experience, I remember an 8 am-3 pm school day, a cross country/track workout from 3 pm-5 pm, a snack until 6pm, and an hour of reading or problem sets. After that, my time was my own to experiment with early microprocessor circuits, tinker with building a hovercraft (powered by a used vacuum cleaner motor) or do personal writing (I entered dozens of essay contests as a teen). Weekends were filled with bike riding up and down the coast of California, SCUBA/snorkeling in local marine preserves, or helping around the house. Summers were filled with outdoor pursuits and low key internships.

My daughter is 16 and is experiencing the typical modern public high school schedule – classes from 7:30 or 8:30 am to 2:30 pm, a bit of after-school community service or exercise, and then 8–9 hours of homework per night, typically ending at midnight or 1 am. I've talked to other parents and found this schedule to be typical. Homework might include hundreds of pages of reading, the creation of a complex research paper, and the self-teaching of advanced genetics. Given that this level of intensity is the norm, colleges consider a high grade point average in honors/AP classes plus near perfect SATs to be just a starting point.

I was not a Pulitzer prize winner, first violin for the local symphony, or the lead in a Hollywood film as a teen, yet this is the kind of achievement that appears on today's college applications. Harvard admits 4% of its applicants.

In my 20s the work day began at 9 am, ended at 5 pm, and did not span into weekends. There was no email. Fax was an emerging technology. Overnight shipping did not exist. Modems were 110 baud.

Today's work day (not just for me but for many) is 24x7x365 with 50% more filling each day than was previously possible because hundreds of email saturate mobile devices with a constant stream of new work.

My Martin Luther King Day ("a national holiday") had three meetings, 500+ email, two conference calls and five projects. People used the day to catch up and now that the office is wherever your laptop and cellular are, it was a full work day for many.

Does this acceleration of stress bother me? Over the years of medical training and leading large complex organizations, I've learned to adapt to just about anything. For every issue there is a process to resolve it.

Is it sustainable for society? I don't think so.

Just as humans were not content to run a four-minute mile or ascend Everest with supplemental oxygen, we seem to be demanding more of ourselves and our families than is rational or healthy. We're becoming a nation of multi-taskers with ADHD,[3] doing more, in shorter time, but not necessarily living happier, more satisfying lives.

Can we sit and enjoy a meal without thinking about work or checking email? Can we go to a movie or concert for an evening without needing to stay connected? Can we turn off our social networks for a week without suffering withdrawal?

The level of stress I see around me is leading humanity to increase consumption of pharmaceuticals (have a problem—take a pill), eat poorly, and reduce the baseline of human kindness (driven in Boston lately?).

> *At some point, we have to wake up, turn off our Blackberries, set limits on tolerable stress in our lives, and regain our civility.*

My grandfather did not attend college. My father completed more education by 21 than my grandfather did in his lifetime. I completed more education by 21 than my father will in his lifetime. My daughter will complete more education by 21 than I will in my lifetime. Where does it stop?

At some point, we have to wake up, turn off our Blackberries, set limits on tolerable stress in our lives, and regain our civility.

Can we reduce the size of our homes, the number of cars in our garages, and our lifestyle burn rates to enable us to work less and improve the quality of life?

I'm not worried about me—I've developed the discipline to leave my stress outside the home. I do worry about my daughter, her future children, and the generations to come.

Just as a parachuter accelerates at 32 feet/second until reaching terminal velocity, there is a point in our existence as humans that stress acceleration will take us to terminal velocity in the quality of our lives.

It is my hope that high schools/colleges, employers, and policymakers think about the terminal velocity we're approaching and open the parachute against stress acceleration before it's too late. ∎

---

3 Attention deficit hyperactivity disorder.

These Are the Good Old Days

How do you think about your past?

If you're like me, I remember the good, but forget the bad. My high school memories are of a simpler time, with fewer responsibilities, and the boundless energy of youth. I've forgotten the worry about college admissions, the ambiguity of the future, and adolescent relationship angst.

College was a time that I courted my wife, saw endless possibilities for the future, and reveled in the joy of unbounded learning. I've forgotten the anxiety of medical school applications, the struggle to build a self-supported household, and the burden of entering the real world.

Each year, month and day that goes by brings its joys and sorrows, its victories and defeats, its anticipation and disappointments. However, I look back and only remember the trajectory, not the day-to-day position on the journey.

It's 2010 and everyone in healthcare IT is complaining. Meaningful Use is too hard. Too many grants have simultaneous deadlines. There are more policy and technology changes than ever before in history.

So how will you remember this stressful time?

Let's consider the past.

In 1981–1982, Kathy, my wife to be and I lived with Frederick E. Terman, former Provost of Stanford University and Silicon Valley pioneer, son of Lewis Terman, inventor of the IQ Test. In his final year of his life, Terman told me of his wartime experiences—innovative radar jammers, tunable receivers to detect radar signals, and anti-radar aluminum chaff, all created at an accelerated pace by his 850-person team at the Harvard Radio Research Laboratory. It was his version of the stimulus bill (ARRA) work we're doing today. Did he remember the stress, the wartime rationing, or emotional cost? No, he remembered only the incredible achievements created in unreasonable timeframes and motivated by the world environment around him.

A turning point in our industry was 2010. There will never again be a time when $46 billion in funding for healthcare IT is aligned with government/industry/academia momentum for change.

The sleepless nights, grant fatigue, policy arguments, and standards debates will all be forgotten.

We'll be telling our grandchildren about 2010 and how we transformed healthcare from a cottage industry of information silos into a connected ecosystem for coordination of care, public health, and patient engagement.

Of course, our grandchildren will claim it's always been that way.

These are the Good Old Days. Trust me. ∎

Resilience

My daughter is 16 going on 17, a junior in high school. We've begun discussions of colleges, SAT scores, and her future.

Many of my peers in healthcare management have college-bound children and are having the same dinner table conversations—what constitutes success, what college to choose, how to work together over the next year to guard against the stress acceleration every high school student is feeling.

College admissions should not be a beauty contest for parents to judge their success in child rearing based on acceptance letters from Ivy League institutions. College admissions should be about matching the needs of the individual with an institutional culture, location, and teaching style that builds self-confidence and resilience.

What do I mean?

I attended Stanford, UCSF, UC Berkeley, UCLA, Harvard, and MIT. My post-secondary education lasted 17 years from 1980–1997.

My personality type was a bit odd—I majored in those topics that were most confusing to me. I speculated that if I could master my weakest areas, I would become a resilient life-long learner of anything that would come my way.

My daughter is talented in ways that I am not (the visual arts, foreign languages, and mathematics that requires spatial sense). No doubt this is because my left brain (math, science, engineering) combined with my wife's right brain (arts, philosophy, creativity) creates a whole brain. My daughter is seeking to define herself, discover those areas in which she can be truly excellent, and build self-confidence.

She would not thrive at a large, urban school, filled with thousands of anonymous peers. She would not thrive in a competitive academic culture which rewards privation, suggesting that if you're not suffering, you're not learning.

She's seeking a school that is small to medium-sized, rural or suburban, located in New England, with a supportive culture that can polish a lovely and intelligent young woman into an assertive but not aggressive adult.

With the right encouragement and opportunities, she'll be challenged but not overwhelmed, hard working but not fatigued, and encouraged to find her unique place in the world.

I do not define success as fame, fortune, or Google hit count. I define success as resilience to navigate the world, enthusiasm to get up each day because you love what you do, and happiness with the people around you.

So, you go girl. Find a college that makes you blossom. Your parents will be there, proud of its fit for you, not its ranking in *US News and World Report*. ■

Where You Start Is Not Where You End

I've written about my daughter's exploration of colleges and my sense that college fit for her including teaching style, student peers, setting, culture, and extracurricular activities is more important than *US News and World Report* rankings or the parental ego boost from the college prestige beauty contest.

As an experiment, I asked several of my staff where they went to college.

There was no correlation between their current roles and the prestige ranking of their college. College was a nurturing experience that enabled them to explore their interests, find themselves, and build the skills to succeed in life. Graduate school did correlate a bit. Aiming for a great Master's program (MS, MBA, MPH, MPA) is an enabler to find a good job.

Interestingly, of the folks I work with in Washington, most identify themselves with the institution of their final degree and not their college experience. After a few years in recognizable positions, any mention of even graduate educational institutions fades away.

From my limited experience of managing 500 people, it's the person and their individual journey that leads to success, not their pedigree.

As I look at my evolving CVs through the years, the pedigree of my 20s is no longer relevant to my trajectory at 50.

The point where you start is not where you end.

I disagree with those who believe the right kindergarten leads to the right elementary school leads to the right high school leads to the famous college, which immediately produces fame and fortune. From my limited experience of managing 500 people, it's the person and their individual journey that leads to success, not their pedigree.

My own life has been filled with twists, random acts of kindness from others, good karma, and Brownian motion that has led me to my current positions.

My daughter's passions are mathematics, Japanese culture/language, archery, the outdoors, and art. Might she be an environmental engineer working in Japan and studying Kyudo, the mediative archery martial art? Could she be the designer of the next generation of Lego toys? Might she teach English to Japanese elementary school students after college, then work in Japanese government as a liaison to visiting technologists? All are possible—the world is her oyster.

In life thus far, I've been a son, programmer, author, editor, manager, winemaker, physician, technologist, politician, husband, and father. Fate usually reinvents my role every few years and the final chapter of my story has not yet been written.

So, Lara, go write your story. You're at Chapter 1. I look forward to reading the novel of your life as you write it, your way, in the years to come. ∎

The Yin to My Yang

Thirty years ago this month (at 17), I won a speaking contest in a California statewide competition. Kathy Greene won a related statewide art competition. At the time I remember marveling at her use of color in oil paintings of California's missions. She recalled a geeky public speaker who could spin an interesting story.

On August 31, 1980, I was assigned to the Lagunita dorm at Stanford. So was Kathy Greene.

We started dating on September 1, 1980. We just celebrated our 25th wedding anniversary.

Within 24 hours of our time together, I realized that she was the Yin to my Yang. I was math, science, engineering, black and white, digital 0s and 1s, Zen, and monk-like asceticism. She was art, music, culture, color, analog, Victorian clutter, and Joie de vivre. I was completely left brain; she was completely right brain. Together we were a whole brain. On September 2, 1980, we agreed to support each other throughout our education—I would do her math and she would do my art. Together, we could do everything.

Back then, Stanford cost almost $15,000 per year and we needed funding after our scholarships ran out. I went to the Stanford Law library, studied the US tax code and wrote a tax computation program (call it early TurboTax) that businesses could use to write payroll checks on CP/M and early DOS computers. Kathy wrote the manual, designed the advertising, and did all the corporate graphics. We sold thousands of copies from my dorm room.

I was asked to create something special for Steve Wozniak's 33rd birthday and I designed electronic greeting cards with synchronized audio and video that ran on 1980s computers. I patented the idea and included the odd concept that someday there will be a big network connecting everyone that would enable sending of electronic greeting cards between computers. (Next time you send an e-card, you can thank me for the royalty-free license!). Kathy created all the graphics and digital artwork.

We've traveled the world, survived medical education, and raised a 17-year-old together. She's introduced me to the cultures of the Far East, the music of Simon and Garfunkel, and the art of Maxfield Parrish.

She's been faculty at the School of the Boston Museum of Fine Arts, faculty at Bentley College, and a studio artist in South Boston.

She recently started her own blog (Art that is Life) and opened the NK Gallery in Boston's South End.

She's my best friend.

It's great to marry the first person you date—I've been able to invest all my energy in a single life relationship. I think it will last. ∎

The Girl with Two Brains

Last Thursday I wrote about the Yin to my Yang, exploring the synergy between my left brain and my wife's right brain.

My daughter Lara turns 17 next week and she's definitely the girl with two brains (or a whole brain).

I cannot draw a stick figure (my attempts at drawing a human look more like a dinner fork than the Venus de Milo).

My daughter took a blank piece of paper and a pencil then drew a self portrait..

Her greatest academic strength is math. She can visualize problems involving vector forces, geometry, or trigonometric functions, then break them into solvable component parts. To me, the hardest part of advanced math and engineering is setting up the problem correctly, not solving it.

She's just completed her first resumé. Today's high school students are expected to master college level topics, develop disciplined work habits at an early age, and complement their academics with sports/music/art/volunteer work, which she's tried to do in a balanced way. My own experience as a student was that I was not the smartest student in the class, but I was the most persistent due to minimal sleep needs, a great tolerance for any kind of discomfort—(cold/fatigue/hunger), and a sense of impatience for the future.

I would like to believe that idealists can succeed through persistence and determination, always staying true to their values.

My daughter has a different set of skills—a whole brain that can process the analytical and visual with equal competency, an ability to think about the greater good rather than personal gain, and a sense that anything is possible. She does not believe in political half truths. She does not judge success by a bank balance. She does not believe the ends justify the means. She believes that the nice guy (or gal) can finish first.

I would like to believe that idealists can succeed through persistence and determination, always staying true to their values. Watching day-to-day activities in Washington has convinced me that it's critically important to have a strong moral compass.

Her current college search criteria on CollegeBoard.com are the following:
- Rural or suburban location

- Under 10,000 students

- Strong Asian studies/Japanese language program (for the right brain)

- Strong environmental engineering program (for the left brain)

- Studio art resources

- If possible, a competitive collegiate archery team (she's ranked 6th in the US)

It's my hope that she has the best of both her parents without the downsides of either.

At very least, she can write a college essay entitled, "Why I have a whole brain"! ∎

My Parents

I've written about being a parent, a husband, and a son.

It's time to write a blog about my parents and their impact on my development, my day-to-day thinking, and my future.

I was born in Des Moines, Iowa, to Dagmar Vanags and John E. Halamka, who were both 20 at the time (typical parenting age for Iowa in the 1950s and early 60s). They are approaching their 50th wedding anniversary. I've blogged about our family history going back to the 1800s. When I was 0-2 years old, we lived with my father's parents as my father finished college. He joined the Air Force and we moved to Colorado Springs, Levittown (Willingboro), New Jersey, and finally Southern California in the mid 1960s. He worked for Aerospace contractors such as CSC, Aerojet General, and TRW.

His engineering work meant that our apartment was filled with tools, various electronic/mechanical surplus, and a culture of inventiveness. On weekends, we went to surplus stores and we built things together including a working wooden model of Da Vinci's catapult, a minibike, and a metal detector.

My father arranged access to the TRW timesharing system via a 110-baud acoustic modem and we worked on FORTRAN, COBOL and BASIC programming. Thus, by 14 I had already spent hundreds of hours developing software (in 1976). As Malcolm Gladwell describes in *Outliers*, having this much computer science and engineering experience in the mid to late 1970s prepared me for success when the personal computer revolution occurred in the early 1980s.

My father became a patent attorney and when I wrote software, he patented the work itself and the business processes, such as my 1984 patent of the electronic greeting card.

In my adult life, he's provided legal advice, financial advice, and feedback on the various career threads I've pursued. His perspective from the eyes of an engineer/attorney is always welcome.

My mother has been a life-long teacher/professor and attorney. She arranged for me to attend a community college physics course when I was in elementary school. She ensured there were books in the house and I learned to read at a very early age. There was no significant family time spent around the television (except watching the original airing of Star Trek from 1966–1969). I went to Broadway plays by the time I was four. I visited major national parks and monuments throughout the country by car by the time I was six.

If my father brought me love of science/technology/engineering/math, then my mother brought me love of learning, writing, and public speaking.

Throughout high school I entered every essay contest I could find and spoke at every speaking competition offered. The ability to think fast on my feet in front of an audience is my mother's skill.

In my adult life, she's provided legal advice, academic career advice, and parenting advice. Her perspective as a teacher, public speaker, and gregarious social person is always welcome.

Today, my parents are retired and have recently moved to a great one-story house. They continue to stay in touch with friends, former students, and colleagues. Over the next few years, I'm sure they will do volunteer work, cultural events, gardening, reading, and travel. We talk every week and they continue to stay involved with everything going on in our extended family.

I look forward to many more years of sharing our journeys together! ∎

Reflections on Being a Father

As Father's Day approaches, I'm off to San Francisco to give Grand Rounds at Lucile Packard Children's Hospital, then to Los Angeles to spend Father's Day with my father.

My daughter is now 17, so I've had nearly 18 years of responsibilities as a father, along with 25 years of being a husband, and 30 years as a companion to my wife.

We live in an era when 50% of all marriages end in divorce and even apparently stable couples like Al and Tipper Gore give up after 40 years together.

> *I am a different person at 48 than I was at 18. The good news is that my wife likes both of those people.*

What are my lessons learned from being a husband and father?

1. I am a different person at 48 than I was at 18. The good news is that my wife likes both of those people. I'm a very different person now than when my daughter was born. We've grown together.

2. I've lived with my daughter through all the stages of her development — from a dependent infant, an inquisitive toddler, an adoring young child, and a spirited teen to a young woman on her way to becoming independent at college in 2011. At each stage she has interacted with me differently. I love her journey to independence as much as I treasured our time together when I was her best friend. Every day I need to recognize and respect her evolution.

3. Communities like Wellesley, Massachusetts, are filled with goal-directed professionals who want to ensure the success of their children. This leads to a fair amount of academic pressure and "helicopter parenting." Although it may seem more expedient to do things for my daughter, it also slows her path of building self-confidence and internal drive. I see my role as helping with her trajectory and providing a safety net, but giving her as much latitude as possible. When my daughter seeks my help, I'm always there as an advisor, counselor, or academic consultant.

4. My values and experiences are different than my daughter's. It's hard to interpret her day-to-day challenges through the lens of my life. The high school and college application process was very different in the 1970s than in the 2010s. I need to accept that my perspective may not be aligned with today's realities. I grew up with land line telephones and IBM Selectric typewriters. She was born in 1993 and thus has not lived a day without the Internet.

5. Life is filled with stresses at work, at home, and with the world in general. It's really important to realize that a year from now, no one will remember today's issues, but family is forever. Being consistent and predictable as a father, immune to whatever external stresses might change my mood, works really well. Raising my voice, being critical, or getting frustrated diminishes me.

Have a great Father's Day and remember that the gift of time is the best present you can give. ∎

Morning Walks with My Wife

From spring until fall, my wife and I rise with the early morning light of dawn (my blog next Thursday will define such seemingly ambiguous terms as dawn, dusk, twilight, etc.) and walk three miles around Lake Waban at Wellesley College.

We have our ritual—we park at the College Club and start walking at the south end of the lake. We check out the family of swans that lives on a protected point to watch the progress of their groaning cygnets. We walk through the Hunnewell estate and its "Dr. Seuss" forest of topiary trees and Japanese tea house. We watch for the purple martins feeding their young in a lakeside meadow. I look for the emerging mushrooms on the west side of the lake so I can prepare for the day's calls from poison control about the mushrooms kids are likely to ingest.

We check out the status of Catbird, Oriole, and Robins' nests, watch the young broods of ducks feeding in the marshlands, and look for muskrats carrying greens to their lodges.

Most importantly, it's a quiet time to connect, reflect on the goals of the day, the state of our family, and plans for the future. In the quiet of the morning mist and blue light of sunrise we can solve every problem and address every concern without the distraction of a screen, a blackberry, or undone house chores.

Having this time is really important. I'm convinced that 90% of stress in life is a result of miscommunication—waiting to speak instead of listening. Walks are a great way to listen—other than birdsong, the splash of fish, or buzz of a dragonfly, there are no distractions. Your muscles are moving, your brain is clear, and stress is low. A few years ago, I wrote about conflict resolution and suggested figurative Walks in the Woods.

Thirty years of walking with my wife has led to a romance, friendship, and partnership that is as strong as when we first met in the summer of 1980. Last week, the *Boston Globe* wrote about the language of marriage. Our walks have been the place where that language has blossomed.

So find your own Lake Waban and make the most of your relationship, footstep by footstep. ∎

Experiencing Healthcare with My Family

I've been lucky when it comes to health issues. In my life, I've had Lyme disease twice (still not out of the woods), a corneal ulcer caused by windblown grit while kayaking across the Baltic Sea, a benign AV nodal reentry tachycardia, a kidney stone from dehydration, and elevated intraocular pressure (multiple generations of males in my family history had glaucoma). I've never broken a bone, had any

GI/neuro/pulmonary/rheumatological issues, or taken any chronic medication, other than Xalatan for my intraocular pressure.

My family history is otherwise unremarkable.

Thus, it came as a complete surprise when the call came in at the end of last week that my father was having a posterior/inferior myocardial infarction and was on his way to the cath lab to be stented.

On Thursday night my wife and I flew to Los Angeles to be with him in the ICU.

The process of medical care is like any complex project—there's a technical part and there's a people part. The doctors and nurses did a remarkable job on the technical part. The role my wife and I played was to manage the people part—building confidence in my parents that everything would be okay, that the quality of life would be just fine, that returning home would be safe, and that the future would be bright.

We stocked the refrigerator with low-fat vegan foods. We helped interpret patient education materials, discussed life-style recommendations, and managed the process of transitioning from inpatient to outpatient.

Hospitals are a great place in a crisis, filled with professionals who can medicate, operate, and heal. But the larger social context of healthcare—the orchestration of emotions, calming of fears, and regaining the cadence of daily life requires a support system.

In the past, extended families lived together or at least clustered together in a community. With increasing specialization of employment, a challenging economy, and the ease of long-distance travel, we've lost many of our family support systems. What I experienced was a remarkable coming together of a virtual extended family in support of my father. Colleagues, former employees, and friends gathered together to support my parents. My father was rarely alone during his ICU stay. In a world that can be filled with road rage, competition for resources, and a lack of civility, I was grateful to experience healthcare supported by the community around my family.

The circumstances, a heart attack, were bad, but the outcome was good. My father is back home, back to his usual routine, and the love and respect of his network of supporters will always be with him. ∎

The Stages of Life

Recently my daughter and I discussed my experience with life, the evolution of my mindset through time, and my thoughts about roles/responsibilities at each age. I summarized life as the following:

- 0-10—A time to master the day-to-day activities of being human

- 11-20—A time to master the process of learning
- 21-30—A time to experience the world, take risks, establish relationships, and seek stable employment
- 31-40—A time to build a household, a family, and a career ladder
- 41-50—A time to build financial security, support growing children, think about wellness, and nurture your relationships
- 51-60—A time to fund college, assist adult children with their increasing responsibilities, and support aging parents
- 61-70—A time to begin the transition to a different phase of life, pursing those activities that you did not have time or resources to do in the past. Note that this phase is getting later and later in life with many people working past 70. A time to start playing with grandchildren and assisting your children's growing families. Continuing to support aging parents, given increasingly long human lifespans.
- 71+—Exploring new ideas, new places, keeping your mind and body healthy, aging well

To which my daughter responded, "How depressing...that you think of life as so linear."

I suggested that life is anything but linear. When I was 5, I wrote a first-grade homework assignment declaring, "I want to be a scientist." When I was 12, computer science seemed like the right direction. When I was 16, medicine and engineering seemed the right approach. Now nearly 50, I'm a CIO, married for 26 years, with a 17-year-old daughter. Completely unpredictable and more of random walk than a linear progression.

Of course, my suggested life timeline is a bit traditional and stereotypical. There are hundreds of variations that may involve zero or multiple marriages, zero or many children, zero or dozen careers. I will not measure my daughter's life success by her adherence to my timeline.

Pondering my life experience, I realize that my current mindset in the 41-50 span includes a different set of challenges, goals, and dreams than in my 21-30 span. I'm continually changing. I remember the pride I felt when I exceeded some of my parents' capabilities when I was in the 11-20 span. I now feel great humility as my daughter begins to exceed some of my capabilities at the same time in her life.

When I'm asked what span is best, my answer will always be, wherever I am now.

When I'm asked what span is best, my answer will always be, wherever I am now. My current experiences, frustrations, and relationships always seem most appropriate to my current condition. I look backwards only to gather lessons learned, not to relive any previous events. I recently skipped my 30-year high school reunion because the joys and sorrows of my 11-20 span are no longer relevant after the experiences of three decades.

At times, I struggle with the politics, conflicts, and uncertainties of daily living. I think back on the challenges of my 20s and 30s and realize that any anxiety I felt earlier in life was over minor and inconsequential events. In my 50s I'm sure I'll feel that same way about my 40's. Realizing that life is a continuous progression with different roles, responsibilities, and expectations at each stage enables us to look forward to the future, relish the present, and learn from the past.

Onward to the stages ahead! ■

The Definition of My Daughter's Success

As I read articles about talented college graduates unable to find work because the US job growth rate is not keeping pace with the college graduation rate, I speculate about the best way to define success for my 17-year-old daughter.

Is it a high-paying job as doctor, lawyer, or stockbroker?

Is it fame resulting from some remarkable talent?

Is it her pursuit of one of my dreams—being a naturalist, an environmental engineer, or outdoor educator?

Is it successfully competing with some local, regional, or national peers to be the best at something?

Should I compare her to the athletes, musicians, performers, artists, and academicians in her school and ask her to be as good or better than they are?

All such measures of success are perilous.

How many doctors, lawyers, or hedge fund traders have you met that are satisfied with their lives and look forward to the challenges of their career every day?

How well does fame really serve anyone? Just ask Paris Hilton, Lindsey Lohan, or Michael Jackson's family.

Imprinting unfilled parental dreams on children is likely not sustainable. Children need to find and pursue their own passions.

Competitive spirit is a great thing to have, except when it leads to a winning at all costs mentality, sacrificing ethics along the way. Just ask the steroid-using baseball players.

Comparing your children to others is an insult to the individuality of your children. When I think back on my own childhood, my peers who could have been held up as ideal comparisons did not end up with happy or fulfilling lives. Some peaked in high school. A journey of continuous optimism and life improvement, striving to be the best you can be on your own terms, seems like a better course than making comparisons to other people along the way.

The bottom line: asking my daughter to fulfill my expectations, follow in my footsteps, or live up to standards I set does not respect her ability to choose and pursue her own dreams.

Thus, my definition of success for my daughter is simple. It's not related to grades, talent, dollars, or fame.

If she can develop a sense of self-worth, pursuing a path designed by her that fuels her self-esteem, then she will be successful.

The world of the 21st century is a complex place. Traditional measures of success—a job, a house, a family—are not necessarily the obvious goals that should be pursued by the next generation.

As she enters the college of her choice (it's up to her), and pursues the educational path of her choice, following her passions and crafting her own life path, I ask only one thing:

If five years from now she can say, "I feel good about me," then she (and I as a parent) have been successful. ∎

Smart Medication Reconciliation and Problem Lists

Last week, I spent a few days in California when both my parents ended up in the hospital with different issues. They're home, settled, and doing well at this point.

Just as when I first wrote about experiencing healthcare with my family, there are important lessons to learn about this trip.

As we strive to achieve Meaningful Use and create health information exchange in the US, the need for smart medication is critical.

Our current national systems do a good job of retrieving a history of medications that were filled or reimbursed, but they do not do a good job of identifying those medications which are active—that is, left to patients or their families. What do you do if the patient is unable to answer, the family is unavailable, or the patient/family does not really know what medications are current?

My family was able to provide history such as "the green capsules, or the pink pill," which was insufficient to achieve accurate medication lists.

Similarly, it can be challenging to retrieve an active problem list from claims data, which is often inaccurate or imprecise.

The result is that my parents received unnecessary medications, as well as did not receive necessary ones.

The hospital focused on the acute inpatient problems without attending to the more chronic outpatient ones.

How do we solve this?

1. Ensure every patient has a personal health record, an electronic medical home with an updated medication list and problem list.

2. Implement novel decision support that infers active medications by examining recent refill history and active problems by examining available data sources such as lab history, recent diagnostic studies which imply active diagnoses (e.g., a recent high hemoglobin A1c in a patient on insulin implies diabetes).

3. At its very simplest, carry a wallet card with an active medication list and problem list.

While in California, I isolated every medication in the house, current and historical. I documented active medications, active problems, and the relationship between the medications and the problems. I reviewed the resulting lists with all family members (with their consent). My parents will ensure all their clinicians update their records to reflect this accurate information. They will carry this information with them to any future hospitalizations. I disposed of historical medications (safely) to prevent any future confusion. I isolated medications for each person so there would be no accidental taking of medications intended for other people.

Admittedly as a clinician, I have the training that enables me to do this.

For families without clinicians, create a shopping bag of medications and take it to a primary care visit for a family medication reconciliation exercise, or ask for the help of a health coach.

As we build electronic systems, the outpatient to inpatient transition will become more seamless and accurate, but during this time of evolving connectivity and less-than-perfect use of electronic health records, I encourage everyone to reconcile their medications and problems, get them into a PHR, and share them widely with family members and caregivers. ∎

Living the Good Life

Last Friday, my daughter was admitted early decision to Tufts University, so the anxiety of the college application process is passed. One of her essays asked her to describe the environment in which she was raised and how it influenced the person she is today. It's worth sharing her observations on what constitute living the good life:

"At this moment, from a room of windows, I can see tall pine trees framing a beautiful, soft green yard. A little vegetable garden lies to my right, with lettuce enduring the brisk autumn wind. Above it stands a lone maple gradually turning brilliant shades of fire. A heavenly light illuminates the clouds passing overhead in the vast baby blue sky. The wisteria climbs the windows to my left, waiting for a warm spring to show its beautiful lavender flowers. The wind passes through the wooden chimes hanging from our crabapple tree, initiating a clonking chorus. Bamboo lines the white rock river with a little wooden bridge. A stone bench rests near the fence, where my father sits and plays his Shakuhachi (traditional Japanese flute). Cardinals, sparrows, and grackles fly overhead, seeking food, warmth, and family. As I open a window, a rush of sweet, crisp autumn cold fills my senses, making me shiver. These wonders surrounding me in such a welcoming, beautiful, and inspiring home and community fostered an appreciation for the subtle things in life. I learned to openly embrace the world around me, understanding and loving its everlasting beauty. Nature is a teacher and a gift, one never to be overlooked. I've grown as a student, an observer, an appreciator, and a believer in the magic and beauty of the world."

As a parent, I want my daughter to feel good about herself. In her essay, she highlighted the simple things that bring richness to her life—a vegetable garden, autumn colors, and a supportive community of family and friends.

I can understand her point of view.

As I write this, I'm sitting in an old Morris chair, sipping Gyokuro green tea, breathing in wisps of smoke from Blue kungyokudo incense. Breakfast will be a bowl of steel cut oatmeal with a few drops of Vermont maple syrup, and soy milk.

The ability to sit quietly and think, enjoy wholesome foods, and enjoy the warmth and comfort of a small home while the weather outside is cold and blustery, gives me an overwhelming sense of well being.

I hope my daughter continues to appreciate that the good life comes from the basics of food/clothing/shelter/family/self-worth.

Tufts University is a great fit for her and I'm confident the next four years will polish and amplify the foundation she's already built. As she creates her own version of the good life, we'll always be available for advice and support, but as of next summer, she's a fledgling, exploring the world on her own. ∎

Reflections on Christmas Eve

As I sit in an old Morris chair, sipping a La Marca Prosecco and watching the glow of the Christmas tree, I'm beginning to unwind and reflect on the tumultuous 2010 that's drawing to a close.

It was a year of thousands of pages of new federal HIT regulations, debate and consensus on standards, new privacy requirements, ever-increasing demand for increasing complex IT services, and escalating expectations for speed/reliability/efficiency in everything that we do.

It was a year of recovery from the economic doldrums of 2009, with a gradual increase in new jobs and budgets, but still a bit of uncertainty.

The stress, the pace, and global competitiveness were unsettling to many, leading to a lack of civility and patience.

Whether you think 2010 was a year of innovation, chaos, or anxiety, there is one thing we can all agree upon—2010 was a year of incredible change.

As I tell my staff and all my colleagues, it's impossible to evaluate a year based on the events of any given day. Don't consider your position today; consider your trajectory over the past year.

My family is all on track. My parents are fully recovered from their November hospitalizations and are healthy and happy. My daughter was admitted to Tufts University. My wife is running the NK Gallery in Boston's South End and she's creating new art. I'm balancing my home life, work life, and personal life in a way that is satisfying and invigorating. I'll be 50 next year and I do have 3 grey hairs but otherwise I'm medication-free and my body mass index is still 20.

Nationally, we've implemented regulations for content, vocabulary, and security standards. We have a consensus approach to transport standards using SMTP/SMIME through NHIN Direct. EHR adoption is climbing steadily. Boards throughout the country are talking about the interoperability, business intelligence, and decision support that are needed to support the healthcare future described in the Affordable Care Act/healthcare reform.

In Massachusetts, we've agreed upon a short-term and long-term HIE governance model. We're procuring workgroup facilitation and a program management office to oversee our statewide "entity level" provider directory, certificate management, and standards/conformance/certification.

At Harvard Medical School, we've created one of the top 100 supercomputers in the world, deployed a petabyte of storage, automated numerous administrative, educational, and research workflows, and established governance committees for all our stakeholders.

At BIDMC, we're on the home stretch of our community EHR rollout, massive lab project, major replacement of our extranet and intranet, and disaster recovery efforts. We've kept our infrastructure stable, reliable, and secure. We enhanced our enterprise clinical, fiscal, administrative, digital library, and media applications in a way that kept most users satisfied. Every compliance, regulatory, and e-discovery need was met.

In many ways, this Christmas is a milestone. My daughter leaves for college next summer, so we'll have an empty nest. This was an especially stressful year due to ARRA-funded projects, Meaningful Use, Harvard's LCME reaccreditation planning, BIDMC's Joint Commission reaccreditation, and more policy/technology change in a single year than any year before.

The details of the good and bad, the joys and sorrows, and the triumphs and defeats, are fading in importance because the trajectory is uniformly good.

Based on my definition of the Good Life, getting the basics right and ensuring every member of your family feels good about themselves, all is calm, all is bright.

So hug your family members, pat yourself on the back, and toast with your favorite beverage. This has been a year of great change, but we did all we needed to do and the world is a better place because of it.

May your next year have satisfying work, a little less anxiety, and a boost to your own sense of self-worth.

Cheers! ∎

Reflections on Being a Parent

Soon my daughter turns 18. She becomes an adult with the ability to vote, take legal responsibility for her actions, and assert her own independence.

In some ways, my job as a parent is done. She has a good moral compass, feels good about herself, and is resilient. She knows when to ask for help and is open with us about her feelings, challenges, and goals. She's decided to skip much of adolescence and go directly from child to adult, bypassing most of the rebelliousness and occasional self-destructive behavior of teens.

She's learned to balance work and play, limit texting and use of electronic devices, and how to build and grow relationships. She has the tools she needs to navigate the next stage of life as she enters college at Tufts University this fall.

What have I learned from our past 18 years together?

1. Create a non-punitive climate of trust. It's far better to encourage discussion of tough issues than to "shoot the messenger" and create a fear of communication.

2. Strike a balance between too much oversight and too little. In four months, she'll leave home and make decisions for herself. She'll decide what to eat and drink, whom to spend her time with, and how to balance academics with leisure. Managing her every moment at home with strict oversight may produce short-term success, but does not enable her to take ownership of the decisions she makes—good and bad. Providing no oversight can lead to risky and destructive behaviors. We've tried to set wide and reasonable limits, then give her free reign to run her life within those limits. She's learned from her mistakes and is a stronger, more self-reliant person because she had the freedom to choose her own path.

3. As with my professional life, I pay more attention to her trajectory than her position. Humans between 12 and 19 can have highly variable moods, rapidly changing ideas, and contrary behaviors. Reacting to

every event day to day is likely to cause frustration on both sides. Chances are that today's troubling issue will be gone tomorrow or next week. Focus on the big picture, not the brushstrokes.

4.   Strong negative emotions accomplish nothing. In the past 18 years, I can remember only a few times that I've raised my voice. Not only was it ineffective, I spent substantial time repairing the emotional damage done. The term I've used before is "Save as Draft." If you ever feel negative emotions and want to yell, Save as Draft. Have a thoughtful discussion and rethink your emotions based on winning the war, not the battle.

5.   Family experiences last a lifetime. Although it may not be immediately clear that time spent together has a profound effect, I can see that my daughter will pursue activities throughout her life inspired by the things we've done together over the past 18 years. Her love of nature, mountains, Japan, gardening, and beaches all come from those hours we spent experiencing the world together.

Of course, she'll have triumphs and tribulations in college. She'll seek our advice and support when she needs it. We'll help her launch a family of her own and continue to share our 50 years of life lessons when they can aid her decision making.

In August, we become empty nesters. Just as we transitioned from the spontaneity of our 20s to the parental responsibilities of our 30s, we're now headed into our next phase.

Thank you, Lara, for the past 18 years. You've made me a better person and I am confident you'll fledge into a magnificent young woman. ∎

Thoughts on My Daughter's Graduation

Recently, my daughter graduated from Wellesley High School.

Just as it was a milestone for her, it was a pivotal life event for her parents.

Lara was born 18 years ago. We had no idea who she would be or what she would become.

During her early years, I was an Emergency Medicine resident. The nature of shift work meant that I could spent at least 12 hours of every 24-hour cycle with her—reading, walking on the beach, going to the park, strolling the Los Angeles zoo, and playing her favorite computer games—Pajama Sam, Freddie Fish, and Spy Fox.

We moved to Massachusetts when she was 3, exactly 15 years ago this week. My Emergency Medicine faculty and Informatics Fellow schedule enabled us to explore nature, hunt geocaches, and camp on the Boston Harbor Islands.

As I became a CIO, life became a bit more complicated, but every weekend we went to Drumlin Farm, Broadmoor, and other Audubon sites.

By the time she was an adolescent, the time spent together evolved to time spent with her friends, extracurricular activities, and schoolwork. I served as her transportation, advisor, and editor.

As she blossomed into an adult, we became peers, having honest and open dialog about relationships, world events, and the challenges ahead.

All along the path, we tried to give her the latitude to celebrate her own successes, learn from her own mistakes, and experience the many facets of the 21st century world—within limits that kept her from going seriously off track.

She begins college in just two short months, making decisions about when to sleep, what to eat, and how to study, all on her own. Her house will be here whenever she wants to visit and her parents will be available whenever she wants to call. We'll not have the pitter-patter of her feet on the stairs, the ebb and flow of her friends, or the vibrant but sometimes unpredictable schedules she added to our lives.

Her parents will garden, travel, rekindle their 30 years of romance together, plan for the future, and write checks for college.

Based on all my conversations with other parents, I know that this transition is truly not saying "goodbye" and declaring the end of parenthood. It's the beginning of another chapter filled with new demands, more complex issues, and expanded possibilities.

As she graduates, the most important things I can offer are my love and support, including a clear expectation of what I believe will constitute success in her next phase of life. This poem by Ralph Waldo Emerson says it better than I can:

Success

To laugh often and much;
To win the respect of intelligent
people and the affection of children;
To earn the appreciation of honest
critics and endure the betrayal of false friends;
To appreciate beauty, to find the best in others;
To leave the world a bit better,
whether by a healthy child, a garden patch,
or a redeemed social condition;
To know even one life has breathed
easier because you have lived.
This is to have succeeded.

So Lara, congratulations on an extraordinary high school career. Now, go define your own success. We'll be here to beam with pride. ∎

Our Lives Together

My wife Kathy and I met at Stanford on September 1, 1980, so we've been together for 31 years. That means that we've spent two-thirds of our lives on this planet together. We've been collaborators, soul mates, homeowners, parents, and friends together. For three decades, our relationship has just worked. Here's why.

My entire life has been math/science/engineering—digital, white and black, linear, orderly, and left-brained.

Kathy's entire life has been the visual arts/humanities/creativity—analog, splashes of color, wabi sabi, Victorian clutter, and right-brained.

Our talents are entirely different, our approaches complementary, and we never compete on any level.

In our 20s we were vigorous hiking partners and built a home together.

In our 30s we focused on raising a young child.

In our 40s we created stability by planning for the future, caring for our parents, and preparing our child to leave the nest.

In our 50s we're likely to travel, create, and tend our garden together.

In our 60s and beyond we're likely to create a Japanese-inspired wilderness retreat to serve as a home base between experiences around the world that are part of our work lives, volunteer lives, and personal lives.

We've evolved together and continue to expand and refine our relationship every day.

When I read literature from the scientific and lay press about the "seven year itch," it makes me realize that needs change, people change, and relationships need to change over time if they are going to last.

In your 20s, you're likely at the peak of your physical life with more endurance, strength, and biological resilience than any other era. You can climb mountains and if you fall, you bounce.

In your 40s, you're likely to be at the peak of your mental life with more experience, intellectual agility, and intuition than any other era. You can climb mountains, but if you fall, you break. You're more likely focused on your 401k than your surfboard.

In your 60s, you're likely to be at the peak of your financial life with more savings, more earning, and more stability than any other area. If you've kept up your workouts and managed your diet, you can climb mountains, but if you fall, you shatter. You're more likely to be focused on supporting your children and aging parents, than thinking about a bleached blonde in a red convertible (unless you're a Congressman...).

If you and your partner were perfect for each other in your 20s, you may not be perfect in your 60s, unless you adapt to your changing bodies, changing needs, and changing abilities together.

Kathy and I have been able to do that.

We've always treated each other as equals— there has never been a superior/subordinate aspect to our home lives, work lives, or family lives. Our division of labor is not cast in stone; it remains fluid based on the schedule and needs of each day. We share housework, we share parenting responsibilities, and we support each other's career.

> *We've always treated each other as equals— there has never been a superior/subordinate aspect to our home lives, work lives, or family lives.*

Of course, we've had stress, anxiety, joy, sadness, and conflict along the way—that's life. But we've been able to weather the challenges, relish the successes, and treat each other fairly along the way.

This month we become empty nesters as our daughter begins her college life at Tufts on August 31. The house will seem quieter, the schedules will change, and our roles will need to evolve again as we focus more time on each other and our careers while our daughter becomes increasingly independent. It's another risky time for relationships.

But we'll navigate the transition, overcome the sense of loss, and plan our future together.

Given human life expectancy, we're likely to live another 31 years (I'm using Japan rather than US because our diet and lifestyle are distinctly Japanese). That means that Kathy and I are only halfway through our life together.

Happy Anniversary, Kathy. The second half of our time together will be even better than the first. I love you and always will. ∎

Preparing for the College Transition

In one week, we drop off our daughter at Tufts University so she can begin the next era of her life as a college woman.

All of us have been preparing.

High school is a time of many emotions—high highs and low lows. It's about discovering independence, making choices, accepting responsibility, developing relationships, and balancing parental authority with the desire for autonomy.

More is expected of today's teens than in my generation. It's very stressful on a young person.

In one week, she'll make decisions on her own. She'll decide what to eat (and drink), when to study, and whom to spend her time with.

Over the past few weeks, she's thought about her transition in a very spiritual way.

I did not approach my college transition formally. I packed my clothes and typewriter the night before and we drove from Los Angeles to Stanford for the drop off. That was 31 years ago this week.

She realizes that she has to prepare for this new era, while bringing closure to her childhood growing up in Wellesley, Massachusetts.

She has thought about all her Wellesley relationships. She's scheduled events with every one of her friends to create positive memories and energy before they go their separate ways. She's arranged hikes, picnics, movies, meals, and sleepovers.

She's taken private walks to her favorite places in Wellesley. She's also made a conscious decision not to visit many of the places she treasured when very young so that she can remember them as they were from a child's point of view.

Yes, she'll stay in touch with friends on Facebook, but that will fade as she develops new relationships, new interests, and new goals. The closure she's bringing now will leave lasting memories among all her friends, creating a sense of optimism and energy for the future ahead.

My wife and I know that next Wednesday will be hard. We'll bring our daughter's carefully packed belongings (four small bins that will fit perfectly in a cozy dorm room) to her new living space, set up her IT infrastructure (the home CIO at your service), and attend a formal matriculation ceremony. My wife and I will give her the space she needs to bond with her new colleagues and we'll retreat to a quiet vegan cafe to reflect on the next era in our lives.

We've already planned a few short trips together. My wife will join me for keynote addresses in Burlington, Vermont; Phoenix, Arizona; and London, England. We've already planned a family get together on Mt. Monadnock over Columbus Day weekend. We've thought about the next few months and years as we've considered the implications of staying close to our daughter, our parents, and our jobs.

The end result is a solid plan that will launch all of us into the next stage of life. For my daughter, it's adulthood. For my wife and I, it's a refocus on each other, the world around us, and our careers. The past 18 years with our daughter have been a gift, but the next era will be positive for all of us too. Our evolution begins next Wednesday.

The College Drop Off

I have a very hard time giving up roles and responsibilities. Rather than change jobs, I add jobs.

In 1996, I oversaw the CareGroup Center for Quality and Value, the data warehousing and analytic operations of a Boston-based integrated delivery system comprised of Beth Israel Deaconess and four other hospitals. When I became the CIO of CareGroup in 1998, it took me a year to separate myself from the operational responsibilities of the CQV.

In 2000, I oversaw the Harvard Medical School learning management system as Associate Dean of Educational Technology. When I become the CIO of HMS in 2001, it took me a year to delegate my educational technology role. Early in my HMS tenure, I was asked to serve as temporary CIO of Harvard Clinical Research Institute (HCRI). That temporary job lasted a year.

Today, my wife and I spent the day at Tufts, helping our daughter move into her dorm and begin her journey as an independent adult. In many ways, my job as parent, that began 18 years ago, fundamentally changed today. It's very hard to let go.

I'll want to hear about my daughter's experiences each day, the decisions she's making, the challenges she's facing, and the successes she's achieving. I'll want to offer advice, assist when I can, and give her the benefits of my 50 years of experience.

However, all of these activities are the wrong thing to do. She needs to fly on her own, knowing that we're here when she needs us.

The Deans at Tufts emphasized three goals for Tufts undergraduates: develop internal curiosity for learning, be responsible for your own actions, and become an advocate for yourself.

The Deans at Tufts emphasized three goals for Tufts undergraduates: develop internal curiosity for learning, be responsible for your own actions, and become an advocate for yourself.

The only way my daughter will become a mature, experienced, and assertive young woman is to do her best, explore a college world that is much more diverse than her high school experience, and be responsible for her own decisions.

Today, my wife and I became a safety net rather than a guiding force.

Lara has fledged and we have an empty nest.

We shed tears of loss when saying goodbye, followed by tears of joy for her new possibilities.

I may have had a hard time leaving my jobs with the CQV, HCRI, and Harvard Medical School, but for Lara, I can morph my parent job so that she can thrive in our increasingly complex and confusing world. My job needs to change, so that she can change.

Lara, we only cried part of the way home. We're ok.

Now do great things. The world is your oyster.

Family Friday

I rarely take vacations and only celebrate major events (like birthdays) when schedules permit my family to assemble, since celebrations are more about the people present than the day of the event.

Thanksgiving weekend is one of those dates when everyone's celebration schedules coincide. It's common to travel on Wednesday, to spend Thursday preparing a meal together, and to take Friday as a vacation day.

This year, I received fewer than 50 emails on Black Friday, down from my usual daily count of 1,000–1,500 messages.

I believe that shopping during the holidays is a contact sport. Traffic slows to crawl, tempers boil, and now there's even pepper spray to worry about.

Unless some twisted souls think of Black Friday as entertainment, I believe the concept should be replaced by Family Friday.

Talk a walk, go to the zoo, play Apples to Apples, talk about the future, have a Kazoo concert.

> *Unless some twisted souls think of Black Friday as entertainment, I believe the concept should be replaced by Family Friday.*

My experience with discounts, sales, and bargains is that they will be offered again or tempt you to buy something unnecessary. A designer tie that's discounted 50% is no bargain if you have enough ties already.

I do not reserve my shopping for any particular day of the year or align it with any retailer's event.

Instead, I use *Consumer Reports* to identify high value products—good quality at reasonable prices. I buy few things, but always buy them to last, given that the real expense is churn—buying a poor quality item ten times is generally more expensive than buying a good quality item once and keeping it for years.

My Prius has 120,000 miles on it and likely will be fine through 200,000 miles. I'll replace it when its total cost of ownership exceeds the value of a replacement, regardless of the date on which that occurs.

I realize there are implications to discouraging a retail frenzy on Black Friday. Sales imply profits which create jobs.

However, if we consider the big picture—that the US needs to move away from a consumer economy back to one in which we create innovative products and services that the world wants to buy—we'll not need Black Friday.

So let's spend time with our families next Black Friday and focus on innovation at work next Cyber Monday.

Our country and our sense of well being will be better for it.

Sustainability

As my daughter begins her adult life (she's in Kanazawa, Japan, this month doing a winter semester Japanese language intensive), I've thought a great deal about the world she will inherit from me.

I've lived in the creatively vibrant 1960s, the economic doldrums of the 1970s, the go-go 1980s, the .com era of the 1990s, the post 9/11 unrest of the 2000s, and the recovery/reform of the 2010s.

During my lifetime, my rubric for success has changed from one that is judged by salary/position/power to one that is measured by making a difference, living with a small footprint, and ensuring sustainability for the next generation.

I usually write about such topics in my Thursday personal blog post, but I think the concept of sustainability impacts the way we work every day so it's worth a Monday discussion.

Over the past 25 years, the US has evolved from a manufacturing economy to a consumer economy that depends upon increasing consumption for success. Unless we grow exponentially—population, sales, and spending—our current economy falters. Since our resources and planet are finite, any strategy based on endless growth will fail.

As I begin the next stage of my life (and we successfully treat my wife's cancer), I believe my best gift to my daughter is sustainability—reducing my consumption of natural resources, reducing my carbon footprint, reducing my contribution to landfills, reducing my belongings/their turnover (what I buy and what I replace), and living closer to the land at a pace supported by nature.

As part of the cancer treatment process, it's important for my wife and me to have long-term goals—what will we be doing in five years and what can we look forward to?

My wife and I have begun looking at land, discussed low-impact/high-energy efficiency-building strategies, and considered how our community gardening/vegan lifestyle can be extended via additional organic farming activities in Eastern

Massachusetts. We've looked at ways to reduce our travel including finding property close to rail lines that will enable us to stop driving in congested traffic and instead take the commuter rail into Boston every day.

Along the way, a few books are guiding our exploration:

- *The Self Sufficient Life and How to Live It* by John Seymour[4]

- *Green from the Ground Up* by David Johnston and Scott Gibson[5]

- *Alternative Construction* by Lynne Elizabeth and Cassandra Adams[6]

- *Back to Basics* by Abigail Gehring[7]

- *Self Sufficiency* by Abigail Gehring[8]

I will strive to apply the same principles in my business life as well. Beyond reducing my commute, I will continue to closely manage the power consumption of the data centers I oversee, eliminate the use of paper in clinical workflows, and embrace recycling/reuse/reduction in procurements.

The best thing I can do to support my daughter's generation is to ensure there is a healthy planet for her to live in.

Serving as Healthcare Navigator for My Father

At the moment, I'm in the ICU watching the rise and fall of my father's chest as he breathes on his own after a night on a BPAP[9] machine. I've taken my mother home to rest. I'm holding my father's hands whenever he becomes agitated. He knows I am here but cannot converse. Today would have been too late to have discussions about his care preferences.

Decisions we've just made are to treat my father per the preferences he wanted—no chest compressions, no intubation, and no pressors.

Difficult discussions our family has had this year included the following:

4   Seymour J. *The Self Sufficient Life and How to Live It.* New York: DK Publishing; 2009.

5   Johnston D, Gibson S. *Green from the Ground Up: Sustainable, Healthy, and Energy-Efficient Home Construction.* Newton, CT: Taunton Publishing; 2008.

6   Elizabeth L, Adams C. *Alternative Construction: Contemporary Natural Building Methods.* Hoboken, NJ: John Wiley & Sons; 2005.

7   Gehring AR. *Back to Basics: A Guide to Buying Working Land, Raising Livestock, Enjoying Your Harvest, Household Skills and Crafts, and More.* New York: Skyhorse Publishing; 2011.

8   Gehring AR. *Self Sufficiency: A Complete Guide to Baking, Carpentry, Crafts, Organic Gardening, Preserving Your Harvest, Raising Animals, and More.* New York: Skyhorse Publishing; 2010.

9   BPAP = bilevel positive airway machine (or portable ventilator).

- Do you want to live at home as long as possible including visiting home care or hospice nurses?

- Do you want to be buried or cremated? A funeral or memorial service?

- Where do you want to live after the death of a spouse?

Now that I'm living through the implementation of these decisions, hour by hour, I am so thankful we had the discussions, created the documents, and shared our work with appropriate lawyers, accountants, and family.

As I sit here, his vital signs are stable, his drips have been stopped, and he is comfortable.

I've worked with a remarkable care team—my mother, a hospitalist, an intensivist, a cardiologist, and nurses to implement our jointly developed care plan.

It's hard to know what the days ahead will bring, but I will sit by father's side, following his wishes, ensuring that he knows that his family loves and supports him. I will ensure he has no pain and no fear. I will celebrate the gifts he has given me and others. I'm reading him notes from my wife and daughter.

It's an awkward time to post a blog, but if my journey over the next several days with my father encourages others to prepare for these events, my father's life will have made an even greater impact. Making a difference is a great legacy.

What Is Compassionate Comfort Care?

Over the past 24 hours, my family and the hospital care team have been guided by my father's healthcare proxy to avoid painful, invasive, or aggressive care at a time when his multiple medical issues have combined to make his health decline irreversible.

The healthcare proxy was extremely clear and enabled us to finalize the do not resuscitate and do not intubate orders. We agreed to stop monitoring and stop all medications except those needed for comfort. We agreed to stop drawing labs.

We want to ensure his comfort and avoid needlesticks/procedures that will cause him anxiety.

But there are other decisions to make.

His bone marrow has stopped producing red blood cells and his hematocrit has dropped to 22.

His heart attack on Friday caused such damage to his heart that the volume of blood per heartbeat is less than half of normal. His lungs initially filled with fluid but are now clearing.

Given his low hematocrit, do we give him blood?

Although it may enhance his overall feeling of well-being, it will likely fluid overload him and make breathing more difficult.

Do we give him IV fluids?

He was fluid positive over the past 24 hours, so we have to delicately balance the notion of keeping him hydrated with fluid overloading him.

Do we consider a feeding tube?

His platelet count is 37 and bleeding caused by the trauma of inserting the tube is a risk. Feeding tubes are irritating and might require us to apply restraints.

These are difficult decisions to make as a doctor and a son. It is very challenging to be objective when the questions are about your own father.

When thinking about what provides him the most compassionate care, there is also a need to weigh the family's beliefs about comfort with my medical experience. Feeding sounds like compassionate comfort, but the pain and anxiety caused by feeding tube insertion and maintenance may not be.

So where are we on the journey and what decisions have we made for my father's care?

At this time we have discontinued all tubes, all wires, all restraints—anything connected to his body except a single IV line which is used for comforting medications.

We've moved him to a sunny room with a wonderful view and enough space for family and friends to visit.

We've changed his comfort medications to a constant infusion rather than as needed dosing.

We're giving him just enough fluids to keep him in even fluid balance.

My mother and I have divided up the 24-hour clock so that we're with him constantly and each of us can get four hours per day of sleep. A rested caregiver is better able to make compassionate decisions.

I wish there was a single definition of compassion comfort care that could simply be ordered. My experience over the past few hours suggests that the patient's wishes, the family's beliefs, and the care team's advice all must be combined to arrive at an optimal answer. Since Friday, we've made stepwise decisions that were not clear or obvious at the beginning of the process.

My father is resting comfortably and I'm telling him stories from the best memories of our lives together. I know he's listening. ∎

Celebrating My Father's Life

As I sit at my father's bedside, managing the increasing heaviness of his breathing, I'm doing my best to keep his lips moist, his extremities warm, and the dosing of his comfort care medications appropriate so there is no air hunger.

People from my parents' past are calling and emailing me, telling me their stories and reveling in the impact my father had on their lives. They've told me:

He inspired them to go into engineering (he's a patent lawyer trained as an engineer).

He inspired them with his kindness and gentleness.

His tenacity living with multiple sclerosis for 23+ years inspired them to approach their own illnesses with vigor.

Some of the stories people remember:

When I was 13 in 1975, my father got my first summer job for me, working at a defense contractor for TRW. I developed satellite telemetry parsing software in Fortran, working in the same building as Chris Boyce (author of *The Falcon and the Snowman: American Sons*). My father's effort to give me powerful computer resources in the 1970s changed the course of my life.

One of my father's friends recalls the joy my father felt when he and I built electronics projects together throughout the 1970s —a metal detector, early analog signal processing experiments such as voice synthesizers, and an Altair 8800.

I have many special memories of life with my father, many of them forever preserved on Kodachrome.

My father was in the Air Force from 1963 to 1968, so we traveled extensively.

One of my earliest memories was playing on a Oahu beach in Hawaii in 1963 with my father when he was stationed near Pearl Harbor. As a child the ocean was always a favorite place.

We typically drove across country in an old Buick from Air Force posting to posting. My father took me on a cross country drive from New Jersey to Colorado Springs via Mt. Rushmore in 1964, and I collected wool souvenir pennants along the way. I learned to love life on the road.

He was stationed near Pensacola, Florida, and we lived on the beach in 1965. We walked the surf line every morning to find sharks, starfish, and conch shells washed upon the shore. I developed a love of natural history and exploring.

In 1966, we sat together to watch a new kind of television program—Star Trek—when it first aired in prime time. Since then, I've watched every Star Trek episode and film multiple times.

In 1968, we moved from Willingboro, New Jersey, to Torrance, California. We lived in a one-bedroom apartment with the family dog, a terrier named Shakespeare. One night Shakespeare became very ill and my father drove with me in the middle of the night, looking for an emergency veterinary hospital, cradling the dog on his lap as he steered the old Buick.

In 1970, I read about linear accelerators in the World Book encyclopedia. I decided to build one at home and my father helped me by going to a local high school machine shop to fabricate parts. I was the only third grader to exhibit atom-smashing technology and won the science fair.

In 1972, my father and I built model rockets together and drove to the desert to launch them. The early 1970s were a different time—somewhat dangerous chemicals and rocket fuel were available without restriction. Luckily, we did no harm to ourselves during our adventures.

In 1973, we built a metal detector together, carefully soldering each transistor into a circuit board. I used it to find lost change on Redondo Beach.

In 1974, I found an old minibike in a local junkyard. The engine was largely destroyed by fire. My father and I rebuilt it, buying parts as spare funds became available. By 1975 I was riding it in a nearby parking lot. Since then I've had a lifelong desire to tinker and fix things.

In 1976, we hiked extensively in the Santa Monica Mountains—the most nature you'll find in Los Angeles (think of the set from M*A*S*H). For most of my life, I've been a hiker, climber, and explorer.

In 1977, we road our bicycles, loaded with gear, from Palos Verdes to Santa Barbara, camping along the way at Point Mugu State Park. I will never forget our attempt at making pancakes on a backpacking stove with a bit too much olive oil. Gooey fried dough is appealing if you are hungry enough.

In 1980, when I graduated from high school, we visited Kauai and hiked the Napali Coast trail. I remember that we confused wild Kukui nuts with Macademia nuts. The laxative properties of Kukui nuts are profound.

In 1980, my adult life began and I attended Stanford, UCSF, and UC Berkeley for years of undergraduate and graduate training. I still shared every experience and tribulation with my father. He subscribed to *Science* and *Nature* so that he could discuss the latest scientific advances with authority.

In 1990, he was diagnosed with multiple sclerosis, and over 23 years progressively lost lower body strength. He fought the good fight and only this year bought his first wheelchair.

My role at the moment is to keep him comfortable and celebrate his life, reflecting on the profound impact he had on everyone around him. Over the past day, I've told him all the stories above. At one time in the night, I told him that I loved him. He opened his eyes and whispered, "I know." Since then, he's been resting. The muscle spasms of multiple sclerosis have stopped, and his breathing remains unlabored. ■

Saying Goodbye to My Father

My father passed away this morning. My mother and I were at his bedside telling him we'd be ok and care for each other. He was 70.

My parents met when they were 17 and I was born when my mother and father were 19.

I've known him for nearly 51 years.

The community recalls him as the kindest most giving lawyer in Southern California.

To me he was a mentor, a friend, and an inspiration.

He told me a story about my early childhood. When I was two years old, I was playing in the backyard of my grandparents' home in Iowa. I fell on the grass and began crying. I was not injured in any way. He watched the incident and decided not to run over and console me. Instead, he let me brush myself off, realize that I could fall, and in a self-reliant way recover from it myself. Within a minute I was ok and back at play. He taught me resilience by being a safety net, but letting me find my own way.

To me he was a mentor, a friend, and an inspiration.

In the entrance to my parent's home, there's a woodcut of Don Quixote. Today, my father's unused cane leans against the wall. I was struck by the resemblance of the lance held by the Man of La Mancha to my father's Leki walking stick. Despite 23 years of multiple sclerosis, with the loss of walking and difficulties with activities of daily living, my father always dreamed the impossible dream. He built a Japanese garden, he turned compost, he grew vegetables, he maintained the house, and continued to build/tinker until the end.

Some have commented that only a cruel god would afflict such a kind man with multiple sclerosis, myelodysplastic syndrome, and severe coronary artery disease. However, my father was stubborn and met the adversity head on. He refused pain medications for dental procedures and declined anesthesia for colonoscopies. He made the best of every day no matter what cards life dealt him.

I will miss him but he will always be a part of me and inspire me to new levels of equanimity and endurance.

Goodbye, Dad. I love you. ∎

Supporting the Living

My father died a month ago and I flew to Los Angeles this weekend to help my mother during the grieving process.

She's doing very well.

The death of a spouse (or father) can be traumatic to everyone involved. The tasks that follow the funeral are numerous—wills/trusts are acted upon, accounts are closed/changed, credit cards are cancelled, insurance policies are claimed or revised, IRAs are transferred, and death certificates are circulated to every appropriate public and private organization that needs legal notification.

But there is much more to supporting the living than the financial and legal "to do" list.

The life tasks performed by two people must now be performed by one.

We all depend on friends, family, and life partners to support our activities in life. This weekend was about empowering my mother to manage my father's tasks.

What are some of those responsibilities that seem trivial but require specialized knowledge?

- The sprinkler system/irrigation controller needs to be managed, ensuring the gardens receive the right amount of water as weather changes.

- The security system and smoke alarms/carbon dioxide detectors need battery changes.

- Printers need toner and paper.

- Internet routers and wireless devices need resetting.

- Plumbing, electrical, and painting tasks need to be managed.

- Light bulbs need changing (and some ceiling fixtures can be very challenging to access).

- Entire digital lives need to be maintained, merged, or erased.

- Many items throughout the house need to be recycled, removed, or stored.

- Cars need to be serviced or sold.

This weekend was about supporting the living as the grieving process evolves into planning for the future.

My mother and I took numerous trips to Home Depot, worked on all the maintenance tasks that had accumulated over the past month, and prepared her to be the steward of the house and everything in it.

I brought her an iPad and an AirPrint-enabled printer to improve her access to media and communications. We worked so closely on planning all aspects of her next stage of life that I'll have no problem supporting her via email, texts, and phone calls.

We both miss my father but know that we cannot bring him back. My mother's resilience and willingness to learn are truly inspiring. I'll be back to Los Angeles again in a few weeks when I lecture at Pri-Med in Anaheim, but I'm completely confident my mother will thrive in my absence. ∎

Making a Difference

In my life on earth, 2013 marked the first time I've had no father with me on Father's Day. For the first time, I've taken on the mantle of "alpha" father for the family.

I celebrated Father's day with my wife, daughter, and her partner David, enjoying a Japanese lunch and helping them rewire the kitchen in their new apartment. They rent one of four units in a 1910-era shingled house in Medford. We braved the dungeon-like basement to find the old breaker box and located the power controls for the kitchen. I taught them how a GFCI[10] receptacle is wired, carefully isolating the load and line sides, the hot wire, the common wire, and the ground. We then built new kitchen shelving for her pots and pans. It was a perfect Father's Day, serving those around me and making my daughter's life easier.

I called my mother, as I have done every day since my father's death, to check on her progress. She's gardening, taking daily walks, and keeping her brain busy with numerous cultural and social activities.

So, what part of this inspired me to think about what really matters?

Will my tombstone read,

"He balanced his budget 20 years in a row."

"He addressed all regulatory requirements for over 2 decades."

"He completed all his annual operating plan goals and more."

Unlikely.

If, in some small way, I empower my daughter to fledge from the nest, taking responsibility for running a household and finding her own way in the world, I will have created a legacy that could last for a century.

If, in some small way, I enable my mother to maintain her wellness, learn new technologies, and experience a rich "act two" after my father's death, I will have made a real impact on her life.

Both are examples of making a difference.

As I look at my weekly calendar, about half my waking hours are spent on operations, a quarter on planning the future, and quarter in service to my family and community.

It's the last quarter, when I give my time, that has the greatest chance of impacting the long-term future of those around me, accelerating the progress of the next generation, and catalyzing good outcomes in the world.

While balancing a budget is a must do, it's quickly forgotten. You're only as good as your last budget cycle or your last successful project.

---

10 GFCI = ground fault circuit interrupter.

However, if your family, your colleagues, and your students feel inspired by something you've said, a situation you've created, or a barrier you've broken down, then you've created a memory that can last a lifetime.

So next time your equanimity is challenged by a person, situation, or event in your job, remember that such issues are transient. Focus your emotional energy on that which really matters and you'll make a difference. That's the pot of gold at the end of my rainbow. ∎

Focus your emotional energy on that which really matters and you'll make a difference.

Chapter 10

The Thursday Blog

This chapter contains my most unusual posts. My background in math, science, and engineering gives me a quirky approach to dressing, eating, making wine, growing mushrooms, and engaging in day-to-day life. Some of these posts have been labeled "weird," "too much information," and "a bit alternative." They are who I am, for better or worse. Enjoy.

My Top Ten Tips for Staying Healthy

I'm learning to appreciate the challenges of staying healthy as I age. Based on my personal experience, here are my top ten tips:

1. Maintain a normal Body Mass Index—A BMI between 18.5 and 24.9 is ideal. An ideal BMI is more about lifestyle than diet. It takes effort! For me, the combination of daily exercise, a vegan diet, and green tea for the past eight years has worked well to keep my BMI in the mid-normal range at 21.7.

2. Exercise daily—I try to exercise every day through a combination of kayaking on the Charles River, cycling through the rural byways of Needham/Dover/Sherborn, hiking in the White Mountains of New

Hampshire, Nordic skiing in Noanet Reservation, and very vigorous gardening (hauling, digging, mulching, etc.) My goal is 3,500 calories burned via exercise every week. This seems to keep my BMI stable.

3. Eat a vegan diet—It's easy to eat badly as a vegetarian. Ben and Jerry's Chunky Monkey is vegetarian. Chili-cheese dip is vegetarian. Eggnog is vegetarian. Try eating badly as a vegan (only foods that grow in the ground). You could drink pure olive oil, but it's really hard to eat badly. If you further limit yourself to locally grown, organic foods (for the majority of your diet; tea and chocolate are not locally grown), you're going to eat a high-fiber, low-calorie, low-fat diet. That's good for your heart and good for your BMI.

4. Drink green tea—I drink two pots of green tea every day, usually Gyokuro Asahi tea from Kyoto. It's very low in caffeine and high in polyphenols, reducing cholesterol and providing anti-oxidants. It has zero calories without the artificial sweeteners and chemicals found in diet drinks. Staying hydrated keeps your energy up and your mind clear.

5. Drink red wine in moderation—I drink six ounces of red wine with dinner each night. I do not consume wine as a thirst quencher or as a stress reliever; I drink it as a complement to food. It's high in polyphenols and reduces heart attack/stroke risk.

6. Eat dark chocolate—Dark chocolate is very high in anti-oxidants and has several health benefits, including reduced cholesterol and blood pressure.

7. Use sunscreen—The time I spend outdoors can dry out my skin and increase my chance of skin cancer. I use SPF 45 on my face, neck, and arms whenever I'm doing outdoor activities.

8. Take vitamin D and a multivitamin daily—Since I use sunscreen generously and do not drink milk, I do not get all the vitamin D I need. Also, as a vegan, I get limited B12 (it does not exist in plants but small amounts are found in soil, which inevitably makes its way into our diet when we eat root vegetables). Taking vitamin D and a Centrum Silver daily works for me.

9. Avoid caffeine and lifestyle medications—Rather than starting each day with a boost of caffeine and ending each day with a mixed drink, I just stay even all the time. I also avoid 'lifestyle medications' such as mood enhancing drugs, nicotine, energy drinks, sleeping aids, etc. Although they may have positive short-term effects, the long-term effects and side effects are ultimately deleterious.

10. Have a positive attitude—Each day is filled with success and failure, joy and sorrow, energy and fatigue. Having a positive attitude about the complexities of life and realizing that all will be well goes far to keep you healthy, active, and energized.

Maybe I should package these ten items into a best-selling book called, "The CIO Diet: A Prescription for a Healthy Lifestyle"! ■

The Joy of a Local Hardware Store

Let me describe two experiences:

I walk into a big box home improvement store and ask for advice about screens for storm windows that were popular in Wellesley, Massachusetts in the 1960s. No one has any idea what I'm talking about. Not just about my storm windows, but any storm windows. The store is 40 aisles of 20-foot-high racks without an easy-to-navigate map. Oddly, screens are not in the Windows section; they're in the Building Materials area. No one knows what tools I need or how much screen I should purchase, so I make several trips back and forth from home to store. I spend hours in the process and throw away an entire roll of screen I've wasted.

I walk into my neighborhood hardware store. A cheerful, experienced salesperson greets me at the door and asks to help with my project. The person instantly knows the type of windows I have, the tools needed, the best materials, and a few tips to get the job done right. The person wanders around the 5,000-square-foot store, picks up all the materials I need and rings me up. I spend minutes in the process, do the job perfectly the first time, and have no waste.

Just as I have extolled the virtues of embracing locavore[1] food culture and community-supported agriculture, I suggest supporting your local hardware store—let's take back the neighborhood from the big box stores.

> *I want to shop locally from farmers, craftsmen, vendors, and salespeople that I know.*

Life is short and I really care about the quality of my day-to-day experiences. I want to shop locally from farmers, craftsmen, vendors, and salespeople that I know. I realize that in our complex world, that is not always possible. If you have a choice of buying a bolt for fifty cents from a helpful, knowledgeable shopkeeper OR buying a bolt of lesser quality for forty

---

1   A locavore is a person interested in eating food that is locally produced, not moved long distances to market. The desired maximum distance for local produce is between 50-100 miles. The locavore movement in the US and elsewhere was spawned as interest in sustainability and eco-consciousness became more prevalent.

cents that takes an hour to find in a big box store, I suggest that you and your wallet shop locally.

I'm so impressed with Green's Hardware in Wellesley that I actually seek out home projects to do on weekends, just so I can enjoy the experience of getting sound advice and quality products from people who teach me how to maintain my home. My house was built in the 1930s but every part of it—from electrical to plumbing to carpentry—is perfectly maintained thanks to the partnership I've developed with Green's, my local hardware store. ∎

In Pursuit of Peace

I've returned from Japan and had many amazing experiences there, both professional and personal. One of the more interesting experiences demonstrated to me that we are truly connected and it is a very small world.

While in Tokyo at a seminar arranged by Fujitsu, I met Yoshio Leeper from the Fujitsu Economic Research Center. He mentioned that his father, Steven Leeper, was Director of Peace Park, the museum/monuments at the site of the Hiroshima atomic bomb blast. I told Yoshio that I would be visiting Hiroshima on February 18 and would welcome the opportunity to meet his father.

Yoshio emailed his father. Steve Leeper graciously offered to take my family to lunch at Okonomi Mura, a building filled with Okonomiyaki restaurants (Okonomiyaki is a remarkable layered pancake with noodles and vegetables that deserves its own blog entry—Hiroshima is famous for them), and give us a guided tour of Peace Park, based on his experience as Director.

We arrived in Hiroshima and went to lunch. Steve described his role as ambassador for peace to the world as Chairperson of the Hiroshima Peace Culture Foundation. He knew of my various roles in technology and policy and asked if I would like to meet the mayor of Hiroshima, Tadatoshi Akiba, PhD, and the CIO of Hiroshima, Asako Toyoda, (who is also Deputy Mayor).

One call to the mayor's office and it was arranged.

We drove to city hall and were escorted to the mayor's private meeting room.

Dr. Akiba is a remarkable man. He's a graduate of MIT and is passionate about technology. Hiroshima is one of the most wired cities in Japan, with near universal Broadband and 3G wireless coverage. He's passionate about peace and specifically hired Steve Leeper to bring strong leadership to Hiroshima's peace activities. Dr. Akiba also has turned the city around financially by trimming expenses, scaling back public works projects, and implementing tight fiscal management.

Asako Toyoda is one of the few CIOs in Japan. Her energy and diligence have led to Hiroshima's IT pre-eminence. It was all accomplished with a very frugal budget.

My conversation with Dr. Akiba ranged from electronic health records and regional information exchanges to personal health records/Google Health. He was very familiar with my background, including the unusual fact that I was Edward Teller's ('father' of the H-bomb) research assistant from 1981–1983. He asked for my help supporting the cause of peace, a critical issue over the next two years as the Nuclear Non-Proliferation Treaty is renegotiated in 2010. Depending on the outcome of that treaty, we can begin a path of global nuclear disarmament or see an increase in countries throughout the world becoming nuclear-weapons capable.

I gave him my commitment to work with my contacts in the House, Senate, and White House staff to raise awareness on this issue. Let's hope that the new administration finds the path to peace appealing as a way to bring stability and economic cooperation to the world.

Japan has high hopes for the Obama administration, and according to all the Japanese senior people I spoke with, there is a fresh look at America now that the administration has changed. The previous administration created a tide of negative public opinion about Americans which is now turning! Just north of Kyoto, there's a town called Obama City. So it's fair to say that while in Japan, I had a visit to see Obama. I hope that Mr. Obama follows Secretary Clinton's lead and visits the Far East. Two of Obama's goal's are ending our unpopular wars and reinvigorating the economy. Pursuing the cause of peace by taking a leadership role in nuclear non-proliferation and strengthening American ties to the second largest economy in the world (Japan also holds much of the US national debt) are two good ways to further the administration's top priorities. ∎

Infinite Growth in a Finite World

We're all aware of the Bernie Madoff Ponzi scheme. He used money from new investors to pay unreasonably high, consistent rates of return to his old investors.

Two articles by Thomas L. Friedman, "The Inflection Is Near?" and "Mother Nature's Dow,"[2] ask if we are engaged in a global Ponzi scheme of accelerating consumption and growth.

Most for-profit companies I've worked with as an advisor or board member measure their success in quarter-per-quarter growth percentages.

---

2   Friedman TL. The Inflection Is Near. *The New York Times.* March 7, 2009; Friedman TL. Mother Nature's Dow. *The New York Times.* March 28, 2009.

In the economy of a bygone era, local businesses were considered successful when they made a high-quality product, maintained the livelihood of a few employees, and built relationships with customers. There was a focus on service to the community rather than endless growth in value for shareholders.

Just as Bernie Madoff promised double-digit returns, the US economy experienced rapid growth (likely unsustainable) via credit cards, speculation, and mortgaging our children's future.

If our resources are finite—we have a limited amount of fresh water, a fixed set of raw materials, and a cap to the population that can be sustained in the environment—infinite growth is not possible.

I believe that the era of "growth is good" is coming to an end. It is my hope that the era of quality, employee retention, customer satisfaction, and sustainability will replace it.

> *If our resources are finite—we have a limited amount of fresh water, a fixed set of raw materials, and a cap to the population that can be sustained in the environment—infinite growth is not possible.*

Call me old fashioned, but does it make sense for hedge fund managers, venture capitalists, and option traders to make such high returns without really contributing to society? Do they create new ideas, innovative products, or value-added services? Or are they no better than sophisticated speculators in a global Ponzi scheme? The vast sums of money they make come from somewhere and we're all paying the price now for their creation of derivative investments that were based on the notion that home prices and businesses would have infinite growth in a finite world.

As I approach 50, my view of the world and my own needs have changed significantly. In my 20s I measured success by the amount of stuff I owned, the size of my house, and the speed of my car. Now I measure my success by the amount of stuff I do not have, the smallness of my house, and the carbon footprint of my car.

If we all endeavor to focus on the quality of life, the sustainability of our environment, and the future of our children, rather than endless growth, the world will be a better place. ∎

Safe Eating Discounts

As I drove into work today, I listened to Boston's WROR FM (105.7) and heard an advertisement for two sausage McMuffins with egg and a cup of Newman's organic coffee.

I had just finished a breakfast of Bob's Red Mill Organic Thick Rolled Oats and a cup of green tea. My breakfast was 190 calories, with 30 of those calories from fat.

The advertised McDonald's special was 900 calories, with 468 of those calories from fat.

Essentially, the McDonald's meal is diabetes and heart disease in a bag, exceeding the entire daily recommendation for saturated fat and cholesterol. And with the sodium load, you'll gain a pound or two of water weight.

While driving, it occurred to me that I get a safe driver discount, since I've never had a moving violation or accident claim.

Why not a safe eating discount from my health insurer?

If I choose to be a vegan and have a diet that has zero cholesterol by definition, essentially no saturated fat, and almost no sodium, I am extending my life by making a disciplined lifestyle choice.

> *Why not a safe eating discount from my health insurer?*

By keeping a body mass index of 20 via veganism and daily exercise, I am preventing future disease.

I know that Charlie Baker, the CEO of my insurer, Harvard Pilgrim Healthcare, is a very smart man and will have a very reasonable analysis. It takes dozens of people like me to support the medical care of the McDonald's eater, so it's really not possible to give a safe eating discount. However, if we're really going to have healthcare reform in the US, I would advocate a carrot-and-stick approach based on personal accountability.

Give folks with low-fat, low-sodium, low-cholesterol diets a safe eating discount.

Put a tax on McDonald's meals, just as we do with tobacco products, to cover the cost of medical care incurred by eating more fat and cholesterol in a single meal than the FDA recommends for the entire day.

I realize that this may sound harsh and I will not make friends in the beef and dairy industry. However, at some point we need to be accountable for our own health.

Just as President Obama has encouraged us to take responsibility for reinventing America, we must take personal action to reduce the healthcare costs that reduce the competitiveness of the economy.

Rewarding healthful behaviors and penalizing harmful ones seem like a good idea.

Next time I see Charlie Baker, I'll ask him. ∎

The Broken Window Effect

As an adult I've returned to various locations from my childhood and found the white picket fences, station wagons, and neighborhood shops transformed into rough, run down, and unsafe neighborhoods. This did not happen overnight. What happened in these places is the same thing that can happen in a business or your personal life. I call it the "broken window effect."

Imagine the perfect "Lake Wobegon" neighborhood where everything is above average. A baseball goes through a window, but the owner decides not to fix it. Then, because the house looks a bit shabby, another neighbor leaves a junked car on the street. Then a bit of graffiti is not cleaned up. Then folks stop picking up garbage from their yards.

This can happen inside a house. One pile on the floor doesn't take too much room, so a few more piles are put around it. Before long, all floor spaces have piles on them. Maintenance items are deferred and junk is not tossed. Years pass and eventually the house is unhealthy to live in, but no one really notices because it happened so gradually.

In IT organizations, the broken window effect can occur when management begins to tolerate downtime, constant workarounds, and broken processes.

How do we prevent the broken window effect?

Every downtime incident is investigated within hours of the problem, and a full report is issued to our weekly change control board meeting. The meeting is not punitive; it is a learning environment attended by all my technical managers so that the entire organization can learn together. Questions include

- Was there a process failure?

- Was there a training failure?

- Was there a policy failure?

- Was there a planning failure?

- Was there a lifecycle maintenance failure?

By examining every incident when it happens and by building a culture that encourages constant improvement based on collective sharing of our experiences, we ensure that "broken windows" are fixed and that problem recurrence is minimized.

The change control board was created after my network collapse in 2002 because at that time we discovered several aspects of the IS organization that needed improvement such as

- Lack of transparency to downtime with details not openly shared among all groups

- Silos of technical knowledge

- A tendency to work around and patch rather than identify and correct root causes of problems

- A lack of planning projects as a coordinated whole with all services—applications, networks, servers, storage, desktop—considered components of a single comprehensive implementation.

The change control board is so rigorous that even I can get into trouble. I recently implemented a health information exchange application update and did not discuss it at the change control board. Thinking that it was just a minor update, I assumed that there were no infrastructure implications. However, given the fact that the application exchanges data securely outside our firewall, involves databases, integration engines, and application teams, it was important to brief everyone first. My next directors meeting will include an overview of all our health information exchange projects—past, present and future—for all IS stakeholders.

On a personal level, I also try to avoid the broken window effect by renewing/ maintaining all aspects of my life.

On a personal level, I also try to avoid the broken window effect by renewing/maintaining all aspects of my life, for example:

- I erase all emails older than 90 days and all files older than one year. It's really rare that an issue has not been resolved after 90 days or someone requests a file older than a year.

- I replace my laptop every two years.

- I replace my mobile device every two years.

- I replace my clothes every three years.

- I keep no paper of any kind in my office and very little in my home. All my reading materials are digital.

Every season has its activities that lead to renewal: spring house cleaning, summer planting, fall yard cleanup, winterization to prep the house for cold weather.

Whether it's your neighborhood, your home, or your office, I recommend you stay vigilant for the broken window effect. Fixing all those broken windows keeps everyone engaged in renewal. ∎

The Personal Genome Project

My genome was recently released publicly at the Personal Genome Project (PGP) site.

As one of the PGP's first ten participants, I contributed my entire medical record, phenotype, and genotype in the hope that this data will support research to enhance personalized medicine for future patients.

The first analysis of my genome reveals:

1. I carry a mutation for hereditary motor and sensory neuropathy with optic atrophy (HMSN VI), also known as Charcot Marie-Tooth disease. Specifically, the base pair change is

Chromosome 1, MFN2 (mitofusin 2 protein)
HEREDITARY MOTOR AND SENSORY NEUROPATHY VI
H T V R A K Q
Reference: CAC ACG GTC CGG GCC AAG CAG
Me: CAC ACG GTC TGG GCC AAG CAG
H T V W A K Q

My father has had multiple sclerosis for 18 years and thus my family has had many discussions about neurological disorders. HMSN typically affects patients in their childhood and thus far, no one in my family or I have been directly affected.

2. I'm heterozygous for severe combined immunodeficiency disease (Boy in a Bubble Syndrome).

Other than two episodes of Lyme disease, I've not had any infections requiring treatment, nor has my daughter.

3. I have 2.23 times average risk for prostate cancer.

The papers about this particular mutation studied two simultaneous mutations and I have only one. Thus, it's unclear if a single mutation has the same risk as two.

4. I have a no Kell antigen which could have implications for future blood transfusions. If I was ever transfused, I could develop antibodies against Kell antigens that could cause a transfusion reaction upon a second transfusion.

5. I have several mutations which put me at increased risk for tuberculosis.

During residency, I led the TB service at Harbor UCLA Medical Center. Several of my fellow residents developed positive PPDs,[3] but I did not seroconvert. Thus, after extensive exposure, I've remained PPD negative, so I appear to be doing well despite the genetic risk.

What does all this mean?

---

3 PPD = purified protein derivative. The PPD skin test is a method used to diagnose silent (latent) tuberculosis (TB) infection.

1. I will certainly be aware of any neurological or ocular findings in any family member.

2. My PSA is .4 and my prostate exam is completely normal. I will take any changes in prostate health more seriously than before.

3. I've encouraged other members of my family to get involved as future PGP subjects. Is there any relationship between my father's MS and the mutation I carry which causes hereditary motor and sensory neuropathy? Is there any relationship between the mutation for severe combined immunodeficiency disease and my mother's celiac disease? These and other research questions will be possible as more people, including those in my family, contribute their lifetime medical records and genomes to PGP.

I'll share all my experiences with the Personal Genome Project and the release of my genome via my blog. ∎

Staying Warm in New England

Now that the leaves are falling and frosts are beginning in New England, it's time to retire my summer wardrobe and prepare for the cold, wet, harsh seasons ahead.

Every year, numerous people die in New Hampshire's White Mountains from hypothermia. It's already snowing on Mt. Washington.

To understand how to keep warm when the weather outside is frightful, you first have to understand how the human body loses heat: conduction, convection, evaporation, radiation, and respiration.

Conduction is heat loss when the body comes into direct contact with a cold object—snow, a metal trekking pole/ice ax, or a cold rock.

Convection is heat loss when air or water passes by the body such as a brisk wind passing by the surface of the skin.

Evaporation is heat loss when moisture on the body becomes airborne—either sweat or rain water on wet clothing.

Radiation is heat loss that occurs when heat escapes directly into the still air.

Respiration is heat loss that occurs when breathing air that is colder than body temperature which is warmed by the body, then exhaled.

Here's my strategy for avoiding hypothermia from any of these causes.

During fall/winter/spring I wear:

- A torso base layer of thin polyester (Arcteryx Rho LT)

- A torso shell layer of Gortex Pro Shell (Arcteryx Alpha LT)

- A lower extremity combination of thin insulation and shell (Arcteryx Gamma MX)
- A head base layer of thin polyester (OR Ninjaclava)
- A warm, windproof hat (OR Windpro Hat)
- A hand base layer of thin polyester (OR PL100 Gloves)
- A waterproof/windproof shell layer (OR Cornice Mitts)
- A belay jacket on my upper extremity when I stop moving (Arcteryx Solo)

How do these work?

- Conduction—The lower extremity insulation layer slows conduction if I sit on the snow or on a rock. I do not lie down on snow, so my upper extremity does not contact anything cold directly.

- Convection—The upper extremity Gortex layer and the lower extremity wind-proof softshell minimize any wind-related heat loss.

- Evaporation—You'll notice that I do not wear any upper body insulation— just a wicking layer of thin polyester. This ensures I do not sweat, even when climbing thousands of feet. I may be a bit cold when I start, but as I climb, the exertion keeps me warm without sweat, minimizing evaporative heat loss.

- Radiation—My multi-layered hats prevent significant radiant heat loss since greater than 50% of the body's radiation occurs through the head. The Belay jacket, which I put on over the Gortex layer when I stop moving, minimizes radiant heat loss.

- Respiration—There's really nothing I can do to eliminate heat loss due to respiration. However, I carry one liter of boiling water and three Lara bars to keep myself fed and hydrated. I carry the hot water in nalgene polyethyelene container (BPA-free) wrapped in an OR water bottle parka. Adding warm liquids to my body during an ice climb or hike maintains my body core temperature.

Dress right, eat right, keep moving, and no matter what the temperature, you'll keep warm.

Remember, in New England there is no bad weather, just poor clothing choices! ∎

100 Things to Do Before You Die

Recently I heard about a sobering accidental death.

Dave Freeman, co-author of *100 Things to Do Before You Die*,[4] a travel guide and ode to odd adventures that inspired readers and imitators, died on August 17 after a fall at his home in the Venice section of Los Angeles. He was 47.

Dave and I were only six months different in age. Over the past ten years, while I've been climbing, hiking, and traveling the world, I've tried to live each day to the fullest, creating my own "100 Things" list. Here are a few completed entries on my list from my recent vacation and previous travels:

1. Explore the excavations of old Jerusalem with an archeologist. I did consulting for the government of Israel on coordinating electronic health records for mass causality incidents. I asked for a day with an archeologist as my compensation.

2. Walk Hadrian's Wall (separates England and Scotland in the UK) coast to coast and have a pint of ale in a rural Scottish pub with farmers who've never met an American.

3. Kayak across the Baltic Sea (it took three days).

4. Gather crawfish by moonlight in Sweden (before I was a vegan).

5. Explore the fiords of Norway on foot.

6. Bicycle throughout East Anglia in England, exploring the backroads and hedgerows.

7. Walk the seven hills of Rome and climb the stairs to the top of St. Peter's Cathedral.

8. Climb the Untersberg in Salzburg, Austria.

9. Play the Turkish Ney in a Mosque in Istanbul.

10. Walk the John Muir Trail.

11. Climb every mountain in New England in every season of the year.

12. Spend a weekend meditating and praying with Buddhist monks at a temple on Mt. Koya.

13. Spend the night on top of Half Dome.

14. Play the Digeridoo in Australia.

15. Scuba dive with Grey Whales.

16. Watch the sunrise from the top of Mt. Fuji.

17. Walk the old city of Prague where my ancestors made Pilsner.

18. Play a flute concert on the top of the Eichorn Pinnacle in Yosemite.

19. Have dinner in the Smithsonian at night after it's closed.

---

4   Teplica N, Freeman D. *100 Things to Do Before You Die: Travel Events You Just Can't Miss.* Boulder, CO: Taylor Trade Publishers; 1999.

20. Walk five miles on the Great Wall of China.

21. Climb the Grand Tetons at dawn.

22. Camp under the stars at 11,000 feet in Yosemite during a meteor shower.

23. Get licked on the face by a giraffe.

24. Watch a sunrise from Machu Picchu.

25. Ride a sleeper train with my family from Tokyo to Sapporo, Japan.

Wherever I wander, I always look for the road less traveled. I never sit in a hotel room or seek the comforts of home—there will be time for that later. By filling each moment with lasting experiences instead of buying 'stuff,' I have very memorable encounters with people and places that provide me with long-term satisfaction when I return home.

Dave, I wish you well and I hope you experienced your 100. I've already made a list for the future that includes sunsets on Santorini, playing the Hungarian Furulya with shepherds near Budapest, and climbing the East Face of Mt. Whitney. Whenever my time comes, I'll know that I balanced each day with work, family, and personal pursuits that include the best things I can find in this world. ∎

Lessons Learned from Alpine Mountaineering

I spent a few days last week in New Hampshire with family. Every hike and climb I do is filled with lessons learned that make me a more responsive CIO.

Here are a few of my experiences.

On Monday, I expected to climb the Whitney Gilman ridge on Mt. Cannon in Franconia Notch. Unfortunately, we've had a very rainy July in New England, filled with pop-up thunderstorms. Monday had a 70% chance of thunderstorms in the Franconia area, which is well known for its uniquely bad weather. Alpine mountaineering is often a race against bad weather, requiring pre-dawn starts and early afternoon descents off the mountain before afternoon thunderstorms put the climbers at risk. On most climbs there is always the possibility of retreat, which is part of the trip planning. Whitney Gilman has a lot of loose rock, no bolted anchors for rappelling, and is bordered by the 1,000-foot 'black dike,' a wet, mossy abyss. There is no retreat from this climb.

In my blog about risk, I described the Morts[5] involved in each of my activities. Risk in my view is the likelihood of a bad event times the consequences of the bad event. Climbing a 1,000-foot rock face without a possibility of descent with

---

5 See the "Risky Business" section of this chapter for an explanation of "Morts" (pages 380–382).

a 70% thunderstorm risk in an area known for very bad weather, created a level of risk that I judged unacceptable. Summitting the mountain is optional, returning to the car is mandatory. I elected to skip all climbing and hike at low elevations on Monday.

The weighing of risks and benefits, evaluation of contingencies, and triage of all available options is something a CIO must do every day. Using my CIO behaviors in the intense world of alpine mountaineering makes me a better climber and vice versa.

On Tuesday, I climbed the Pinnacle Buttress (8 pitches, 5.8) to the summit of Mt. Washington. Although 5.8 climbing is only moderately difficult, the week of thunderstorms had created a thin sheet of moss over the entire climb, making handholds and footholds very tenuous. There were two options—become overwhelmed by the poor climbing conditions or just focus, trust myself, and move to the top step by step. Often, when doing projects as a CIO, the politics, limited resources, software quality issues, and changes in scope can be very daunting. By focusing on the task at hand, realizing there is a process for everything, projects eventually succeed. Applying the same patience and perseverance I use in climbing to my work as an IT leader makes me a better CIO.

On Thursday, I hiked Mt. Monadnock from each compass direction, doing four ascents over the course of the day. On my final descent, I passed a gentleman who was moving slowly with his two young children, one age five and one age eight. The five-year-old was quite tired and having difficulty with the trail. The eight-year-old asked her father which direction to go and he told her to follow me as I seemed to know where I was going. She took this as a command and ran down the mountain with me for three miles. It was 6 pm, most hikers had left for the day, and I was alone with an eight-year-old girl I did not know, who was probably going to have to wait two hours for her family. I accepted responsibility for the situation, ensured she was fed and hydrated, then explained the situation to her. We walked to the Mt. Monadnock State Park headquarters where I filled out an incident report, asked the state park rangers to supervise her, gave them all my contact information, and asked them to follow-up. At 11 pm, her father called me to say that the family was down the mountain, reunited, and all was well.

By accepting responsibility for situations that are often not caused by me or are beyond my control (whether in the office or in the wild), I can ensure the satisfaction of all stakeholders.

A great vacation in New Hampshire. My next excursion into the wild begins on August 8 with the John Muir trail. ∎

My Closet

Many people ask me about my black wardrobe, which I've written about as simply practical for the 24x7x365 CIO and not a *Gentleman's Quarterly* fashion statement. I was recently asked to share a glimpse of my closet.

I know this sounds like a strange blog topic, but my closet provides an insight into my brain, demonstrating that every minute of my existence is part of a complex lifestyle. Hopefully, the detail below will not sound too obsessive-compulsive. Call it "the examined life."

My closet is organized into clothing for my lower extremity and clothing for my torso.

Everything I own for the lower half of my body is black. It's practical. Whether business attire, climbing clothing, or alpine ascent gear, various kind of black pants work well. For the office, my pants are rayon (it's vegan and derived from wood fiber). For climbing, I wear all Arcteryx gear made of thin but durable nylon. For alpine ascents, I wear Arcteryx gear made from Powershield, a Polartec softshell.

For my torso, I wear all black linen fabrics (a 5,000-year-old textile made by weaving flax) in the office, since they are easy-care, cool in summer, and warm in winter. For the outdoors, all my upper extremity clothing is red for visibility. I have base layers of polyester, mid layers of Polartec Powerstretch, and outer layers of Gortex. Each layer is engineered for specific temperatures and humidity conditions.

For footwear, I have specific shoes for specific tasks: vegan microfiber polyester Monk shoes and Dealer Boots for the office, Five-ten climbing and approach shoes for the Crag, and Scarpa Double Plastic boots for Alpine travel.

My closet also stores my ropes, packs, climbing hardware, and helmet.

All of my clothing and most of my belongings fit into this one eight-foot space.

Over the years, I've tried to refine what I own and approach all my clothing from an engineering perspective, only carrying what is minimally necessary for the range of climatic conditions I'll encounter. I use my engineering approach to clothing, taking into account specific temperature and humidity conditions for each piece of clothing. This philosophy works very well in an era when travel is so expensive and difficult. Wearing black, and using the durable, breathable fabrics I've chosen, a week in Europe can be done from a single carry-on satchel. A week in Yosemite takes a bit more, since I have seven pounds of rope and climbing hardware to carry along, but one small duffel will do the trick.

That's my closet—another expression of my lifestyle that does not separate work, family, job, and avocations but comingles them all into one continuum. ∎

Mushroom Season

As part of my duties as an Emergency Physician, I do 200 toxicology consultations each year for patients in New England who eat wild mushrooms and seek medical care.

There are three basic types of patients whom I treat via Regional Poison Control Centers referrals:

1. Toddlers—Two- to four-year olds wander out to the lawn and munch a mushroom. They usually eat small quantities and most often parents find unchewed pieces in their children's mouths. Common mushroom types are the Fairy Ring (Marasmius oreades) and "little brown mushrooms" (Mycena), both non-toxic. I generally try to avoid treating toddlers with activated charcoal, the common treatment for poisonings, by rapidly identifying the mushroom as non-toxic. My experience with activated charcoal in pediatric poisoning is that more charcoal ends up all over the parents than in the patient.

2. Teenagers—14- to 18-year-olds who search cow pastures looking for blue-staining mushrooms (e.g., "Hey man, do THOSE shrooms grow around here?"). Yes, various hallucinogenic mushrooms grow in New England—Psilocybe species, Panaeolus, and Amanita Muscaria abound. The challenge for these teenagers is that these mushrooms contain wildly variable amounts of toxins. One mushroom may contain virtually no toxin and another may contain an overdose. I remind teenagers that "intoxicate" contains the word "toxic." The treatment for overdose of hallucinogens is largely supportive—a quiet dark place and the use of anti-anxiety drugs to treat a truly bad trip.

3. Gourmets—The 20+ educated amateur mushroom hunter with an Audubon field guide who looks for mushrooms based on pictures in the book. There are 2,500 species of mushrooms in North America, of which 35 are great to eat and a dozen are lethal. Edible mushrooms and toxic mushrooms can look similar. A mushroom expert considers the time of year, where the mushroom is growing, and trees growing near the mushroom when picking edible mushrooms. A photo from a field guide is really not that helpful. The only deaths I've had in my consulting practice are the gourmet amateur mushroom hunters. A typical story is that an educated person picks two pounds of wild mushrooms, makes stroganoff, gets ill 12 hours later, waits a few days, feels better, then suddenly develops seizures, liver failure, kidney failure, and seeks medical care. By that time it's too late and not even a liver transplant works. If you want to pick mushrooms to eat, learn from an expert how to identify a few key species such as morels, chantrelles, and porcini. Learn where they grow and pick them

from the same patch year to year. Avoid eating any mushrooms with white gills (the underside of the cap). Not all white-gilled mushrooms are poisonous, but Amanitas are white-gilled mushrooms that can kill you.

How am I consulted? Today, I've received four consults already. Doctors throughout New England call Poison Control Centers, which refer callers to me. The doctors use their cell phones to take pictures of the mushrooms and patients, then email them to me. On my Blackberry, I can view the mushroom, determine the species, outline a course of treatment, and follow-up with the patient to ensure all is well.

Mushroom season runs from June to October in New England. Based on the volume of incoming consultants, I can tell it's going to be a busy year! ∎

Go Climb a Rock

At times I get quizzical looks for being vegan, playing the Japanese flute, or wearing black. However, the most unusual looks from my peers occur when they see photos of me rock climbing.

Winter mountaineering is a good way to get away from your cell phone (the battery life is two minutes at -40F), but why climb a rock?

Think of climbing a mountain as a giant Rubik's cube—a wonderful mental exercise. Climbing requires a well-orchestrated combination of gear, route finding, movement, and teamwork to make it to the top.

Here's how it's done:

1. Make the approach—Some climbs are a five-minute walk from the road and some are ten miles through bush, over stream crossings, and up thousands of feet. The Grand Teton is usually a day of hiking followed by a 2 am departure, which puts you at the base of the technical portion of the summit pyramid at sunrise. The climb to the top takes until 8 am or so, enabling a retreat before the usual afternoon thunderstorms hit the summit. Many Yosemite approaches, such as Half Dome, require hours of tricky route-finding on poorly marked trails before the climbing begins. Of course, you must carry everything with you—climbing shoes, harness, rope, food, water, and extra clothing during the approach.

2. Prepare to climb—At the base of the climb, you put on your harness, unwind your rope, put on your climbing shoes, and do safety checks with your partner. Safe climbing requires at least two people—one to

climb and one to control the rope, catching the leader if a fall occurs. Once gear and knots are checked, climbing can begin.

3. Lead the pitch—The leader uses a combination of footholds, handholds, cracks, and friction to climb up the rock face. Every ten feet or so, the leader places a piece of protection into a crack and clips the rope to that protection. Modern climbing is "clean climbing" that does not involve pitons or any gear that damages the rock. Spring-loaded cams, metal nuts/stoppers, and slings around natural features such as trees provide temporary protection that supports the rope so your climbing partner can catch a fall.

   If you consider the physics of leading, it's where the bulk of the risk of climbing occurs. If you place a piece of protection every ten feet, you'll fall 20 feet if you slip off the rock, since ten feet of rope to the last piece of protection means you'll fall ten feet below that piece before you stop. A 170-pound climber falling 20 feet generates a lot of force on the climber's body, the rope, and the person controlling the rope.

   Routes are divided into segments of under 200 feet in length because that is the length of the most common climbing rope.

   Route difficulty is graded on a scale from 5.1 (climbing a ladder) to 5.15 (basically climbing an inverted slab of glass with butter on your hands). I lead 5.8 and follow 5.10a, which is climbing a vertical to overhanging wall with dime-sized handholds and footholds.

4. Prepare the belay—Once you've climbed the pitch, you must set up a safe and secure attachment to support your climbing partner as he or she climbs. Typically, I place three pieces of protection in the rock for redundancy, then use a 16-foot loop of rope or sling material called a cordelette to provide a secure attachment point for me and my climbing partner. Once I'm safe and I've prepared the rope to support my climbing partner, I give the signal to my partner to begin climbing.

5. Bring up your partner—When your partner climbs, it's called seconding the pitch, since you were the primary or lead climber. Seconding is not particularly risky because you are supported by a rope from above if you fall. Mentally it's easier, but it has the same physical challenges as leading the climb.

6. Repeat—My climbing partner and I do swinging leads, alternating leading and seconding, so we each take half the risk. We do this until we're at the top of the mountain. Some major climbs in Yosemite can be 15 pitches or more, which can take half a day to climb. We do not typically do "big walls" which require you to sleep on a portaledge

strapped onto the face of the mountain. We'd rather have a very long climbing day and then descend before nightfall.

7.   Descent—In some ways, descent is the most dangerous part of the climb. Rappelling down the mountain is risky because a gear failure means death or injury. When we're climbing up, we typically do not fall—the gear is there for safety just in case. When you rappel down the mountain, the gear is all that is keeping you from falling. For this reason, we typically walk off most climbs, down hiking trails rather than rappelling. We always carry headlamps and a rain jacket in our packs when doing long alpine routes, just in case we're delayed or trapped by a storm.

Great climbing areas in the Northeast are the Shawangunks in New Paltz, New York; Cathedral Ledges and Whitehorse Slabs in North Conway, New Hampshire; Franconia Notch near Lincoln, New Hampshire; and Rumney near Plymouth, New Hampshire.

In the US, places like Red Rocks, Nevada; Joshua Tree, California; and the Tetons, Wyoming are extraordinary. However, nothing quite measures up to grandeur of Yosemite and the Eastern Sierra. Here's my typical Yosemite climbing schedule

August 12: Tenaya Peak

- August 13: Cathedral Peak/Eichorn Pinnacle (per my New Year's resolutions, I'll play a Japanese flute concert from the top of Eichorn Pinnacle if the weather holds)

- August 14: Fairview Dome

- August 15: North approach to Mt. Conness

- August 16: Tioga Crest

Rock climbing is an incredible way to focus the mind, experience the outdoors from a new perspective, build teamwork, and work with technical gear, all at the same time. As I age, the routes I'll attempt will likely get easier, but whether they are 5.5 or 5.10a, the joy of a mile of air under your feet is the same! ∎

Risky Business

This is one of those episodic blog entries that delves into some aspect of my personal life. I've often asked if I'm a risk taker, given my alpine mountaineering passion, rock/ice climbing activities, and my travel around the world

Here's the way I think about my life. Let's say there is an activity that results in 100% chance of death (mortality). Let's call that 1 Mort.

Is it possible to skydive without a parachute and survive? Highly unlikely, so such an activity is probably .99999 Mort.

How about flying on domestic airlines? Over the past 20 years, the fatalities per plane flight in the US have been 1 in 7 million. This means that if I took a non-stop flight every day, I would average 19,000 years before succumbing to a fatal crash. Even frequent flyers face minimal cumulative risk over their careers. What's my risk? Last year I took 166 non-stop flights which is .0000237 Morts - 23.7 microMorts.

I'm 45 years old, so let's look at the CDC mortality rate data:

All causes of death 3.52 milliMorts

1. Malignant neoplasms .867 milliMorts

2. Diseases of heart .696 milliMorts

3. Accidents (unintentional injuries) .426 milliMorts

4. Intentional self-harm (suicide) .169 milliMorts

5. Chronic liver disease and cirrhosis .151 milliMorts

6. Cerebrovascular diseases .119 milliMorts

7. Human immunodeficiency virus (HIV) disease .115 milliMorts

8. Diabetes mellitus .10 milliMorts

9. Chronic lower respiratory diseases (J40-J47) .056 milliMorts

10. Assault (homicide) .053 milliMorts

The National Safety Council (NSC) publishes an annual summary of fatalities and accident statistics called "Injury Facts."

All accidents have a risk of .56 milliMorts, which is very close to the CDC accident data above for 45-year-olds of .426 milliMorts.

Motor vehicle accidents are .15 milliMorts per year.

My life insurance policy prohibits me from operating a private plane, skydiving, and scuba diving. Per my review of the literature:

Operating a single engine private aircraft has a risk of .35 milliMorts.

Skydiving has a risk of .30 milliMorts.

Scuba diving has a risk of .02 milliMorts.

Thus, perceived high-risk behaviors are just twice as risky as driving in Boston and are half the risk of having a 45-year-old heart.

The medical literature suggests that alpine mountaineering causes 1.87 deaths per 1,000 climbing days. Last year, I did five days of alpine climbing. That's 9.35 milliMorts compared to the baseline all-cause rate for 45-year-olds of 3.52 milliMorts.

The bottom line is that my highest risk behavior is just 2.65 times more risky than breathing as a 45-year-old.

Thus, for the moment, I'll continue to climb, fly commercial aircraft, and do a few alpine ascents every year. At 9.35 milliMorts per year, I've got 107 years to go before I reach a Mort! ■

An Engineering Eye for the Average Guy

This is one of my more unusual blog entries, so I'll start with a disclaimer that I do have a life and I'm not obsessive compulsive. What follows is an engineering version of "clothes make the man."

When I lost 60 pounds through a combination of vegan diet and exercise, I began to look for new clothes from an engineering standpoint, not a fashion standpoint. To work 20 hours a day and fly 400,000 miles a year, I need very practical clothing that fits well, survives abuse, and works in a multitude of settings. Here are my lessons learned about men's clothes, from toe to head.

First, a comment about the color black. Black is formal and informal. I've worn it to the stuffiest supper clubs on Beacon Hill and to rock concerts. It's the choice of savvy business travelers and the always hip Steve Jobs. It does not show dirt or wrinkles. At 3 am half way around the world, you do not have to think about color matching. It never goes out of style.

Shoes—Most shoes are made in a single average width. This means that men with wide feet (I'm 9 EE) buy shoes that are too long so that the width feels right in the shoe store. However, just about all shoes stretch in one direction—the width expands with wear. If wide shoes are not available, buy shoes that are the right length and the width will expand by stretching in a few days. I used to wear size 10D shoes that were too long but the right width. I now wear size 9 shoes (European 42/UK size 8) and after a day or two of wear, they are perfect. Since I'm a vegan, I only buy non-leather shoes, which is not as hard as it sounds. Take a look at Mooshoes, Vegetarian Shoes, and Novacas. My choice is a simple black office shoe for day to day, and a simple dress boot for New England winters.

Socks—Why do we wear socks? Since mankind evolved to walk on two feet without the encumbrance of shoes, our feet are not optimized to manage temperature/moisture/friction encased in a shoe. A sock should keep feet dry all year long, warm in the winter, and cool in the summer. Hence, a few thoughts about socks. Cotton as a fabric is like a sponge. Once wet, it takes days to dry. Just dunk Levis in water and see how long they stay wet. Does it make sense to put your feet in a sponge and then encase them in a shoe? Cotton socks are not a good choice. A wicking combination of polyester/nylon/wool is ideal. Polyester wicks, nylon provides strength, and wool provides temperature regulation. I wear black Smartwool liner socks. From a vegan standpoint, this is an interesting moral dilemma. Animals are not intentionally killed in the wool-making process (unlike leather), but the use of any animal products is not consistent with veganism. Since veganism is a journey toward a goal in the modern industrial world, I have accepted the fact that until I find a better-performing material for temperature regulation, a small percentage of wool in my long lasting socks is acceptable.

Pants—Have you ever looked at a group of men walking down the street? Half have pants that are too long, creating large clumps of fabric falling over their shoes. Half have pants that are too short, exposing socks and looking like capris. Why is this? Typically men's pants off the rack are sized in even-numbered lengths (i.e., 32, 34, 36), so it means that a person with a 33-inch inseam cannot get a good fit. Also, pants are cut from templates based on an average-sized thigh, seat, hip, etc. Buying pants turns out to be very challenging because they are a three-dimensional object sold with two-dimensional measurements. The way that pants are constructed is that they have an inseam, a rise (from crotch to navel), and an outseam (from shoe to waist). Here's the engineering: the inseam is not a straight line and pants measurements are related by this equation: outseam=rise+inseam-1.

Purely by luck, 32 waist/34 length Levi's Button Fly 501's (in black of course) have an outseam of 44, a rise of 11, and an inseam of 34, which are exactly my measurements. However, no such luck with dress pants. A typical 32x34 dress pant has an outseam of 44, a rise of 12.5, and an inseam of 32.5, making me wear the pants about two inches above my navel because of the 12.5 rise, but that makes the pants too short. Wearing the pants below the navel makes them long enough, but then the crotch sits two inches below my body, creating a "gangsta" look. The bottom line of all of this is that men need to determine the rise (where on the waist they wear their pants), then find a pair with the right outseam to give them the right inseam. Unfortunately, pants do not have published rises or outseams. In my case, finding a pair of dress pants that fits was not possible and I had to find a company that creates pants based on body measurements. The cost of these is not much higher than typical off-the-rack dress pants. My belt is not leather: it's microfiber polyester from Vegetarian Shoes.

Shirts—Finding a shirt that fits well is very challenging. Collars are sized by inches (e.g., 15 or 16), sleeves are often sized by multiple inches (e.g., 34/35), and just about all shirts follow a typical template that creates a waist with way too much extra fabric. A tailor's template for a 16-inch-collar includes a 40-inch waist measurement—you have no choice. For me to find a shirt that fits a 32-inch waist, I'd have to buy a 13-inch collar, which would asphyxiate me. How can I find a shirt with a 15.75-inch collar, a 34-inch sleeve, and a 32-inch waist? Only two choices: a polyester mock turtleneck that stretches, or a company that creates shirts based on your measurements. I have black mock turtlenecks off the rack and black linen shirts made to my measurements.

Jackets—Many suit jackets and sport coats have the same problem as shirts. I wear a 40 long, which automatically comes with sleeves about 35 or 36 inches long. I buy black Nehru jackets made of rayon/polyester that fit my chest and body length, then have the sleeves altered.

Thus, my office wardrobe is black, mostly vegan, and fitted to my measurements by ordering custom shirts/pants, wearing Levis 501s, and alteration.

My outdoor wardrobe for ice climbing, rock climbing, and mountaineering is made of form-fitting synthetic materials by Arcteryx, which by random chance has outdoor clothing that matches my every measurement. Although I wear all-black in the office, I wear red shirts (no Star Trek jokes allowed) outdoors for visibility.

Clearly this is more information that anyone wants to know about clothing, but it works for me! ∎

The Number 5

In the movie, "The Number 23," the main character played by Jim Carrey is obsessed with the idea that all incidents and events are directly connected to the number 23, some permutation of the number 23, or a number related to the number 23.

I'm not obsessed, nor do I have OCD in any way, but much of my life is neatly organized into groups of five.

Why five?

I find that five is the maximum number of tasks I can do simultaneously without losing track of the details. Here's my framework for my career and personal life:

Career

1. BIDMC—As CIO of BIDMC, I have five direct reports:
    a. Clinical Systems
    b. Financial Systems
    c. Infrastructure
    d. Knowledge Services (includes medical library and all online)
    e. Media Services
2. Harvard Medical School—As CIO of HMS, I have five direct reports:
    a. Administrative IT
    b. Educational IT
    c. Informatics
    d. Infrastructure
    e. Research IT

3. Standards—Chair of HITSP and Vice-chair of the HIT Standards Committee (Although the work we're doing includes five Tiger Teams, that was not a conscious choice on my part!)

4. Healthcare Information Exchange—Chair of NEHEN and CEO of MA-Share (MA-Share and NEHEN merger will be finalized in June) which supports five different use cases for data sharing.

5. Advisory Councils—I have five advisory positions:

   a. Food and Drug Administration Subcommittee on IT

   b. Social Security Administration Future Technology Advisory Panel

   c. Anvita Health Board of Directors

   d. Epocrates IT Advisory Council

   e. Robert Wood Johnson Foundation National Advisory Committee for Project HealthDesign

Personal Life

1. Family - (wife, daughter, mother, father, and me)

2. Home and garden (my Thursday blog will describe my five small gardens)

3. Japanese flutes (I have five instruments)

4. Outdoors - (hiking, kayaking, climbing, running, and biking)

5. Writing (blogs, IT journals, academic publications, popular press, lectures)

Each night before bed, I review my five career organizations and my five direct reports in each of my jobs to ensure I've resolved all the issues of each day. By always balancing five tasks, five people, and five projects in every area, I maximize my breadth without sacrificing the depth of my attention span.

There's no need to worry about my sanity: the number five is just a convenient mnemonic and not a prerequisite for getting through the day. And now it's time to prepare for my five meetings tomorrow... ∎

The Road Less Traveled

I'm back from Japan, physically and spiritually refreshed, ready to embrace my jobs, my blogging, and my outdoor activities with new vigor.

In previous years, my vacations have been about movement—hiking the John Muir trail, climbing in Yosemite, and exploring the outdoors with my family.

This year's trip to Japan was about people. My family and I had remarkable experiences that were not about traveling to every tourist spot, taking a few photographs, then shuttling to the next location. Instead, we based ourselves in Kyoto for two weeks and in the Inland Sea (Miyajima) for three days, spending time with shopkeepers, craftsmen, and friends. Here are a few examples:

- We had the opportunity to spend a few hours with the President of Shoyeido Incense, Masataka Hata, the 12th generation leader of the company. He led us in a traditional Japanese incense ceremony (Koh-do), teaching us the details of refined arts from the 1600s.

- We had the opportunity to meet with the owner of Horaido Tea, Nagahiro Yasumori, whose family has sold tea in Kyoto since 1803. He taught us how to make the ideal cup of Gyokuro and Sencha green tea.

- We spent an afternoon with Ken-ichi Utsuki, owner of Aizenkobo workshop, a traditional Japanese natural indigo dying and textile firm. He and his son fitted me with a Samue (Japanese workclothes for Zen monks and tradespeople).

- We met with Kunimi Naito and her family, makers of traditional Japanese Geta (wooden sandals) in the Gion (Geisha) district of Kyoto. They carefully studied my feet and are making a custom pair of geta for my 27cm western-sized foot.

- We met with a sake brewer and tasted the range of his handmade Ginjo and Daiginjo sakes.

- We viewed the bonfires of Obon with faculty members from Kyoto and Keio University.

- I played Shakuhachi in a 500-year-old mountaintop temple overlooking the Inland Sea with a Zen monk who played a Conch shell.

- We made traditional Japanese sweets (Wagashi) with a master craftsman.

- We had incredible Zen meals in small, family-run restaurants such as Kiko.

I want to thank our Japanese hosts, Dr. Hiroyuki Yoshihara and Michiko Yoshida, for making it all possible.

There are so many memories and spiritual experiences to describe that I will use the next several months on my Thursday blogs to share everything I learned about traditional Japanese culture from the master craftsman who taught me over the past two weeks. ■

The Experience of Tea

Some of my favorite Japanese traditions are tea (cha-no-yū), incense (Kōdō), Japanese textiles (Samue and farmer's jackets called Noragi), Zen cuisine (Shojin Ryori), and music (Shakuhachi).

While in Kyoto, I spent an afternoon with Nagahiro Yasumori, owner of Horaido Tea on the Teramachi shopping street in Kyoto. I traveled to the oldest tea store on the planet, Tsuen, located next to the Uji River bridge for the past 850 years. I also walked the hillsides of Uji to wander among the bushes that produce the world's finest tea.

I drink four kinds of Japanese tea—Sencha, Gyokuro, Genmaicha, and Houjicha. I'll cover Matcha and the tea ceremony in its own blog entry.

Sencha is traditional Japanese green tea. The leaves are picked, steamed, rolled, shaped, and dried. It has a grassy aroma and a bitter taste. Sencha Fukamushi is steamed a bit longer than regular Sencha and has a more intense flavor.

Gyokuro is a rare/fine tea grown in the shade rather than full sun. It's brewed in small quantities at lower temperatures and has a sweet, intense taste.

Genmaicha is Sencha mixed with roasted rice. It has a light, mellow flavor.

Houjicha is a roasted tea with a smoky flavor.

To make tea, I use a traditional Japanese ceramic teapot (a Kyusu) made of Banko ware. I preheat the teapot and brew the tea with dechlorinated hot water. I keep all my teas in airtight cherry bark tea caddies. Here are the proportions of water/tea, and the temperature I use:

Sencha

> Tea leaves: 3 teaspoons (7-8 g)
> Water temperature: 176°F (80°C)
> Amount of water: 200 ml (7.04 fl oz)
> Brewing time: 1 minute

Sencha Fukamushi

> Tea leaves: 3 teaspoons (7-8 g)
> Water temperature: 176°F (80°C)
> Amount of water: 20 ml (7.04 fl oz)
> Brewing time: 40-45 seconds

Gyokuro

> Tea leaves: 3 teaspoons (7-8 g)
> Water temperature: 104°F
> Amount of water: 100 ml (3.5 fl oz)
> Brewing time: 2 minutes

Genmaicha

> Tea leaves: 3 teaspoons (7-8 g)
> Water temperature: 176°F (80°C)
> Amount of water: 200 ml (7.04 fl oz)
> Brewing time: 1 minute

Houjicha

> Tea leaves: 3 teaspoons (7-8g)
> Water temperature: boiling water
> Amount of water: 200 ml (7.04 fl oz)
> Brewing time: 15-30 seconds

Nagahiro Yasumori made us an extraordinary pot of Gyokuro by brewing it for several minutes at a very low temperature. The flavor was sweet, intense, and almost wine-like in its persistent finish. We bought Kame-no-yowai Gyokuro and I'm sure I'll be buying from him frequently.

During my travels I consumed many great cups of tea and learned how to choose my tea wisely (buy from Horaido or Tsuen), care for my tea (use only fresh tea, kept in airtight containers), and brew the perfect cup (as above). If you visit me in any of my offices, you can be sure I'll greet you with a fresh pot of Sencha. ■

How I Eat

I've written about what I eat and where it's from, but not about how I eat.

What do I mean?

In the US, meals are often considered a meat-based main dish plus sides or trimmings (e.g., we're having chicken for dinner).

Taking a lesson from Japanese cuisine, there is no main dish to any of my meals. I typically have four or five small plates that include salad, soup, rice, and vegetables.

Here's tonight's dinner:

1. A bowl of coconut barley pilaf with corn, tofu and cashews (I replaced the chicken in the recipe with tofu)

2. A bowl of braised yuba and bok choy from our CSA

3. A bowl of curried summer squash with yuba and cilantro

4. A cup of Sencha Fukamushi green tea

I savor every dish equally and consider them part of the palette which makes up the meal. The family gathers to discuss the events of the day, the schedule for the next day, and the challenges/frustrations we face at school/office/studio. We often read the Dave Barry calendar page of the day at dinner and comment how the day's Dilbert parallels real life. We serve ourselves individually in the kitchen, picking from a large assortment of random Japanese bowls and plates, so that every meal is a completely different visual experience, sized to the appetite of the day, the seasons, and personal whim.

Grazing rather than eating, enjoying several small plates rather than a main dish, and making dinner the family time of the day work well to keep us together, keep us communicating, and keep us appreciating the wonderful myriad of foods available to vegans. ∎

Of Bicycles and Printers

Bicycles and Printers? It's a parable, so humor me.

I ride a Trek 7.5 Fx Hybrid mountain bike. When I bought it in 2007, it cost $700 and it had Shimano Deore derailleurs, which are the lower end of Shimano's component sets. Although I have a great deal of experience adjusting bicycle components, I had many drivetrain problems—gears skipping, ghost shifting, low gears overshifted, high gears undershifted. No amount of adjustment left me with a stable, reliable ride.

Last weekend, I replaced the Deore components with Shimano XT, a higher-end product. The difference between Deore and XT for my bike was about $100 or 15% of the cost of the bike. The new components worked perfectly and since I started using XT, I've not had a flawed shift or any adjustment problems. When I bought the bike, I would have happily paid 15% more to get a bike with a problem-free drivetrain. The Deore components are now in the Wellesley Recycling Center and I'm a happy Shimano XT user.

And now, the analogy. At home, I've always used inkjet printers such as the HP K550 and HP K5400 Pro. I spent very little buying these printers but filled them with expensive cartridges. HP printer drivers seem to have one purpose in life—to tell you to order new supplies. Each year the inkjet print heads fail and no amount of head cleaning/alignment can revive them. Since the cost of print head supplies exceeds the cost of the printer, I just replace the printer yearly. It seems that the lifecycle of a printer model is about a year, so I cannot even replace the printer with a similar model. Often that means that existing cartridges are no longer usable in the new model.

This weekend, I decided to get off the inkjet revolving door. I will never use an inkjet printer again because they are not eco-friendly, not cost effective, not easily maintainable, not reliable, and have poor life-cycle management.

At BIDMC our printer lifecycle is seven years with the following equipment:

Color Laser

HP Color LJ4700N (Departmental)
HP Color LJ CP3525N (Work Group)
HP Color LJ CP1215 (Single)

Black and White

HP LJ p4015N/TN (Departmental)
HP LJ p2055DN/X (Work Group)
HP LJ p2035N (Two-person)

I purchased an HP P2035N black and white laser printer at Staples and turned in my inkjet for recycling, getting $50 cash back. Yes, this printer costs a bit more up front, but it has the reliability, cost effectiveness, and life-cycle management I need.

Just as with my bike, buying the right parts the first time to meet your requirements is the right thing to do.

I now have a small laser printer on my home network and not a single inkjet cartridge left in the house. ∎

The Pleasures and Risks of Solo Hiking

In my travels around the world, I'm always looking for the road less traveled. In the past few years, that's included walking the Seven Hills of Rome, exploring archeological sites in the Middle East, climbing mountains in Austria, and kayaking across the Baltic Sea.

Because of the logistics, physical conditions, and specialized gear needed to do these activities, I've often traveled alone, going Into the Wild.

When I travel alone I take extra precautions, packing a bit of extra food and a spare layer of warm clothing, and posting my itinerary with someone who can call for a rescue party if needed.

I will not do solo unroped climbing, solo travel in avalanche areas, or solo kayaking in water that is colder than 50 degrees.

There are a few pleasures to traveling alone—a pace that you define yourself based on your personal energy level, no time commitments, and simpler logistics.

There are risks—an injury while on a cold mountain ridge can lead to hypothermia, frostbite, or death. The margin of safety while hiking alone in wilderness areas, especially in winter, can be thin.

A hiking partner enables you to share the memories and relive the experiences. This winter, I've hiked alone many weekends, but also hiked with one of my colleagues from BIDMC who is an experienced alpinist.

My hike in Japan will cover 20 kilometers of the North Takao Ridge, from Mt. Takao to Jimba-san, traversing three peaks and stretching my knowledge of the Japanese rail and bus systems to get to the trailhead.

So, I'm off to experience the Japanese wilderness alone, with minimal risk, and play my Japanese flute from the peaks.

Buckaroo Banzai would be proud. ■

Geeks, Dorks, and Nerds

My daughter and I were recently discussing the precise definitions of Geeks, Dorks, and Nerds.

When I first started this blog, I could have called it NerdDoctor or DorkDoc, but luckily I chose Geekdoctor, since it aligns well with the definition of a Geek.

Here's the key vocabulary:

- Geek—Someone who is passionate about some particular area or subject, often an obscure or difficult one, such as healthcare IT

- Dork—Someone who has difficulty with common social expectations and interactions

- Nerd—Someone who loves learning and academics

My daughter and I agree that we're an admixture of all these qualities.

In high school, I was part of a small cohort of computer geeks who used MITS Altair 8800, Wang word processors, and 110 baud dial-up teletypes with thermal paper instead of video displays. We were obsessed with the potential of early microcomputers, an esoteric subject that meets the definition of geeky behavior.

In elementary and high school, I wore shirts buttoned to the top and had no sense of fashion or rhythm. I was definitely socially awkward—a dork.

I spent 30 years in academics as a student, so I guess that makes me nerdy.

Of course, I've long exhibited other characteristics that are badges of courage for geeks, dorks, and nerds:

- Watched every Star Trek episode multiple times and can recite most dialog from memory

- Played Dungeons and Dragons and Magic: The Gathering

- Favorite books include *Lord of the Rings* and just about any science fiction

- Favorite TV series include Twilight Zone, Outer Limits, and Dr. Who.

- Favorite movies include Star Wars, Blade Runner, and bad Japanese monster films. ■

What Makes Me Happy

I was recently in a meeting with senior managers who commented on my generally even temperament. I rarely express extremes of emotion (joy, sadness, anger, despair) in the workplace. They asked me what makes me happy.

Here's my own version of "Raindrops on roses and whiskers on kittens," or, what makes me happy:

1. Innovation—Operations is really important, but if I can spend dedicated time each week creating something new, I feel invigorated and inspired.

2. Focusing on one thing and doing it really well—In our multitasking world, it's hard to meet everyone's expectations for real-time response if you are focused on a single task at a time.

3. Teaching a willing student—Sharing the lessons I've learned with my family, friends, and colleagues is very fulfilling for me. Teaching my daughter has been one of my life's great joys.

4. Experiencing the world with a friend—I enjoy exploring exotic locales from museums to mountaintops with my best friend, my wife.

5. Time in the wilderness and outdoors in general—Every week I try to spend time hiking, biking, skiing, kayaking, or climbing.

6. A breakfast of rice, tsukemono, vegan miso soup, and big cup of Gyokuro green tea from Uji—It's healthy, low calorie, and satisfying.

7. Vegan pot pie or split pea soup after a day working outside—These are definitely my comfort foods.

8. A Saturday morning at home with a coil of blue incense from the Kungyokudo Incense shop (near the Kyoto train station).

9. A glass of red wine on a cold winter's night.

10. Growing Japanese cucumbers, eggplant, and shiso. The taste of cucumber salad (sunomono), grilled eggplant with miso (nasu dengaku), or shiso on soft tofu reminds me of summer nights in Japan.

What makes me unhappy:

1. Unplanned work that increases scope without a change in resources or timeline.

2. Needless administrative or bureaucratic processes imposed by those who are not actually doing the work.

3. The guy behind you who honks two milliseconds after the light turns green.

4. Flights that are delayed or cancelled due to equipment failure when the airlines run so lean that no spare aircraft or parts are available.

5. Cold callers from organizations you do not support.

6. Your neighbor whose dog barks continuously and whose children play loud musical instruments, but who objects to the sounds created by garden maintenance at noon on a Saturday.

7. Staff at home improvement stores who have never done home improvement.

8. Monday morning quarterbacks who lack the expertise to do work but are happy to criticize others' work.

9. People who believe that the louder they yell, the faster those around them will work.

10. Machiavellian people who use politics, relationships, and manipulation rather than hard work to get ahead.

There you have it. ∎

The Adjustment Bureau

On a flight to Tokyo, I watched The Adjustment Bureau, a Philip K. Dick-inspired film about a supernatural team of agents who ensure each person's path through life (their fate) is followed according to plan.

I've written about Regression to the Mean and the need for constant reinvention which makes life seem entirely non-linear. When I consider the circuitous path I've taken in my career, it's interesting to think about the inflection points—my own adjustment bureau that led me to where I am today.

Here are five random but pivotal events:

1. In the early 1970s, my parents were admitted to law school in Southern California. I had free time after school to explore my own interests while they were taking classes. I rode my bicycle to a local surplus store that specialized in integrated circuits that were discarded by local defense contractors but were still completely functional. By the age of 12, I taught myself digital logic, analog signal processing, and the basics of microprocessors. I learned to program in machine language and built an Altair microcomputer in 1979, becoming the first student with a dorm room-based computer at Stanford University. My parents' law school admission led to my IT expertise—a non-obvious association.

2. While I was an undergraduate at Stanford and a medical student at UCSF, I ran a 35-person company which specialized in business process automation software. It enabled me to purchase a house in Marin Country and anchored me to the San Francisco Bay area. The Dean of Students at UCSF during that time did not believe that a medical student doing advanced clinical rotations should be allowed to run a company simultaneously and gave me a choice—divest the company or defer medical school. I recognized that medicine was my future and divested the company, which eliminated my Northern California ties and ultimately led to my taking a job at Beth Israel Deaconess and Harvard. A Dean of Students with a strong opinion about medical student entrepreneurial activities led to my career in Boston—another non-obvious association.

3. On December 10, 1997, while working in the Emergency Department at BIDMC, my cell phone rang and the CEO of CareGroup informed me that I was going to serve as the CIO of CareGroup beginning at 8 am the next day. The external auditors at the time told the CEO that giving a CIO job to an unproven Emergency Physician was administrative malpractice. The CEO firmly believed that a clinically focused, web-savvy risk taker was better than a traditional process-oriented CIO. Nearly 15 years later, many people believe he was right. A CEO who took a very controversial risk on a 35-year-old with limited leadership experience resulted in my career as a CIO—a challenging outcome to predict based on my life history up to that point.

4. In 2001, the new Dean for Medical Education at Harvard Medical School had a dream—moving the entire medical school curriculum to the web and mobile platforms (early Palm technology). He asked for my advice given my experience at BIDMC moving clinical records to the web. Although I had no experience in educational technology, I worked with a team of students, faculty, and IT developers to collaboratively create the MyCourses learning management system, serving as a part-time Associate Dean in addition to my CareGroup CIO role. The project went well and I was eventually asked to serve as part-time Harvard Medical School CIO, which the CareGroup board gave me permission to do (I became a 1.5 FTE, 100% at CareGroup and 50% at Harvard simultaneously). A sojourn into educational technologies led to my becoming responsible for ten years of infrastructure and application work at Harvard Medical School, including the evolution of high-performance computing and storage clusters to support the life sciences, unique challenges that were not even imagined in 2001—a definite non-linear path.

5. In 2005, I took a call from ANSI, asking if I would attend a meeting to discuss harmonizing standards as part of a program conceived by the first national coordinator for IT, David Brailer. Although I did not consider myself a standards expert, I agreed to serve as chair of HITSP. As a consequence of five years of work with healthcare standards, I became part of many national, regional, and state healthcare IT projects. A phone call about standards led to my federal and state roles, which became the basis for my Harvard professorship. A call from ANSI and a Harvard professorship—very hard to predict that!

What's next? At BIDMC, the Chief Executive Officer selection process will result in new leadership this fall. New mergers and acquisitions will result in an accountable care organization built around BIDMC. Complex health information exchange, registries, and business intelligence tools needed to support healthcare reform will accelerate my hospital CIO, state, and national activities.

All of this is happening while I'm working on replacing my Harvard Medical School CIO role with a full-time successor.

It's July of 2011 and hard to know exactly how the inflection point of my evolving Harvard role will affect the future, but I feel powerful forces are aligning to create a quantum leap forward in electronic health records and health information exchange technology.

A year from now, I'll look back and assess what The Adjustment Bureau had in mind for me. ∎

There Is Hope

Every Thanksgiving I reflect on the state of the world, the state of healthcare IT, the state of my various roles, my family, and my life.

My message this year—there is hope.

Some may think that the tone of my blog changed in 2011—from a focus on cutting-edge technology that will revolutionize healthcare to themes of compliance, limited resources, unbridled demand, urgent unplanned projects, and security challenges.

That's a valid observation.

In my 15 years as CIO, I've evolved from creating innovative applications to maintaining customer relationships. I've gone from strategic visionary to resource planner.

This transformation is not about me or my jobs—it's about the world we live in. According to the Center for Health System Change, households with Broadband in the US increased from 47% to 66% from 2007–2010. Smartphones are ubiquitous and the majority of households in the US are IT savvy. That creates a very different expectation for healthcare IT service delivery.

When I first started as a CIO, mobile devices had not yet been invented, computers were the domain of geeky early adopters, and solutions to problems involved workflow change, not automation.

Today, most of my work is managing demand. I aim to complete 80% of the requests I'm given. I've been told that 50% is typical. Few other industries move so fast and yet have so little tolerance for mistakes.

So, why do I have hope?

I recently met with a Clinical Fellow who is very likely going to be chair of an academic department or a senior hospital administrator some day.

We spoke about the need to understand workflow, the need to change behavior, and the critical role of piloting new processes before automating them.

We talked about the need to balance functionality, security, and maintainability. We talked about defining requirements before selecting a solution.

In my blog about "Content versus Context," I described the job of the CIO as becoming increasingly impossible because many people expect flying cars when we live in an era of IT bicycles.

However, it is clear that the next generation of leaders, who were born in the 1980s' personal computing era, understand that technology is the easy part—policy and process are the hard part.

Also, I have hope because I believe the BIDMC FY12 IT Operating Plan is well aligned with the needs of the business. Today I did a "Venn analysis" of five resources:

1. The BIDMC FY12 IT Operating Plan

2. BIDMC FY12 requirements from key customers

3. The BIDMC FY12 Annual Operating Plan

4. The Meaningful Use Stage 1 and recommended Stage 2 Standards and Certification criteria

5. Emerging compliance projects

I found that the existing BIDMC FY12 IT Operating Plan addresses the needs of all these stakeholders. There are only a few items to defer or reconsider.

Today, the CEO of BIDMC, Kevin Tabb, sent out his Thanksgiving message and highlighted BIDMC Information Systems: "We were named the #1 health care IT organization in the United States for 2011 by *Information Week 500*, and BIDMC was the first hospital in the country to achieve Meaningful Use of electronic health records, meeting a key set of new federal government standards."

I'll transition my Harvard Medical School CIO role by February 2012. I serve on the search committee, which is following a multi-stakeholder process to find a visionary CIO to lead a great organization.

In my international, national, and state lives, I've worked with incredible people and the trajectory is very good. In 2011, we completed a healthcare IT plan for Japan and for New Zealand. The content, vocabulary, and transport standards for the US are submitted to ONC, completing the foundational work for Meaningful Use Stage 2. The State of Massachusetts has submitted a new State Medicaid Health Plan and completed a new HIT Strategic and Operational plan.

But most importantly, my family life is earning an "A."

My daughter has blossomed into a resilient college woman with clear goals, deep friendships, and a very positive self-worth. She's excelling in her coursework, immersing herself in the culture of Tufts University, and traveling to Japan as part of a study abroad program this winter. I'm so proud that she has left the nest and is building a life on her own.

My wife and I are planning the next stage of our lives and we'll be in Vermont this weekend visiting farm properties. I'll be 50 this year and although I have many years to go before retirement, it seems the right time to find a property to grow organic vegetables, raise chickens/goats/llamas, and revel in a self-sufficient lifestyle, learning to live nearly off grid.

My parents are doing well in a new house and enjoying time with friends, cultural events, and gardening time.

So, there is hope. The world is experiencing a challenging time marked by economic fragility and social unrest. The Occupy movement is raising our consciousness about the disparities in the US. However, it is possible for a strong team of people working hard to excel in healthcare IT. It is possible for your family to thrive based on love, trust, and lifelong learning.

Revel in the next few days of Thanksgiving (we're roasting root vegetables, brussel sprouts and tofu). When you receive your next challenging email or are asked to define a timeline before you understand requirements, scope, or resources, take a breath. There is hope! ■

On Turning 50

Is it your work life and the trajectory of your career? No, but it is important to spend your day doing something that is intellectually challenging and offers you the potential for personal growth.

Is it the awards and accolades you accumulate through strength of will and persistence against adversity? No, but it is important to feel recognized for your successes.

In my multiple roles living, working, and playing over 50 years, I've spent time with presidents, Nobel Laureates, and tycoons. Some have risen and some have fallen. I've watched my mentors in life triumph and I've watched them fail.

So after 50 years what really matters?

I've said that the difference between an expert and novice is not the detail they notice, but what they choose to ignore. For example, when I do a toxicology consult, I focus less on the exact subspecies of mushroom the patient has ingested, and more on ensuring it is not one of the few that kill humans.

I ignore the day-to-day frustrations, bureaucratic hassles, and conflicts in my work life. People leave, projects end, and no one remembers the details of last year's urgencies.

What really matters is happiness at home.

Jobs may change but family is forever. The life events surrounding your parents, your spouse, and your children are the palette that colors the stages of life.

If your relationships with those who are important to you are positive and supportive, you will feel a sense of optimism and life energy that empowers all the other aspects of your life.

You'll be able to share all your life joys, be supported through your sorrows, and look forward to the sanctuary that is your home life.

When my mentors have stumbled in the workplace, they've generally been forgiven. However, when they've had challenges in their home lives (affairs, violence, or public conflict), they've been judged harshly.

> *If your relationships with those who are important to you are positive and supportive, you will feel a sense of optimism and life energy that empowers all the other aspects of your life.*

As I've approached 50, I've worked hard to build a haven at home. I married the first person I dated in college and we've created homes together since 1980. Our relationship has always been based on loyalty. I call my parents every week and we have an open, loving relationship. My 19-year-daughter still believes her parents are reasonable people. Tonight and for much of the summer, our household will be multi-generational since my daughter will be home from college, and my father-in-law recently moved in with us. My wife is cancer-free and our new farm is bursting with healthy young animals, fresh hay in our meadow, and the spring vegetables we planted.

Yes, I will be engaged and passionate in my work life as I begin my 50th year, but my reputation, integrity, and sense of equanimity derive from my happiness at home. ∎

Living Things First

When a young animal is hungry and cold, it can begin to fade, exhausting its minimal reserves.

Similarly, the people in our work lives need our support and attention.

Budgets, strategic plans, policymaking, interviews, and innovation can wait. Patients, employees, and colleagues with urgent issues should not.

When I scan my email, I look for those issues that involve the well-being of the people I serve. Some of those emails ask for urgent help with challenging political issues. Some express anxiety or anticipation about upcoming meetings, complex projects, or new regulations.

I vow never to be the rate-limiting step for people issues (or supporting any living thing). I'll rapidly respond with my best answer, even if a complete answer will take a few days to research. It's far easier to defuse an emotional situation or steer events back on course by acting rapidly instead of waiting for the situation to get worse.

As an emergency physician, I often make decisions with incomplete information and need to tolerate ambiguity. Focusing on the living things and keeping them stable in the golden hours when problems are still minor create ample time for addressing less urgent issues when time permits.

Every ten years I reinvent my lifestyle—from entrepreneur, to winemaker, to Japanese flute player, to alpinist, and now to farmer. I expect the lessons learned from the farm over the next few years will make me a better technology leader. Even the few short weeks tending the chickens has given me the perspective of the importance of serving living things first. ∎

Joyful Chaos

My daughter recently returned from a month-long stay in Long Island to rejoin Kathy and me at the farm we've been creating since May. She walked the barn, paddocks, new pasture, new buildings, and new trails, then concluded, "There's so much happiness and energy infused into a whirlwind of change—it's joyful chaos."

In past personal blogs about our cancer journey, I've explained the "why"— looking forward to a vision of a bucolic future made the six months of cancer treatment a lot more tolerable.

I've never explained the "how." In a new series of Thursday blogs, beginning today, I'll recount what we've done and what we're doing to turn 15 acres of Sherborn, Massachusetts into a productive working farm providing a non-stressful environment, numerous animals, and a nurturing ecosystem for a bountiful fruit/vegetable harvest.

The property we purchased in April, 2012, has all the right ingredients—former pastureland filled with 1700s rock walls; flat, sunny, well-drained soil with generous sun exposure; forest; a meadow; and a stream/wildflower wetland.

Over the past hundred years, the pastures have filled with second growth trees—pines, oaks, and black birch. The rock walls have been lost in a sea of bittersweet, wild grape, and poison ivy.

Our first task was to re-open the pastures. We cleared over 50 trees including numerous invasive/non-native plants. We used an expert tree contractor for the large trees and for the smaller trees I used a Stihl MS290 chainsaw, a Gransfors Bruks splinting maul/Swedish forest axe, and a steel farm push cart capable of hauling 800 pounds.

Our next task was to clear debris—fallen branches and deadwood. I created a pile 50-feet long and 10-feet high, which we chipped into mulch.

Then we created paths throughout the property which enabled us to manage the land. We covered the paths with the mulch we created from chipping.

Once the rough clearing was done, we had to move rocks. New England is full of rocks. Although I hand-carried many and used a heavy-duty wheelbarrow for others, we used a small front loader (Bobcat) for the really large ones.

Once the topography of the land was more obvious, we planned our planting areas, buildings, and fences.

A wetland engineer is working with the town of Sherborn to plan our future planting areas—likely an orchard of heirloom apples and a meadow filled with high bush blueberries.

We created a 10x12 chicken coop and a loafing shed to keep animals warm in winter/cool in summer. We planned 1,000 feet of fences and chose to use 5-foot woven wire fence supported by posts at 20-foot intervals, topped by a hot wire (9,000 volts, low amperage) to keep the predators out.

The end result was two-quarter-acre paddocks—one for males and one for females, and a half-acre pasture, connected with a series of eight gates that support manure management, hay storage, and easy movement of animals.

A friend gave us a rooster. We named him "Lucky" since he'll be living with vegans/vegetarians.

We then planned the barn. The property included a barn, but it was originally designed as more of a garage than a barn. We added hay loft doors, thick rubber mats for the stalls, a water hydrant with a French drain, fans to keep animals cool in summer, and wall-mounted feeders. We painted the building red with black trim and added barn lights above each door.

With this layout done, we had the infrastructure in place to complete our animal strategy. We raised 12 chickens from 3-day-old chicks indoors and moved them to the coop at 6 weeks. A friend gave us a rooster. We named him "Lucky" since he'll be living with vegans/vegetarians.

We raised 22 guinea fowl from 3-day-old chicks and moved them to the coop at 6 weeks.

By pure happenstance, my Telecom manager is selling her herd of eight alpaca. After meeting them, we purchased the entire herd—three males and five females.

Realizing that alpacas need guardians because they do not defend themselves well against the coyotes, fisher cats, and other predators on our property, we researched llamas. We found an ideal guard llama that has lived with alpaca for many years. She also happens to be pregnant.

The female llama will guard the female alpaca.

For the male alpaca, we chose an experienced female Great Pyrenees mountain dog, the livestock guardian used by Basque shepherds. We also chose a male Great Pyrenees puppy that will keep the female company and learn how to guard from her.

On August 18, the alpaca arrive. On August 20, the female Great Pyrenees arrives. On August 23, the male Great Pyrenees arrives. On August 26 the llama arrives.

The journey of joyful chaos at Unity Farm has replaced the cancer journey and our property is about to blossom with new arrivals. ∎

A Time for Boundless Energy and Optimism

2012 was a challenging year for me.

On the personal side, my wife had cancer. Together we moved two households, relocated her studio, and closed her gallery. This week my mother broke her hip in Los Angeles and I'm writing from her hospital room as we finalize her discharge and home care plan before I fly back to Boston.

On the business side, the IT community around me has worked hard on Meaningful Use Stage 2, the Massachusetts State Health Information Exchange, improvements in data security, groundbreaking new applications, and complex projects like ICD-10 with enormous scope.

We did all this with boundless energy and optimism, knowing that every day we're creating a foundation that will improve the future for our country, communities, and families.

My personal life has never been better—Kathy's cancer is in remission, our farm is thriving, and our daughter is maturing into a fine young woman at Tufts University.

My business life has never been better—Meaningful Use Stage 2 provides new rigorous standards for content/vocabulary/transport at a time when EHR use has doubled since 2008, the state HIE goes live in one week, and BIDMC was voted the number #1 IT organization in the country.

It's clear that many have discounted the amazing accomplishments that we've all made, overcoming technology and political barriers with questions such as, "How can we?" and "Why not?" rather than, "Why is it taking so long?" They would rather pursue their own goals—be they election year politics, academic recognition, or readership traffic on a website.

As many have seen, a letter from the Ways and Means Committee makes comments about standards that clearly have no other purpose than election year politics. These House members are very smart people and I have great respect for their staff. I'm happy to walk them through the Standards and Certification Regulations (Meaningful Use Stages 1 and 2) so they understand that the majority of their letter is simply not true—it ignores the work of hundreds of people over thousands of hours to close the standards gaps via open, transparent, and bipartisan harmonization in both the Bush and Obama administrations.

I spoke with the authors of the *Wall Street Journal* article, "A Major Glitch for Digitized Health-Care Records,"[6] and discovered that their issue was not interoperability standards but a lack of usability in non-standard EHR user interface design. When a clinician goes from Epic to Cerner to MEDITECH and tries to perform the same task (e-prescribing, managing a problem list, or looking up a lab), the learning curve can be steep. The authors and I reviewed the Consolidated CDA specification that is required by Meaningful Use Stage 2 and they are completely satisfied that interoperability standards gaps are no longer a rate-limiting step.

Many reporters have asked me about *The New York Times* article, "Medicare Bills Rise as Records Turn Electronic."[7]

I've said three things:

1. In the past, paper documentation lacked details to accurately document acuity. As we make the multi-year journey from simple EHRs that support electronic billing to complex EHRs that include decision support, interoperability, and patient/family engagement, there will be an interim period when increasing detail in documentation results in higher acuity, which results in increased reimbursement.

---

6   Soumerai S, Koppel R. A major glitch for digitized health-care records. *Wall Street Journal*. 2012.

7   Abelson R, Cresswell J, Palmer G. Medicare bills rise as records turn electric. *The New York Times*. September 21, 2012.

2. These trends long pre-date the health IT incentive program. Meaningful Use re-orients the healthcare IT industry away from EHRs supporting billing, to EHRs which focus on prevention, care coordination, and population health management. It is these functionalities that will both enable, and be incentivized by the shift in payment policies towards value, and away from volume. In a healthcare reform world, clinicians will be paid for wellness, not sickness, and the EHR will help them increase efficiency, safety, and quality, which will be required for reimbursement.

> *In a healthcare reform world, clinicians will be paid for wellness, not sickness, and the EHR will help them increase efficiency, safety, and quality, which will be required for reimbursement.*

3. As quoted in the Center for Public Integrity's Cracking the Code series, Donald Berwick said he believes that only a small portion of the upswing in coding is the result of fraud. In most cases, he said, the hospitals have learned "how to play the game," and are targeting the vulnerabilities of the Medicare payment system. "If you create a payment system in which there is a premium for increasing the number of things you do or the recording of what you do, well, that's what you'll get."

Our current society tries to find fault in everyone and everything. Social media and our increased connectedness have turned criticism into a spectator sport.

If everyone could align their efforts into an agenda of optimism, we'd all be better for it.

I may be asking too much to expect positive energy and optimism from Congress, the *Wall Street Journal*, and *The New York Times*, but anything is possible if you try hard enough. ∎

Conclusion

I've posted over a million words in my blog to date. So what does it all mean? Here's my top ten list corresponding to the chapters in this book:

1. You can successfully lead healthcare organizations as long as you keep your equanimity, listen, and realize that there is a process for everything.

2. Implementing electronic health records requires a strictly controlled process that standardizes work and ideally uses a cloud-based, web-friendly, mobile-enabled record.

3. Modern CIOs know that there are rarely easy answers, but engaging stakeholders through governance and communicating broadly makes the job possible.

4. Security is a process, not a product. You'll never be done but you can reduce risks.

5. Balancing job and home life is increasingly difficult, but they are two sides of the same coin. It's hard to be successful in one without being successful in the other.

6. Innovators take risks and as with an investment portfolio, a balance of safe and speculative activities often has the consistently highest yield.

7. Substantial progress has been made to implement EHRs, engage patients/families, and enhance interoperability. However, the combined burden of ICD-10, Meaningful Use, the Affordable Care Act, and the HIPAA Omnibus rule on the same timeframe is straining the resources of many healthcare organizations.

8. Bad things happen, but often adversity creates an opportunity for leaders to shine.

9. In the natural timeline of our lives, we will experience many transitions of our loved ones, some joyful and some sorrowful. It's part of the journey and we should treat every event as a step along the path.

10. Our personal lives define our character. Never lose your individuality.

Let me leave you with a Zen fable. An aging master grew tired of his apprentice's complaints. One morning, he sent him to get some salt. When the apprentice returned, the master told him to mix a handful of salt in a glass of water and then drink it.

"How does it taste?" the master asked.

"Bitter," said the apprentice.

The master chuckled and then asked the young man to take the same handful of salt and put it in the lake. The two walked in silence to the nearby lake and once the apprentice swirled his handful of salt in the water, the old man said, "Now drink from the lake."

As the water dripped down the young man's chin, the master asked, "How does it taste?"

"Fresh," remarked the apprentice.

"Do you taste the salt?" asked the master.

"No," said the young man.

At this the master sat beside this serious young man, and explained softly, "The pain of life is pure salt; no more, no less. The amount of pain in life remains exactly the same. However, the amount of bitterness we taste depends on the container we put the pain in.

"So when you are in pain, the only thing you can do is to enlarge your sense of things. Stop being a glass. Become a lake."

I can only hope that by sharing every aspect of my life as a CIO, I have demonstrated that you are not experiencing any bitterness alone. Working together, we collectively become a lake.

So become a lake and make a difference. ∎

Index

I